W0036149

SAGE was founded in 1965 by Sara Miller McCune to support the dissemination of usable knowledge by publishing innovative and high-quality research and teaching content. Today, we publish over 900 journals, including those of more than 400 learned societies, more than 800 new books per year, and a growing range of library products including archives, data, case studies, reports, and video. SAGE remains majority-owned by our founder, and after Sara's lifetime will become owned by a charitable trust that secures our continued independence.

Los Angeles | London | New Delhi | Singapore | Washington DC | Melbourne

KERALA'S ECONOMIC DEVELOPMENT

Thank you for choosing a SAGE product!
If you have any comment, observation or feedback,
I would like to personally hear from you.

Please write to me at **contactceo@sagepub.in**

Vivek Mehra, Managing Director and CEO, SAGE India.

Bulk Sales

SAGE India offers special discounts
for purchase of books in bulk.
We also make available special imprints
and excerpts from our books on demand.

For orders and enquiries, write to us at

Marketing Department
SAGE Publications India Pvt Ltd
B1/I-1, Mohan Cooperative Industrial Area
Mathura Road, Post Bag 7
New Delhi 110044, India

E-mail us at **marketing@sagepub.in**

Get to know more about SAGE

Be invited to SAGE events, get on our mailing list.
Write today to **marketing@sagepub.in**

This book is also available as an e-book.

KERALA'S ECONOMIC DEVELOPMENT

EMERGING ISSUES AND CHALLENGES

Edited by
B. A. Prakash
Jerry Alwin

Los Angeles | London | New Delhi
Singapore | Washington DC | Melbourne

Copyright © B. A. Prakash and Jerry Alwin, 2018

All rights reserved. No part of this book may be reproduced or utilised in any form or by any means, electronic or mechanical, including photocopying, recording, or by any information storage or retrieval system, without permission in writing from the publisher.

First published in 2018 by

SAGE Publications India Pvt Ltd
B1/I-1 Mohan Cooperative Industrial Area
Mathura Road, New Delhi 110 044, India
www.sagepub.in

SAGE Publications Inc
2455 Teller Road
Thousand Oaks, California 91320, USA

SAGE Publications Ltd
1 Oliver's Yard, 55 City Road
London EC1Y 1SP, United Kingdom

SAGE Publications Asia-Pacific Pte Ltd
3 Church Street
#10-04 Samsung Hub
Singapore 049483

Published by Vivek Mehra for SAGE Publications India Pvt Ltd, typeset in 10.5/13 pts Bembo by Zaza Eunice, Hosur, Tamil Nadu, India and printed at Chaman Enterprises, New Delhi.

Library of Congress Cataloging-in-Publication Data

Names: Prakash, B. A., editor. | Alwin, Jerry, editor.
Title: Kerala's economic development: emerging issues and challenges/
    edited by B. A. Prakash and Jerry Alwin.
Description: New Delhi, India: SAGE Publications India, 2018. | Includes
    bibliographical references and index.
Identifiers: LCCN 2018022466 | ISBN 9789352807659 (print (hb)) | ISBN
    9789352807666 (e-pub 2.0) | ISBN 9789352807673 (e-book)
Subjects: LCSH: Economic development—India—Kerala. | Kerala
    (India)—Economic policy. | Kerala (India)—Economic conditions. | Kerala
    (India)—Social conditions.
Classification: LCC HC435.2 .K459 2018 | DDC 338.954/83—dc23 LC record available at https://
lccn.loc.gov/2018022466

ISBN: 978-93-528-0765-9 (HB)

SAGE Team: Rajesh Dey, Alekha Chandra Jena, Madhurima Thapa and Ritu Chopra

Contents

Part IV: Industry and Infrastructure

Part V: Tourism and Banking

Part VI: Education and Health

Part VII: State Finance and Planning

Preface

Kerala completes six decades as a state of Indian Union as well as a regional economy in 2016. The state remained a backward economy with a low rate of growth during the pre-liberalisation period (1956–1990) when the state followed the excessive market intervention type of economic policies and neglected private investment. The volume of investment was too small to break the vicious circle of the low rate of growth, technological backwardness and low level of productivity in all sectors. But the state's economy achieved a higher rate of investment, technological change and a rate of growth during the post-liberalisation period (1991–2016), when liberalisation policies were implemented and promotion was given to private investment. The state witnessed rapid urbanisation, development of motor transport, technological change in all sectors, leading to reduction in poverty and rise in consumption levels during the post-liberalisation period. But the liberalisation and globalisation policies have created negative effects in the agricultural sector such as the fall in price of cash crops and marginalisation of some sections of people. During the post-liberalisation period, an international factor which adversely affected the growth process as well as the migration prospects and remittances from West Asia was the Global Economic Crisis of 2008 and subsequent years. In this context, the volume examines the development of the state's economy since 2001 and the emerging development issues and challenges.

In this volume, 19 original essays are presented to examine the emerging development issues and challenges. In the first part, we present an overview containing the summary of all the essays and an essay examining the economic liberalisation and economic growth of Kerala, focusing on the growth during post-liberalisation period. In the second part, emerging issues in demographic front such as fall in share of young population, increase in share of old age-people, paradoxical situation of shortage of manual labour and high rate of unemployment of educated labour, immigration of casual workers from other states to Kerala and fall in the trends in emigration to West Asia are examined. The third part discusses the recent changes in production, productivity and cropping pattern in agriculture, impact of globalisation policies on the plantation crops and farmers, and the marginalisation of agricultural households due to overall agrarian changes. The fourth part presents emerging trends in IT services sector, an analysis of the radical restructuring of power sector and the rapid growth and emerging issues in road, water, air and rail transport.

The fifth part examines Kerala's achievements in tourism sector, contributions of the sector, constraints in development and negative effects of the sector and current problems and emerging issues in the development of banking and causes for low credit deposit ratio. The sixth part presents an analysis on the issues in higher education such as wide disparity in the location of number of higher educational institutions in southern and northern regions and gross enrolment ratio among students belonging to different social groups and a profile of health care development and emerging issues. The seventh part examines the acute fiscal crisis, Goods and Services Tax, an analysis of the performance of Eleventh Five-Year Plan of the state and plan performance of grama panchayats. Excessive and uncontrolled growth in non-plan revenue expenditure, and the failure of successive governments to curtail it, is found as the root cause of the acute fiscal crisis of the state.

The three edited volumes on Kerala's economy by B. A. Prakash and published by SAGE examined the economic change of Kerala from 1956 to 2002, the beginning of the new millennium. The volumes are: (a) *Kerala's Economy: Performance, Problems and Prospects* (1994); (b) *Kerala's Economic Development—Issues and Problems* (1999); and (c) *Kerala's Economic Development—Performance and Problems in the Post-Liberalisation Period* (2004). But absence of serious work relating to the later period has been identified as a gap in the literature on Kerala's economic development. This is the context in which the book is edited. With the publication of this volume, literature will be available examining the economic change of Kerala for the last six decades.

As the book is addressed to a wide audience, we have provided a data-based analytical account of the economic issues and problems. A reference at the end of each chapter has been included for those who wish to use the book for further empirical research. In order to facilitate easy understanding of large numbers for Indian and foreign readers, we have used two units of measures such as lakh and crore in tables and million, billion and trillion in explanations. This book is the outcome of the collaborative efforts of 20 scholars who have made significant research contributions to Kerala's economic issues. Shri Bijil Babu R. gave research support for this edition. We take this opportunity to express our gratitude to all of them.

Thiruvananthapuram   **B. A. Prakash**
June 2018   **Jerry Alwin**

PART I

Introduction

Chapter 1

Introduction and Overview

B. A. Prakash and Jerry Alwin

Kerala completes six decades as a state of Indian Union as well as a regional economy in 2016. The development of the state's economy may be broadly divided into two periods based on the nature of economic policies pursued, namely, pre-liberalisation period (1956–1990) and post-liberalisation period (1991–2016). During the pre-liberalisation period, the state pursued economic policies of excessive state intervention in market, development through economic planning using the state's meagre resources, public investment in education and health, expansion of social welfare measures, etc. The second phase, since 1991, witnessed a radical change in economic policies, and market-oriented liberalisation and globalisation policies were implemented. Besides the domestic factors, a factor which gave the biggest push to Kerala's economic change since the mid-1970s has been the large-scale emigration of Keralite workers to foreign countries and the receipt of large amount of foreign remittances, especially from West Asian countries. Kerala remained as a backward economy with a low rate of growth during the pre-liberalisation period. But the state's economy achieved a higher rate of investment, technological change and rate of growth during the period since 1991, when liberalisation policies were implemented and promotion was given to private investment. During the post-liberalisation period, an international factor which adversely affected the growth process as well as the migration prospects was the

Global Economic Crisis of 2008 and subsequent years. In this context, the volume examines the development of the state's economy since 2001 and the emerging development issues and challenges.

The volume starts with a chapter by B. A. Prakash and Jerry Alwin. In Chapter 2, B. A. Prakash examines the economic policies and economic growth during the pre- and post-liberalisation periods. It is pointed out that Kerala remained as a backward economy with low rate of growth during the pre-liberalisation period (1956–1990) when the state followed excessive market intervention type of economic policies and neglected private investment and technological development. It is argued that the volume of investment was too small to break the vicious circle of low rate of growth, technological backwardness and low level of productivity in all sectors. But the state's economy achieved higher rate of investment, technological change and rate of growth during the period since 1991, when liberalisation policies were implemented and promotion was given to private investment. The state witnessed rapid urbanisation, development of motor transport, technological change in all sectors, leading to reduction in poverty during the post-liberalisation period. But an external factor which adversely affected the growth process was the Global Economic Crisis of 2008 and subsequent years. But the liberalisation policies have created negative effects in agricultural sector such as fall in price of cash crops and marginalisation of some sections of people.

Chapter 3 by S. Irudaya Rajan and S. Sunitha discusses the demographic change in Kerala focusing on change in age structure and its effects on future population growth. Demography of Kerala is an exceptional case in India with its peculiar features such as low birth and death rate, longer life span of the individual and sex ratio which has been favourable to females. Another feature of the state's demography that stands out is the migration of its youth, mainly for employment purposes. The process of ageing is considered to be an end product of demographic transition in Kerala. The increase in life expectancy and the below replacement level of fertility comprises the growth in population of Kerala. There were 53 older persons for every 100 children in 2011. Every five working Keralites may have to take care of one elderly person in 2011. As far as the share of young and youth population has been decreasing, there are concerns regarding the capacities of societies to address the challenges associated with these demographic shifts. In order to face these challenges, the authors point out the need for a new approach to ensure a successful aging. They suggest that when people live longer, the society should make use of this longevity dividend by recognising older people as a resource and not as a burden.

Chapter 4 by M. P. Abraham and A. S. Shibu presents the trends, patterns and structure of employment and unemployment in Kerala since 2000. Based on the National Sample Survey definition and data, Chapter 4 examines the trends and patterns of rural and urban employment and unemployment in Kerala. Kerala's labour market has a paradoxical situation of high rate of unemployment among the educated labour force on the one hand and acute shortage of manual workers on the other. In spite of the economic development and structural transformation, there has not been much change in the pattern of rural employment in Kerala since 2000. Kerala's rural labour market is still dominated by self-employment and casual labour with a small share of regular employment. Compared to the rural labour market, more changes have occurred in the urban labour market. Kerala has a higher rate of rural and urban unemployment compared to other states in India. The categories of labour force which have very high rate of unemployment are youth and educated. Lack of generation of regular and remunerative employment for them is the most critical problem faced by Kerala in the employment front.

Chapter 5 by B. A. Prakash on emigration examines the trends, patterns of emigration of Keralite workers to West Asian countries and its economic impact. As contract migration is temporary type and the entire savings of the migrant is sent to his or her home country, the economic impact is substantial in labour sending countries. Of the total Indian migrant workers in West Asia, Kerala's share has been nearly half since mid-1970s. The large-scale emigration of workers is identified as the crucial and biggest factor that contributed to the biggest economic change of Kerala during the last four decades. It is argued that the large-scale migration and flows of remittances had resulted in unprecedented economic changes in Kerala since the mid-1970s. Based on empirical support, the author presents the following hypothesis to explain the economic impact of emigration. 'The factor which had the greatest impact on the state's economy, especially on labour market, consumption, savings, investment, poverty, income distribution and economic change during the last four decades has been the Gulf migration and migrant remittances'.

Chapter 6 by V. Prakash on interstate migration of workers discusses the structure and characteristics of Kerala's labour market, the profile of the workers, recruitment process, wages, working and living conditions and the effects of migration on migrant households. The major conclusions of the study are the following. The labour shortage of manual categories of workers, high wage rate compared to other states and better working conditions which prevailed in the state contributed to the migration of casual workers from other states to Kerala. Migrants belonged to poor households and migrated mainly from Bihar, Odisha and West Bengal. Migrants were economic migrants, and migration was prompted by monetary considerations. Some of them migrated to other states in India and learnt that the wages and working conditions in Kerala were better and decided to migrate here. Migrant labourers were recruited and employed by local subcontractors and they were assigned labour-intensive and low-skilled jobs. There were no pre-migration expenses because the workers arrived without undergoing any special training or paying any amount. They were forced to live in rented accommodations which were poor in all respects.

Chapter 7 by K. P. Mani on agriculture presents the performance of Kerala's agriculture since the dawn of this century with respect to cropping pattern, production, productivity, input use, commodity prices, export and imports. Kerala's agriculture underwent structural changes since the implementation of the economic reforms in 1991. A major change was shift in cropping pattern in favour of cash crops. There had been a steep fall in the area under paddy and other food crops which affected the food security of the state. At the same time, cash crops were not getting remunerative prices because of non-availability of processing and value addition facilities. In spite of the agricultural development, the productivity of food and non-food crops did not improve to a satisfactory level. On the input side, seeds, fertilisers, irrigation facilities and credit were not efficiently used. There was only limited evidence to show that the technology use was very effective and sustainable in agriculture. The launching of WTO and the associated clauses adversely affected our exports. The study concludes that if we want to make Kerala's agriculture globally competitive, earnest efforts are needed from the side of policy makers, government, parastatals, farmers and institutional agencies.

Chapter 8 by K. J. Joseph and Brigit Joseph examines the growth performance of plantation crops during the last two and a half decades after the implementation of economic liberalisation. It is pointed out that during the post-liberalisation period, there has been a shift in the policy pendulum from protection to open competition under globalisation, brought about by WTO and Free Trade Agreements along with the withdrawal of the state and greater play of market forces. As a result, the sector has got integrated with the world economy and exposed to heightened international competition from low-cost producers. This in turn has had its implications on the plight of plantation sector in general and the livelihood of the million small growers and workers in particular. The central message that emerges from the study is that the poor state of plantation sector is on account of a host of factors that include varied structural rigidities and spaces of exclusion in the different spheres of plantation sector such as production, processing, marketing and trade along with the generation and diffusion of knowledge. In a context wherein such structural infirmities remain unaddressed, the sector has been exposed to heightened international competition. This in turn has led to added challenges such as increasing price volatility, heightened import competition and more importantly unprecedented decline in prices.

Chapter 9 by P. Aravindh and S. Harikumar discusses the marginalisation of agrarian households in Kerala by looking at the changing pattern of land use, cropping pattern, agricultural wages, crop prices and indebtedness. The authors argue that the agricultural sector has been on a continuous downslide since the implementation of land reforms in 1970. The total area under cultivation came down steadily as a result of mounting population pressure and declining profitability from agriculture. The cropping pattern shifted from low profitable food crops to high profitable commercial crops. The rise in farm price of paddy was unable to consistently keep up with the rising labour cost in its cultivation. There had been a fall in price of cash crops, a shift of young labour force from agriculture to non-agricultural occupations and migration to foreign countries. These changes had heavily marginalised agrarian households, which were marginal or small. The marginalisation was further aggravated by rising level of indebtedness, which forced the abandonment of agriculture on a large scale in Kerala. The fact was that the indebted amount was used more for non-agricultural purposes and did very little to improve the state of agriculture of the indebted households.

Tomy Joseph's Chapter 10 on information technology (IT) analyses the policies of the successive governments in Kerala to promote IT development and points out the constraints and problems of the industry. The major conclusions of the study are the following. A number of policy initiatives have been taken by the successive state governments to leverage the benefits of the IT boom starting with the IT Policy of 1998, exempting labour laws and offering a number of concessions and incentives. The major thrust of these policies was to make Kerala an IT destination to make digital technology for overall development of the state and to ensure quick and efficient delivery of all essential services. The IT industry is still in the infant stage and Kerala is not in a position to compete with the IT-developed states such as Karnataka, Tamil Nadu and Telangana. The IT sector is facing challenges globally especially due to the recessionary trend, cutting down costs and profits along with local employment issues. The need of the hour seems to be shifting to a remodelled IT growth based on innovation and technology on the one hand and the boost of digitisation drives in all spheres to give fillip to the domestic market on the other.

Chapter 11 by Vijayamohanan Pillai presents the growth, performance, emerging issues and problems of power sector in Kerala since 2000 and argues for the need for suitable power sector reforms. It is pointed out that power sector in India has been undergoing a radical restructuring for quite some time. What was once in the realm of a vertically integrated public sector monopoly undertaking has now become functionally unbundled and independent corporations/companies in some of the states in India. It is generally recognised that distribution is the weakest link in the whole structure of power supply system. The massive leakage from this inefficient outlet in the form of subsidised sales and distribution loss, including technical loss and theft, illegal drawal and so on, under protective patronage has been steadily sapping the state electricity boards (SEBs), thus taking it to a no-return point of forced reforms. It is argued that the problems confronting the SEBs are just internal to them, and hence what the system requires is not any market-oriented restructuring but an essence-specific reform that can remove the impediments that stand in the way of the SEBs' improved performance.

Arun Shyamnath's Chapter 12 on transport sector examines the growth and development of this sector, emerging issues, constraints and the problems faced by different modes of transport. The major conclusions of the study are the following. The transport sector in Kerala has made considerable progress since 2000. But the focus of the growth has been primarily on roads and road transport. While there are hurdles in the expansion of road transport, other modes of transport such as waterways and railways which hold potential for growth are not utilised properly. The existing transport infrastructure, especially road, in the state is under severe strain and unable to meet the fast-growing transportation requirement. Current pattern of growth has led to emerging issues such as increasing congestion, pollution and accidents. Poor maintenance of existing transport infrastructure, lack of coordination between various departments and stakeholders, scarcity of finance and difficulty in land acquisition are major problems in the sector. There is a need to develop an intermodal transport network integrating various modes of transport, tapping the advantages and potential of each mode.

Chapter 13 by Rony Thomas Rajan and Shijo Philip discusses the development of tourism sector by focusing on the issues, problems and prospects. The major conclusions of the study are the following. Kerala has emerged as one of the prime tourist destinations in the international tourist map within a short span of time. The presence of natural resources, skilled manpower, niche health holidays, monuments, supportive government and multitude of micro enterprises along with responsible media have created a conducive atmosphere for tourism to grow and flourish. The sector makes some significant contributions towards earnings of foreign exchange, generation of employment and income as well as regional development. The following factors were identified as the major constraints of tourism development in Kerala: ineffective utilisation of available resources, poor management of waste by different local governments (LGs), stray dog menace, frequent strikes and bandh resulting in sudden stoppage of economic activities, lack of adequate training institutions to train youth for tourist jobs, poor marketing of tourism, etc. Major negative aspects of the tourism development related to destruction of environment and ecology. The excessive growth of tourism such as backwater tourism using house-boats, hill station tourism leading to encroachment of forest areas and environment destructing construction and growth of beach tourism destroying the environment are a few examples.

Chapter 14 by Jerry Alwin on banking presents the growth of banking sector since 2000, deposits, non-resident deposit (NRD), advances and credit deposit ratio (CDR) and location-wise analysis of banking activities. The major conclusions of the study are following. The major factor which contributed to the development of banking in Kerala has been the emigration of Keralites to Gulf countries since the mid-1970s and the receipt of large amount of foreign remittances. The major share of deposits and advances in the banking sector of Kerala are in public sector banks, followed by private sector, cooperative and foreign banks. The low CDR of Kerala may be attributed to low credit absorption in productive sectors, low rate of private investment, poor infrastructural facilities, etc. Though there has been an increase in growth of NRD, its share in total deposit has been showing a decline in the recent years. The banking activities such as bank branches, deposits and credit distribution are concentrated in urban and semi-urban areas. District-wise distribution of scheduled commercial banks also reveals that bank branches, deposits and CDR are higher in urban districts such as Ernakulam, Thiruvananthapuram and Thrissur.

Chapter 15 by Abdul Salim examines the nature and extent of expansion of higher education in southern and northern regions of Kerala and equity in access to higher education between the regions and socio-economic groups. The major conclusions of the study are the following. Though the expansion of higher education is very impressive in Kerala, the institutions are largely located in the southern region (Travancore and Cochin) compared to north (Malabar). Not only number of colleges but also the number of courses and sanctioned seats in the Travancore–Cochin region is large. Thus, the students of Travancore–Cochin region have easy access to higher education, while the access is a big issue for students of Malabar region. It is disturbing to note that most of the courses offered in the colleges were conventional categories and did not meet the requirements of the fast-growing knowledge economy. The major share of professional and technical education institutions in Kerala are private self-financing run by communal organisations and the students belonging to that community get more chances for getting admissions. The author argues that due to this, the gross enrolment ratio is the highest among General category students compared to Other Backward Community and Schedule Caste and Schedule Tribe students. A positive thing is the achievement of gender equality among all types of colleges in Kerala.

Chapter 16 by K. Gangadharan presents a profile of health care development and emerging issues in Kerala in the new era. The study also focuses on the problems of the health care of tribal people in Kerala. The major conclusions of the study are the following. Kerala has made significant gains in health indices such as infant mortality rate, birth rate, death rate and expectancy of life at birth. The challenges before the state are to sustain the achievements in the health sector and to tackle the problems of lifestyle diseases such as diabetes, coronary heart disease, renal disease, cancer and geriatric problems. Checking the spread of communicable diseases such as chicken guinea, dengue, leptospirosis and swine flu is emerging as major challenge. The medical services provided by Primary Health Centre (PHC) are poor or unsatisfactory due to a number of factors such as lack of periodic maintenance of buildings, sufficient equipment and furniture, basic clinical investigation facilities, shortage of medicine, inadequate staff, etc. The percentage share of delivery of child at home in the case of tribal people was found very high mainly due to lack of accessibility of health institutions, facilities and poor medical services.

Chapter 17 on fiscal crisis by B. A. Prakash and Jerry Alwin examines the nature, magnitude and causes of the acute fiscal crisis of Kerala. In order to explain the causes of the crisis, the authors present the following hypothesis.

[T]he successive governments in Kerala have been following fiscal policies neglecting resource mobilization for political gains on the one side and resorting to fiscal extravagance to satisfy the demands of powerful vested interest and pressure groups on the other, leading to a vicious circle of persistent low revenue receipts, higher non-plan revenue expenditure (NPRE) and higher rate of revenue and fiscal deficits.

The study found that slump in resource mobilisation, lack of periodical revision of rate of taxes and non-taxes, fall in the growth of tax revenue, underperformance of the Commercial Taxes Department in collection of sales tax and VAT, non-realisation of additional resource mobilisation targeted in the budget, inflated plan outlays, fall in dividends and profit from public sector undertakings, accumulation of arrears of revenue, and inefficient and poor collection of taxes and non-tax items have contributed to the crisis on the revenue side. Excessive and uncontrolled growth in non-plan revenue expenditure (NPRE) and the failure of successive governments to curtail this is the root cause of the present acute fiscal crisis on expenditure side. Among the items of NPRE, the single largest item is salary and pension expenditure.

Chapter 18 by Jose Sebastian on Goods and Services Tax (GST) discusses economic rationale and relevance of GST, its salient features and the impact of GST on India's economy in general and Kerala's economy in particular. The major observations of the chapter are the following. The vast diversity and complexity of the country and federal polity prevented India from keeping the GST very simple. While most developed countries have two GST rates, India has five rate categories. Petroleum and petroleum products are kept outside the GST. This means that those manufacturers who use these as intermediate products will not be eligible for input tax credit. All these rob our GST much of its benefits and render tax administration and compliance difficult. But these deficiencies can be rectified in course of time, and the country can look forward to a GST which is closer to the ideal. As a regional economy importing most of the manufactured commodities from other states, GST is likely to benefit Kerala immensely. The additional revenue that Kerala can count on in the GST scenario will be mostly from the goods sector and not from service sector. GST also offers a big opportunity for Kerala to kick-start its lost industrialisation opportunity.

Chapter 19 by Jerry Alwin on Eleventh Five-Year Plan examines strategies and objectives, financing plan and plan outlays, priorities in plan allocation, plan outlay and expenditure, execution of annual plans and plan performance. The major conclusions of the study are the following. The practice of fixation of unrealistic and inflated plan outlays without adequate resource support has led to poor achievement of targeted outlays. The practice of introduction of the supplementary projects and schemes subsequent to the passing of budget resulted in non-completion of projects in the budget within the stipulated time frame. The sector-wise outlay on infrastructure items such as irrigation and flood control, power, industry, transport and communications, urban infrastructure, scientific research, etc., shows that only a small amount is spent on these sectors and the share of them had been showing a decline. The plan performance was poor for the key sectors such as power, social and community services. Bunching of plan expenditure towards the last quarter of the financial year is the common practice followed by the government departments.

Chapter 20 by B. A. Prakash on decentralised planning presents an analysis of plan performance of grama panchayat in Kerala, based on a sample survey. The major conclusions of the study are the following. The irrational and irrelevant plan formulation guidelines giving too much emphasis on pre-project preparation activities and low priority for project preparation, getting approvals, timely execution of projects, etc., are the important causes for the poor plan performance. It was found that the root cause of the poor plan performance is the implementation of a large and unmanageable number of projects by the LGs. The execution of projects through beneficiary committee, lack of adequate staff for plan preparation and execution also contributed to the poor plan performance. Projects implemented gave overemphasis on ward-wise interests and neglected the overall development of the LG. Due to the enormous delay in completing the pre-execution formalities of projects, they were hastily executed during the last quarter or last month of the financial year. And bunching of plan expenditure to last quarter or the last month of the financial year is a common practice.

Chapter 2

Economic Liberalisation and Economic Growth in Kerala

B. A. Prakash

INTRODUCTION

Kerala completes six decades as a state of Indian Union as well as a regional economy in 2016. The development of the state's economy may be broadly divided into two periods based on the nature of economic policies pursued. During the first period between 1956 and 1990, the state pursued economic policies of excessive state intervention in market, development through economic planning, public investment in education and health, and expansion of social welfare measures. The second phase, since 1991, witnessed a radical change in economic policies, and market-oriented liberalisation and globalisation policies were implemented. Besides the domestic factors, the large–scale emigration of Keralite workers to foreign countries and the receipt of large amount of foreign remittances also influenced the growth and development of the economy. In this chapter, an attempt is made to examine the economic policies under the pre–liberalised and post–liberalised period. Our hypothesis is 'the state achieved higher investment, technological change and economic growth and speedy structural transformation during the post–liberalisation period compared to earlier period'. This chapter discusses the economic policies of central government, Kerala government and economic growth prior and after liberalisation. For the analysis, we use the state income data and other data published by the state government.

Theoretical Framework

The following frameworks are used for the analysis of economic growth and economic policies. Simon Kuznets (1974) has defined a country's economic growth as 'a long term rise in capacity to supply increasingly diverse economic goods to its population, this growing capacity based on advancing technology and the institutional and ideological adjustments that it demands'. Based on the economic growth perspectives of Third-World countries, Michael P. Todaro identifies three crucial factors of economic growth: (a) capital accumulation, including all new investment in land, physical equipment and human resources; (b) population growth and the associated eventual increase in the labour force; and (c) technological progress. There are three basic classifications of technological progress: (a) neutral, (b) labour savings and (c) capital savings (Todaro, 1998).

The policy instruments widely used in developed and underdeveloped countries are general and specific instruments (Chenery, 1976 [1958]). The general instruments act as broad aspects of economy: the money supply, the government budget, investment, consumption, etc. The specific instruments are applied differently to individual sectors of the economy, as illustrated by subsidies, tariffs, etc. To achieve a given effect on production, or use, of any commodity, there is a choice between controlling a price and controlling a quantity, by using either price or quantity variables as instruments. Thus, the main issues of economic policy are concerned with the choice between using general and specific instruments and between using prices and quantities as control variables. Though market intervention is essential to provide social goods, social welfare, protection of environment, etc., the experience of many developing countries suggests that excessive market intervention especially using quantity type of policy instruments retards economic growth.

ECONOMIC POLICIES OF THE CENTRAL GOVERNMENT

After the attainment of freedom from British colonial rule in 1947, India aimed to achieve rapid economic development through economic policies giving emphasis on excessive intervention in the market, centralised economic planning, expansion of public sector undertakings and public investment in infrastructure, education, health, etc. These policies were pursued from 1947 to 1990. India wanted to achieve socialistic pattern of society in a mixed economy framework by giving emphasis for private and public sectors in the production and distribution of goods and services. The key elements of the mixed economy of India were the following: (a) a framework of private agriculture based on public investment support; (b) the adoption of centralised planning aimed at coordinating large-scale investment in different sectors and regions of the economy; (c) assignment of major role to public sector; (d) regulation of external trade, foreign exchange and private foreign capital; (e) promotion of small and medium industries; and (f) adoption of a regime of administered prices in key sectors to regulate both the instabilities and the presumed inequalities of the market system.

The objectives of the industrial policy between 1948 and 1980 were to increase production and productivity, regionally balanced industrial development, encouraging small-scale industries, preventing concentration of economic power by the control of monopolies, controlling foreign investment in the domestic industry, pursing self-reliance through import substitution–oriented policies and assigning a central role for the public sector. A system of industrial licensing and a system of import licensing were introduced. These policies created barriers to entry, provided indiscriminate protection to domestic industries, prevented the existence of sick and non-viable units, imposed a system of physical controls, provided incentives for rent-seeking and acted as obstacles to technological development.

In the external sector, the choice between import substitution–oriented strategies and export promotion–oriented strategies or combination of the two was followed. The imposition of import controls, licensing and restrictions were widely used to restrict imports. A fixed exchange rate regime was also pursed. Thus, the excessive intervention in the market to regulate the domestic economy and external sector distorted the market prices, interest rates, wages, foreign exchange rates, created incentives for entrepreneurs for rent-seeking and corruption and prevented modernisation and technological change. The continuous deficits in balance of payments were financed through external borrowing resulting in huge and unmanageable level of foreign debt. These had led to an unprecedented balance of payment crisis in 1990. The crisis was so grave that access to the external commercial credit was completely denied. For getting a bank loan, the Government of India was forced to transport gold and pledge it in a foreign bank.

In the context of unprecedented economic crisis arising due to domestic and external factors, the Congress government, which came in to power in the centre in 1991, implemented market-oriented economic reforms, namely, structural adjustment reforms (SARs). The four major policy initiatives taken by the government were fiscal correction, trade policy reforms, industrial policy reforms and public sector reforms. An important element in the fiscal policy was to restore fiscal discipline in the context of the acute balance of payment crisis and the persistent inflationary situation that prevailed due to large budgetary fiscal deficits. The objective of the trade policy reforms was to create an environment which would provide a stimulus to exports while at the same time reduce the degree of regulations and licence control of foreign trade. The industrial policy announced in July 1991 sought to substantially deregulate industries so as to promote the growth of a more efficient and competitive industrial economy. The objective of the public sector reforms was to improve the operational efficiency of the public sector units whose performance was very poor and to implement a limited disinvestment of public sector equity. In March 1993, India moved from the dual exchange rate regime to a single, market-determined exchange rate system. The second phase in which the economic reforms were expanded was the period of the Bharatiya Janata Party rule between 1998 and 2004. The liberalisation, privatisation and globalisation process were further accelerated during the phase. The successive governments which came to power at the centre also pursued the liberalisation policies.

ECONOMIC POLICIES OF KERALA GOVERNMENT

Since the formation of the state in 1956, political parties or groups which came into power either believed in communist or socialist ideologies. Hence, excessive state intervention in market, development through economic planning, promotion of public sector undertaking, public investment in education and health, and expansion of social welfare measures were the cardinal elements of economic policy. Compared to the economic policy framework of the central government, more market intervention types of policies were pursued by the successive governments in Kerala between 1956 and 1990. For example, during the first five Five-Year Plans (1951–1979), the broad plan objectives were to increase per capita income to that of the national level, to attain self-reliance in food by increasing rice production, to terminate the tenancy system, to create employment opportunities for solving the unemployment problem, to reduce regional disparities and to uplift the vulnerable sections of society, especially Scheduled Castes and Tribes (State Planning Board, 1978). The basic weakness of the policy pursued was that it ignored the vital role of private investment in accelerating the economic growth and development.

The strategy pursued for economic development between 1956 and 1990 was state sponsored and state funded through planning and public investment. It was believed that, with the small amount of public investment, the state can achieve rapid economic growth and development. The policies pursed were inward-looking, excessive state intervention in market, more emphasis for equity and social welfare and ignored private investment, production, productivity, employment generation and technological development. Mechanisation of activities in agriculture, industries and tertiary sectors were considered anti-labour as it affected the employment opportunities of workers. It was believed that development means starting more government departments, public sector undertakings, semi-government institutions, etc., and generation of employment in public sector. These policies had suppressed the initiatives of investors and discouraged investment, production and technological development and failed to accelerate the growth process in a big way. The introduction of computers in banks, public sector undertakings and government departments were strongly opposed by the trade unions in the 1980s.

The implementation of market-oriented economic reforms by the central government since 1991 was not welcomed by the political parties, especially Left parties in the state of Kerala. They conducted constant agitations against the reforms during the first half of the 1990s when United Democratic Front (UDF) government was in power. When the Left parties came to power during the second half of the 1990s, they said that they were not going to implement these policies, which were harmful to Kerala and had unfavourable impacts on poor and weaker sections. In spite of this, the liberalisation policies implemented by the central government since 1991 made revolutionary changes in the promotion of private investment, production, productivity and technological development in the state in all sectors (Prakash, 1994).

ECONOMIC GROWTH PRIOR TO LIBERALISATION (1956–1990)

We may start the analysis with a discussion of economic situation that prevailed at the eve of the formation of the state. The state of Kerala came into existence by integrating three regions, namely, Travancore, Cochin and Malabar, with some other minor territorial adjustments in 1956. At the time of the formation of the state, the economic conditions of Travancore and Cochin regions were better compared to Malabar. Prior to independence, Malabar region was under the British colonial rule and remained very backward. In 1956, Kerala was the smallest, but most densely populated, state of India. The total population of Kerala was around 150 lakhs. The economy was basically rural and the share of urban population was below 15 per cent. The major socio-economic problems faced by Kerala were acute economic backwardness, massive poverty and unemployment. Kerala was identified as a state having very high incidence of poverty among the states in India. According to one estimate, the percentage of poor below poverty line in Kerala was as high as 90.75 per cent in 1960–1961 (Dandekar & Rath, 1971).

An analysis of the various sectors of the Kerala's economy indicates that the state had the characteristics of a backward economy. The agriculture sector remained backward, followed traditional methods for cultivation and was characterised by low productivity levels. Major agricultural products were produced and sold as agricultural raw materials in domestic and foreign markets. Majority of the farmers had very small, marginal or tiny agricultural holdings which made agricultural operations uneconomic. Due to the relative profitability in cultivation of plantation and commercial crops, the farmers were interested in the cultivation of cash crops, and cropping pattern shifted from food to cash crops. The animal husbandry sector was poorly developed and the milk yield per cow in Kerala was the lowest in the country. Kerala has a long coastline and produced nearly 30 per cent of the total marine fish production of the country during the mid-1950s. The widespread use of non-mechanised and indigenous fishing crafts were cited as the major reasons for the low productivity. Lack of modernisation of activities connected with fishing, preservation of fish, marketing and processing were cited as the major constraints for fisheries development.

Regarding the generation of electricity, the state was in the infant stage. The electricity was generated from a few hydroelectric stations and distributed only in 846 places in 1956. The mechanisation of road transport was also at the infant stage and the total number of motor vehicles was only 24,480 in 1961. In mid-1950s, Kerala remained as an industrially backward state with the dominance of traditional and labour-intensive industries such as coir, cashew, handloom, etc. Of the 9.7 lakh persons engaged in industrial sector, 17.5 per cent were engaged in factory-type industries and the rest were engaged in unorganised small-scale and cottage industries. Predominance of technologically backward small-scale units which created a meagre re-investable surplus and poor entrepreneurial talents were identified as the major causes for industrial backwardness.

Based on the state income data, an attempt is made here to examine the aggregate and sector-wise growth of the state economy during the pre-liberalised period. The average annual growth rate of the net domestic product (NDP) for the decade 1960s and 1970s is given in Table 2.1.

Except the second half of the 1960s, the annual average rate of growth was below 2.6 per cent in the 1960s and 1970s. This low growth rate can be attributed to heavy reliance of state on the meagre state resources for investment, excessive intervention in market discouraging private investment, slow pace of development of power, road transport, motor transport and other items of core infrastructure. The policies had given heavy emphasis on achieving social welfare and totally neglected the vital role of private investment. The state's

Table 2.1 *Annual Average Growth Rate of Net Domestic Product of Kerala (%)*

Period and Constant Prices	Sector-wise Growth Rate			
	Primary	Secondary	Tertiary	Total
(1) At 1960–1961 prices				
1960–1961 to 1965–1966	0.4	5.8	4.4	2.5
1965–1966 to 1970–1971	5.1	4.3	5.6	5.1
(2) At 1970–1971 prices				
1970–1971 to 1975–1976	1.6	4.0	3.3	2.6
1975–1976 to 1980–1981	−1.2	5.6	4.1	2.0

Sources: Bureau of Economics and Statistics (1977) and Department of Economics and Statistics (1986).

Table 2.2 *Sector-wise Distribution of Net Domestic Product of Kerala (%)*

Period and Constant Prices	Primary	Secondary	Tertiary	Total
(1) At 1960–1961 prices				
1960–1961	56.0	15.2	28.8	100.0
1970–1971	50.5	17.1	32.4	100.0
(2) At 1970–1971 prices				
1970–1971	49.4	16.3	34.2	100.0
1980–1981	40.3	20.6	39.2	100.0

Sources: Bureau of Economics and Statistics (1977) and Department of Economics and Statistics (1986).

economy also witnessed a structural change indicating a steep fall in share of the primary sector on the one hand and an increase in the share of secondary and tertiary sectors on the other during the decades 1960s and 1970s (Table 2.2).

We may also examine the economic growth and structural change of the state's economy during the decade 1980s. During the decade 1980s, a major factor which influenced economic growth had been the large-scale migration to Gulf countries and its impact on state's economy (Prakash, 1998). The total net state domestic product (NSDP) of Kerala at constant prices increased from ₹30,198 crore in 1980–1981 to ₹37,478 crore in 1990–1991 (Table 2.3). The compound annual growth rate of the state economy and its sectors and subsectors for the decade 1980s is given in Table 2.4.

During the first half of the 1980s, the annual growth rate of the state's economy was 1.14 per cent and during the second half 3.59 per cent. The primary sector witnessed a negative growth during the first half of the 1980s followed by a marginal growth during the second half. The secondary sector witnessed a higher growth rate in the second half of 1980s. Industry and construction are the two sub-sectors that registered an increase in the growth rate during the period. Compared to the secondary sector, the tertiary sector witnessed a steady growth during the 1980s. Some of the sub-sectors which witnessed a fairly high rate were transport, storage and communication, banking and insurance, and public administration. During the decade 1980s, the state's economy witnessed a structural change similar to that which occurred during the decade 1970s. The economy witnessed a decline in the share of the primary sector and an increase in the share of secondary and tertiary sectors (Table 2.5). A notable development was the steep increase in the share of the tertiary sector from 45 per cent to 51 per cent.

Table 2.3 *Net State Domestic Product of Kerala in Constant Prices*

Year	NSDP (₹ crore)	Growth (%)	Per Capita Income (₹)
1980–1981	30,198★	–	11,909
1985–1986	30,532★	1.11	11,260
1990–1991	37,478★	22.75	12,929
1995–1996	50,603★	35.02	16,592
2000–2001	62,909★	24.32	19,809
2005–2006	91,884★	46.06	27,714
2011–2012	328,021★★	257.00	97,912
2015–2016 (Q)	426,131★★	29.91	124,773

Source: Department of Economics and Statistics (2010) and State Planning Board (2017).

Notes: ★ Base year 1999–2000, ★★ Base year 2011–2012, Q Quick Estimate.

Table 2.4 *Compound Annual Growth of Net State Domestic Product of Kerala (%)*

| S. No. | Sector and Year | Constant Prices (Base Year 1999–2000) | | | | |
		1980–1985	1985–1990	1990–1995	1995–2000	2000–2005
1	Agriculture and allied activities	0.37	3.28	6.13	0.42	1.97
2	Forestry and logging	−15.21	−6.59	4.43	−0.28	0.44
3	Fishing	−1.73	−1.93	9.50	−0.74	0.12
4	Mining and quarrying	2.80	12.66	2.69	10.05	2.80
	Subtotal of primary sector	−3.03	1.74	6.26	0.39	1.69
5	Manufacturing	4.47	6.36	7.39	3.98	2.48
6	Electricity, gas and water supply	−1.49	6.99	2.15	15.36	9.66
7	Construction	1.24	3.46	11.32	1.90	13.31
	Subtotal of secondary sector	2.47	5.05	8.92	3.64	8.48
8	Transport, storage and communication	8.75	6.31	10.20	11.06	13.55
9	Trade, hotel and restaurants	1.68	3.35	4.99	6.12	4.51
10	Banking and insurance	8.79	16.20	8.45	14.94	9.49
11	Real estate, ownership of dwellings and business services	3.12	3.12	3.06	4.22	9.70
12	Public administration	9.83	8.41	5.96	9.94	7.14
13	Other services	5.04	1.95	4.23	6.54	4.07
	Subtotal of tertiary sector	3.79	4.16	5.39	7.52	7.37
	Net state domestic product	1.14	3.59	6.36	4.82	6.42
	Per capita income (in ₹)	1.50	1.41	1.04	0.86	0.84

Source: Department of Economics and Statistics (2010).

An attempt is also made to examine the growth in employment, urbanisation, reduction in poverty and mechanisation in motor transport sector during the pre-liberalised period. A review of the growth in employment shows that the decadal growth rates of employment in the 1960s were 10 per cent, in the 1970s 25 per cent and in

Table 2.5 *Sectoral Share of Net State Domestic Product at Constant Price (%)*

S. No.	Sector and Year	Constant Prices (Base Year 1999–2000)				Constant Prices (Base Year 2011–2012)
		1980–1981	1990–1991	2000–2001	2005–2006	2015–2016 (Q)
1	Agriculture and allied activities	21.00	23.05	17.05	13.43	9.48
2	Forestry and logging	11.36	1.89	1.81	1.33	–
3	Fishing	3.92	3.83	2.13	1.33	–
4	Mining and quarrying	0.24	0.56	0.29	0.46	1.14
	Subtotal of primary sector	36.52	29.32	21.28	16.55	10.62
5	Manufacturing	7.65	9.24	8.91	6.37	9.76
6	Electricity, gas and water supply	0.54	0.41	1.17	1.07	0.89
7	Construction	10.33	9.72	9.89	15.85	15.73
	Subtotal of secondary sector	18.52	19.37	19.97	23.29	26.38
8	Transport, storage and communication	2.32	4.03	8.61	10.88	8.61
9	Trade, hotel and restaurants	22.80	23.10	22.87	22.12	18.27
10	Banking and insurance	1.10	2.98	5.26	5.64	5.10
11	Real estate, ownership of dwellings and business services	6.77	7.69	7.69	7.52	15.70
12	Public administration	2.46	4.25	4.33	4.52	3.58
13	Other services	9.51	9.26	9.99	9.47	11.74
	Subtotal of tertiary sector	44.96	51.31	58.75	60.16	63.00
	Net state domestic product	100.00	100.00	100.00	100.00	100.00*

Source: Department of Economics and Statistics (2010).

Notes: Q = Quick Estimate

*denotes net state value added.

the 1980s 18 per cent. While the growth rate of employment was very low in the primary sector, the secondary sector achieved comparatively better growth rates. Among the three sectors, the sector that achieved a very high rate of growth in employment was the tertiary sector. The structure of employment also witnessed somewhat similar changes to the structural changes of the state's economy. There had been a steady decline in the share of employment of the primary sector between 1961 and 1991. The share of employment of the secondary sector remained almost at the same level during the period. But the share of employment of the tertiary sector witnessed a continuous increase during the three decades. It increased from 20 per cent in 1961 to 34 per cent in 1991. The large-scale migration to the West Asia and the flow of large volume of remittances have also contributed to economic change in all fronts since the mid-1970s.

Urbanisation is an indicator of economic development. Between 1951 and 1981, the growth in the share in urban population was very small. It increased from 13.48 per cent in 1951 to 18.74 per cent in 1981. This indicates that the state's economy remains stagnant without much economic change. However, the decade 1980s witnessed an increase in urbanisation process. Estimates on poor people based on the official poverty line of the planning commission indicate that the incidence of poverty in Kerala was very high during the 1970s. Nearly 60 per cent of the people were below the poverty line in 1973–1974. But there had been a steep decline in the poverty during the late 1970s, 1980s and later periods. A major reason for this can be attributed to the large-scale migration of Keralite workers to Gulf countries and receipt of huge amount of remittances since the mid-1970s.

The growth in the number of motor vehicles will give an idea about the mechanisation in road transport sector. During the 1960s, Kerala had a small number of motor vehicles, and people relied on manual and animal-driven vehicles for transporting goods and passengers. The total number of vehicles was only 24,480 in 1960–1961. But the post-liberalisation period witnessed an unprecedented increase in the number of personalised category of motor vehicles such as motor cars, auto-rickshaws, motorcycles, etc.

Thus, the aforementioned review of the growth rate during the three decades, namely, the 1960s, 1970s and 1980s prior to the introduction of the liberalised economic reforms indicates that the growth rate was below 5 per cent except the period of the second half of the 1960s. This can be considered as low rate of growth of the economy. Though a number of reasons can be attributed to the low growth rate, the most important reason was the policies of excessive intervention of the market resulting in distortion of market prices, impositions of controls and the total neglect of private investment in the economic policies of the state.

ECONOMIC GROWTH AFTER LIBERALISATION (1991-2016)

In this section, an attempt is made to analyse the rate of growth of state's economy, different sectors and sub-sectors using NSDP at constant prices during the post-liberalisation period. The liberalised and market-oriented policies pursued since 1991 had stimulated the growth process in primary, secondary and tertiary activities. The state's economy also registered a higher rate of growth during the post-liberalisation period compared to earlier period. But the trend in growth was arrested due to the global economic crisis of 2008. This is due to the fact that the state economy had been integrating more with the world economy since 1991. The Global Economic Crisis of 2008 had inflicted severe damage to the state's economy. In this section, we examine a comparative analysis of the growth trends during the pre- and post-liberalisation period and trends in growth rate since the global crisis year of 2008.

A noticeable development was that the state's economy achieved a higher rate of economic growth during the post-liberalisation period compared to pre-liberalisation period (Tables 2.4 and 2.6). The liberalised policies stimulated the growth process in all sectors, namely, primary, secondary and tertiary. The rate of growth of primary activities, especially agriculture and allied activities, registered a higher rate of growth in certain years. The industrial growth was also higher during the post-liberalisation period. The construction is a sub-sector which registered a spurt in growth during the first half of the 1990s due to market-oriented policies. The liberalisation policies had accelerated a higher rate of growth in the tertiary sector activities. The sub-sector, transport, storage and communications registered the highest growth rate during the period. Banking and insurance, real estate, ownership of dwelling and business services and public administration also witnessed a higher rate of growth during the post-liberalisation period.

The policies also accelerated a process of structural change of the state's economy at a faster rate. There had been a steep fall in the share of the primary sector comprising agriculture and allied activities, forestry, fishing, mining and quarrying. The share of the primary sector declined from 29.32 per cent in 1991 to 16.5 per cent in 2006. It further declined to 10.6 per cent in 2016 (Table 2.5). On the other hand, the share of the secondary sector comprising manufacturing, electricity, gas and water supply and construction registered an increase during the post-liberalisation period. It increased from 19.37 per cent in 1991 to 23.29 per cent in 2006. The sector further increased to 26.38 per cent in 2016 (Table 2.5).

The most important structural change occurred during the period was the emergence of the tertiary sector as the dominant sector of the state. The share of the tertiary sector increased from 51.31 per cent in 1991 to 60.16 per cent in 2006. It further increased to 63 per cent in 2016 (Table 2.5). Trade, hotels and restaurants became the single sub-sector contributing for the largest share of the state's income. There was also substantial increase in the share of transport, storage and communications, real estate, ownership of dwellings and business services and other services (Table 2.5).

We may examine the impact of the Global Economic Crisis of 2008 on the growth rate of the state's economy. The crisis of 2008 is considered as the worst global crisis since the Great Depression of the 1930s. As the Indian economy is integrated with the world economy, the crisis had affected the national as well as the state's economy very badly. During the first decade of the present century, the state achieved a fairly high rate of growth till the year of Global Crisis of 2008. During the period between 2000 and 2005, the compound annual growth rate of the state's economy was 6.42 per cent (Table 2.4). In the subsequent two years, the rate of growth registered a steady increase. But the rate of growth fell from 8.9 per cent to 6.5 per cent during 2008–2009 (Table 2.6). A steep fall in the growth rate of the secondary sector is a major cause for this. There was also a fall in tertiary activities such as trade, hotels and restaurants, banking and insurance, real estate sector, public administration and other services.

Table 2.6 *Annual Growth Rate of NSDP of Kerala (%)*

S. No.	Sector and Year	Constant Prices (Base Year 2004–2005)					
		2006–2007	2007–2008	2008–2009	2009–2010	2010–2011	2011–2012
1	Agriculture	−11.06	−1.07	8.22	−5.14	−10.37	5.58
2	Forestry and logging	0.35	5.59	3.17	3.03	−1.16	2.15
3	Fishing	5.39	−0.57	−0.17	−0.45	−3.62	2.73
4	Mining and quarrying	−12.76	−22.84	15.03	28.62	−1.52	26.84
	Subtotal of primary sector	−8.54	−0.74	6.94	−2.98	−8.29	5.47
5	Manufacturing	7.23	20.79	−1.48	−0.28	12.36	4.52
6	Construction	6.71	1.99	2.39	9.26	16.74	4.16
7	Electricity, gas and water supply	2.15	3.53	−21.90	17.99	4.86	0.56
	Subtotal of secondary sector	6.70	8.21	0.10	6.07	14.88	4.18
8	Transport, storage and communication	17.22	14.45	17.96	19.82	12.96	13.53
9	Trade, hotels and restaurants	10.28	7.70	3.28	12.03	−3.04	0.36
10	Banking and insurance	17.12	15.86	12.10	10.47	13.15	10.27
11	Real estate, ownership of dwellings and business services	13.15	10.56	8.82	3.14	8.30	2.68
12	Public administration	13.36	14.61	6.47	−2.18	−1.91	28.47
13	Other services	8.92	11.83	3.89	20.36	13.51	2.22
	Subtotal of tertiary sector	12.53	11.17	7.97	12.15	6.32	6.38
	NSDP	7.90	8.93	6.15	9.04	6.40	5.82

Source: Department of Economics and Statistics (2015).

A review of the trends in growth rate suggests that the adverse impacts of the Global Crisis continued till the end of 2013–2014. Between 2008–2009 and 2013–2014, the growth rate was lower in all the years except 2009–2010 (Tables 2.6 and 2.7). Industry is one of the sub-sectors which was severely affected due to the Global Economic Crisis. Electricity, gas and water supply is another sub-sector which experienced a fall or negative growth rate. In the tertiary sector, except transport, storage and communications, and banking and insurance, all the other sub-sectors were adversely affected during the period. Available state income data suggest that the state's economy achieved a revival from the adverse effect of Global Crisis only during the year 2014–2015 (Table 2.7).

We may also examine the recent trends in the structural change of the state's economy between 2006 and 2016 (Table 2.5). The state has been witnessing a structural change, and the share of the primary sector has been declining. The share of the secondary sector registered a marginal fall due to the fall in the activities of construction. On the other hand, there has been a steep increase in the share of the tertiary sector due to the expansion of all sub-sectors except public administration and other services. Among tertiary sub-sectors, the sector which registered the largest increase in its share was real estate, ownership of dwellings and business services.

But the liberalisation and globalisation policies have created negative effects in some fronts. These policies have led to substantial import of agricultural produce and resulted in the fall in the price of cash crops in Kerala. Rubber, the major crop, was severely hit due to the price fall. The policies also contributed to the marginalisation of certain sections of the society such as landless agricultural labourers, marginal farmers, tribal people and workers solely depend on agriculture and allied activities. The anticipation of substantial private investment in infrastructure through public–private participation (PPP) mode was not materialised. Though these policies have created some negative effects, the policies have laid the foundation for higher rate of investment, higher growth, generation of more employment opportunities, reduction of poverty and increase in consumption levels of common people.

Table 2.7 *Annual Growth Rate of NSDP of Kerala (%)*

S. No.	Sector and Year	Constant Prices (Base Year 2011–2012)			
		2012–2013	2013–2014	2014–2015 (P)	2015–2016 (Q)
1	Agriculture, forestry and fishing	−3.07	−3.82	−0.53	−2.55
2	Mining and quarrying	−16.03	48.40	37.98	5.94
	Subtotal of primary sector	−3.80	−1.26	2.31	−1.71
3	Manufacturing	13.46	−5.22	3.08	12.65
4	Electricity, gas and water supply	−2.53	13.17	−4.22	3.34
5	Construction	−3.66	8.67	7.04	6.45
	Subtotal of secondary sector	2.52	3.32	5.16	8.55
6	Trade, repair, hotels and restaurants	13.88	2.52	8.43	8.05
7	Transport, storage and communication	5.67	9.10	5.88	8.63
8	Financial services	6.61	11.19	8.26	8.37
9	Real estate, ownership of dwellings and business services	14.56	16.65	13.30	12.06
10	Public administration	0.18	2.19	5.49	3.93
11	Other services	5.21	3.68	7.64	6.82
	Subtotal of tertiary sector	9.50	7.34	8.86	8.64
12	Total net state value added at basic prices	5.67	5.14	7.08	7.42
13	Taxes on products	12.35	0.81	12.45	12.45
14	Subsidies on product	9.87	7.48	−7.81	−7.81
15	NSDP	6.28	4.62	7.95	8.24

Sources: State Planning Board (2017) and Economic Review (2016).

Note: P=Provisional Estimate, Q=Quick Estimate.

CONCLUSION

The aforementioned analysis may be concluded with the following observations. Kerala remained as a backward economy with low rate of growth between 1956 and 1990, when the state followed excessive market intervention type of economic policies and neglected private investment. The volume of investment was too small to break the vicious circle of low rate of growth, technological backwardness and low level of productivity in all sectors. But the state's economy achieved higher rate of investment, technological change and rate of growth during the period since 1991, when liberalised policies were implemented and promotion was given to private investment. The state witnessed rapid urbanisation, development of motor transport, technological change in all sectors, leading to reduction in poverty and rise in consumption levels during the post-liberalisation period. The large-scale emigration to the Gulf, the receipt of large amount of remittances and the spending of it in the state's economy increased consumption level and created the demand for goods and services, leading to and expansion of economic activities. During the post-liberalisation period, an international factor which adversely affected the growth process was the Global Economic Crisis of 2008 and subsequent years.

REFERENCES AND SELECT BIBLIOGRAPHY

Bureau of Economics and Statistics (BES). (1977). *Statistics for planning 1977.* Thiruvananthapuram: BES.

Census of India. (1961). *General economic tables* (Vol. 7, Part II B (i), Kerala). Thiruvananthapuram: Director of Census Operations.

———. (1981a). Series 10, Kerala, Part III (A and B) (i). *General economic tables.* Thiruvananthapuram: Director of Census Operations.

———. (1981b). *Final population tables* (Series 10, Paper 3, Kerala). Thiruvananthapuram: Director of Census Operations.

———. (1991). Series 12, Kerala, paper 1 of 1991. *Provisional population totals.* Thiruvananthapuram: Director of Census Operations.

———. (2001). Series 33, Kerala, Paper 1 of 2001. *Provisional population totals.* Thiruvananthapuram: Director of Census Operations.

Chenery, H. B. (1976 [1958]). Policy instruments and development alternatives. In G. M. Meir (ed), *Leading issues in economic development* (pp. 807–811). New York, NY: Oxford University Press.

Dandekar, V. M., & Rath, N. (1971). *Poverty in India*. Pune: Indian School of Political Economy.

Department of Economics and Statistics (DES). (1986). *State income and related aggregates of Kerala for the years 1983–84 and 1985–86*. Thiruvananthapuram: DES.

———. (1999). *Statistics since independence*. Thiruvananthapuram: DES.

———. (2001). *Statistics for planning 2001*. Thiruvananthapuram: DES.

———. (2010). *Gross state domestic product of Kerala from 1970–71 to 2008–09 (base year 1999–2000)*. Thiruvananthapuram: DES.

———. (2015). *GSDP of Kerala and India from 2004–05 to 2013–14*. Thiruvananthapuram: DES.

Kuznets, S. (1974). *Economic growth and structure*. New Delhi: Oxford and India Book House.

Planning Commission. (2014). *Report of the expert group to review the methodology for measurement of poverty*. New Delhi: Planning Commission.

Prakash, B. A. (ed). (1994). *Kerala's economy: Performance, problems and prospects*. New Delhi: SAGE Publications.

———. (1998, 12 December). Gulf migration and its economic impact. *Economic and Political Weekly*, *33*(50), 3209–3213.

———. (ed). (1999). *Kerala's economic development: Issues and problems*. New Delhi: SAGE Publications.

———. (ed). (2004). *Kerala's economic development: Performance and problems in post-liberalisation period*. New Delhi: SAGE Publications.

———. (ed). (2012). *The Indian economy since 1991: Economic reforms and performance*. New Delhi: Pearson.

State Planning Board. (1978). *Draft five-year plan (1978–83)* (Vol. I). Thiruvananthapuram: State Planning Board.

———. (2006). *Economic review for the years 2005*. Thiruvananthapuram: State Planning Board.

———. (2014). *Perspective plan 2030—Kerala* (Vols. 1–4). Thiruvananthapuram: State Planning Board.

———. (2017). *Economic review 2016* (Vol. 2). Thiruvananthapuram: State Planning Board.

Todaro, M. P. (1998). *Economic development*. Harlow, England: Addison–Wesley.

Zachariah, K. C., & Rajan, S. I. (2012). *Kerala's gulf connection, 1998–2011: Economic and social impact of migration*. New Delhi: Orient BlackSwan.

———. (2014). *Dynamics of emigration and remittances in Kerala: Report on Kerala migration survey 2014 (draft report)*. Thiruvananthapuram: Centre for Development Studies.

PART II

Demography, Employment and Migration

Chapter 3

Demographic Change in Kerala

S. Irudaya Rajan and S. Sunitha

INTRODUCTION

The economic development of any country depends on its demographic trends. India has the second largest population in the world and is passing through the third stage of demographic transition, which is indicated by a reduction in birth and death rates. Age structure of the population determines the impact of population growth. The state-level data indicates that the pace of demographic transition varies across the states. The four southern states, namely, Kerala, Tamil Nadu, Karnataka and Andhra Pradesh, have been far behind from its co-runners in the field of demographic advancement to achieve magnificent economic development. Kerala is a forerunner among these states, which has an atypical structure of development through its demographic advancement.

The 2011 Census explains the age structure of the population as children accounted for 23.4 per cent (0–14 age group), working age group accounted for 63.9 per cent (15–59 age group) and the elderly comprised 12.6 per cent (age 60 years and above) of the total population. Median age of population is increasing faster with the reduction of number of children and growth of older population. In 'young' populations, the median age is typically below 25 years. Kerala has a median age of 31 years which is higher than the national average (25.5 years), pointing to the growth of population towards old. This higher median age is achieved through an age structural transition from the first stage of demographic transition (high birth rate and high death rate) at the beginning of the last century to the last stage of demographic transition (low birth rate and low death rate) at the beginning of the present century. This age structure is similar to that of developed countries. Till 1971, the state had highest population growth rate, which was above the national level and thereafter it showed a declining trend. By controlling the mortality factor, this population in 1971 will become aged at 2031 and this would lead to a boom in the aged population. This chapter envisages how the changes occurred in the age structure from the past and how it is consecutive at present and how this will affect the future population growth. Here, we discuss three major demographic inputs, namely fertility, mortality and migration, and their related components and determinants.

Demographic Terms

To be affluent with this chapter, it is necessary to get acquainted with certain demographic terms. The definitions are borrowed from the book written by Ramakumar (1986).

1. Median age—the age that divides a population into two numerically equal groups; half the people are younger than this age and half are older.
2. Population momentum—the tendency for population growth to continue beyond the time that replacement-level fertility has been achieved because of the relatively high concentration of people in the childbearing years.
3. Replacement-level fertility—the level of fertility at which a couple has only enough children to replace themselves, or about two children per couple.
4. Total fertility rate (TFR)—the average number of children that would be born alive to a woman during her lifetime if she passes through her childbearing years conforming to the age-specific fertility rates of a given year.

5. Age-specific fertility rate—the number of live births per 1,000 women in a specific age group during a given year. The age interval is 15 to 49 years.
6. Crude birth rate (CBR)—the number of births per 1,000 population in a year.
7. Crude death rate (CDR)—the number of deaths per 1,000 population in a year.
8. Infant mortality rate (IMR)—the number of deaths of infants under age 1 per 1,000 live births in a given year.
9. Nuptiality—the frequency, characteristics and dissolution of marriages in a population.
10. Natality—births as a component of population change.
11. Mortality—deaths as a component of population change.
12. Maternal mortality ratio—the number of women who die as a result of pregnancy and childbirth complications per 100,000 live births in a given year.
13. Expectation of life—the average number of additional years a person could expect to live if current mortality trends were to continue for the rest of that person's life.

POPULATION SIZE AND GROWTH

The population of Kerala has almost doubled (in 2011) since its formation as a state in 1956. There was 8.4 per cent increase even in the epidemic period of 1911–1921. In the very next period, there was a sudden rise in the population and it stood at 17.9 per cent. The highest percentage of increase over the period was of 20.8 per cent during 1961–1971. In 2011, the increase in percentage was just 4.7. Unlike other parts of India, female population has dominated over the years, especially since the beginning of the last century (Table 3.1). In 1901, there were 4 more females to 1,000 males, whereas in 2011 there were 84 more females to 1,000 males. This difference is attributed to both higher life expectancy among females and larger international migration among males (Bhat & Rajan, 1990). Kerala's population was 2.1 times more from 1901 to 1951, whereas there was an increase of 2.5 times in between 1951 and 2011.

Table 3.1 *Population and Its Growth, Kerala, 1901–2011*

Year	Male	Female	Total	Sex Ratio	Annual Exponential Growth Rate	Density
1901	3,191,466	3,204,796	6,396,262	1,004	–	165
1911	3,559,425	3,588,248	7,147,673	1,008	1.1	184
1921	3,879,458	3,922,669	7,802,127	1,011	0.9	201
1931	4,702,951	4,804,099	9,507,050	1,022	2.0	245
1941	5,443,296	5,588,245	11,031,541	1,027	1.5	284
1951	6,681,901	6,867,217	13,549,118	1,028	2.1	349
1961	8,361,927	8,541,788	16,903,715	1,022	2.2	435
1971	10,587,851	10,759,524	21,347,375	1,016	2.3	549
1981	12,527,767	12,925,913	25,453,680	1,032	1.8	655
1991	14,288,995	14,809,523	29,098,518	1,036	1.3	749
2001	15,468,600	16,372,800	31,841,400	1,058	0.9	819
2011	16,027,412	17,378,649	33,406,061	1,084	0.5	860

Source: Compiled from various Censuses, 1901–2011, Registrar General of India.

Kerala is one of the most densely populated states of India. The increase in population density was at its peak in 1971 and 1981. According to 2011 Census, population density of Kerala was 860 persons per square kilometre and the most densely populated districts are Thiruvananthapuram, Alappuzha and Kozhikode. Urban share of population has had a huge growth during the last decade from 26.0 per cent in 2001 to 47.7 per cent in 2011. The shift of labour force from agriculture sector to the tertiary sector is the reason for high urbanisation in Kerala.

Interestingly, when India had a negative growth rate during 1911–1921, due to the spread of communicable diseases, Kerala had a positive growth rate of 0.9 per cent (Figure 3.1). The state had a sudden rise in the growth rate in 1931, which continued up to 1961–1971. After 1971, there was a gradual reduction in the growth rate and it was 0.5 per cent in 2001–2011.

Religious customs mould the shape of the population. The population control methods are not accepted by many religions which

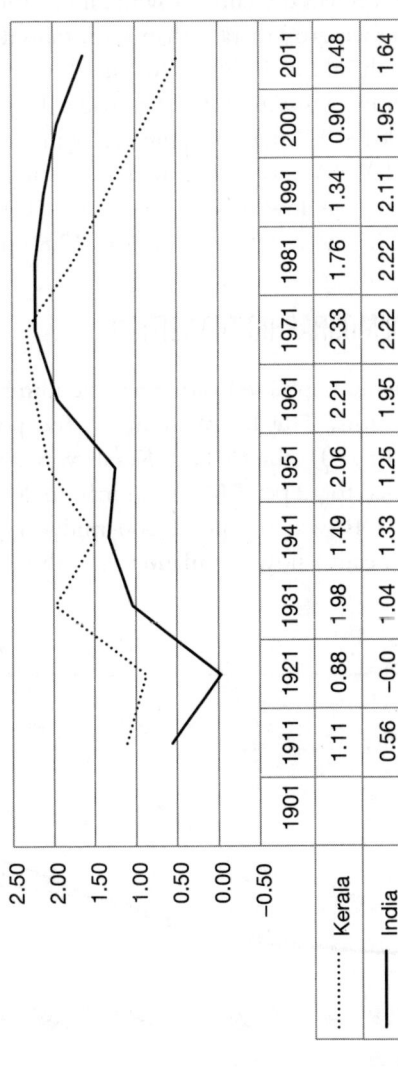

	1901	1911	1921	1931	1941	1951	1961	1971	1981	1991	2001	2011
Kerala		1.11	0.88	1.98	1.49	2.06	2.21	2.33	1.76	1.34	0.90	0.48
India		0.56	–0.0	1.04	1.33	1.25	1.95	2.22	2.22	2.11	1.95	1.64

Figure 3.1 *Annual Exponential Growth Rate of India and Kerala, 1901–2011*

Source: Compiled from various Censuses, 1901–2011, Registrar General of India.

accelerates the growth of population. After 1921, Muslim population lagged behind Christian population, which overtook in 1981 and continues to increase (Figure 3.2).

Muslims and Christians had the same growth rate in 1961, but after that Muslims had a higher growth rate than Christians and Hindus. Even though the growth rate is declining for the three religions, the reduction rate is less among Muslims. Christians had a drastic reduction in the growth rate in 1981–1991 period, compared with less than half of the growth rate of 1971–1981 period (Figure 3.3). During 2001–2011 period, the growth rate was low among Christians (1.38 per cent) followed by Hindus (2.23 per cent) and Muslims (12.80 per cent).

DEMOGRAPHIC TRANSITION

The determinants of demographic transition are the number of births and the number of deaths. The health status of the population is reflected by its IMRs. In 1901, the IMR of Kerala was 240 per 1,000 live births which declined to 12 per 1,000 live births in 2011. In 2014, CBR was 14.8 and CDR was 6.6 per 1,000 midyear population. Decline in the rates indicate a slow population growth (Table 3.2).

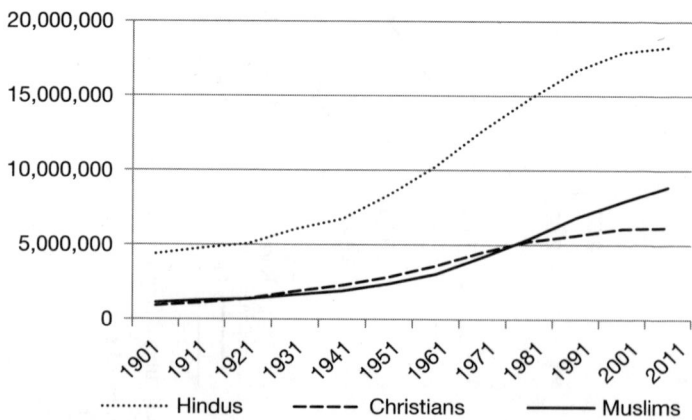

Figure 3.2 *Population Growth of Kerala by Religion, 1901–2011*

Source: Compiled from various Censuses, 1901–2011, Registrar General of India.

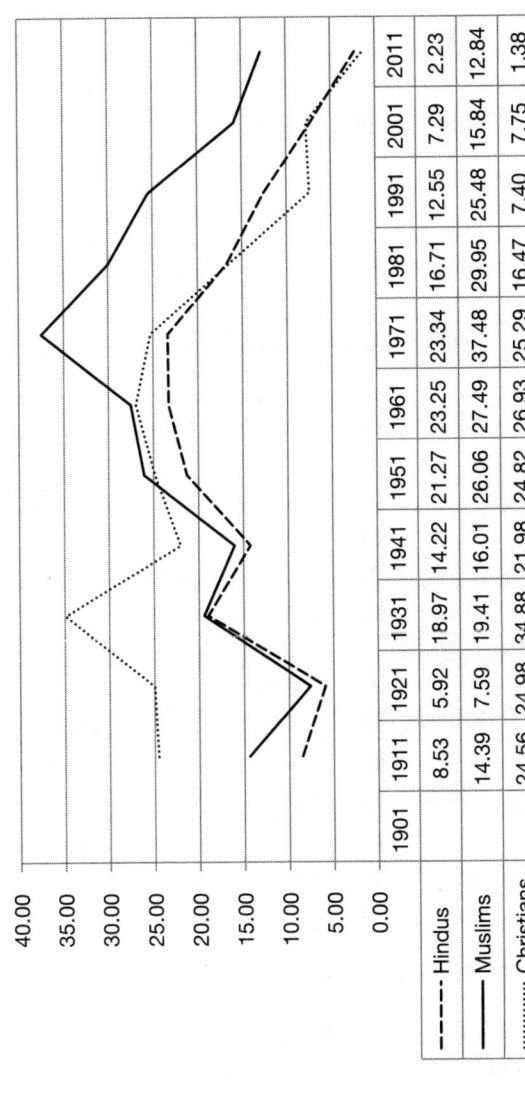

	1901	1911	1921	1931	1941	1951	1961	1971	1981	1991	2001	2011
Hindus		8.53	5.92	18.97	14.22	21.27	23.25	23.34	16.71	12.55	7.29	2.23
Muslims		14.39	7.59	19.41	16.01	26.06	27.49	37.48	29.95	25.48	15.84	12.84
Christians		24.56	24.98	34.88	21.98	24.82	26.93	25.29	16.47	7.40	7.75	1.38

Figure 3.3 *Population Growth Rate of Kerala by Religion, 1901–2011*

Source: Compiled from various Censuses, 1901–2011, Registrar General of India.

Table 3.2 *Crude Birth and Death Rates, Infant Mortality Rates, 1971–2015*

Year	CBR	CDR	IMR	Year	CBR	CDR	IMR
1971	31.1	9.0	58	1996	18.0	6.2	14
1972	31.2	9.2	63	1997	17.9	6.2	13
1973	29.2	8.5	54	1998	17.9	6.2	13
1974	26.8	7.8	54	1999	17.9	6.2	14
1975	28.0	8.4	54	2000	17.9	6.4	14
1976	27.8	8.1	56	2001	17.2	6.6	11
1977	25.8	7.3	47	2002	16.8	6.4	11
1978	26.7	7.0	42	2003	16.7	6.3	11
1979	25.6	6.9	43	2004	15.2	6.1	12
1980	26.7	7.0	40	2005	15.0	6.4	14
1981	25.6	6.6	37	2006	14.9	6.7	15
1982	26.2	6.6	30	2007	14.7	6.8	13
1983	24.9	6.7	33	2008	14.7	6.8	12
1984	22.9	6.4	29	2009	14.6	6.6	12
1985	23.3	6.5	31	2010	14.8	7.0	13
1986	22.5	6.1	27	2011	15.2	7.0	12
1987	21.7	6.1	28	2012	14.9	6.9	12
1988	20.3	6.4	28	2013	14.7	6.9	12
1989	20.3	6.1	21	2014	14.8	6.6	12
1990	19.6	6.0	17	2015	14.8	6.6	12
1991	18.3	6.0	16				
1992	17.7	6.3	17				
1993	17.4	6.0	13				
1994	17.4	6.0	16				
1995	18.0	6.0	15				

Source: Sample Registration Survey (SRS), India, 1971–2015.

Demographic transition is a change from high birth and death rates to low birth and death rates. This has five stages. Kerala is in the fourth stage of late transitional phase with continuing decline in birth rates and slowdown in the fall in death rates. Due to the technological advancement in various fields, including the medical treatment or the health care, the transition has been much faster than any other part of India. The decline in birth and death rates almost ceased in 2004 and 1982, respectively. As long as the birth rate and death rate continue to remain at the same level, the population growth rate will be zero.

Female literacy had an important role to play in the transition of the health sector. The educated females are more aware of the healthy ways to look after their children and more alert in taking vaccination for their children. Due to these reasons, the IMR of Kerala came down. Though the rate is declining over the years after 1971, the 21st century is witnessing IMR of Kerala as the lowest in India.

DEMOGRAPHIC CHANGE IN THE 21ST CENTURY

The drastic change in all aspects of development in the last century was reflected in the population of the 21st century as a peaceful momentum phase. Population of Kerala experienced the reduction in fertility to replacement level of fertility, resulting in a population momentum. Districts in southern part had the lowest decadal growth rate during 2001–2011 period, in which Pathanamthitta (–3.0 per cent) and Idukki (–1.8 per cent) had negative growth rates.

Malappuram had the highest growth rate with 13.4 per cent followed by Kasaragod (8.6 per cent) and Palakkad (7.4 per cent). However, the overall decadal growth rate of Kerala was 4.9 per cent which is at least half of the previous decade. How Kerala achieved these demographically unique features will be explained in the following sections.

NUPTIALITY

Age at marriage and proportion of unmarried women are important determinants of fertility. Parents preferred to get their daughters married at younger ages than their sons. According to NFHS II (1999), median age at marriage for women aged between 25 and 49 years is 20.2 years and percentage of unmarried women of 15 to 19 years age group is 85.9.

According to 2011 Census, there are 86.7 per cent women in the age group of 15 to 19 years who are unmarried. About 31 per cent females who are married fall between the age group of 18 to 19 years,

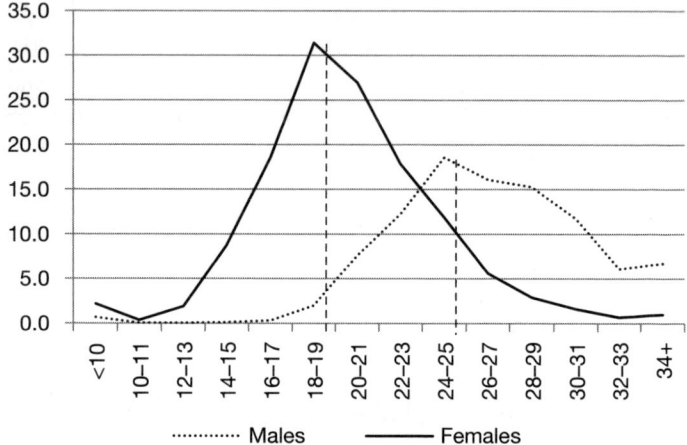

Figure 3.4 *Age at Marriage in Kerala by Sex, 2011*

Source: Census of India 2011, Registrar General of India.

whereas there are a higher proportion of males married between the age group of 24 to 25 years (Figure 3.4). Among Muslims, 52.8 per cent of women were married between 16 to 19 years and men were married between 20 to 25 years, respectively. Among Hindus, 44.7 per cent women were married between 18 to 21 years, whereas 49.7 per cent men who were married aged between 24 and 29 years.

Men in Kerala married at the average age of 28.7 years compared to women who married at the age of 21.7 years as per estimates based on 2011 Census (Rajan, Nair, & Anil Chandran, 2016). Age at marriage of women seems stabilised at age 22 years, over the period, which was 22.3 years in 1991, falling slightly to 21.7 years in 2011 (Bhagat, 2016). On the other hand, the mean age at marriage of men increased from 27.7 years in 1991 to 28 years in 2001 and 28.7 years in 2011. Thus, we can conclude that mean age for marriage of women is falling, whereas for men it is going upward. However, there has been a rise in age at marriage from the 20th century to the 21st century. Increasing proportion of never-married women and the high mean age at marriage has caused the fertility to remain low or to decrease. The highly educated men and women postponed their marriages to late 20s. More than half of the men who graduated married between 26 and 31 years, while women graduates married between 22 and 25 years (Census 2011).

NATALITY

The continuous decline in fertility has changed the age structure of population in Kerala. The child–woman ratio (CWR) is a good indicator of measuring the fertility level, though it is not an accurate measure of fertility. It is used as an indirect estimate of the TFR. Table 3.3 reveals a spike in fertility reduction (even though it is a small reduction) during 1961–1971 period, which continued in the successive years. The highest reduction can be seen during 1981–1991 period. However, in the beginning of the 21st century, the reduction in fertility was slow.

The percentage increase in ever-married women in the two successive Census years (13.1 per cent) is higher than the percentage increase in ever-born children (0.7 per cent). This shows the decline in fertility. The mean number of children to the women who have completed the age of childbearing (age group 45–49 years) has decreased from 2.9 in 2001 to 2.3 in 2011 (the rate of decline is 0.6 per cent; Table 3.4). Among the different religious groups, Muslim women who have completed the age of childbearing have had the highest average number of children ever born (3.2) compared to Hindu and Christian women (2.1 each). The same group among the graduated women has an average of 1.8 children, whereas among the illiterate women the average number of

Table 3.3 *Changes in Child–Woman Ratio in Kerala, 1951–2011*

	CWR 0–4	Percentage Change	CWR 5–9	Percentage Change
1951	501		481	
1961	622	24	657	37
1971	591	−5	682	4
1981	482	−18	605	−11
1991	329	−32	408	−33
2001	303	−8	382	−6
2011	263	−13	282	−26

Source: Various Censuses 1951–2011.

Note: CWR 0–4 is obtained by dividing population of 0–4 years by number of women in the age interval 15–49 years. CWR 5–9 is obtained by dividing population of 5–9 years by number of women in the age interval 20–54 years.

Table 3.4 *Average Number of Children per Ever-married Woman*

Age	Mean Number of Children in 2001	Mean Number of Children in 2011
15–19	0.4	0.3
20–24	1.0	0.8
25–29	1.6	1.4
30–34	2.1	1.9
35–39	2.3	2.1
40–44	2.6	2.2
45–49	2.9	2.3
All ages	2.7	2.3
Total number of ever-married women	9,877,605	11,368,550
Total children ever born	26,390,638	26,575,512

Source: Compiled from Census of India 2001 and 2011.

children is 2.7 (Census 2011). So it is clear that education of females has a reflection on childbearing through postponement or family planning.

REPRODUCTIVE HEALTH

The reproductive age group is 15 to 49 years, a period in which women are fertile. The reduction in childbearing needs results in better health care for women in the reproductive ages. In view of this, the National Reproductive and Child Health Programme had been launched in 1997 to provide health and family welfare services for women and children. The National Population Policy (NPP) adopted in 2000 had a long-term objective of stabilising population by 2045 at a sustainable level. Later in 2002, national health policy was launched with the objective of dispersing the network of comprehensive primary health care services linked with health education. In 2005, the National Rural Health Mission (NRHM) was launched with a goal to provide effective health care facilities and universal access to rural population.

Reproductive health care services include family planning, antenatal care, natal and postnatal care. National family health surveys identified that almost all the women in Kerala had at least one antenatal care visits to hospital. These services changed the place of delivery to institutions from home. NFHS III data show that 99.3 per cent of deliveries took place in some health care institutions. Compared to the figures in District Level Health Survey (DLHS) 3 survey (2007–2008), there was a rise in the percentage of delivery at government health institutions in DLHS-4 (2012–2013) and the percentage was high in urban areas (48.2 per cent) compared to rural areas (43.5 per cent). In the meantime, the proportion of caesarean in the government hospitals has increased over the survey period (from 9.6 per cent to 15 per cent). However, caesarean section is higher in private hospitals compared to public hospitals. Several reasons are attributed to the high caesarean rate in Kerala. They include high rate of institutional delivery and higher dependence on private hospitals. It could be the profit motive operating in private sector institutions that resulted in a higher volume of elective caesarean sections. The one-child norm is cited as another reason for higher proportion of caesareans. It is pointed out that in such a situation, the child and the mother are very precious and the doctor does not have much elbow space (Kumar & Devi, 2010).

FAMILY PLANNING

Family planning has an effect on the reduction in fertility. It helps to limit the fertility which will help to improve the health of both mother and child. We can classify the married women into three categories: those who are sterilised and have desire of no more children; those using temporary family planning methods to limit or to adjust the space between the births and those who are neither sterilised nor use any temporary method. DLHS figured out that during 2012–2013 period, 60 per cent of the women used any type of contraception and 39.7 per cent had female sterilisation. It is noticeable that the female sterilisation has decreased over the survey period and there has been an increase in use of temporary methods. Also, unmet needs increased over the period. About 19 per cent fecund women were not using any method of family planning for limiting or spacing the birth compared to 16.8 per cent in the previous survey period.

TOTAL FERTILITY RATE

TFR is the total number of children a woman would have when she completes her reproductive age. It is a useful indicator of population stabilisation prospects. In Kerala, TFR (1.6) has decreased to below replacement level of 2.1 by the last decades of the 20th century (Table 3.5). Among the 14 districts, 6 districts have TFR below 1.5 (Guilmoto & Rajan, 2013). These are all southern districts of Kerala which attained the replacement-level fertility by the late 1980s (Nair & Laya, 2004). Pathanamthitta district has the lowest TFR in Kerala (1.3).

MORTALITY

Mortality influences the health and vitality of the population. There are two hypotheses concerning the effect of IMR on fertility. First is

Table 3.5 *Total Fertility Rate by Districts, 2011 and 2001*

Districts	2011	2001
Thiruvananthapuram	1.4	1.6
Kollam	1.4	1.6
Pathanamthitta	1.3	1.5
Alappuzha	1.4	1.5
Kottayam	1.4	1.6
Idukki	1.4	1.6
Ernakulam	1.5	1.5
Thrissur	1.5	1.6
Palakkad	1.6	1.8
Malappuram	2.2	2.4
Kozhikode	1.6	1.7
Wayanad	1.7	2.0
Kannur	1.6	1.7
Kasaragod	1.8	1.9
Kerala	1.6	1.7

Source: Guilmoto and Rajan (2013).

the 'child survival hypothesis', which argues that if parents live in an era of high child mortality, they will have more children because they expect to lose a high percentage of these offspring by death (Birdsall & Griffin, 1988). Second is the 'child replacement hypothesis', which assumes that if a child dies, parents are anxious to replace the loss by another child as soon as possible (Scrimshaw, 1978). It depends on the socio-economic development and quality of life of the population. Modern and advanced health facilities reduced the maternal, infant and child mortality rates as well as the overall death rates. According to the latest estimates of infant and child mortality rates by Rajan, Sunitha and Arya (2017), Kerala has the lowest infant and child mortality rate in India. In 1991, highest IMR occurred in Kozhikode and Idukki districts (43). In 2001, it was highest in Thiruvananthapuram, Palakkad and Wayanad (21). In 2011, IMR was highest in Wayanad (18) followed by Idukki and Alappuzha (15). Some districts have had a drastic change in between the decades. Among the 640 districts of India, 6 districts of Kerala were figured in the list of top 10 districts with low IMR (Rajan, Sunitha, & Arya, 2017).

The mortality experience of males and females are different in any population. The age structure of both sexes, considered simultaneously in an age pyramid, explains how the population grows under the influence of births and deaths. The decline in younger age group is evident from 2011 pyramid with its narrowing base compared to that of 1961. Also, there is an increase in elderly female proportion in 2011 compared to 1961. An age pyramid has a wide base and rapidly narrows down towards its apex to a barrel-shaped pyramid with shortened base and slowly tapers off towards its apex (Figure 3.5).

MATERNAL MORTALITY

Maternal mortality occurs as part of childbearing which is measured as the number of women aged between 15 and 49 years dying during maternity per 100,000 live births. Cardiac disease was the leading medical cause of maternal deaths. Clinical causes such as haemorrhage and hypertensive disorders continue to be the main medical causes of death. In 2011–2012, the epidemic of H1N1 pneumonia accounted for 24 maternal deaths in the state (Paily, Ambujam, Nair, & Thomas, 2014).

According to the SRS 2011–2013, Kerala's maternal mortality rate (MMR) has shown an impressive drop of 15 points from 81 per 100,000 live births in 2007–2009 to 66 in 2010–2012 and came down to 61 in 2011–2013. In the beginning of the 21st century, the MMR was 110 per 100,000 live births. Ensuring 100 per cent institutional deliveries, reducing the number of C-section deliveries, improvements in antenatal care, reduction of maternal deaths, clinical protocols and quality standards to improve delivery care are some of the major initiatives in maternal health care (*The Hindu,* 2014).

Overall mortality rate is low among females compared to their male counterparts. But the IMR was 13 among females compared to 15 among males in 2000. But later, the male IMR declined compared to the female IMR. After 2005, there is visible gap in between male and female IMR, and in 2013, male IMR was 10 and female IMR was 13. The female mortality rate among the age group of 0–4 years is higher than the male mortality rate of the same age group. In 2001, male mortality rate among the age group of 0–4 years was 3.3, while the female mortality rate of the same age group was 1.8. There was a sudden hike in the female mortality rate, which reached at 3.4 in 2006. The survivorship of the females at the infant stage will definitely affect the future population growth.

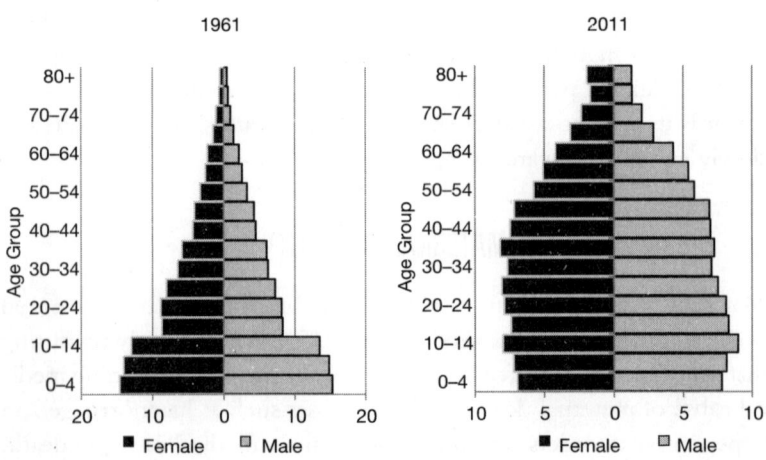

Figure 3.5 *Population Age Pyramid*

Source: Compiled from 1961 and 2011 Censuses, Registrar General of India.

EXPECTATION OF LIFE AT BIRTH AND AT 60

Apart from the practice of allopathic system, Ayurveda is also diligently practised in Kerala. The new medical interventions and advanced developments in treatment affected mortality and morbidity in Kerala. Decline in mortality and a decline in birth rates have led to a more adult and aged population, which increases the prevalence of chronic diseases.

The female life expectancy is always high compared to the life expectancy of males. In the beginning of the 21st century, the average age of females expected to live was 74.7 years and that of males was 68.7 years which increased to 77.8 for females and 71.8 for males in 2013. An average of 6-point gap in between male and female expectation of life can be seen in 2013. An elderly at the age of 60 years was expected to live 20 years more from 2013 (for females 21.6 years and males 18.0 years).

SOCIO-ECONOMIC INDICATORS

Kerala's fertility and mortality levels are mostly spelled out by its socio-economic levels such as literacy level of female population, education level of both male and female population, place of residence, religion and occupational levels. The trends in the level of education revealed the male–female disparity in attaining education.

Level of Education

The literacy rate has increased over the period and the male–female literacy gap was declined from 5 point in 2001 to 2.5 point in 2011. About 19 per cent of the males have completed their middle school education, while 18 per cent of the females have completed higher secondary level (Table 3.6). There were more females with afore-mentioned graduation level compared to their male counterpart. The female education has a significant role in delaying the marriage as well as the followed childbirth.

Theoretically, the level of education of women could influence age at marriage in four ways (Caldwell, Reddy, & Caldwell, 1983; Shapiro, 1996). First, there might exist more opportunities for higher education or employment outside the home that may delay marriage for the woman outside marriage if she was educated. Second, education

Table 3.6 *Percentage Distribution of Education Levels in Kerala, 2011*

Education Level	2011		2001	
	Male	Female	Male	Female
Below primary	15.2	16.1	18.9	19.8
Primary	18.4	17.6	24.3	23.2
Middle	18.9	17.1	24.2	23.1
Matric/Secondary	13.9	13.5	17.6	17.9
Higher secondary/Intermediate	16.8	17.9	5.3	6.9
Non-technical diploma	0.3	0.3	0.1	0.3
Technical diploma or certificate	3.7	2.7	2.9	1.7
Graduate and above	8.3	9.7	5.5	5.8
Unclassified	0.2	0.2	0.0	0.0
Total	100.0	100.0	100.0	100.0
Illiterate	14.5	17.0	17.6	22.2
Literate	85.5	83.0	82.4	77.8

Source: Compiled from Census of India 2001 and 2011.

might enable a woman to obtain a well-educated husband or one with an urban job, and increase in search time delaying marriage. Third, the employment prospects of women improved if they were better educated. Women are able to support themselves economically while being single. Finally, education might also influence women's ideas about marriage via learning the values (Keeley, 1977).

Labour Force Participation

Population, workforce and employment are closely interrelated, that is, the change in size, composition and distribution of the population will alter the demographic structure of the labour force. On the other hand, a change in the size of the labour force, level of employment and job opportunities will affect components of population change, particularly fertility and migration (United Nations, 1976). The total workforce in Kerala was 10.3 million, out of which 7.8 million were males and only 2.5 million were females (Census 2011). In 2011, the

Table 3.7 *Work Participation Rate and Annual Exponential Growth Rate in Kerala by Sex, 1991–2011*

	Percentage of Workers		Exponential Growth Rate	
	Male	Female	Male	Female
1991	74.3	25.7	–	–
2001	75.7	24.3	1.36	0.63
2011	72.7	27.3	–0.21	1.52

Source: Compiled from three successive Censuses 1991, 2001 and 2011.

total labour force has a slight increase of 10.5 million—76.3 million males and 29.1 million females.

Work participation rate of Kerala in 2011 was 49.4 per cent. Among this, 72.7 per cent were males and 27.3 per cent were females (Table 3.7). The female work participation rate is increasing over the period. Annual exponential growth rate of female work participation is 1.52 per cent during 2001–2011 period, whereas males have a negative growth rate of –0.21 per cent. About half of the population among the total labour force was unemployed in 2011. Migration is a fact among the youth to tackle the unemployment problem in the state. Most of the job seekers prefer to work abroad in line with the unemployment problem.

Migration has had a positive impact on unemployment and has been a major factor in keeping unemployment rate low in Kerala. Kerala Migration Survey 1998 noted that the unemployment rate in Kerala fell by about 3 per cent due to migration. In a study, Zachariah and Rajan (2012) have concluded, 'Had there been no migration, the unemployment rate in Kerala would have been 16 per 100 in the labour force. With the extent of migration that took place, the actual unemployment rate was only 10.5'.

MIGRATION

According to Kerala Migration Survey conducted in 2014 by the Centre for Development Studies, estimated number of emigrants was 24 lakhs. As per the study in 1998, it was 13.6 lakhs. There was a steady increase in the number of emigrants over the period. These migrants are always male dominated. However, there is an increase in female emigration over the period. All these emigrants will spend their prime youth in destination countries and most of them will return back after attaining their goals or at their retirement ages with some health problems. One out of five households in Kerala has one or more emigrants, and one out of ten households has one or more return emigrants (Zachariah & Rajan, 2015). Migration leads to remittances, and remittances lead to socio-economic impact on human resource development on land ownership, housing, lifestyle, etc., individually as well as generally and directly as well as indirectly. Partly as a result of emigration, the average size of households in Kerala has decreased and the number of very small households increased. Migrants are ambitious to give better education to their children resulting in more than 60 per cent of the emigrant households using remittance for education. Also, people are migrating to other parts of India. Anyway, these migrations had some significant change in the age structure of population in Kerala. Nowadays, a new pace of replacement migration has come to Kerala. The replacement migration refers to migration occurring as a result of age structure changes. Educated youth, moreover, are reluctant to do manual jobs and refrain from physical labour in Kerala. The scarcity of labour force has been replaced by the migrants from other parts of India. The 2011 Census says there has been a significant inflow of migrants to Kerala. The influence of Gulf remittances changed the wages also. The high differences in wage between Kerala and other states attracted the other states' inhabitants to Kerala (Rajan, Prakash, & Suresh, 2015).

In 2013, the stock of domestic migrant labourers was 25 lakhs. The net growth rate would be 6.87 per cent or 11.82 per cent. The net addition to the stock of migrant labourers is 182,300. The largest proportion of migrants are from West Bengal (20 per cent) followed by Bihar (18 per cent), Assam (17 per cent) and Uttar Pradesh (15 per cent). This migrant stock is predominantly male, within the age group of 18–29 years (Narayana & Venkateswaran, 2013).

THE DEMOGRAPHIC DIVIDEND

Demographic dividend refers to the larger proportion of working age group compared to younger and older age groups. The demographic dividend emanates from rapid changes in fertility. The proportion of working age group is increasing over the period. This impact of age structure can properly be used to change the economic growth of the state. By giving good quality education and skill levels, the state can reap the yield of the labour force.

OTHER EMERGING ISSUES

The demographic dividend is of a shorter duration and eventually the state will move into an ageing population. The proportion of the elderly will increase up to 34.3 per cent by the year 2050. This proportion will cross over the young by the year 2021 (Figure 3.6). The expected life span for males will be 75.2 years and that females will be 78.6 years in 2030.

As the longevity increases, the major challenge would be regarding the care of the elderly. Demographic and economic changes accompanied by enhanced migration of people in search of better and quality employment results in the elderly being left behind. The living arrangement pattern of the elderly are expected to undergo rapid changes during this period.

Majority of these elderly are females and widows. According to a study done by Rajan, Sunitha and Arya (2017), 75 per cent of those who lived alone were widowed. Living arrangements determine who will

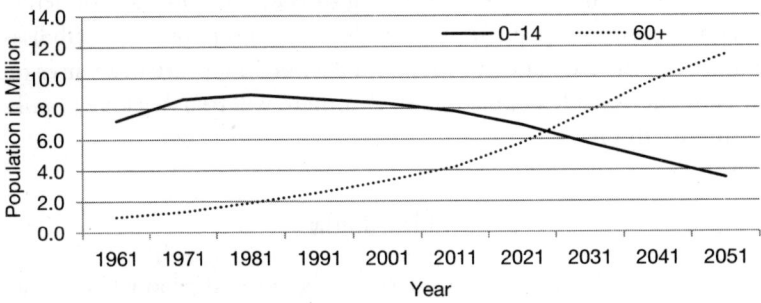

Figure 3.6 *Expected Cross over Between Young and the Aged in Kerala*

Sources: Compiled from the successive Censuses 1961–2011. Compiled from the Population Projections 2021–2051 based on 2011 Census (unpublished).

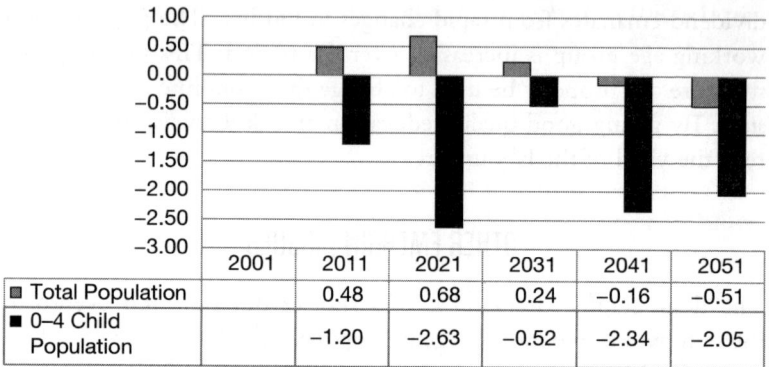

	2001	2011	2021	2031	2041	2051
▣ Total Population		0.48	0.68	0.24	−0.16	−0.51
■ 0–4 Child Population		−1.20	−2.63	−0.52	−2.34	−2.05

Figure 3.7 *Growth Rate of Population and Children, 2001–2051*

Sources: Compiled from the successive Censuses 1961–2011. Compiled from the Population Projections 2021–2051 based on 2011 Census (unpublished).

provide care at the time of need for special care. The study shows that compared to female elderly, male elderly have less chance to live alone. The elderly living with spouse were of the opinion that the elderly should be independent rather than be taken care of by their children.

The growth rate of 0–4 child population is continuous to be negative and by 2041, both population and 0–4 child population will be negative (Figure 3.7). So there is a fall in birth rate to below replacement level and reduction in the proportion of the population in the reproductive age group (55.8 per cent in 2001 and 53.7 per cent in 2011). As a result, the state is running through the last stage of demographic transition, population growth ceases and population stabilises. Figure 3.7 shows that there may be a decline in fertility even after the attainment of stable population, so that there will be a negative population growth phase.

CONCLUSION

The process of ageing is considered to be an end product of demographic transition in Kerala. The increase in life expectancy and the below replacement level of fertility comprises the growth in population of Kerala. There were 53 older persons for every 100 children in 2011. Every five working Keralites may have to take care of one elderly person in 2011. As far as the young and youth population is decreasing, there are concerns regarding the capacities of societies to address the challenges associated with these demographic shifts. In order to face these challenges, we need a new approach to ensure a successful aging. So it is important to make better use of the longer life span rather than view ageing as a quandary, that is, when people live longer, the society should make use of this longevity dividend by recognising older people as a resource and not as a burden. This implies that the elderly should continue to be productive for an unprecedented period of time.

REFERENCES AND SELECT BIBLIOGRAPHY

Bhagat, R. B. (2016). *The practice of early marriages among females in India: Persistence and change* (Working Paper No. 10). Mumbai: International Institute for Population Sciences (IIPS).

Bhat, P. N. Mari, & Rajan, S. I. (1990). Demographic transition in Kerala revisited. *Economic and Political Weekly, 25*(35–36), 957–980.

Birdsall, N. M., & Griffin, C. G. (1988). Fertility and poverty in developing countries. *Journal of Policy Modelling, 10*(1), 29–55.

Caldwell, J. C., Reddy, P. H., & Caldwell, P. (1983). The causes of marriage change in South India. *Population Studies, 37*(3), 353–355.

Guilmoto, C. Z., & Rajan, S. I. (2013). *Fertility at district level in India: Lessons from the 2011 Census* (Working Paper No. 30). Paris: Centre Population and Development (CEPED).

Rajan, S. I., Prakash, B. A., & Suresh, A. (2015). Wage differentials between Indian migrant workers in the Gulf and non-migrant workers in India (Chapter 20). In S. Irudaya Rajan (ed), *India migration report 2015: Gender and migration* (pp. 297–310). New Delhi: Routledge.

Rajan, S. I., Sunitha, S., & Arya, U. R. (2017). Elder care and living arrangement in Kerala. In S. Irudaya Rajan & Gayathri Balagopal (eds), *Elderly care in India: Societal and state responses* (pp. 95–116). Singapore: Springer.

Rajan, S. I., Nair, P. M., & Anil Chandran, S. (2016). *Infant and child mortality in India: District level estimates.* Estimates based on 2011 Census. New Delhi: Population Foundation of India.

Keeley, M. C. (1977). The economics of family formation. *Economic Enquiry, 15*(2), 238–250.

Kumar, N. A., & Devi, D. R. (2010). *Health of women in Kerala: Current status and emerging issues* (Working Paper No. 23). Kerala: Centre for Socio-economic and Environmental Studies.

Ministry of Home Affairs. *Maternal mortality ratio (MMR), maternal mortality rate and life time risk; India, EAG & Assam, South and other states, 2011–13.* Retrieved

23 March 2018, from http://www.censusindia.gov.in/vital_statistics/mmr_bulletin_2011-13.pdf

Ministry of Home Affairs. *SRS based life table 2011–15*. Retrieved 23 March 2018, from http://www.censusindia.gov.in/Vital_Statistics/SRS_Life_Table/Srs_life_Table_2011-15.html

————. *B-1 main workers, marginal workers, non-workers and those marginal workers, non-workers seeking/available for work classified by age and sex*. Retrieved 23 March 2018, from http://www.censusindia.gov.in/2011census/B-series/B-Series-01.html

Nair, P. M., & Laya, K. S. (2004). Fertility change in South India: A district level Analysis. In Audinarayana, S. Krishnamoorthi, P. M. Kulkarni & C. P. Prakasam (eds), *Perspectives on population gender employment and health in South India* (pp. 252–277). Mumbai: Research Book Centre.

Narayana, D., & Venkateswaran, C. S. (2013). *Domestic migrant labour in Kerala*. Report submitted to the Labour and Rehabilitation Department, Government of Kerala, Gulati Institute of Finance and Taxation.

NFHS II (1999). *National Family Health Survey, Kerala 1998–1999*, pp. 36–37. Mumbai: International Institute for Population Sciences.

Paily, V. P., Ambujam, K., Nair, V. R., & Thomas, B. (2014). Confidential review of maternal deaths in Kerala: A country case study. *Journal of Obstetricians and Gynaecologists* (BJOG), *121*(Suppl. 4), 61–66.

Ramakumar, R. (1986). *Technical demography*. New Delhi: New Age International (P) Limited, Publishers.

Scrimshaw, S. W. M. (1978). Infant mortality and behaviour in the regulation of family size. *Population and Development Review, 4*, 383–403.

Shapiro, D. (1996). Fertility decline in Kinshasa. *Population Studies, 50*(1), 89–103.

The Hindu. (2014, 5 January). Kerala's MMR comes down to 66. Thiruvananthapuram: *The Hindu*.

United Nations. (1976). Population aspects of manpower and employment: A regional overview. *Asian Population Studies, 35* (Chapters I, III, VII and IX). Bangkok: ESCAP.

Zachariah, K. C., & Rajan, S. I. (2012). *A decade of Kerala's Gulf connection*. New Delhi: Orient BlackSwan.

————. (2015). *Dynamics of emigration and remittances in Kerala: Results of the Kerala migration survey 2014* (Working Paper No. 463). Thiruvananthapuram: Centre for Development Studies.

Chapter 4

Employment and Unemployment in Kerala

M. P. Abraham and A. S. Shibu

Generation of decent gainful employment is both a mean and an end of any just and equitable society. Lack of employment opportunity breeds poverty, deprivation and consequently creates ground for social unrest.

—Indian Labour Year Book 2011 and 2012

INTRODUCTION

A basic deficiency of the development process in Kerala has been its failure to generate adequate regular and remunerative jobs in the organised sector. Lack of adequate employment opportunities and chronic unemployment of certain categories especially educated labour have resulted in large-scale migration of educated labour to other parts of India and abroad. The feature of labour market is characterised by excess supply of educated labour on the one side and shortage of manual labour on the other. The labour market in Kerala is characterised by the dominance of casual and self-employment, with a small share of regular employment. Kerala is identified as one of the states having high rate of rural, urban and educated unemployment.

A few attempts were made to study the trend and pattern of employment and unemployment and offer some explanations (Prakash, 1989, 1990, 2004; Mathew, 1997). Excess supply of young labour force, the low growth in labour demand arising due to low economic growth of state's economy and restrictive labour practices distorting the operation of labour market were cited as the causes of growing unemployment (Prakash, 1989). Based on the data of National Sample Survey (NSS) another study presents the broad changes in employment and unemployment and attributes it to the socio-economic factors (Mathew, 1997). Educated and urban unemployment are the other topics studied (Prakash, 1988, 2002; Mathew, 1995). A study on urban unemployment in Kochi city, came to the conclusion that urbanisation has been associated with a process of casualisation of labour and fail to generate rapid growth in regular employment for educated labour (Prakash, 2002).

The objectives of this chapter are to examine the trends, pattern, and structure of employment and unemployment of Kerala, especially after 2000. For our analysis, we have used the conceptual framework and data of the NSSO.

CONCEPTUAL FRAMEWORK

We have used the NSSO definitions to measure employment, unemployment, labour force and out-of-labour force. The persons surveyed are classified into various categories on the basis of the activities pursued by them during certain specified reference periods. Three reference periods are used in these surveys: (a) one year, (b) one week and (c) each day of the week. Based on these three periods, three different measures are arrived at: (a) usual status (US), (b) current weekly status (CWS) and (c) current daily status (CDS).

Classification According to Usual Status

Usual Status: Principal Status

1. Employed: A person is considered 'working' or 'employed' if the person was engaged for a relatively longer time during the past year in any one or more work-related activities.

2. Unemployed: A person is considered as 'seeking or available' for work or 'unemployed' if the person was not working but was either seeking or was available for work for a relatively longer time during the past year.
3. Out-of-labour force: If a person was engaged in any non-economic activity for a relatively longer time of the reference year, he or she is considered as 'out-of-labour force'.

Usual Status: Principal and Subsidiary Status (PS + SS)

This specific activity category is determined on the basis of the time spent criterion, that is, the activity on which major time was spent. A person categorised as 'employed' on the basis of the principal status (PS) is called as 'PS employed'. A person categorised as a non-worker who pursued some economic activity in a subsidiary capacity is called a 'subsidiary status employed'. These two groups—PS workers and subsidiary status workers—together constitute 'all workers'.

Classification According to Current Weekly Status

For classification of persons according to the CWS approach, they are assigned a unique activity status with reference to a period of seven days preceding the date of survey.

1. Employed: According to this status, a person is considered working or employed if the person was engaged for at least one hour on any one day of the previous week in any work-related activity.
2. Unemployed: A person who had not worked for even one hour on any one day of the week, but had been seeking or had been available for work at any time for at least one hour during the week days, is considered 'seeking or available for work'.

Classification According to Current Daily Status

The workforce measured in CDS gives the average picture of the person-days worked in a day during the survey period. For each person, activity status according to the CDS approach was recorded for each of the seven days preceding the date of survey. If a single activity was recorded in a day, 1.0 intensity was assigned against that activity status and if two different activities were recorded in a day, 0.5 intensity was assigned for each of these two activity statuses. Based on the activity statuses and the intensities recorded for the seven days of the reference week, total number of person-days corresponding to the different activity statuses was estimated for a period of seven days. If a person worked for four hours or more on a day, 1.0 intensity was assigned against work activity status on that day and if the person worked for at least one hour but less than four hours on a day, 0.5 intensity was assigned against work activity status on that day. The estimate of the number of person-days employed in the reference week was obtained by considering the number of person-days which were in work activity during the reference week. The number of person-days employed on a day during the survey period is obtained by dividing the estimated number of person-days employed in a week by seven.

The NSSO's definitions of employed, unemployed, labour force, self-employed, regular employed, casual labour and unemployment rate are given as follows:

1. Employed: Persons who are engaged in any economic activity or who, despite their attachment to economic activity, have abstained for reasons of illness, injury or other physical disability, bad weather, festivals, social or religious functions or other contingencies necessitating temporary absence from work constitute workers.
2. Unemployed: Persons who, owing to lack of work, had not worked but either sought work through employment exchanges, intermediaries, friends/relatives or by making applications to prospective employers or expressed their willingness or availability for work under the prevailing condition of work and remuneration are considered as those seeking/available for work or as unemployed.
3. Labour force: Persons who are either working, or seeking or available for work (i.e., unemployed) during the reference period constitute the labour force.
4. Self-employed: Persons who operate their own farm or non-farm enterprises or are engaged independently in a profession or trade on own account or with one or few partners. The essential feature of

self-employment is that the remuneration is determined wholly or mainly by sales or profits of the goods or services being produced.

5. Regular employed: Persons working in others' farm or non-farm enterprises, both household and non-household, and getting in return salary or wages on a regular basis (and not on the basis of daily or periodic renewal of work contract).

6. Casual labour: A person casually engaged in others' farm or non-farm enterprises (both household and non-household) and getting in return wage according to the terms of the daily or periodic work contract.

7. Unemployment rate: Unemployment rate is defined as the percentage of unemployed persons in the total labour force.

TRENDS AND STRUCTURE OF EMPLOYMENT

In this section, we examine the trends and changes in the structure of employment after 2000. We present trends in the workforce participation rate (WFPR), the structure of rural and urban employment based on industrial classification, and occupations and changes in employment in the organised sector.

Workforce Participation Rate

The number of persons/person-days employed per thousand persons/person-days is referred to as WFPR or worker–population ratio (WPR). The WFPR provides an idea about the participation of the labourers in economic activities.

Table 4.1 gives the sex-wise WFPR for rural and urban India from 1999–2000 to 2009–2010. Regarding the trends and pattern of WFPR, we may draw the following observations. The WFPR rate of the male workers in rural India is more or less steady, and there is slight increase during the period from 1999–2000 to 2009–2010. However, at first, there has been an increase from 29.9 to 32.7 per cent during the period 2000–2005 and then there has been a substantial reduction in the WFPR from 32.7 per cent to 26.1 per cent of female workers in rural India during the same period. In urban India also, female WFPR

Table 4.1 *Workforce Participation Rates—Kerala and India, Usual Status (PS + SS)*

	Kerala		India	
Year	Rural	Urban	Rural	Urban
Male				
1999–2000	55.3	55.8	53.1	51.8
2004–2005	55.9	54.7	54.6	54.9
2009–2010	56.4	54.7	54.7	54.3
Female				
1999–2000	23.8	20.3	29.9	13.9
2004–2005	25.6	20.0	32.7	16.6
2009–2010	21.8	19.4	26.1	13.8
Persons				
1999–2000	38.7	37.3	41.7	33.7
2004–2005	40.0	37.1	43.9	36.5
2009–2010	38.3	36.3	40.8	35.0

Sources: National Sample Survey Organisation (2000, 2001, 2006, 2011).

at first increased (from 13.9 per cent to 16.6 per cent) and then showed a decline (from 16.6 per cent to 13.8 per cent) during this period.

The female WFPR for rural and urban areas was much lower compared to that of male workers. Average urban male WFPR is above 50 per cent, while that for female is below 20 per cent. This shows a higher level of gender bias in the WFPR. The rural WFPR rate in Kerala was lower compared to other states and the all-India average. Compared to other states and all-India average, the urban WFPR was marginally higher in Kerala.

Socio-economic and demographic factors determine the level of work participation of any population in economic activities. Factors such as the decline in agricultural activities, small and marginal nature of agricultural holdings, decline in traditional and rural industries, changes in occupational preferences of young rural labour force and migration to other parts of India and abroad have contributed to the lower WFPR in rural Kerala. Besides economic factors, a number of social factors such as marriage and child rearing, unconducive factors for promoting occupational and geographic mobility, withdrawal of educated labour from manual works and the general reluctance to engage in self-employment have contributed to the low WFPR among females.

PATTERN OF RURAL AND URBAN EMPLOYMENT IN KERALA

Let us examine the pattern of male and female employment in Kerala. There is a decline in the employment of both male and female workers in the primary sector. In rural Kerala, the primary sector employment decreased from 50.0 per cent in 1999–2000, to 36.8 per cent in 2009–2010 (Table 4.2). In the case of the secondary sector, there is an increase in the employment of both male and female workers in the same period. The secondary sector employment increased from 22.0 per cent in 1999–2000 to 27.5 in 2009–2010. A similar trend can be observed in the case of the tertiary sector also. Employment in the tertiary sector increased from 28.0 per cent in 1999–2000 to 35.7 per cent in 2009–2010.

In rural Kerala, during 1999–2000, 42.8 per cent of the male workers were engaged in agriculture. The other major activities in which males are employed are manufacturing, construction, trade and commerce, transport and other services. There is a slight difference in the pattern of employment of the women. During 2009–2010, 42.8 per cent of the female rural workers were engaged in agriculture. The other major activities in which females are employed are manufacturing and services. The proportion of females employed in construction trade and commerce, and real estate is comparatively lower.

One visible change in the pattern of employment in rural Kerala is the substantial reduction in the employment of workers in the agricultural sector and moderate progress in other two sectors. This may be due to the paralysis of the agricultural activities in the last two decades and progress of the other two sectors.

The pattern of urban employment in Kerala is quite different from that of rural employment. According to NSSO survey 2009–2010, 57 per cent of workers were engaged in the tertiary sector activities, 31.2 per cent in the secondary sector and 11.7 in the primary sector.

Table 4.3 reveals that there is a declining trend in the employment provided by the primary sector in urban Kerala after 2004–2005.

Table 4.2 *Distribution of Rural Workers in Kerala by Industrial Category (%), Usual Status (PS+SS)*

Sector	Rural Males			Rural Females			Rural Persons		
	1999–2000	2004–2005	2009–2010	1999–2000	2004–2005	2009–2010	1999–2000	2004–2005	2009–2010
Agriculture	42.8	37.1	32.8	59.8	51.7	42.8	48.3	42.0	35.7
Mining and quarrying	2.1	1.9	1.4	0.8	0.2	0.5	1.7	1.3	1.1
Primary	44.9	39.0	34.2	60.6	51.9	43.3	50.0	43.3	36.8
Manufacturing	9.4	10.1	8.7	19.3	20.9	18.6	12.6	13.7	11.7
Electricity, water, etc.	0.3	0.3	0.3	–	0.2	0.5	0.2	0.2	0.4
Construction	12.6	15.1	19.2	2.7	1.7	6.7	9.2	10.6	15.4
Secondary	22.3	25.5	28.2	22.0	22.8	25.8	22.0	24.5	27.5
Trade, hotels and restaurants	15.8	15.6	15.8	3.7	5.2	6.8	11.9	12.2	13.1
Transport	9.0	9.9	10.0	0.2	1.4	0.7	6.2	7.0	7.2
Real estate and business services	2.1	2.9	4.0	1.1	1.6	2.9	1.8	2.5	3.6
Services (public administration, etc.)	6.0	7.1	8.0	12.5	17.1	20.7	8.1	10.5	11.8
Tertiary	32.9	35.5	37.8	17.5	25.3	31.1	28.0	32.2	35.7
Total	100.0	100.0	100.0	100.0	100.0	100.0	100.0	100.0	100.0

Sources: National Sample Survey Organisation (2000, 2001, 2006, 2011).

Table 4.3 *Distribution of Urban Workers in Kerala by Industrial Category (%), Usual Status (PS+SS)*

Sector	Urban Males			Urban Females			Urban Persons		
	1999–2000	2004–2005	2009–2010	1999–2000	2004–2005	2009–2010	1999–2000	2004–2005	2009–2010
Agriculture	7.4	14.0	11.7	14.6	19.8	9.2	9.5	15.7	11.0
Mining and quarrying	0.4	0.6	0.9	0.2	0.0	0.2	0.3	0.5	0.7
Primary	7.8	14.6	12.6	14.8	19.8	9.4	9.8	16.2	11.7
Manufacturing	17.4	14.1	14.8	27.2	23.4	22.0	20.2	16.6	16.8
Electricity, water, etc.	0.6	0.4	0.3	0.2	0.2	0.4	0.5	0.4	0.3
Construction	14.2	15.0	18.2	2.1	2.9	3.3	10.7	11.7	14.2
Secondary	32.2	29.5	33.3	29.5	26.5	25.7	31.4	28.7	31.3
Trade, hotels and restaurants	32.7	26.5	22.9	25.1	11.5	15.5	30.5	22.5	20.9
Transport	11.5	13.5	12.1	1.8	1.7	2.3	8.7	10.3	9.4
Real estate and business services	4.6	5.7	9.1	3.7	5.2	9.0	4.4	5.6	9.1
Services (public administration, etc.)	11.2	10.0	9.8	25.1	35.2	37.9	15.2	16.9	17.6
Tertiary	60.0	55.7	53.9	55.7	53.6	64.7	58.8	55.3	57.0
Total	100.0	100.0	100.0	100.0	100.0	100.0	100.0	100.0	100.0

Sources: National Sample Survey Organisation (2000, 2001, 2006, 2011).

During 2004–2005, 16.2 per cent of the urban workers were engaged in the primary sector, which reduced to 11.7 per cent in 2009–2010. On the other hand, we can see an improvement in the provision of employment by the other two sectors after 2004–2005. The secondary sector employment increased from 28.7 in per cent in 2004–2005 to 31.2 per cent in 2009–2010 and the tertiary sector employment increased from 55.3 per cent in 2004–2005 to 57.0 per cent in 2009–2010.

In urban Kerala, more than 20 per cent of the workers were engaged in activities such as trade hotels and restaurants and nearly 20 per cent were engaged in manufacturing activities. The other sub-categories that provide sizable employment are other services, transport and construction. The broad structural change that occurred in 2000s were a substantial fall in the share of primary employment and a moderate increase in the share of secondary and the tertiary sector workers.

It is clear from Table 4.3 that the pattern of urban employment in Kerala is quite different from that of rural employment. The major categories of employment in which urban male workers were engaged were manufacturing, construction, trade and commerce, transport and services.

Now we have a comparative analysis of the structure of employment in Kerala and all India. Table 4.4 gives the sector-wise distribution of workers for Kerala and all India.

The major differences in the structure of employment in Kerala and all India reflected in Table 4.4 are the following. The percentage of primary workers in rural Kerala was comparatively much lower than the all-India average which indicates a faster structural transformation of rural Kerala. Second, the share of secondary and tertiary rural workers was higher in rural Kerala compared to the all-India average. This indicates that rural Kerala has achieved faster economic changes compared to national growth. The structure of urban employment in Kerala shows more or less the same pattern to that of national level. This suggests that Kerala's position is somewhat similar to the all-India position in the case of urban employment.

INFORMAL NATURE OF EMPLOYMENT

The characteristic feature of employment in Kerala is its informal nature. Casual and self-employed workers constitute the major category of workers. In spite of the economic growth and the structural

Table 4.4 *Sector-wise Distribution of Workers: Kerala and All-India (%) Usual Status (PS+SS)*

Sectors	Kerala						All India					
	Rural			Urban			Rural			Urban		
	1999–2000	2004–2005	2009–2010	1999–2000	2004–2005	2009–2010	1999–2000	2004–2005	2009–2010	1999–2000	2004–2005	2009–2010
Primary	50.0	43.3	36.8	9.8	16.2	11.7	76.8	73.2	68.5	9.6	9.6	8.1
Secondary	22.0	24.5	27.5	31.4	28.5	31.3	10.9	13.2	16.8	31.4	33.3	33.8
Tertiary	28.0	32.2	35.7	58.8	55.3	57.0	12.4	13.6	14.7	59.2	57.2	58.2
Total	100.0	100.0	100.0	100.0	100.0	100.0	100.0	100.0	100.0	100.0	100.0	100.0

Sources: National Sample Survey Organisation (2000, 2001, 2006, 2011).

transformation of the rural economy, 80.6 per cent (2009–2010) of the rural workers are either self-employed or casual labourers (Table 4.5).

The share of 'regularly employed' in the rural workforce was only 19.4 per cent in 2009–2010. Among the male and female workers, majority of rural workers were casually employed. The NSSO data of the workers during the 2000s show that there is a fall in the number of self-employed female workers in this period and at the same time there is an increase in the category of casual labour. In 1999–2000, 53 per cent of the females are in the category of self-employed which declined to 42.1 per cent in 2009–2010. At the same time, the number of casual female workers increased from 32 per cent to 34.2 per cent during the same period. A similar trend can be noticed in the case of male workers also during the same period though at a slow pace. In regular employed, there is stagnation in the case of male workers during the period. On the other hand, the number of female workers employed in regular category increased from 15 per cent in 1999–2000 to 19.3 per cent in 2004–2005 and further to 23.8 per cent in 2009–2010.

Compared to the rural labour market, more changes have been taking place in the urban labour market in Kerala. Of the total work-force in urban area, the self-employed account for 34.0 per cent in 2009–2010 and 34.2 per cent were in the category of regular workforce (Table 4.6). Only 31.8 per cent were engaged in the casual category of workforce. We can see a downward trend in the self-employed category over the years 1999–2000 to 2009–2010. On the other hand, regularly employed and casually employed category (persons) increased from 29.1 and 29.6 per cent in 1999–2000 to 34.2 and 31.8 per cent, respectively, in 2009–2010.

The structural transformation that has been taking place in Kerala's economy is now capable of shifting workers from one category to another. Very slow or negative growth in the agriculture and slow growth of manufacturing shifted workers from self-employed category to casual category. Small and medium industries also remained more or less stagnant without generating new regular employment.

Let us now analyse the common features of unemployment in Kerala with other southern states and all-India average. Out of the total rural workforce, majority of the workers in southern states were engaged in the self-employed or casual category. In the case of urban workforce,

Table 4.5 *Distribution of Rural Workers in Kerala as per Usual Status (PS + SS) (%)*

Category	1999–2000			2004–2005			2009–2010		
	Male	Female	Persons	Male	Female	Persons	Male	Female	Persons
Self-employed	38.1	53.0	42.9	41.5	53.1	45.4	38.8	42.0	39.8
Regular employed	13.0	15.0	13.7	15.0	19.3	16.5	17.6	23.8	19.4
Casual labour	48.9	32.0	43.4	43.5	27.6	38.1	43.6	34.2	40.8
Total	100.0	100.0	100.0	100.0	100.0	100.0	100.0	100.0	100.0

Sources: National Sample Survey Organisation (2000, 2001, 2006, 2011).

Table 4.6 *Distribution of Urban Workers in Kerala as per Usual Status (PS+SS) (%)*

Category	1999–2000			2004–2005			2009–2010		
	Male	Female	Persons	Male	Female	Persons	Male	Female	Persons
Self-employed	37.4	50.9	41.3	40.5	42.6	41.1	34.5	32.9	34.0
Regular employed	28.0	31.9	29.1	25.2	38.1	28.7	28.8	48.1	34.2
Casual labour	34.6	17.2	29.6	34.2	19.3	30.1	36.7	19.0	31.8
Total	100.0	100.0	100.0	100.0	100.0	100.0	100.0	100.0	100.0

Sources: National Sample Survey Organisation (2000, 2001, 2006, 2011).

majority of the workers in the southern states except Kerala were engaged in the regular employed category.

Regarding self-employment, the proportion of rural and urban workers was lower in Kerala compared to national average. Regular employment in rural Kerala was considerably higher than that of the national average. On the other hand, the same was comparatively lower in urban Kerala. Compared to all-India average, the share of casually employed labourers in rural and urban Kerala was very high. In rural Kerala, 40.7 per cent labourers were engaged in the casual employment category, while only 19.5 per cent labourers were engaged in the regular employment category. However, we can see a more or less equal distribution of labourers in urban Kerala.

TRENDS AND CHARACTERISTICS OF UNEMPLOYMENT

The unemployment of a large section of the active labour force has been the most serious socio-economic problem of Kerala during the last four decades. Due to enormous and alarming increase in unemployment, the unemployment issue has emerged as the foremost political issue of Kerala today. In this section, we present the characteristics and trends in unemployment in India and southern states including Kerala based on the NSSO data.

Let us analyse the trends in unemployment from 1999 to 2010. Table 4.7 gives the unemployment rates in all India based on US, CWS and CDS definition.

NSSO Surveys conducted throughout the country during the 2000s shed light on the unemployment situation in India. As per the CDS, 7.1 per cent of the rural labour force was unemployed in 1999–2000 which increased to 8.2 per cent in 2004–2005 and finally decreased to 6.4 per cent in 2009–2010 (Table 4.7). A more or less similar trend can be observed in the urban unemployment also. In 1999–2000, urban unemployment as per the CDS declined from 7.7 per cent to 5.8 per cent.

RURAL AND URBAN UNEMPLOYMENT IN KERALA

The NSSO survey report shows that there has been a decrease in the rates of rural unemployment in Kerala during the second half of the

Table 4.7 *Unemployment Rates in All-India (%) Usual Status (PS+SS) Current Weekly Status and Current Daily Status*

Category	Usual Status (PS+SS)			Current Weekly Status			Current Daily Status		
	1999–2000	2004–2005	2009–2010	1999–2000	2004–2005	2009–2010	1999–2000	2004–2005	2009–2010
Rural									
Male	0.9	1.6	1.6	2.1	3.8	3.2	7.2	8.0	6.4
Female	0.3	1.8	1.6	1.0	4.2	3.7	7.0	8.7	8.0
Person	0.6	1.7	1.6	1.5	3.9	3.3	7.1	8.2	6.8
Urban									
Male	2.4	3.8	2.8	3.0	5.2	3.6	7.3	7.5	5.1
Female	0.8	6.9	5.7	1.0	9.0	7.2	9.4	11.6	9.1
Person	1.7	4.5	3.4	2.1	6.0	4.2	7.7	8.3	5.8

Sources: National Sample Survey Organisation (2000, 2001, 2006, 2011).

2000s. The unemployment rates based on CDS has decreased from 21.7 per cent in 1999–2000 (persons) to 17.3 per cent in 2009–2010 (Table 4.8).

A gender-wise analysis as per the CDS shows that the rural unemployment rate for males was 12.9 per cent and for females it was 27.4 per cent in 2009–2010. The unemployment rates (CDS) for rural male showed a declining trend from 20.0 per cent in 1999–2000 to 12.9 per cent in 2009–2010, whereas there was a marginal increase in the unemployment rate of females from 26.1 to 27.4 per cent during the same period. The principal reason for the decrease in rural male unemployment has been the revival of Indian economy during this period and rapid expansion of construction and service sectors.

According to NSSO surveys, the urban unemployment rates based on CDS has decreased from 19.2 per cent (persons) in 1999–2000 to 14.3 per cent in 2009–2010 (Table 4.8). The survey reveals that 12.1 per cent of urban male labour force and 21.3 per cent of the female labour force in Kerala were unemployed as per CDS in 2009–2010. The unemployment rates for males as well as females registered a decrease during the period 1999–2000 to 2004–2012. A notable feature of urban unemployment is the high incidence of unemployment among females compared to males.

UNEMPLOYMENT RATES IN KERALA AND OTHER MAJOR STATES—A COMPARISON

Both in the rural and in urban areas unemployment is highest in Kerala among the major states of India. In the case of rural Kerala, as per the CDS, 12.9 per cent of the male workers were unemployed, while the rate of unemployment among the female workers was 27.4 per cent. These rates were very high compared to the national average of 6.4 per cent for the male workers and 8.0 per cent of the female workers. Unemployment among persons as per this definition was 17.3 per cent in Kerala, while it was 6.8 per cent at the national level, which is nearly three times of the national average.

Similarly, the unemployment in the urban Kerala is also very high compared to the major states of India. Unemployment among the male and female workers in Kerala was 12.1 per cent and 21.3 per cent,

Table 4.8 *Rural and Urban Unemployment Rates in Kerala (%) Based on US, CWS and CDS*

Category	Usual Status (PS+SS)			Current Weekly Status			Current Daily Status		
	1999–2000	2004–2005	2009–2010	1999–2000	2004–2005	2009–2010	1999–2000	2004–2005	2009–2010
Rural									
Male	–	5.1	3.2	10.1	9.8	4.7	20.0	21.1	12.9
Female	–	20.1	16.1	18.0	26.0	19.9	26.1	34.6	27.4
Person	–	10.7	7.5	12.5	15.6	9.5	21.7	25.6	17.3
Urban									
Male	–	6.2	2.9	9.7	9.1	5.2	15.5	17.4	12.1
Female	–	33.4	16.8	23.5	36.5	18.1	28.2	42.3	21.3
Person	–	15.6	7.3	13.8	18.0	9.1	19.1	25.2	14.8

Sources: National Sample Survey Organisation (2000, 2001, 2006, 2011).

respectively, in 2009–2010. The corresponding national averages were 5.1 and 9.1 per cent, respectively. Among the persons, 14.8 per cent workers were unemployed in Kerala, while the national average was 5.8 per cent. We can also see that unemployment in Kerala as per CDS is more than two times that of the national average.

UNEMPLOYMENT AMONG YOUTH AND EDUCATED

In India, persons aged 15–29 years, who were considered as the youth, accounted for 26 to 29 per cent of the total population. A substantial proportion of them attain some level of education and enter into the labour market while they are in the age group of 15–29 years, whereas some of them may be chronically unemployed—remaining unemployed for a longer period of the year. Some others, though usually employed, become intermittently unemployed during some weeks or days of the year due to seasonal fluctuations in the labour market.

One of the characteristic features of unemployment in developing countries is the high incidence of unemployment among young people. The same characteristic feature is evident in the labour market of Kerala. The NSSO survey results suggest that the rate of unemployment is very high among young people belonging to the age group of 15–29 years (Table 4.9).

The incidence of unemployment was found very high in the age group of 15–19 years, the phase when youth first enter into the labour force. The incidence of youth unemployment is very high both in rural and urban areas. More than one-third of the young labour force in rural and urban areas in Kerala is unemployed.

Another characteristic feature of unemployment in the developing countries is the high incidence of unemployment among the educated youth. Table 4.10 shows that 18 per cent of the rural and 13.7 per cent of the urban educated labour forces were unemployed in 2009–2010.

A notable characteristic of unemployment among the educated is the high incidence of female unemployment in urban as well as rural areas. The NSSO survey results (2009–2010) suggest that 35.2 per cent and 27.9 per cent of educated females in rural and urban Kerala, respectively, are unemployed. On the other hand, the incidence of male unemployment in this category is 8.3 per cent and 6.2 per cent, respectively. This

Table 4.9 *Unemployment Rates (%) Among Youth in Kerala (CDS)*

Category	Age Group (Years)											
	1999–2000				2004–2005				2009–2010			
	15–19	20–24	25–29	15–29	15–19	20–24	25–29	15–29	15–19	20–24	25–29	15–29
Rural												
Male	43.7	32.6	26.4	32.3	49.0	32.4	24.5	31.9	42.7	29.3	12.5	23.0
Female	50.6	53.8	33.8	45.8	59.1	65.2	56.1	60.6	75.3	58.1	44.1	52.7
Person	45.9	38.9	28.5	36.3	52.1	44.5	36.0	42.1	53.1	39.1	24.2	33.5
Urban												
Male	44.7	30.3	15.7	26.6	46.0	28.5	21.0	28.3	28.3	25.6	14.0	19.9
Female	48.4	61.9	38.8	50.4	83.4	60.0	72.2	68.5	25.6	58.0	39.4	45.9
Person	45.7	41.8	22.7	34.3	56.1	39.8	38.6	41.8	27.6	36.0	22.9	28.4

Sources: National Sample Survey Organisation (2000, 2001, 2006, 2011).

Table 4.10 *Educated Unemployment Rates According to Usual Principal Status in Kerala*

Category	1999–2000 (%)	2004–2005 (%)	2009–2010 (%)
Rural			
Male	1.5	13.4	8.3
Female	4.9	53.3	35.2
Person	25.3	29.6	18.0
Urban			
Male	9.9	12.6	6.2
Female	41.9	55.5	27.9
Person	21.2	29.6	13.7

Sources: National Sample Survey Organisation (2000, 2001, 2006, 2011).

means the incidence of educated female unemployment in Kerala is four to five times that of educated males. From Table 4.10, it is also clear that both male and female educated unemployment shows a declining trend. Educated unemployment (persons) in rural Kerala declined from 25.3 per cent in 1999–2000 to 18.0 per cent in 2009–2010 and in urban Kerala, it declined from 21.2 per cent to 13.7 in the same period.

CONCLUSIONS

The aforementioned analysis may be concluded with the following observations. In spite of the economic change and structural transformation, there has not been much change in the pattern of rural employment in Kerala since 2000. Kerala's rural labour market is still dominated by self-employment and casual labour with a small share of regular employment. The only visible change in the rural labour market is a small increase in the share of the secondary and tertiary sector employment. Compared to the rural labour market, more changes have occurred in the urban labour market. However, the structure of the urban labour market is still dominated by self-employment.

Kerala's unemployment—both urban and rural—has been growing and reached at high rate by the beginning of the millennium. The findings of nationwide surveys show that the rates of urban and rural unemployment in Kerala are among the highest in the country. The high incidence of unemployment in rural Kerala may be attributed to factors such as the fall in the prices of agricultural commodities, the shift in the occupational pattern from agriculture to non-agriculture avenues, small and tiny nature of agricultural holdings, decline in all-traditional labour intensive industries and the economic consequences created due to the exodus of Kerala emigrants from the Gulf countries. The incidence of urban unemployment is high due to the urban labour market being characterised by self- and casual employment. Kerala also has high incidence of unemployment among youth and educated people. Another notable feature of educated unemployment in Kerala is the very high incidence of female unemployment.

Employment creation and labour absorption is a zigzag process which may vary as per the variations in macroeconomic variables. As the state's economy is more integrated with world economy compared to other Indian states, the impact of the Global Economic Crisis of 2008 and afterwards on the labour market has been severe. In a state following a traditional pattern of higher education, the shift of focus to skill training is a crucial factor. The state needs to promote entrepreneurship, innovation and skill development to accelerate the process of investment and employment generation.

REFERENCES AND SELECT BIBLIOGRAPHY

Census of India. (2011). *Kerala part.* Thiruvananthapuram: Director of Census Operations.

Mathew, E. T. (1995, 11 February). Educated unemployment in Kerala: Some socio economic aspects. *Economic and Political Weekly, 30*(6), 325–335.

———. (1997). *Employment and unemployment in Kerala.* New Delhi: SAGE Publications.

Government of India. (2015). *Ministry of Labour and Employment. Indian labour year book 2011 and 2012.* Shimla: Labour Bureau.

National Sample Survey Organisation. (2000). *Employment and unemployment in India, 1999–2000: Key results* (Report No. 455). New Delhi: National Sample Survey Organisation.

———. (2001). *Employment and unemployment situations in India, 1999–2000* (Report No. 458). New Delhi: National Sample Survey Organisation.

———. (2006). *Employment and unemployment situations in India, 2004–05* (Report No. 515). New Delhi: National Sample Survey Organisation.

National Sample Survey Organisation (2011). *Employment and unemployment situations in India, 2009–10* (Report No. 537). New Delhi: National Sample Survey Organisation.

———. (2014). *Employment and unemployment situations in India, 2011–12* (Report No. 554). New Delhi: National Sample Survey Organisation.

Prakash, B. A. (1988). *Educated unemployment in Kerala: Some observations based on a field study* (Working Paper No. 224). Thiruvananthapuram: Centre for Development Studies.

———. (1989). *Unemployment in Kerala: An analysis of economic causes* (Working Paper No. 231). Thiruvananthapuram: Centre for Development Studies.

———. (1990). Growing unemployment in Kerala, a study of nature and magnitude. *Manpower Journal, 26*(3), 67–78.

———. (1999). *Kerala's economic development: Issues and problems.* New Delhi: SAGE Publications.

———. (2002, 28 September). Urban unemployment in Kerala: The case of Kochi City. *Economic and Political Weekly, 37*(39), 4073–4078.

———. (2004). *Kerala's economy performance, problems, prospects.* New Delhi: SAGE Publications.

Prakash, B. A. and Abraham, M. P. (2004). Employment and unemployment in Kerala. In B. A. Prakash (ed). *Kerala's economic development: Performance and problems in post liberalisation period.* New Delhi: SAGE Publications.

State Planning Board. (2016). *Economic review, 2016.* Thiruvananthapuram: Kerala State Planning Board.

Chapter 5

Emigration of Keralite Workers to West Asia
Trends, Patterns and Economic Impacts

B. A. Prakash

The large-scale emigration of Keralite workers to West Asian countries during the last four decades has contributed to the biggest socio-economic change in Kerala. This has resulted in an unprecedented increase in emigration, receipt of migrant remittances and widespread change in the economic and social fronts. In this context, this chapter examines the trends, patterns of emigration of Keralite workers to West Asian countries and its economic impacts. In order to explain the economic impacts of emigration, we present the following hypothesis. 'The factor which had the greatest impact on the state's economy especially on labour market, consumption, savings, investment, poverty, income distribution and economic change during the last four decades has been the migration to Gulf and migrant remittances'. The chapter is presented in four sections. In the first section, we present a review of research and framework of analysis. In the subsequent sections, we examine Indian emigrants in West Asia, trends in emigration from Kerala and economic impacts.

REVIEW OF RESEARCH AND FRAMEWORK OF ANALYSIS

The economic impact of Gulf migration on Kerala is a topic which attracted considerable attention from economists and demographers (Gopinathan Nair, 1989; Prakash, 1978, 1998a; Thomas, 1993; Zachariah, Mathew, & Irudaya Rajan, 2003). A hypothesis put forward in one of the studies is that 'Since the mid-1970s, the factor which had the greatest impact on Kerala's economy especially on labour market, consumption, savings, investment, poverty, income distribution and economic growth has been the Gulf migration and migrant remittances' (Prakash, 1998a). A similar conclusion was arrived by another study based on a statewide survey (Zachariah, Mathew, & Irudaya Rajan, 2003). Issues connected with return emigration such as the causes of return, socio-economic background of the return emigrants, the current activity status of the return emigrants and the problems faced by them is another area where a number of studies are available (Prakash, 2000, 2013; Zachariah, Gopinathan Nair, & Irudaya Rajan, 2006).

In Kerala, migration to the West Asia continued to be an important topic of research during the first decade of the present century. Among the studies, a notable one is *Kerala's Gulf Connection*, a compilation of studies on Keralite emigration to the Gulf (Zachariah, Kannan, & Irudaya Rajan, 2002). Other studies also examine aspects such as trends, patterns, socio-economic impacts, profile of emigrants and return emigrants (DES, 2013; Zachariah & Irudaya Rajan, 2009, 2012a, 2012b, 2014; Zacharia, Prakash, & Irudaya Rajan, 2004).

The aforementioned review may be concluded with the following observations. Keralite migration to the Gulf is an area where fairly good amount of literature is available on trends and patterns of migration, profile and problems of migrants, return migration, global crisis and the socio-economic aspects of migration.

Framework of Analysis

Settlement Migration

In settlement migration, people especially with better skills from less developed countries migrate to developed countries to avail better jobs, opportunities, living conditions and to settle there. They migrate with their family members and settle in the foreign country. They usually spend their entire earnings in the foreign country and their native country is not benefited much from the migration. This type of migration results in brain drain in backward countries.

Contract Migration

In contract migration, the workers are hired for contractual jobs for a definite time period and are expected to return after the expiry of the period. Usually during the period of stay abroad, they leave their families behind in their home country. In order to support their family, the emigrants send remittances on a regular basis which is spent by the households. The economic impact of this spending will be substantial on the domestic economies of the labour exporting countries. The areas which experience substantial impact are labour market, balance of payments, consumption, savings, investment, distribution of income and economic growth.

Concepts and Sources of Data

- Emigrants are defined as members of the household who had moved out of Kerala and were living outside India.
- Return emigrants are members of the household who had emigrated out of India but returned to Kerala and live as members of the households.
- Total remittances include remittances received directly by the households and also by any institution in Kerala from all parts of the world.

Both secondary and primary data are used for the study. For presenting the trends and patterns of emigration, we have used the data from the migration surveys conducted by the Centre for Development Studies in 1998, 2003, 2008, 2011 and 2014.

INDIAN EMIGRANTS IN WEST ASIA

According to the High Level Committee on Indian Diaspora, the total stock of Indian emigrants in the West Asia was 5.31 lakh in 1979

(Table 5.1). The principal destination of Indians during the second half of 1970s was the United Arab Emirates (UAE), Saudi Arabia, Kuwait and Oman. There had been a continuous increase in the Indian emigration to the Gulf during the 1980s. The Committee estimates that the total Indian emigrants in West Asia increased to 30 lakhs in 1999. Of the total emigrants in West Asia, the share of Saudi Arabia was 40 per cent, the UAE 25 per cent and Oman 15 per cent in 1999. The other West Asian countries such as Bahrain, Kuwait and Qatar accounted for 20 per cent of the total emigrants.

According to another estimate of Indian Council of Overseas Employment, the total stock of Indian emigrants in India increased to 49 lakh in 2008. The country-wise distribution of the stock of Indian emigrants is given in Table 5.2.

The data on the annual migration of unskilled and semi-skilled categories of labourers who require permission from the Protector General of Emigrants (PGE) to migrate to foreign countries indicate that there had been a steep decline in Indian migrants to West Asia since 2008, the year of Global Economic Crisis. The number of workers being granted emigration clearance declined from 8.48 lakh in 2008 to 6.10 lakh in 2009 (Ministry of Overseas Indian Affairs, n.d.).

The Global Economic Crisis which spread throughout the world since 2008 was considered as one of the worst global crisis since the Great Depression of the 1930s. As a result of global crisis, there was a massive decline in construction activities, trade and commerce, services and manufacturing in Gulf Cooperation Council countries. A large proportion of migrant workers in construction, trade, manufacturing, agriculture and domestic service sectors had lost their jobs and were

Table 5.1 *Estimates of the Total Stock of Indian and Keralite Emigrants in the Gulf*

Year	Indian Emigrants	Keralite Emigrants*
1979	531,000	265,500
1983	916,000	458,000
1991	1,505,000	752,500
1999	3,000,000	1,500,000

Source: Government of India (2002).

Note: *Keralite's share was calculated as half of the total Indian emigrants.

Table 5.2 *Stock of Indian Emigrants in West Asia (2008)*

Country	Number of Indian Emigrants (in Lakh)	Per Cent
Bahrain	3.1	6.3
Kuwait	5.8	11.8
Oman	5.5	11.2
Qatar	4.0	8.2
UAE	15.0	30.6
Saudi Arabia	15.6	31.8
Total	49.0	100.0

Source: Indian Council of Overseas Employment (2009).

forced to return home. Those who remained in the Gulf countries were affected by reduction in wages, longer working hours and deterioration in working conditions.

WAGE STRUCTURE OF INDIAN EMIGRANT WORKERS IN THE UAE AND KUWAIT

A study on the profile of Indian workers in the UAE and Kuwait gives an idea about the wage structure of the workers in 2013. Indian emigrant workers in the UAE can be classified into five categories based on the monthly wage they receive, namely, those who earn UAE dirham below 600, 601–1,200, 1,201–4,000, 4,001–10,000 and above 10,000 (Table 5.3). Nearly half of the total migrants can be classified in the first two categories. The third and fourth categories are the middle income groups who can save after meeting their consumption expenditures and other items of expenditure and account for about 35 per cent. On the other hand, the fifth group may be considered as a high income group, accounting for about 15 per cent.

The wage structure of Indian emigrant workers in Kuwait is classified into four categories (Table 5.4). The first category consists of those Indian emigrants getting monthly wages between 50 and 150 Kuwaiti dinars. This is the lowest earning category of workers in Kuwait and they account for about one-third of the total workers. The second category is those getting a monthly wage ranging between

Table 5.3 *Wage Structure of Indian Emigrant Workers in the UAE in 2013*

S. No.	Monthly Wage in UAE Dirham	Category of Indian Workers
1	Below 600	Unskilled construction worker, household worker, cleaner, etc.
2	601–1,200	House maid, servant, cook, construction labourer, sweeper, office boy, watchman, waiter in small tea shops, salesman in small shops, delivery boy, cleaner, etc.
3	1,201–4,000	Tailor, welder, steel fixer, draftsman, mason, teachers, salesman, watchman, clerk, office assistant, electrician, etc.
4	4,001–10,000	Foreman, draftsman, heavy vehicle driver, store keeper, cashier, manager, sales executive, accountant, marketing manager, lab technician, plant operator, small businessman and traders.
5	Above 10,000	Doctor, engineer, IT professional, bank manager, professional, top executive, businessman and investor.

Source: Rajiv Gandhi Institute of Development Studies (2014).

151 and 400 Kuwaiti dinars. Another one-third workers belong to this group. The third category is the emigrants getting a wage ranging between 401 and 600 Kuwaiti dinars and accounts one-fourth of the total emigrant workers. The rest of them belong to the high income group of above 600 dinars.

TRENDS IN EMIGRATION FROM KERALA TO WEST ASIA

The High Level Committee on Indian Diaspora had estimated that Keralite emigrants accounted for half of the total stock of Indian emigrants in the Gulf countries. Accordingly, the stock of Keralite emigrants was 2.65 lakh in 1973. There had been a continuous increase in the stock of emigrants in the 1980s and 1990s (Table 5.1). Five statewide surveys on migration conducted by the Centre for Development Studies in 1998, 2003, 2008, 2011 and 2014 give somewhat better

Table 5.4 *Wages Structure of Indian Emigrant Workers in Kuwait in 2013*

S. No.	Monthly Wage in Kuwaiti Dinar	Category of Indian Workers
1	50–150	House maids, servants, cooks, drivers, unskilled construction workers, waiters, cleaners, salesman, delivery boys, sweepers, watchmen, office boys, etc.
2	151–400	Technicians, masons, welders, foremen, mechanics, heavy vehicle operators, sales assistants, sales executives, office assistants, accountants, clerks, lab technicians, nurses, plant operators, junior managers, etc.
3	401–600	Engineers, nurses in public hospitals, IT professionals, middle-level managers, sales executives, plant operators, etc.
4	Above 600	Engineers, doctors, bank managers, senior managers, high grade executives, sales executives, professionals, businessmen and investors.

Source: Rajiv Gandhi Institute of Development Studies (2014).

estimates about the international migration from Kerala. Compared to the previous estimates, the survey used better concepts of migration and statistical methods to collect data. And for the same reasons, these surveys provide more realistic, reliable and comparable estimates about the trends in emigration from Kerala. On the basis of these surveys, we present the trends and patterns of emigration from Kerala from 1998 to 2014 (Table 5.5).

According to the migration survey of 1998, the total emigrants from Kerala were estimated as 13.62 lakh. The subsequent surveys had estimated the total emigrants as 18.38 lakh in 2003 and 21.83 lakh in 2008. The latest survey conducted in 2014 estimates the total emigrants as 23.63 lakh of which 86 per cent belonged to Gulf countries.

A major change has occurred in the trend in migration to the West Asia since the Global Crisis of 2008. During the pre-global crisis period (up to 2008), there had been a continuous growth in the migration from Kerala to the West Asia. Between 2003 and 2008, the migration to the Gulf countries increased by 18.6 per cent. On the other hand, the post-global crisis period witnessed a substantial decline. Between

Table 5.5 *Country of Residence of Kerala Emigrants*

Countries	Number				
	1998	2003	2008	2011	2014
UAE	421,959	670,150	918,122	883,313	886,968
	–	(58.8)	(37.0)	(–3.8)	(0.4)
Saudi Arabia	510,895	489,988	503,433	574,739	514,976
	–	(–4.1)	(2.7)	(14.2)	(–10.4)
Oman	139,571	152,865	167,628	195,300	185,996
	–	(9.5)	(9.7)	(16.5)	(–4.8)
Kuwait	68,163	113,967	129,282	127,782	180,765
	–	(67.2)	(13.4)	(–1.2)	(41.5)
Bahrain	74,654	108,507	101,344	101,556	146,472
	–	(45.3)	(–6.6)	(0.2)	(44.2)
Qatar	62,969	98,953	121,613	148,427	104,623
	–	(57.1)	(22.9)	(22.1)	(–29.5)
Other West Asia	–	2,047	–	6,696	13,368
	–	–	–	–	(99.6)
Total Gulf countries	1,278,211	1,636,477	1,941,422	2,037,813	2,033,168
	–	(28.0)	(18.6)	(5.0)	(–0.2)
Other countries	83,744	202,001	251,993	242,730	330,143
	–	(141.2)	(24.7)	(–3.7)	(36.0)
Total	1,361,955	1,838,478	2,193,415	2,280,543	2,363,311
	–	(35.0)	(19.3)	(4.0)	(3.6)

Source: Zachariah and Irudaya Rajan (2014).

Note: Figures in brackets are growth rate in per cent.

2008 and 2011, the growth in migration to the Gulf was only 5 per cent. The latest statewide survey on migration in 2014 indicates that the growth in the migration was negative between 2011 and 2014 (Table 5.5). This indicates a major shift in trends and patterns of emigration from Kerala to the Gulf. This is a disturbing development that has been taking place in a state, which heavily relies on migration and foreign remittances for its survival.

During the post-global crisis period, there was a change in the share of Kerala emigrants in the different Gulf countries. In 2008, the Global Crisis year, the UAE accounted for the largest share of Kerala emigrants. But the share of migrants registered a decline since then (Table 5.6). Saudi Arabia, which ranked second with respect to the share of Kerala emigrants registered a decline of its share between 2011 and 2014. Similar change occurred in the case of Qatar. On the other hand, the share of Kerala emigrants registered an increase in the case of Oman, Kuwait and Bahrain.

A structural change that had occurred in Kerala's migration front was the decline in the share of migration to the Gulf countries and increase in the share of non-Gulf countries. The share of migrants to the Gulf countries witnessed a steady decline from 93.8 per cent in 1998 to 88.5 per cent in 2008 and to 86 per cent in 2011 (Table 5.6). On the other hand, the share of migrants to non-Gulf countries witnessed a steady increase from 6.2 per cent in 1998 to 11.5 per cent in 2008 and 14 per cent in 2014. The non-Gulf countries to which sizable

Table 5.6 *Country of Residence of Kerala Emigrants (Percentage Share)*

Countries	Percentage Share				
	1998	2003	2008	2011	2014
UAE	31.0	36.4	41.9	38.7	37.5
Saudi Arabia	37.5	26.7	23.0	25.2	21.8
Oman	10.2	8.3	7.6	8.6	7.9
Kuwait	5.0	6.2	5.9	5.6	7.6
Bahrain	5.5	5.9	4.6	4.5	6.2
Qatar	4.6	5.4	5.5	6.5	4.4
Other West Asia	0.0	0.1	0.0	0.3	0.6
Total Gulf countries	93.8	89.0	88.5	89.4	86.0
Other countries	6.2	11.0	11.5	10.6	14.0
Total	100.0	100.0	100.0	100.0	100.0

Source: Zachariah and Irudaya Rajan (2014).

numbers of workers migrate from Kerala are the United States, Canada, the United Kingdom, other European countries, Malaysia, Australia, New Zealand and other South Asian countries.

District-wise Distribution of Emigrants

An analysis of the district-wise emigration from Kerala shows that emigration is not uniform in all districts or regions. The districts which are having large share of emigrants are Malappuram, Kannur, Thiruvananthapuram, Thrissur and Kozhikode. On the other hand, the share of emigrants in Wayanad and Idukki districts are very small. The other districts have moderate rate of emigration. The 2014 survey on migration shows that there has been a substantial fall in emigration between 2011 and 2014 in five districts of Kerala (Tables 5.7 and 5.8).

The districts which experienced negative growth are Alappuzha, Kottayam, Palakkad, Wayanad and Kasaragod. The districts which registered a substantial increase in emigration are Pathanamthitta, Idukki and Ernakulam. It is likely that the increase in the migration in these districts may be due to the migration to Gulf as well as to non-Gulf countries. The economic and social impacts of migration in districts will differ depending on the number of migrants and volume of remittances.

Return Emigrants

The migration surveys have estimated the return emigrants from the foreign countries to Kerala for the years 1998, 2003, 2008 and 2011. According to the survey of 1998, the total return emigrants were 7.39 lakh in Kerala. It increased to 8.93 lakh in 2003, 11.57 lakh in 2008 and to 11.50 lakh in 2011.

A noticeable point is that there has been a marginal decline in the number of return emigrants during post-global crisis period. This can be largely attributed to the steep fall in fresh emigration and the absence of immediate return of the new migrants due to adjustability problems during the post-global crisis period.

Table 5.7 *Emigrants by District of Origin*

Districts	1998	2003	Number 2008	2011	2014
Thiruvananthapuram	130,705	168,046	308,481	229,732	248,852
Kollam	102,977	148,457	207,516	167,446	197,014
Pathanamthitta	97,505	133,720	120,990	91,381	137,730
Alappuzha	62,870	75,036	131,719	144,386	89,905
Kottayam	35,494	106,569	89,351	117,460	110,411
Idukki	7,390	7,880	5,792	7,690	23,945
Ernakulam	103,750	121,237	120,979	136,113	186,765
Thrissur	161,102	178,867	284,068	198,368	224,978
Palakkad	116,062	177,876	189,815	142,020	69,186
Malappuram	296,710	271,787	334,572	408,883	444,100
Kozhikode	116,026	167,436	199,163	206,719	224,638
Wayanad	4,552	7,704	13,996	26,874	20,511
Kannur	88,065	202,414	119,119	283,045	290,335
Kasaragod	38,747	71,449	67,851	120,425	93,598
Kerala	1,361,955	1,838,478	2,193,412	2,280,543	2,361,968

Source: Zachariah and Irudaya Rajan (2014).

Table 5.8 *Emigrants by District of Origin (Percentage Share)*

Districts	Percentage Share				
	1998	2003	2008	2011	2014
Thiruvananthapuram	9.6	9.1	14.1	10.1	10.5
Kollam	7.6	8.1	9.5	7.3	8.3
Pathanamthitta	7.2	7.3	5.5	4.0	5.8
Alappuzha	4.6	4.1	6.0	6.3	3.8
Kottayam	2.6	5.8	4.1	5.2	4.7
Idukki	0.5	0.4	0.3	0.3	1.0
Ernakulam	7.6	6.6	5.5	6.0	7.9
Thrissur	11.8	9.7	13.0	8.7	9.5
Palakkad	8.5	9.7	8.6	6.2	2.9
Malappuram	21.8	14.8	15.2	17.9	18.8
Kozhikode	8.5	9.1	9.1	9.1	9.5
Wayanad	0.3	0.4	0.6	1.2	0.9
Kannur	6.5	11.0	5.4	12.4	12.3
Kasaragod	2.9	3.9	3.1	5.3	4.0
Kerala	100.0	100.0	100.0	100.0	100.0

Source: Zachariah and Irudaya Rajan (2014).

Households with and Without Emigrants

The proportion of households with one or more emigrants to total will give an idea about the intensity of migration. The economic and social impact of migration will differ depending on the intensity of migration. The surveys on migration give the percentage of households with one or more emigrants or return emigrants. According to the migration survey 2014, the percentage of households with one or more emigrants is 19 (Table 5.9).

A notable aspect of the pattern of emigration is the relative constancy of the proportion of households with migrants in various surveys. Second aspect is the wide variations in the percentage of migrant households among districts in Kerala. For instance, Malappuram district has 35 per cent of households having one or more emigrants. On the other hand, Idukki district has only 6.2 per cent of the households having

Table 5.9 *Percentage of Households with One or More Emigrants or Return Emigrants by Districts*

Districts	Emigrants (EMI)			Return Emigrant (REM)		
	2008	2011	2014	2008	2011	2014
Thiruvananthapuram	24.2	18.7	17.4	22.6	22.4	23.1
Kollam	21.0	19.7	20.0	14.8	15.9	15.5
Pathanamthitta	22.1	18.6	27.2	14.6	4.4	10.4
Alappuzha	14.6	15.1	14.1	6.8	9.1	11.4
Kottayam	12.1	12.9	12.4	4.5	2.2	5.8
Idukki	1.3	2.2	6.2	1.0	2.1	1.1
Ernakulam	9.8	9.3	12.7	7.5	5.8	6.5
Thrissur	26.1	21.1	19.2	20.4	17.7	14.4
Palakkad	17.5	14.8	9.9	13.0	10.4	1.9
Malappuram	36.8	35.9	34.9	28.8	17.7	28.2
Kozhikode	21.2	21.8	20.2	10.2	15.8	13.2
Wayanad	5.9	10.0	9.2	1.0	7.5	6.6
Kannur	15.5	27.3	28.9	4.3	16.4	15.6
Kasaragod	19.6	25.7	22.8	9.9	12.6	13.7
Kerala	18.0	18.2	19.0	11.8	11.7	12.7

Source: Zachariah and Irudaya Rajan (2014).

emigrants. Among the districts, those having 20 per cent or more households with migrants are Kollam, Pathanamthitta, Malappuram, Kozhikode, Kannur and Kasaragod. It is likely that the economic impact of migration will be higher in these districts compared to other districts. If we take both emigrants and return emigrants, the total emigrant households were 30.7 per cent in Kerala in 2014.

Remittances

These surveys have estimated the total remittances received in Kerala from the emigrant workers. According to the survey of 1998, the total remittances received in Kerala from the migrant workers were ₹13,652 crore which was equivalent to 22 per cent of the gross domestic product of Kerala (Table 5.10). The remittances increased to ₹43,288 crore in 2008, ₹49,695 crore in 2011 and ₹72,680 crore in 2014. The amount of remittances received was equivalent to 15.6 per cent in 2014.

The post-global crisis period (2008 to 2011) witnessed a decline in the rate of growth of remittances. Another notable thing is that the migrant remittances received in Kerala were more than the total annual expenditure of the state government comprising revenue and capital expenditure except one year, that is, 2011 (Table 5.11).

Table 5.10 *Remittance and Gross Domestic Product of Kerala*

Year	Remittance (₹ in Crore)	GSDP (₹ in Crore)	Remittance as Percentage of GSDP	Remittances per Household (₹)
1998	13,652	62,286	21.9	21,469
2003	18,465	96,698	19.1	24,444
2008	43,288	202,782	21.3	57,215
2011	49,695	307,906	16.1	63,315
2014	72,680	465,041	15.6	88,720

Source: Zachariah and Irudaya Rajan (2012a, 2014).

Table 5.11 *Remittance and Total Expenditure of Government of Kerala*

Year	Remittance (₹ in Crore)	Total Expenditure of Government of Kerala	Remittance as Percentage of Total Expenditure
1998	13,652	9,880	138.2
2003	18,465	17,427	105.9
2008	43,288	30,904	140.1
2011	49,695	50,896	97.6
2014	72,680	67,713	107.3

Source: Zachariah and Irudaya Rajan (2012a, 2014).

ECONOMIC IMPACT IN KERALA

In this section, the impact of emigration on the state's economy is examined. As the rate of emigration among districts is different, the economic impact emigration is different in the districts of Kerala. The latest data suggest that the intensity of emigration is fairly high in eight districts of Kerala where the emigration rate is more than 15. The emigration rate which denotes the number of emigrants per 100 households ranged between 17 and 34 per cent in these districts (Table 5.9). The districts which have highest intensity of emigration are Malappuram, Kannur, Pathanamthitta, Kasaragod, Kozhikode and Kollam. On the other hand, the districts such as Alappuzha, Kottayam, Ernakulam and Palakkad have moderate level of migration. But the economic impact due to migration is very small or marginal in the districts such as Idukki and Wayanad.

An estimate about the district-wise receipt of total remittances showed that there were wide variations in the amount received. One can notice a correlation between the emigration rate and amount of remittances received in the district (Table 5.12). Malappuram, Ernakulam, Kannur, Thiruvananthapuram and Kollam have received large amount of remittances. This denotes that the economic impact of migration is large in northern region compared to southern region.

From Table 5.12, it is clear that the economic effects of migration are different among different regions or districts of Kerala. This shows that the economic changes in the labour market, consumption, savings, investment, income distribution and factor prices are different in the districts of Kerala. We have already seen that the volume of remittances received in Kerala due to migration was larger than the total expenditure of Kerala government.

The large-scale inflow of remittances had resulted in substantial growth in the number of branches and banking activity in Kerala since the mid-1970s. The non-resident external (NRE) deposit was ₹18,724 crore accounting for 48 per cent of the total deposit in the banks in Kerala in 2000. And the total NRE deposits increased to ₹66,190 crore accounting for 29 per cent of the total bank deposits in 2013 (State Planning Board, 2014). The flow of remittances had contributed to a substantial growth in the bank branches in Kerala.

Table 5.12 *Remittance by Districts in 2003 and 2011*

Districts	2003 (₹ in Crore)	2011 (₹ in Crore)	2003 Share (Per Cent)	2011 Share (Per Cent)
Thiruvananthapuram	1,926	4,740	10.4	9.5
Kollam	1,813	4,423	9.8	8.9
Pathanamthitta	955	2,079	5.2	4.2
Alappuzha	1,339	2,296	7.2	4.6
Kottayam	580	2,419	3.1	4.9
Idukki	39	182	0.2	0.4
Ernakulam	1,515	6,127	8.2	12.3
Thrissur	3,235	4,293	17.5	8.6
Palakkad	1,149	3,293	6.2	6.6
Malappuram	2,893	9,040	15.7	18.2
Kozhikode	1,358	3,904	7.3	7.9
Wayanad	68	578	0.4	1.2
Kannur	976	5,145	5.3	10.3
Kasaragod	623	1,176	3.4	2.4
Total	18,469	49,695	100.0	100.0

Source: Zachariah and Irudaya Rajan (2012a).

The total number of bank branches of state bank groups, nationalised bank, regional rural banks and private sector banks was 5,027 in 2014. Except the districts such as Kasaragod, Wayanad and Idukki, all the other districts have more than 300 bank branches.

Impact on Labour Market

A major impact on labour market was the reduction of unemployment among youth through migration of unemployed persons. Available evidences suggest that a substantial share of migrants were unemployed prior to migration. According to migration survey conducted by the Centre for Development Studies, 24 per cent of emigrants were unemployed prior to the migration in 2007 (Zachariah & Irudaya Rajan, 2007).

The migration has resulted in reduction in supply and increase in the demand for certain categories of workers, especially construction workers. Many parts of Kerala began to experience severe shortage of construction workers since the mid-1970s due to large increase in construction activities because of receipts of remittances, migration of construction workers to Gulf resulting in shortage of workers and lack of interest of educated youth to engage in manual work.

From the 1970s to the 1990s, the major share of the migrant workers came from the state of Tamil Nadu. But during the first decade of the 21st century, there occurred a change in the origin of migrant workers, and major share of workers came to Kerala from other states such as Uttar Pradesh, Assam, West Bengal, Bihar and Odisha. According to one estimate, the total stock of migrant workers belonging to other states in Kerala was 25 lakh in 2013 (Gulati Institute of Finance and Taxation, 2013). Currently, these workers are working in construction sector, quarries, agriculture, industry, trade and service as unskilled, semi-skilled and skilled workers. And Kerala heavily relies on migrant workers from other states. The shortage of construction workers and increase in wage have led to introduction of capital-intensive technique since the early 1990s in construction and allied activities. Another change that occurred in labour market due to Gulf migration was the introduction of vocational education and training in skills.

Impact on Consumption, Saving and Investment

Impact of migration on consumption, saving and investment is largely determined by the amount of remittances sent by migrants as well as the utilisation pattern of remittances. The surveys on migration indicate that there had been a steady increase in remittances per household (Table 5.10). The per household remittances had increased from ₹21,469 in 1998 to 57,215 in 2008 and 88,720 in 2014. Available evidences suggest that the income of the migrant household is high compared to non-migrant households. Due to this, the monthly expenditure is higher in the case of migrant households compared to non-migrant households. The migrant households incurred higher expenditure on food, clothing, education, fuel, lights, travel and entertainment, medical expenses, etc. The household also spent more money

Table 5.13 *Percentage of Households in Possession of Consumer Durables with Non-residential Keralites (NRK) and Others (Non-NRK)*

Consumer Items	2008			2014		
	NRK	Non-NRK	All	NRK	Non-NRK	All
Motor car	10.8	6.1	7.4	22.3	15.9	17.7
Taxi, truck	2.4	1.9	2.0	6.6	6.4	6.5
Motorcycle	28.9	21.1	23.2	41.8	34.6	36.7
Land phone	77.5	51.7	58.6	53.0	37.7	42.1
Mobile phone	77.3	68.3	70.7	92.7	86.9	88.6
Television	88.1	77.8	80.5	90.6	86.0	87.3
MP3/DVD/VCD	54.8	37.5	42.1	54.1	43.6	46.6
Refrigerator	56.2	28.4	35.8	72.3	48.6	55.4
Computer/laptop	10.5	4.8	6.3	26.6	18.0	20.5
Microwave oven	2.0	0.2	1.3	11.2	6.9	8.1
Net connection	–	–	–	14.7	10.0	11.3

Source: Zachariah and Irudaya Rajan (2014).

on consumer durables. Migration surveys indicate that the migrant households have better possession of consumer items such as motor car, motorcycle, land phone, mobile phone, television, refrigerator, computer, microwave oven, net connection and so on (Table 5.13).

To conclude, the migrant households had higher income, better consumption level and asset position compared to the non-migrant households.

Impact on Poverty and Income Distribution

The impact on poverty and income distribution may be classified into direct and indirect impacts. The direct impact is on the migrant households which received remittances. The indirect impact includes all those spillover effects such as increased wages, employment opportunities, increase in the price of land, consumer items, services, etc. The impact has affected the welfare of the migrant and non-migrant households differently.

The micro level studies on the socio-economic status of the migrants on the eve of the migration showed that majority of the migrants were poor at the time of migration, especially during the 1970s. A study based on a sample of about 700 returned migrants in 1984 revealed that nearly 58 per cent of the migrant households were classified as poor households (Gopinathan Nair, 1989). Another study conducted in four districts in 2013 covering 800 returned emigrant households revealed that 24 per cent of them belonged to the category of Below Poverty Line (BPL) households (Prakash, 2013). Thus, a good percentage of the emigrants who migrated to West Asia belonged to the category of poor households. These households are the beneficiaries of higher income and consumption.

The large inflow of remittances had resulted in a spurt in construction activities and generation of employment. Similarly, large employment opportunities were generated in tertiary activities such as transport, communication, trade, commerce, education, health, service, banking, etc. There was increase in wage rate of all categories of casual workers. Thus, the receipt of remittances to the poor households, the generation of employment in construction and tertiary sectors and increase in wage rate have resulted in the increase in income levels of poor households in Kerala. The estimates on poverty also support the aforementioned change. According to the poverty line of the Planning Commission, the people BPL in Kerala had declined from 53 per cent in 1977–1978 to 13 per cent in 1999–2000 and 7.1 per cent in 2011–2012. The most important factor contributing to the poverty reduction is the large-scale emigration and flow of remittances.

The hike in price of land, commodities and services due to the inflow of remittances has affected distribution on income in favour of some sections of people while adversely affecting others. Available information suggests that the inflow of remittances had pushed up prices of land in urban and rural areas in those districts where the intensity of migration has been high. It is reported that there had been a continuous increase in the price of land in rural and urban areas of Trivandrum district between 1975 and 1983 (Gopinathan Nair, 1989).

The impact of the continuous increase in price of land was different on different sections of people. With the steep increase in price of land, the owners of the land got a windfall when they sold their land. Prior to the mid-1970s, there was not much demand for land in rural area, and the increase in price of land was only small. On the other hand, the post-mid-1970s period witnessed continuous rise in price of land in all parts of Kerala. The land was considered as a speculative asset witnessing continuous value appreciation. Due to this spurt in price of land, the poor, middle class and fixed-income group of people found it very difficult to purchase land for construction of houses and other purposes. This was a negative consequence of the economic effect of the emigration.

CONCLUSION

Among the total Indian migrants to the Gulf, Keralites account for nearly half. The large-scale migration and flows of remittances resulted in unprecedented economic changes in Kerala. Widespread changes had taken place in labour market, consumption, savings, investment, poverty, income distribution and economic growth. The migration resulted in reduction of unemployment, shortage of workers in all sectors, upgraded skills, increased wage rates and immigration of workers from other states to Kerala. Available evidences suggest that the migration helped the migrant households to attain higher levels of income, consumption and acquisition of assets compared to non-migrant households. As sizeable section of migrants belonged to poor households at the time of migration, the receipt of income through migration improved their economic status.

As the volume of remittance received in Kerala was very large, the impact of it on the state's economy was obviously very great. Compared to the annual total expenditure of government of Kerala, the remittances received in Kerala were large. These evidences support the hypothesis that the factor which had the greatest impact on the state's economy, especially on labour market, consumption, saving, investment, poverty, income distribution and economic change during the last four decades, has been the Gulf migration and migrant remittances.

REFERENCES AND SELECT BIBLIOGRAPHY

Department of Economics and Statistics (DES). (2013). *Pravasi Malayali census 2013* (Vol. 1). Thiruvananthapuram: DES.

Gopinathan Nair, P. R. (1989). Incidence, impact and implications of migration to the Middle East from Kerala. In Rashid Amjed (ed), *To the Gulf and back*. New Delhi: ILO-ARTEP.

Government of India. (2002). *Report of the high level committee on the Indian diaspora*. New Delhi: Government of India.

Gulati Institute of Finance and Taxation (GIFT). (2013). *Domestic migrant labour in Kerala*. Thiruvananthapuram: GIFT.

Indian Council of Overseas Employment. (2009, 21–22 July). *Impact assessment of global recession on Indian migrant workers*. Paper presented in the International Conference, Centre for Development Studies. Thiruvananthapuram.

Ministry of Overseas Indian Affairs (n.d.). *Annual reports for the years 2004–05 to 2010–13*. New Delhi: Government of India.

Prakash, B. A. (1978, 8 July). Impact of foreign remittances: A case study of Chavakkad Village in Kerala. *Economic and Political Weekly, 13*(27), 1107–1111.

———. (1998a). Gulf migration and its economic impacts: The Kerala experience. *Economic and Political Weekly, 33*(50), 3209–3213.

———. (ed). (1998b). *Indian migration to the Middle East*. Rohtak: Spellbound Publications.

———. (2000, 16 December). Exodus of Gulf emigrants—Return emigrants of Varkala Town in Kerala. *Economic and Political Weekly, 35*(51), 4534–4540.

———. (2013). *Return emigration of Indian emigrant workers from the West Asia: Report on a survey of return emigrants in Kerala*. Thiruvananthapuram: Rajiv Gandhi Institute of Development Studies.

Rajiv Gandhi Institute of Development Studies. (2014). *Indian migrant workers in West Asia* (Unpublished). Thiruvananthapuram.

State Planning Board. (2014). *Economic review report 2013* (Vols. 1 and 2). Trivandrum: State Planning Board.

Thomas, Issac T. M. (1993). Economic consequences of Gulf crisis: A study of India with special reference to Kerala. In Eickramsekhara Proyasinin (ed), *The Gulf crisis and South Asia* (pp. 59–97). New Delhi: UNDP-ARTEP.

Zachariah, K., Kannan, K. P., & Irudaya Rajan, S. (eds). (2002). *Kerala's Gulf connection*. Thiruvananthapuram: Centre for Development Studies.

Zachariah, K. C., Gopinathan Nair, P. R., & Irudaya Rajan, S. (2006). *Return emigrants in Kerala: welfare, rehabilitation and development*. New Delhi: Manohar.

Zachariah, K. C., & Irudaya Rajan, S. (2009). *Migration and development, the Kerala experience*. New Delhi: Danish Books.

———. (2012a). *Inflexion in Kerala's Gulf connection—Report on Kerala migration survey 2011* (Working Paper No. 450). Thiruvananthapuram: Centre for Development Studies.

Zachariah, K. C., & Irudaya Rajan, S. (2012b). *Kerala's Gulf connection, 1998–2011.* New Delhi: Orient BlackSwan.

———. (2014). *Dynamics of emigration and remittances in Kerala: Report on Kerala migration survey 2014.* Thiruvananthapuram: Centre for Development Studies (Draft Report).

Zachariah, K. C., Mathew, E. T., & Irudaya Rajan, S. (2003). *Dynamics of migration in Kerala, dimensions, determinants and consequences.* New Delhi: Orient Longman.

Zachariah, K. C., Prakash, B. A., & Irudaya Rajan, S. (2004, 29 May). Indian workers in U.A.E: Employment, wages and working conditions. *Economic and Political Weekly, 39*(22).

Zachariah, K. C., & Irudaya Rajan, S. (2007). *Migration, remittances and employment: Short term trends and long term implications.* Working paper 395. Thiruvananthapuram: Centre for Development Studies.

Chapter 6

Interstate Migration of Workers
A Study of Migration of Casual Workers to Kerala

V. Prakash

INTRODUCTION

For nearly three decades, Kerala has been witnessing a large inflow of migrant labour from different parts of the country. Although during the early part it was an influx from the neighbouring state of Tamil Nadu, later it turned to be an all-India phenomenon with Uttar Pradesh, West Bengal, Odisha, Assam and Bihar accounting for the major share. What is the estimated size of this labour? What are the push and pull factors behind this phenomenon? How do the in-migrants live? What impact have they made in their home states as well as in the host state of Kerala? These are issues that attract scholarly attention. Equally important is the fact that migration has a rich theoretical tradition. Given the extremely complex and in many ways paradoxical nature of Kerala's migration, there is a great potential for building theories and formulating hypotheses.

Migration has emerged as a major concern in many developing countries along with the levels of economic development and population growth. Over the last few decades, most industrialised countries have experienced zero population growth, resulting in a severe shortage of manpower. On the other hand, inadequate economic growth coupled with rising populations have left many of the less developed nations with a considerable surplus of labour. The net result has been the movement of people across borders—through legal as well as illegal channels—for employment. Globalisation, aided by rapid advances in information and communication technology, has accentuated this process. This has changed the demographic and cultural characteristics of both countries sending and receiving migrants and led to considerable debate and discussion.

In economic theory, migration is treated as an integral part of the development process. According to Ravenstein (1885, 1889), the founding father of modern migration research and analysis, migration is a consequence of economic development. He points out that migration largely takes place from areas of low opportunity to areas of high opportunity, and the process accelerates with the growth of transport, communication, trade and industry. Both the neoclassical and new economics approaches to the study of migration have highlighted its role in the transformation of traditional rural societies after people move to new centres of influence or 'modernisation', primarily town and cities. A host of non-economic factors along with improved transportation and communication facilities, the influence of the print and electronic media and an urban-oriented education with the changes in values and attitudes that it brings seem to trigger migration.

Historical evidence suggests that inter-regional migration has been almost a permanent feature of the Indian society. After Independence, the process of planned economic development further accelerated the pace of inter-regional migration. Growth of cities such as Bombay, Calcutta, Madras, Delhi and Ahmedabad attracted more people from all over the country. Geographical and occupational mobility of labour takes palace everywhere with the changing conditions of the labour market. Geographical mobility denoting mobility of labour force within different regions in the state or to other parts of India and abroad is a process by which labour supply adjusts to the demand for labour. Demand for labour increases in any area due to industrial development. As the supply cannot increase in the short run, this will result in shortage of labour and rise in wages in the locality. Labour theories support the idea that labour in the neighbouring region at first and later from far of areas will be attracted to the industrial centres because of the information about the high wage rate. In-migration of people from other parts of India to Kerala is not a new development. Sizeable number of Tamilians migrated to Travancore area between 1901 and 1931, a period which witnessed rapid expansion of plantations. More workers from the regions of Tamil Nadu and Karnataka migrated to Kannur, Calicut and Kottayam districts of Kerala with the development of plantation.

Objectives of the Study

Though there are numerous studies on the many facets of out-migration from Kerala, there are virtually no scientific studies worth mentioning on the emerging phenomenon of in-migration to the state. An exception is a case study of migrant construction workers from Kanyakumari district in Tamil Nadu (Anand, 1986). Another study which gives a rough estimate of the stock of migrants is the study of Gulati Institute of Finance and Taxation (GIFT) (Narayana & Venkiteswaran, 2013). This is the context in which the study is attempted. The objectives of the study are (a) to examine the structure and characteristics of Kerala's labour market and shortage of workers; (b) spatial and occupational distribution of migrant workers; (c) reasons and process of migration; and (d) effects of migration on the individual, family and society.

STRUCTURE AND CHARACTERISTICS OF LABOUR MARKET IN KERALA

Kerala's labour market displays socio–economic characteristics that are very different from those seen in the all-India pattern. When employment and unemployment is considered, the state economy has an excess supply of educated manpower. At the same time, employment generation is not on a par with the rate of growth of the labour force. In a competitive market, the wage rate is adjusted to take care of the imbalance between the supply of labour and the demand for it. But in Kerala, there exists the paradox of an excess supply of labourers and a high level of wages. This abnormal coexistence of a high wage rate and unemployment has to be explained with the help of economic and sociological factors (Kannan, 1988; Krishnan, 1991). These include political mobilisation, collective bargaining by labourers, improvements in their educational level, migration to countries abroad and so on. Further, it is seen that even though the state has a labour surplus economy, there is large-scale in-migration of workers from other states. A detailed analysis of the changes that have taken place in the state's socio-economic circumstances in the last few decades is attempted to uncover the reasons that have promoted the migration of labourers to the state, especially in the construction sector. Because of stagnation in the productive sectors, the rate of growth of employment in Kerala has been very low, making it the state with highest rate of unemployment (Mathew, 1995, 1997; Oommen, 1992; Prakash, 1988).

In a perfectly competitive labour market, the supply–demand imbalance would have resulted in a lowering of real wages but the labour market in Kerala presents the paradox of high unemployment coexisting with high real wages. Studies show that both economic and sociological factors can be cited to explain why labourers in Kerala do not offer themselves for work at lower wages even in the face of acute unemployment (Krishnan, 1991). The most important factor behind this is political mobilisation and collective bargaining by labourers, which has forced the state to intervene in the labour market from time to time with several progressive legislations to improve wages and working conditions (Kannan, 1995; Mohanakumar & Sharma, 2000). The large-scale migration to the Gulf also contributed to substantial increase in construction since the mid-1970s (Zachariah, Mathew, & Irudaya Rajan, 2003). The connection between remittances and the construction boom in Kerala has been well examined (Gopikkuttan, 1988). Remittances created a demand–supply gap for workers in the construction sector also.

Trends in Unemployment

The cumulative effect of the decline in the labour-intensive manufacturing sector, crop-cultivating agricultural sector and the failure to attract industrial investments has been the acute unemployment in Kerala. Unemployment, especially educated unemployment, is a very grave problem the state faces. It was generally three to five times more than the all-India average (Mathew, 1995; Oommen, 1992; Prakash, 1988). It can be seen that when the rate of growth of employment generation was 1.07 per cent at the all-India level during the period 1993–1994 to 1999–2000, it was only 0.07 per cent in Kerala. At the same time, the increase in unemployment was 20.97 per cent in the state against an all-India rate of 17.32 per cent. Kerala has the lowest growth rate in employment and the highest rate of unemployment among all major states in India.

High Wages and In-migration

The wage rate in Kerala has been consistently higher than that of its counterparts in other Indian states. As of 2001, the wage in Kerala at ₹185 was more than four times higher that of Madhya Pradesh at ₹46. Similar differences exist in the case of Odisha, Bihar and West Bengal as well. The reasons for agricultural wage rates in Kerala not declining even in the face of acute unemployment demands deeper study. The trigger for large-scale in-migration from neighbouring states in the beginning and later on from far-off states such as Odisha, Bihar and West Bengal has been the remittances from abroad flowing into Kerala. A good portion of these remittances are spent on constructing new houses and buildings in Kerala (Gopikkuttan, 1988). Acute shortage of unskilled workers resulted in an increase in the local wage rate in so many sectors such as construction, mining and quarrying, trench making and road works. It was this shortage in supply of labour and the simultaneous rise in demand for casual workers which attracted labour from nearby regions in the 1980s.

SPATIAL AND OCCUPATIONAL DISTRIBUTION OF MIGRANT WORKERS

Migrants are now employed in almost all sectors of Kerala's economy. However, construction is the one important sector that has absorbed migrant workers on a large scale. Migrants in Kerala were mostly from the poorer states of Bihar, Odisha and West Bengal. Their places of origin were mainly Ganjam district in Odisha, Siwan district in Bihar, Malda and Jalpaiguri districts in West Bengal and the districts of Tirunelveli and Kanyakumari in Tamil Nadu. Only 2 per cent of the sample migrants were from an urban background and the remaining

98 per cent were from rural backgrounds. That there were only a few workers from Kerala's neighbouring states such as Tamil Nadu and Karnataka needs explanation. The flow of Tamil workers to Kerala ebbed during the late 1990s when the construction sector in Tamil Nadu, especially in the districts bordering Kerala, began picking up, creating more opportunities for masons and others to work in their home state. When the supply of labour from Tamil Nadu decreased, contractors of civil works as well as brick makers in Kerala began thinking of bringing in workers from North Indian states. A few workers from Rajasthan, who had come on trucks bringing marble to Kerala, were already working in the flooring segment of the construction sector. Gradually, more people from the northern states began arriving in Kerala in search of jobs in the construction sector. They were later followed by migrant workers from the eastern states of Bihar, West Bengal and Odisha. The flow of workers from North India was initiated in the 1990s by construction companies from the region that carried out the civil works for the Kayamkulam thermal power project in Alappuzha district and work related to the national highways in Ernakulam district.

Migrant workers are visibly present everywhere in Kerala. But the density of migrant population varies with the growth rate of construction activities in different districts. The number of migrant workers seems to be very high in Kannur, Thrissur, Ernakulam, Alappuzha, Kollam and Thiruvananthapuram districts. No reliable data on the number of migrant workers in the state is available. Ramanthali, Chavakkad, Chalakudy, Perumbavoor, Kozhencherry, Kunnanthanam, Paravur, Kazhakoottam, Chirayinkeezhu, etc., are the localities in various districts of Kerala where the migrant workers are concentrated. A study (Narayana & Venkiteswaran, 2013) based on the railway passengers incoming from outside Kerala estimated the stock of migrant labourers in Kerala as 25 lakh. But the actual figure may be much higher.

Occupational Distribution

It is interesting to observe that the migrant workers have come to fill almost all occupations and sectors of the economy. Their largest concentration is in the construction sector (60 per cent). Substantive number of migrants is seen in the manufacturing, hotels and restaurants, trading and the loading/unloading sectors. Majority of the migrants are doing the work of helpers in the construction sector, and large numbers are engaged as carpenters, masons, flooring installers and stone cutters, electricians, tailors, suppliers in restaurants, cooks and salesmen.

Level of Education and Skills

Migration usually necessitates at least some level of literacy. But since internal migration does not involve any formal procedures and formalities, even illiterates can choose to migrate if they possess saleable skills. However, it has to be pointed out that literacy can be instrumental in empowering a person and instilling a determination to migrate in him or her. In reality, the level of literacy did not have much to do with the kind of work the migrants were called upon to do. What was important perhaps was that they had the ability to do the manual work they were assigned. Though literacy empowers a worker to bargain and get a better wage, the job profile of these migrant workers did not offer much scope for this.

Economic Status and Asset Position

It is generally held that poverty is the main cause of rural–urban migration. Poverty caused by natural calamities such as famines, floods or droughts can also force the migration of entire families. The migration to Kerala, at least in the construction sector, is different from such poverty-linked migration. As seen earlier, most of the migrants were unmarried and those who were married were not accompanied by their spouses and children. This suggested that along with their low-income status, the urge to uplift their family's economic status was a major factor in making them migrate. At the time of migration, the income of the sample migrants ranged between ₹1,000 and ₹2,000 (2003 or earlier). Besides the level of prevailing wages, the number of days one had to work also determined total monthly earnings. Interactions with the sample migrants revealed that they would probably not have migrated had there been regular work in their own villages. Agricultural operations were seasonal and the number of days a worker got to work depended on the season.

The asset position—possession of land—of the sample migrants indicated that 26 per cent of them were landless. Even among those who possessed land, only a small proportion had irrigated landholdings. Even with irrigated land, the earnings were not sufficient for meeting a family's expenses and marginal farmers tended to work as agricultural labourers or construction workers in some months. The data suggested that it was not only the poorest of poor that migrated. People with a little land and other assets also did migrate, presumably to improve their economic and social status by acquiring more land and other assets.

Living Conditions

Though poverty is the principal reason for rural–urban migration, there are other factors that motivate it. One major reason is living conditions and the quality of life. The desire to construct a more suitable dwelling or to purchase modern consumer goods prompts even comparatively better-off workers to resort to migration. A definite indicator of the living standard of a migrant at the time of migration is the status of the dwelling in which his family lives.

As mentioned, the survey of sample migrants showed that it was not always the poorest of the poor that migrated. Those who lived in houses with a thatched roof and mud flooring were only 27.5 per cent of the sample. In a majority of the migrants, social pressure to improve their living conditions played a role in the decision to migrate. The survey further showed that 72 per cent of the sample migrants were first-timers, whereas 28 per cent had earlier migrated to other places. The first-timers were encouraged by the better travelled ones to migrate to Kerala. The experiences of the latter seemed to have instilled confidence in the new bees to migrate.

REASONS OF MIGRATION AND PROCESS OF MIGRATION

Migration anywhere is a painful process. The compelling reasons for migration are essentially economic. In the Indian context, the migration of poor people from villages to cities is triggered by unemployment, poverty and sometimes natural disasters. The sample migrants were economic migrants in the sense that they were mainly motivated by monetary considerations. Some of them migrated to various places and learnt that the wages and service conditions in Kerala were better and decided to migrate there. It was evident from the data that the primary reason for migration, in the case of 44.5 per cent of the sample migrants, was inadequate earnings. For 27.5 per cent, unemployment was the principal reason. Inadequate infrastructural facilities and inadequate educational opportunities were some of the other reasons mentioned for migration. We find that 85 per cent of the sample migrants heard about the migration opportunity from friends and relatives who had migrated to Kerala. Surprisingly, the percentage of sample migrants who migrated through formal channels such as labour contractors was negligible.

It was observed that the majority of migrants were from poor backward caste communities in Bihar, Odisha, West Bengal and Tamil Nadu. Occupationally, the migrants were mostly agricultural labourers and construction workers, though there were a few who had been marginal farmers and artisans in their places of origin. A significant portion of the migrants possessed some land but most of it was not capable of generating an income sufficient to meet their needs. The living conditions in the houses they had migrated from suggested that most of them lived in dwellings with a thatched roof and cement flooring. Their average monthly income at the time of migration was between ₹1,000 and ₹2,000. The evidence showed that a majority of the sample migrants were motivated by an urge to better their living conditions.

Use of Labour in Construction

Workers in the construction sector can be divided into two very broad skill categories—masons and helpers. At the lower end are unskilled workers who do the carrying and carting, and at the other end are the semi-skilled workers who mix cement and sand in the right proportion, supply the mixed cement to masons and help them at times with measuring evenness and water levels. The use of labour in the construction sector offers considerable scope for paying wages in accordance with skill levels. Depending on productivity and workmanship, wages can differ, and to that extent the scope for collective bargaining as a group is limited. The physically demanding tasks are very often assigned to migrant workers. An analysis of the primary data gives one the feeling that it is migrant labourers from Bihar, Odisha, West Bengal and Tamil Nadu who are vital cogs of the construction engine in Kerala.

Recruitment, Wages and Conditions of Work

Individuals who construct bungalows in rural areas either entrust the work to local contractors or directly supervise the work, hiring the services of workers and buying the materials. In both cases, there are bound to be different layers of subcontracts. The wages paid by contractors and subcontractors to labourers is always lower than the wages received by them from the owner. However, with construction companies now dominating the construction scene in Kerala, several changes have taken place in the manner in which houses and buildings are built in the state. Big outfits from metropolitan cities such as Mumbai and Bangalore have launched projects in the major towns and cities of Kerala, offering independent villas and flats. Here the wages and working conditions are determined by a new system of recruitment that allows the employers substantial liberty. In the construction of independent residential buildings, the work is carried out by labour contractors under the supervision of the owner or a person authorised by the owner. It avoids the paper work and processes associated with Inter-State Migrant Workmen (Regulation of Employment and Conditions of Service) Act, 1979. Migrant labourers are employed through local subcontractors and they are assigned to do labour-intensive and low-skill tasks.

The vast majority of the migrant workers were recruited to work as helpers. A majority of the workers had a low level of education and were unskilled. Interaction with the masons revealed that most of them were from Tamil Nadu and Bengal. Talking to the helpers, it emerged that some of them expected to graduate to the level of mason in two to three years. Be that as it may, the extent to which on-the-job upgradation of skills actually takes place. Looking into the process of migration of the workers, it emerged that recruitment agencies had played no role in it. Interstate migration in India does not involve such formalities and expenses as in the case of international migration. There were no pre-migration expenses because the workers arrived in Kerala without undergoing any special training in construction activities. They were all absorbed into construction sites in Kerala as casual labourers. In most cases, there was no guarantee that they would get regular employment or a certain sum as wages. After reaching Kerala, they had, with the aid of local subcontractors, entered into different types of employment relations with their employers. Of the sample migrants, 66.5 per cent were casual labourers on daily wages and 16.5 per cent were labourers on piece wages. Only 17 per cent workers were long-term workers. Enquiries revealed that the long-term employees were trusted associates of the migrant subcontractors who regularly supplied manpower to the local subcontractors.

The migrants worked on various sites without any formal contracts or agreements. The long-term employees helped them negotiate their wages and conditions of work with the local subcontractors. Interaction with the migrant labourers showed that none of the procedures and formalities prescribed in the Inter-State Migrant Workmen (Regulation of Employment and Conditions of Service) Act, 1979 was involved in this system of labour recruitment. Though it saved both the workers and their employers the hassles of tiresome procedures and formalities, the workers were ultimately the losers.

Dual Wage System

'One' phenomenon that needs to be explained is that of local labourers employed in the same type of work as migrant labourers being paid higher wages. While local labourers were paid ₹300 to ₹750 per day, migrant workers got only ₹250 to ₹500 under contractors. The migrant labourers worked longer hours for lower wages and were apparently meek and docile compared to the local labourers. What made entrepreneurs in the construction industry pay higher wages to the local labourers? Discussions and interviews revealed that there were several reasons for this contradiction. Entrepreneurs said that though local labourers were more costly, they were more productive when it came to certain tasks that demanded creativity, innovation and application of the mind. Migrant labour was preferred where the turnover or volume of the work was more important than quality. It appeared that if local labour was fully replaced, it could cause resistance and this could lead to law and order problems.

Living Conditions

The living conditions of migrant labourers the world over seem to be pathetic. To get a feel of the living conditions of the sample migrant workers, their places of residence were visited by the survey team. Their poor living conditions, almost in complete isolation from the local population, presented a very dismal picture. The situation was in blatant violation of the provisions of the Inter-State Migrant Workmen (Regulation of Employment and Conditions of Service) Act, 1979. Workers either lived on work sites or in dilapidated or rundown houses, which resembled sheds, with no real facilities for human habitation. In one place, about 15 to 25 workers shared a shed with an area of 300 square feet. The newcomers joined the existing ones and shared whatever facilities there were. All crowded into a small area, there were no beds or mattresses and they slept on the floor using their small suitcases as pillows. In many places, there were no real sanitation facilities and the labourers used any vacant land nearby or the space beside roads and railway lines and river banks for fulfilling their primary needs, causing inconvenience and creating a health hazard to the local communities and themselves.

Pros and Cons

An analysis of the wages and working conditions of the sample migrant construction workers in Kerala revealed that in terms of earnings they were now much better off than what they were in their respective home states. They were able to save substantial amounts by putting in long hours of work and working overtime. The migrant workers led very frugal lives to save as much money as possible. At the same time, it cannot be overlooked that they were discriminated against at work sites when it came to wages and working conditions. The survey also brought to light blatant violations of the provisions of the Inter-State Migrant Workmen (Regulation of Employment and Conditions of Service) Act, 1979. Close interaction with the migrants showed that they worked and lived in what most labourers in Kerala would consider subhuman conditions. Though they were overwhelmingly appreciative of the cosmopolitan society they saw around them in Kerala and the state's infrastructure, they also realised that they were isolated from the local community. The perception that their fellow local workers treated them as inferiors was a major grievance among them.

EFFECTS ON INDIVIDUAL, FAMILY AND SOCIETY

Migration almost always has far-reaching effects on a migrating individual, his or her family and the society from which he or she comes. Most of the sample migrants did not maintain any record of their expenses or the remittances they had made, and some of those who did were not willing to disclose details. Only 50 per cent of the sample migrant workers responded to these questions. It is evident that a major portion of the remittances was spent on day-to-day consumption. This was understandable as most of the migrants belonged to poor families. It was quite common among migrant households to spend money on many items that the family members had wanted for long but could not afford earlier. The possession of these items enhanced the prestige of the family in society and, in turn, the migrant's prestige as well. The impact of migration is not only confined to an individual but also on the local economy and society from which the migrant comes.

The sample migrants were requested to list out the changes that had taken place in their locality and society after people began migrating from there to various places. The data showed that the vast majority of migrants noticed changes in their villages, which they attributed to migration and the remittances that followed. But it is very difficult to isolate the effects of migration from other factors that contribute to growth of an area such as development activities undertaken by the central, state and local governments. The savings of individual migrants were too small to make any investment worth the name. It seemed that if concerted efforts were made by governmental or community agencies to mobilise the small savings of the migrants to channel into productive investment, it would benefit the workers and their societies.

On Migrants' Values and Attitudes

'Migration', as mentioned earlier, has tangible and intangible effects. A major effect of migration is on the values and attitudes of migrants. The vast majority of migrant construction workers in Kerala are from the so-called Bihar, Madhya Pradesh, Rajasthan and Uttar Pradesh (BIMARU) states. Societies in these states are still in the clutches of the caste system, their literacy levels are dismaying. The age of marriage is also low in these states, and the practice of child marriages has not been totally eradicated. Due to tardy progress of the family planning programme, family sizes in these states are large compared to Kerala. Kerala's sociopolitical environment had a huge impact on the outlook of the sample migrants. Some of them admitted that years of life in Kerala had instilled in them the courage to oppose the 'unwritten laws' on caste and community that prevailed in their villages. Several migrants admitted that migration had enhanced their standing in society. They had also realised the importance of education and encouraged family members, neighbours and relatives to provide their children with a good education. The sample migrants who had stayed for more than five years had learnt the local language and begun communicating with local workers. The impact of the local culture and values seemed to be stronger in their case. They, however, said that though their values and attitudes had changed, they were not very hopeful about changing age-old customs and traditions in their villages.

Evidence from the survey of the sample migrants suggested that some of the negative aspects of Kerala's society such as heavy drinking and conspicuous consumption had affected them to some degree. To quote a press report, one reason for the big jump in liquor consumption could be the heavy drinking by the lakhs of migrant workers from Bihar, Tamil Nadu and Odisha who splurged the high wages they have got on the bottle. In Angamaly, Chalakudy and Perumbavoor, three of the dozen major drinking centres in the state, migrants employed in building construction made a sizeable proportion of the drinkers (Basheer, 2008).

Kerala is the state with the highest per capita consumption of liquor in India. The proportion of migrants who picked up the habit of regular drinking while in Kerala was higher than the proportion that used to only have an occasional drink while in their home state.

Apart from consuming alcohol, the only pastime that the migrants had was going for movies or watching television. A common grouse was that the local cinemas did not exhibit Hindi films, which were their favourite watching. Only in two migrant settlements were at least a black and white television seen. It seemed that drinkers in the groups had introduced non-drinkers to liquor. Some of the migrants said that it was the local workers who introduced them to liquor. There was also reason to suspect that the comparatively high wages in Kerala had made liquor more affordable.

Another negative influence on the sample migrants, which they generally owed up to, was the culture of spending. Though the propensity of the migrants in Kerala was to save, a high percentage of their savings was used by their households for consumption. Many migrants admitted that they had not been exposed to the kind of lifestyle Kerala had before coming to the state. It is worth pointing out that Kerala tops the list in household consumption in India. It seemed that the 'demonstration effect' had made a dent in the volume of savings of the migrants.

CONCLUSION

Though Kerala has a history of welcoming migrants, the state has not witnessed in-migration of this magnitude in the recent past. Some unofficial estimates put the number of migrants in Kerala at around a million. The labour shortage of manual categories of workers, high wage rate compared to other states and better working conditions prevailing in the state have contributed to the migration of casual workers from other states to Kerala. Migrants belonged to poor households and migrated mainly from Bihar, Odisha and West Bengal. Migrants were economic migrants, and migration was prompted by monetary considerations. Some of them migrated to other states in India and learnt that the wages and working conditions in Kerala were better and decided to migrate here. Migrant labourers were recruited and employed by local subcontractors and they were assigned labour-intensive and low-skilled jobs. There were no pre-migration expenses because the workers arrived without undergoing any special training or paying any amount. They were forced to live in rented accommodations which were poor in all respects.

REFERENCES AND SELECT BIBLIOGRAPHY

Anand, S. (1986). *Migrant construction workers: A case study of Tamil workers in Kerala* (MPhil thesis). Thiruvananthapuram: Centre for Development Studies.

Basheer, K. P. M. (2008, 7 April). *Social barriers to drinking crumbling.* Retrieved on 27 March 2018, from http://www.thehindu.com/todays-paper/tp-national/tp-kerala/Social-barriers-to-drinking-crumbling/article15198745.ece

Gopikkuttan, G. (1988). *Housing boom in Kerala, causes and consequences* (PhD thesis). Thiruvananthapuram: University of Kerala.

Kannan, K. P. (1988). *Of rural proletarian struggles: Mobilisation and organisation of rural workers in south-west India.* New Delhi: Oxford University Press.

———. (1995). State and union intervention in rural labour: A study of Kerala. *Indian Journal of Labour Economics, 38*(3), 42–64.

Krishnan, T. N. (1991). Wages, output and employment in interrelated labour markets in an agrarian economy. *Economic and Political Weekly, 26*(26), 113–146.

Mathew, E. T. (1995). Educated unemployment in Kerala: Some socio-economic aspects. *Economic and Political Weekly, 30*(6), 325–35.

———. (1997). *Employment and unemployment in Kerala.* New Delhi: SAGE Publications.

Mohanakumar, S., & Sharma, R. K. (2000). Minimum wage legislation and its impact on rural wage formation: A study of agricultural labourers in Kerala. *Indian Journal of Labour Economics, 43*(2).

Narayana, D., & Venkiteswaran, C. S. (2013). *Domestic migrant labour in Kerala* (Report). Thiruvananthapuram: Gulati Institute of Finance and Taxation.

National Sample Survey Organisation. (2001). *Migration in India, 1999–2000* (55th Round, Report No. 470). New Delhi: Ministry of Statistics and Programme Implementation, Government of India.

Oommen, M. A. (1992). The acute unemployment problem of Kerala: Some exploratory hypothesis. *IASSI Quarterly, 10*(3), 422–446.

Prakash, B. A. (1988). *Educated unemployment in Kerala: Some observations based on a field study* (Working Paper No. 224). Thiruvananthapuram: Centre for Development Studies.

Ravenstein, E. G. (1885). The laws of migration. *Journal of the Royal Statistical Society, 48*(2), 167–235.

———. (1889). The laws of migration. *Journal of the Royal Statistical Society, 52*(2), 241–305.

Zachariah, K. C., Mathew, E. T., & Irudaya Rajan, S. (2003). *Dynamics of migration in Kerala: Dimensions, differentials and consequences.* New Delhi: Orient Longman.

PART III

Agriculture

Chapter 7

Performance of Agriculture in Kerala

K. P. Mani

At the time of Independence in 1947, the present state of Kerala comprised of three regions, namely, Travancore, Cochin and Malabar. While Travancore and Cochin were ruled by native kings, the Malabar region was under the direct British rule. One of the first steps taken by Independent India was to amalgamate small states so as to make them viable administration units. Accordingly, Travancore and Cochin states were integrated to form the Travancore Cochin state on 1 July 1949. However, Malabar remained as part of the Madras state. Under the States Reorganisation Act of 1956, Travancore Cochin state and Malabar were united to form the state of Kerala on 1 November 1956. Although the state represents only 1.18 per cent of the total area of the country, it has about 3.50 per cent of its total population. Just like all-India trends, the agriculture sector of Kerala also underwent structural, unique and interesting changes. The broad objective of this chapter is to examine the performance of Kerala's agriculture sector since the dawn of this century with respect to cropping pattern, production, productivity, input use and input use efficiency, commodity prices, exports and imports. An attempt is also made into the prospects of the agriculture sector in the backdrop of reforms.

AGRICULTURAL SCENARIO IN KERALA

Table 7.1 presents the state domestic product (SDP) scenario of the state from 1960–1961 to 2015–2016. In current prices, agriculture and allied activities sectoral SDP represents 54.97 per cent in 1960–1961. At the start of economic reforms, the share declined to 20.82 per cent. By 2015–2016, this share came down to 10 per cent in current prices. These trends indicate that the share of agriculture and allied activities in the total SDP is coming down steadily. This is in tune with national picture also, but causes panic. The situation will be more revealing when we look into trends in agricultural income in Kerala (Table 7.2).

The agriculture sector in Kerala has undergone significant structural changes in the form of decline in the share of gross state domestic product (GSDP), indicating a shift from agrarian economy towards the service sector-dominated economy. The contribution of agriculture in the GSDP of the state has witnessed a decline to 11.59 per cent in 2009–2010. The agriculture sector suffered a setback in recent years and the slowdown had several structural consequences including agrarian

Table 7.1 *State Domestic Product in Kerala (1960–1961 to 2015–2016)*

Years	GSDP (₹ Crore Current Prices)	Agriculture and Allied Activities (GSDP) (₹ Crore Current Prices)
1960–1961	461.98	254.08
1970–1971	2,207.21	620.47
1980–1981	6,189.18	1,399.33
1990–1991	18,591.44	3,872.54
2000–2001	72,658.83	11,424.49
2014–2015	519,895.85	59,076.77
2015–2016	588,336.59	58,719.58

Source: Government of Kerala, Department of Economics and Statistics (various years).

Table 7.2 *Trends in Agricultural Income in Kerala (at Constant Prices)*

	Year	Agricultural Income (₹ in Crore)	Rate of Change over Previous Year	Percentage Contribution to State Income
Base year 1993–	1993–1994	6,256	–	26.23
1994 prices	1995–1996	6,947	0.72	25.78
	1997–1998	6,777	–4.75	23.67
	1999–2000	7,017	1.70	21.45
	2001–2002	5,312	–2.50	15.39
Base year 1999–2000 prices	2003–2004	12,819	–2.38	15.04
Base year 2004–	2005–2006	18,041.97	6.25	16.67
2005 prices	2007–2008	16,196.60	–2.24	13.15
	2009–2010	16,236.47	–1.79	11.59

Source: Government of Kerala, Department of Economics and Statistics (various years).

distress. The agricultural performance is subject to year-to-year fluctuations due to vagaries of nature as well as high degree of price volatility mostly due to international market price behaviour of the commodities. It is a great challenge and formidable task to arrest the decline and reverse the slowing growth of the agriculture sector in the state.

LAND USE PATTERN IN KERALA

Any discussion on the agriculture sector starts with an examination of the land utilisation pattern and the profile of landholdings in Kerala which is available from Table 7.3. It is seen that since 1990, the gross cropped area made a notable decline. This is mainly due to the shifts of the farmers from agricultural operations to non-agricultural use. It is seen that the land area put to non-agricultural use in 1980–1981 (269,824 hectares) increased to 297,381 hectares in 1990–1991, the net change

Table 7.3 *Pattern of Land Utilisation in Kerala (in Hectares)*

Classification	1980–1981	1990–1991	2000–2001	2005–2006	2010–2011	2015–2016
Total geographical area	3,885,497	3,885,497	3,885,497	3,886,287	3,886,287	3,886,287
Forest	1,081,509	1,081,509	1,081,509	1,081,509	1,081,509	1,081,509
Land put to non-agricultural use	269,824	297,381	381,873	370,322	384,174	434,646
Barren and uncultivated land	85,770	58,308	29,318	26,457	19,573	13,100
Net sown area	2,179,590	2,246,774	2,206,126	2,132,483	2,071,507	2,023,073
Area sown more than once	705,250	773,206	815,546	853,244	575,954	604,504
Total cropped area	2,884,840	3,019,980	3,021,672	2,985,727	2,647,461	2,627,576
Total cropped area as percentage to total geographical area	74.24	77.72	77.76	76.84	68.12	67.61

Source: Kerala State Board in association with Government of Kerala, Department of Economics and Statistics.

during decade being 27,557 hectares, percentage change being 10.21. Between 1991 and 2001, the increase is found to be 28.41 per cent and from 2001 to 2016 being 13.81 per cent. These trends indicate that the area of land put to non-agricultural use is significantly increasing. There are many reasons for this trend, the major being agricultural operations are becoming uneconomic due to escalating input prices, stagnating output price, diseconomies of scale, etc. Another notable feature is the significant shift in the cropping pattern skewed towards cash crops, which is discussed in detail in the succeeding paragraphs.

CROPPING PATTERN IN KERALA

The cropping pattern has undergone significant changes over the last six decades in the state. In the following section, an attempt is made to analyse the growth pattern in terms of area, production and productivity of major crops cultivated in the state. Agricultural crops in the state are broadly classified as food crops and non-food crops. Food crops are cereals and millets, sugar crops, spices and condiments, fresh fruits, vegetables, etc. The major non-food crops are rubber, betel leaves, lemon grass, etc. Another classification of crops is seasonal crops, annual crops and plantation crops which are based on their lifetime. Seasonal crops are paddy, pulses, tapioca, vegetables, sweet potato, tubers, groundnut, ginger, turmeric, cotton, tobacco, onion, tur, etc. Annual crops include sugarcane, banana, plantain, pineapple, betel leaves, etc. Plantation crops cover coconut, areca nut, cashew nut, mango, jackfruit, tamarind, pepper, rubber, tea, coffee, cardamom, cloves, nutmeg, cinnamon, cocoa, papaya, etc.

TRENDS IN AREA, PRODUCTION AND PRODUCTIVITY OF FOOD GRAINS

Among the food grains, rice occupies the predominant position in the state. Among the districts, Palakkad, Ernakulam, Thrissur, Alappuzha, Wayanad and Malappuram are the major rice-growing regions (Mani, 2005). These districts account for nearly 73 per cent of the total area under rice cultivation in the state. Food crops comprising rice, pulses, etc., occupy only 10.32 per cent. After a long period of continuous decline, area under rice increased from 2.29 lakh ha in 2007–2008 to 2.34 lakh ha in 2008–2009 but it sharply declined by 20,828 ha in 2010–2011 period over to the previous year. Similar tendencies of deceleration were noted in the area under jowar, ragi, cereals and pulses. Consequently, the relative area under food grains fell from 38.73 per cent in 1960–1961 to just 10.32 per cent in 2013–2014. The area under food grains is depicted in Table 7.4.

The production of food grains is depicted in Table 7.5. The production of rice showed an increasing trend during the period 1960–1961 to 1975–1976. From mid-1970s onwards, a continuous decline in production was noticed. Except jowar, all other food grains depicted a fall in production with slight variations. In 2013–2014, food crops in general showed an increasing trend in production as the production of rice as well as tapioca increased, while that of the pulses recorded a marginal decline. This could be more on account of increase in productivity rather an increase in acreage as the area under rice has recorded only a marginal increase, while that of tapioca has, in fact, declined (Table 7.6).

Table 7.4 *Area Under Food Grains (Area in Hectares)*

Year	Rice	Jowar	Ragi	Other Cereals	Pulses	Total Food Grains
1960–1961	778,910	1,470	5,370	5,850	44,120	835,720
1965–1966	802,330	1,240	5,100	6,720	43,310	858,700
1970–1971	874,930	1,520	5,030	5,330	39,540	926,350
1975–1976	885,000	–	–	–	–	885,000
1980–1981	801,699	–	1,471	0	33,859	837,029
1985–1986	678,300	–	–	–	–	678,300
1990–1991	559,450	4,527	1,272	1,455	23,385	590,089
1995–1996	471,150	5,454	2,025	3,173	20,990	502,792
2000–2001	347,455	463	1,955	2,071	6,986	358,930
2005–2006	275,742	2,450	414	110	10,562	289,278
2010–2011	213,185	2,208	263	243	3,824	219,723

Source: Government of Kerala, Department of Economics and Statistics (various years).

Table 7.5 *Production of Food Grains (Production in Tonnes)*

Year	Rice	Jowar	Ragi	Other Cereals	Pulses
1960–1961	1,067,530	640	8,010	2,910	17,550
1965–1966	997,490	450	7,030	3,120	16,900
1970–1971	1,298,010	840	4,880	3,170	13,050
1975–1976	1,364,867	–	–	–	–
1980–1981	1,271,962	–	–	–	–
1985–1986	1,173,051	–	–	–	–
1990–1991	1,086,578	2,305	1,042	1,131	16,544
1995–1996	953,026	2,776	1,638	2,463	14,994
2000–2001	751,328	236	1,582	1,605	5,472
2005–2006	629,987	1,248	335	215	7,940
2010–2011	522,738	1,128	212	187	2,908

Source: Government of Kerala, Department of Economics and Statistics (various years).

Table 7.6 *Productivity of Food Grains (in kg/ha)*

Year	Rice	Jowar	Ragi	Other Cereals	Pulses
1960–1961	1,371	436	1,438	NA	398
1965–1966	1,243	364	1,390	NA	390
1970–1971	1,483	553	971	596	354
1975–1976	1,542	NA	NA	NA	NA
1980–1981	1,587	–	769	–	664
1985–1986	1,729	NA	NA	NA	NA
1990–1991	1,942	509	819	777	707
1995–1996	2,023	509	809	776	714
2000–2001	2,162	510	809	775	783
2005–2006	2,285	509	809	1,909	752
2010–2011	2,452	511	806	770	760

Source: Government of Kerala, Department of Economics and Statistics (various years).

TRENDS IN AREA, PRODUCTION AND PRODUCTIVITY OF ANNUAL CROPS

The production, area and productivity of annual crops are given in Tables 7.7, 7.8 and 7.9, respectively. Among the annual crops, coconut occupies predominant position accounting for 41.96 per cent of the area during 2013–2014. This could be because a part of the paddy fields were reclaimed and planted with coconut during the period. From 3,220 million nuts in 1960–1961, the production increased to 5,536 million nuts in 2000–2001. The increase in output is more on account of increase in acreage as the productivity of the crop is very low in the state. In 2013–2014, there was a marginal increase in the production from 5,799 million nuts in 2012–2013 to 5,921 million nuts. The main cause for falling productivity is the prevalence of root wilt disease, poor management and existence of unproductive palms. Hence, massive replanting of root wilt palms by elite palms and elimination of senile palms, setting up of nurseries for production of quality seedlings and their subsequent distribution are required for increasing productivity.

The area under cashew nut, a major cash crop produced in the state, started declining in absolute and relative terms from the early 1980s. Pepper and areca nut are two crops, which showed an increasing trend in area over the years. A slump in the production was observed in the case of cashew nut; productivity started increasing in the latter half of the 1980s and showed a declining trend in the 1990s.

The total area under annual crops increased during the time period 1960–1961 to 1975–1976, declined in the decade 1975–1976 to 1985–1986 and started increasing from the latter half of the 1980s. The relative share of area under annual crops increased from the early 1960s to mid-1970s and declined in the latter half of the 1970s. The proportion of area recovered in the decade 1980–1981 to 1990–1991 and slumped again in the 1990s.

TRENDS IN AREA, PRODUCTION AND YIELD OF PLANTATION CROPS

Plantation crops in general are either export oriented or import substi-tuting and therefore assume special significance from the national point

Table 7.7 *Production of Annual Crops (in Tonnes)*

Year	Sugarcane	Pepper	Ginger	Areca Nut (Million Nuts)	Banana and Other Plantains	Cashew Nut	Tapioca	Coconut (Million Nuts)	Cotton (Bales of 170 kg)
1960–1961	38,090	27,030	11,270	7,737	327,850	84,630	1,683,000	3,220	1,970
1965–1966	40,950	21,690	11,190	9,681	361,120	98,030	3,095,660	3,293	1,250
1970–1971	37,630	25,030	19,680	12,738	368,980	115,240	4,617,190	3,981	1,290
1975–1976	41,831	24,580	22,840	11,387	395,042	122,360	5,390,217	3,439	1,710
1980–1981	48,178	28,519	32,039	10,805	317,405	81,900	4,060,911	3,008	9,847
1985–1986	42,560	33,121	44,466	10,664	361,126	80,203	3,276,877	3,377	9,624
1990–1991	51,977	46,802	45,685	13,074	491,935	102,771	2,803,001	4,232	1,732
1995–1996	28,313	68,568	46,455	19,204	592,410	82,760	2,500,113	5,155	1,720
2000–2001	27,555	60,929	42,699	87,947★	731,650	66,178	2,586,903	5,536	6,209
2005–2006	9,165	87,605	56,288	119,309★	987,156	68,262	2,568,284	6,326	3,452
2010–2011	2,908	45,267	33,197	99,909★	837,439	34,752	2,408,962	5,287	731
2013–2014	2,210	29,408	21,521	100,018★	893,694	33,375	2,479,070	5,921	284

Source: Government of Kerala, Department of Economics and Statistics (various years).

Note: ★ Tonnes.

Table 7.8 *Area Under Annual Crops (in Hectares)*

Year	Sugarcane	Pepper	Ginger	Areca Nut	Banana and Other Plantains	Cashew Nut	Tapioca	Coconut	Cotton
1960–1961	9,150	99,750	12,000	54,260	44,420	54,320	242,200	500,760	9,820
1965–1966	9,190	99,700	11,850	64,480	47,780	87,370	229,680	586,310	7,160
1970–1971	7,650	11,754	12,170	85,820	48,760	102,710	293,550	719,140	7,260
1975–1976	7,600	108,300	11,700	76,600	52,300	109,100	326,900	692,900	7,562
1980–1981	8,041	108,073	12,662	61,242	49,262	141,277	244,990	651,370	–
1985–1986	7,800	121,600	15,700	58,700	43,000	137,700	202,900	704,700	–
1990–1991	7,625	168,507	14,143	64,817	65,637	115,621	146,493	870,022	252
1995–1996	5,623	191,596	12,925	70,899	72,681	103,284	113,601	914,370	152
2000–2001	3,367	202,133	11,612	87,360	99,412	92,122	114,609	925,783	213
2005–2006	1,222	237,998	12,226	108,590	116,622	78,285	90,539	897,833	2,655
2010–2011	2,845	172,182	6,088	99,834	107,800	43,848	72,284	770,473	501
2013–2014	–	84,065	4,538	100,008	116,773	49,105	67,589	808,647	177

Source: Government of Kerala, Department of Economics and Statistics (various years).

Table 7.9 *Productivity of Annual Crops (kg/ha)*

Year	Sugarcane	Pepper	Ginger	Areca Nut	Banana	Cashew Nut	Tapioca	Coconut (Nuts per Hectare)	Cotton
1960–1961	4,165	271	938	–	7,381	1,558	6,949	6,430	192
1965–1966	4,454	281	945	–	7,558	1,122	13,478	5,616	174
1970–1971	4,917	213	1,617	–	7,568	1,122	15,729	5,536	178
1975–1976	5,504	227	1,952	–	7,553	1,122	16,489	4,963	NA
1980–1981	5,992	264	2,530	–	6,443	580	16,576	4,618	1,580
1985–1986	5,456	272	2,832	.	8,398	582	16,150	4,792	NA
1990–1991	6,816	278	3,230	–	13,355	888	19,134	5,239	1,614
1995–1996	5,035	358	3,594	1,213	13,816	801	22,008	5,638	1,614
2000–2001	8,184	301	3,677	1,007	7,360	718	22,572	5,980	1,614
2005–2006	7,500	368	4,604	1,099	8,010	872	28,367	7,046	1,300
2010–2011	9,555	263	5,453	1,001	8,244	793	33,326	6,862	1,459
2013–2014	–	350	4,742	1,000	8,533	680	36,678	7,322	1,604

Source: Government of Kerala, Department of Economics and Statistics (various years).

of view (George, 1999). It is estimated that nearly 14 lakh families are dependent on the plantation sector for livelihood. Kerala has a substantial share in the four plantation crops, that is, rubber, tea, coffee and cardamom. These four crops together occupy 7.04 lakh ha, accounting for 26.88 per cent of the gross cropped area in the state. Kerala's share in the national production of rubber, coffee and tea is 72.02 per cent, 22 per cent and 6.3 per cent, respectively, during the year 2013–2014.

The area, production and productivity of plantation crops are given in Tables 7.10, 7.11 and 7.12.

In the case of tea, Kerala accounts for 5.03 per cent of the area and 6.3 per cent of the total domestic production, and it has been falling continuously for the last three years. In 2012–2013, the tea production recorded an increase of 5,059 MT compared to previous year mainly on account of increase in productivity. In 2013–2014, there has not been much change in the area, production and productivity of tea compared to the previous year. The major issues plaguing the tea industry are stagnant productivity, acute labour shortage, high cost of machines and non-availability of original machinery.

Table 7.10 *Area Under Plantation Crops (in Hectares)*

Year	Rubber	Tea	Coffee	Cardamom	Total Plantation
1960–1961	122,870	37,630	16,800	28,610	205,910
1965–1966	149,630	39,470	23,600	28,680	241,380
1970–1971	179,260	37,590	31,560	47,490	295,900
1975–1976	206,700	37,700	41,800	54,004	340,204
1980–1981	237,800	36,164	57,564	56,376	387,904
1985–1986	330,300	34,800	65,600	60,628	491,328
1990–1991	384,000	34,706	75,057	66,890	560,653
1995–1996	448,988	36,775	82,348	44,248	612,359
2000–2001	474,364	36,847	84,735	41,288	637,234
2005–2006	494,400	35,043	84,644	41,367	655,454
2010–2011	534,230	36,965	84,931	41,242	697,368
2013–2014	548,225	30,205	85,359	39,730	703,519

Source: Government of Kerala, Department of Economics and Statistics (various years).

Table 7.11 *Production of Plantation Crops (in Tonnes)*

Year	Rubber	Tea	Coffee	Cardamom
1960–1961	23,040	40,370	7,410	1,280
1965–1966	46,950	39,150	9,880	1,610
1970–1971	78,730	41,450	12,570	1,250
1975–1976	128,769	43,264	12,570	1,250
1980–1981	140,333	50,716	36,475	3,100
1985–1986	184,700	52,628	23,550	3,340
1990–1991	307,521	63,416	35,700	3,450
1995–1996	474,555	64,794	45,000	5,380
2000–2001	579,866	69,132	70,550	7,580
2005–2006	739,225	56,384	60,175	9,765
2010–2011	770,580	57,291	65,650	7,935
2013–2014	648,220	62,937	66,645	14,000

Source: Government of Kerala, Department of Economics and Statistics (various years).

Table 7.12 *Productivity of Plantation Crops (kg/ha)*

Year	Rubber	Tea	Coffee	Cardamom
1960–1961	187	1,073	442	45
1965–1966	314	992	418	56
1970–1971	439	1,103	430	26
1975–1976	623	1,148	344	38
1980–1981	590	1,402	634	55
1985–1986	559	1,512	359	55
1990–1991	800	1,827	475	52
1995–1996	1,057	1,762	546	122
2000–2001	1,222	1,876	833	184
2005–2006	1,495	1,609	711	236
2010–2011	1,442	1,550	773	192
2013–2014	1,182	2,084	781	352

Source: Government of Kerala, Department of Economics and Statistics (various years).

The area under coffee plantations has been increasing in the state both absolutely and relatively. Although a fall in production was seen in the 1980s, the situation improved in the 1990s. The productivity of coffee showed high variations over the years. It decreased from early 1960s to mid-1970s. The productivity improved in the latter half of the 1970s and showed a declining trend in the early 1980s. The share of Kerala in total coffee production in the country is around 22 per cent during 2013–2014. Major variety grown in Kerala is Robusta with a share of 97.1 per cent in planted area. Productivity of the crop is 808 kg/ha which is lower than the national level of 852 kg/ha during 2011–2012. Among the states, Kerala stands next to Karnataka which produces 70.4 per cent of total coffee production.

Cardamom, another major plantation crop cultivated in the state, showed an upward trend in the area from the early 1960s to early 1990s. In the 1990s, the area under cardamom fell both absolutely and relatively. The production and productivity of cardamom showed a downward trend in the decade 1960–1961 to 1970–1971. Thereafter, a continuous increase in production and productivity was observed. During 2013–2014, there is a decline in the area of 4.5 per cent from the previous year in spite an increase of 36 per cent in production.

In the previous paragraphs, we have seen the major trends in area, production and yield of major food and non-food crops. The changes and improvements in output depend on inputs and input use efficiency. The major inputs relevant to Kerala agriculture are credit, fertilisers and extend of irrigation. In the following text, an attempt is made to examine the recent changes in the quantity and use of these inputs.

SOURCES OF FINANCE FOR INVESTMENT IN AGRICULTURE

On the basis of the recommendations of the All-India Rural Credit Survey (1954), the Government of India made elaborate arrangements for the disbursement of rural credit primarily directed towards agriculture and allied sectors. Over the years, the sources and regulations changed and also multiplied. The initiatives got a setback since 1991 because of the changed scenario of the economy as a consequence of reform process.

Table 7.13 *Institutional Flow of Agriculture Credit in Kerala (₹ Crore)*

Years	Commercial Banks	Cooperative Banks	RRB	Total
1990–1991	269.20	179.40	40.20	488.80
	(55.1)	(36.7)	(8.2)	(100)
2001–2002	1,231.04	1,208.31	388.27	2,827.6
	(43.53)	(42.74)	(13.73)	(100)
2011–2012	23,889	8,367	2,807	35,063
	(68.13)	(23.86)	(8.01)	(100)
2012–2013	25,780	8,557	2,807	37,144
	(69.41)	(23.04)	(7.56)	(100)

Source: Government of Kerala, Department of Economics and Statistics (various years).

Note: RRBs=Regional Rural Banks; figures in brackets give percentage to total source.

Over a period of 25 years from 1991, the share of agricultural advances significantly reduced from 17.4 per cent to just 13.0 per cent, while the RBI prescription for the agriculture sector advances is 18 per cent of the total advances. Multiple factors would have contributed to this and will be revealed only if we go for a more microscopic look into the institutional credit flow to agriculture in the state. Table 7.13 presents the institutional flow of agriculture credit from 1990–1991.

In 1990–1991, total agriculture credit from commercial banks, regional rural banks (RRBs) and cooperatives reached ₹488.80 crores, the respective shares being 55.1 per cent, 8.20 per cent and 36.70 per cent, respectively. In 1995–1996, the volume of agricultural credit increased to ₹1,056.52 crore, the five-yearly increase being 2.16 times. Source-wise, the increased shares are 2.19 per cent, 2.37 per cent and 2.05 per cent, respectively, for commercial banks, RRB and cooperative banks. It is important to note that the role of cooperatives has reduced over a span of five years. From 1995–1996 to 2000–2001, commercial banks credit increased by 64.95 per cent followed by 138.33 per cent increase in RRB credit and 184.80 per cent in cooperative credit. Total credit improved by 112 per cent. From 2001–2002 to 2012–2013, it is evident from Table 7.13 that the cooperative bank's credit to agriculture is declining and credit from commercial banks shows an increasing trend only because of the increase in bank branches. When we look at the average size of the credit, one can understand that per hectare credit from the commercial bank is also decreasing. The agriculture credit from RRBs depicts a slight increase over the years.

One of the serious and current issues threatening the prosperity and prospects of the agricultural credit is the low share of investment credit. The necessity of investment credit was felt at large in the early 1970s as a consequence of green revolution which necessitated investment in agriculture for technological upgradation. The tempo was continued until the middle of the 1980s and since then there is stagnation in the investment credit. One of the probable reasons for this trend is the strategy of globalisation and reforms. The reforms compelled the commercial banks and other sources of agricultural credit to think and act in new directions—quick profit-generating activities (Mani, 2008). These apprehensions are well documented in Table 7.14 and Figure 7.1.

Although the overall credit flow to the agriculture sector in India has increased over the years, the share of term loan in agriculture

Table 7.14 *Flow of Production and Investment Credit to the Agriculture Sector in Kerala (₹ Crore)*

Year	Production Credit	Investment Credit	Total
1990–1991	349	140	489
	(71)	(29)	(100)
2001–2002	2,311	550	2,861
	(81)	(19)	(100)
2011–2012	27,728	3,901	31,629
	(88)	(12)	(100)
2012–2013	32,651	5,059	37,710
	(87)	(13)	(100)

Sources: 1. State Planning Board (Report of the task force on agriculture financing 1997). 2. Government of Kerala, Department of Economics and Statistics (various years).

Note: Figures in brackets give percentage distribution between production credit and investment credit.

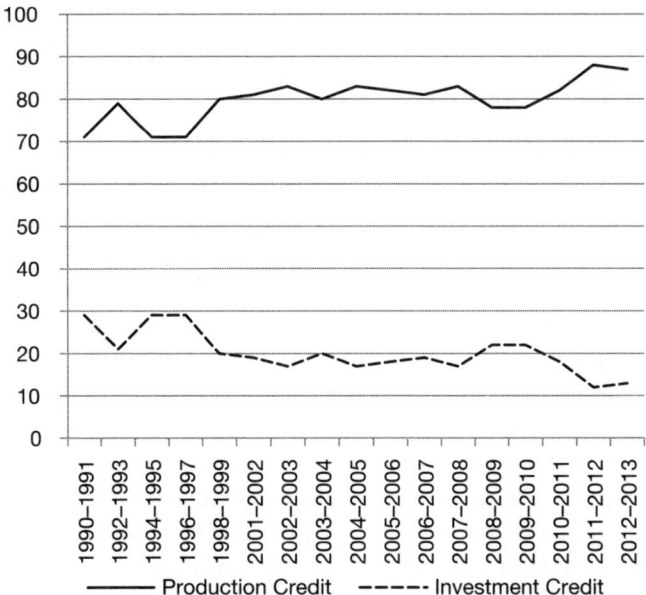

Figure 7.1 *Percentage Share of Production and Investment Credit to the Agriculture Sector*

Sources: 1. State Planning Board (Report of the task force on agriculture financing 1997). 2. Government of Kerala, Department of Economics and Statistics (various years).

credit or investment credit declined from 39.3 per cent in 2004–2005 to 19.5 per cent in 2013–2014. But looking at the trend, 2014–2015 witnessed an increase in the share of term loan to 24.3 per cent from 19.5 per cent in 2013–2014, depicting a growth rate of 47.5 per cent.

In Kerala, the production credit increased from ₹349.10 crore in 1990–1991 to ₹950.48 crore in 1996–1997 and ₹2,310.97 crore by the end of 2001–2002. Between 1990–1991 and 1996–1997, the production credit increased by 2.72 times, and between 1996–1997 and 2001–2002, the improvement was by 2.43 times. On the other hand, investment credit increased by 2.73 times and 1.43 times between 1990–1991 to 1996–97 and 1996–1997 to 2001–2002, absolute figures being ₹382.91 crores and ₹550.39 crore, respectively. The share of the investment credit to agricultural credit disbursement declined from 20 per cent during 2000–2001 to 17 per cent during 2002–2003 and slightly increased to 18.13 per cent in 2005–2006 and 19 per cent in 2006–2007. Out of the total credit flow, the share of production credit has marginally increased from 2004–2005 onwards. From 2007–2008, the share of production credit has increased by 6 per cent, while investment credit diminished by 6 per cent during 2011–2012. Hence, it can be argued that there is a significant fall in the volume of investment credit over the years (it has picked up albeit marginally to 13 per cent in 2012–2013). This is not favourable for accelerating agricultural growth.

Dividing between production credit and investment credit, it was found that in 1990–1991, production credit recorded 71.40 per cent of agriculture credit which increased to 80.76 per cent in 2001–2002, with marginal variations in between. It is heartening to observe that the share of the investment credit which touched 28.60 per cent in 1990–1991 declined to 20.16 per cent in 1998–1999 and later to 19.24 in 2001–2002. These trends are really bad, while the agriculture sector of the economy is setting ready for a take-off to achieve the long-run objectives of food security, value addition, exports and ultimately profitability, productivity and efficiency in the farm sector.

FERTILISER CONSUMPTION IN KERALA

Table 7.15 explains the growth in the use of chemical fertilisers in Kerala. It is seen that until the late 1980s, the use of chemical fertilisers was very minimum; per hectare use was only 16.13 kg in 1960–1961 and 19.10 kg in 1970–1971. In 1990–1991, the use went up to 203,000 tonnes, the per hectare use being 66.62 kg. In 2001–2002, the volume of use declined and this was due to reduction in area under crops, but the per hectare use increased to 76.25 kg; this further changed to 109.6 kg by 2015. But these usage rates were low compared to the average rates in certain other parts of the country and other countries. Again, the important question was not whether per hectare use was high or low, but whether the use was efficient or not. Mere increase in quantity would not ensure quality. The quality in fertiliser application was very much linked to the problem of fertiliser nutrients such as nitrogen, phosphorous and potash. Whenever we apply fertilisers, first we should go for soil testing and find out which fertiliser nutrient is absent in the soil and must apply the fertiliser rich in that nutrient. But

Table 7.15 *Consumption of Fertilisers in Kerala*

Year	Consumption ('000 Tonnes)	Per Hectare (kg) (NPK)
1960–1961	58	16.13
1970–1971	77	19.17
1980–1981	94	32.82
1990–1991	203	66.62
2000–2001	173	76.25
2004–2005	192	74.28
2014–2015	224	109.6

Source: Government of Kerala, Department of Economics and Statistics (various years).

Table 7.16 *Irrigated Area in Kerala ('000 Hectares)*

Year	Gross Sown Area	Net Irrigated Area	Net Irrigated Area as Percentage of Net Sown Area
1960–1961	456.25	318	16.57
1970–1971	601.38	431	20.50
1980–1981	380.90	237.90	22.61
1990–1991	383	333	14.84
2000–2001	396	347	14.95
2014–2015	406	353	14.75

Source: Economic Review.

reports indicate that only less than 10 per cent farmers go for soil tests. Thus, soil testing should be made mandatory through Krishi Bhavans.

IRRIGATION FACILITIES

The use of chemical fertilisers and the area under irrigation are highly correlated. In 1960–1961, the gross irrigated area was reported to be 456.25 thousand hectares and net irrigated area 218.00 thousand hectares (Table 7.16). These areas respectively increased to 466 thousand hectares and 357 thousand hectares in 1997–1998. In absolute terms, the change was only marginal but this was due to a total reduction in area under crops. In later years, it was seen that the area under irrigation remained stagnant. Other than the reduction in area under crops, another reason attributed is the fall in capital formation in agriculture and also the absence of complementarities between public investment and private investment. All these are burning issues in Kerala agriculture which need detailed investigations and research.

AGRICULTURE COMMODITY PRICES

One of the challenges of agricultural activities in any country or state is the declining or stagnating output prices compared to escalating input prices. Kerala agriculture is also not an exception to this. When we look into the agricultural commodity prices since 2000, it is seen that the commodity prices are either declining or are stagnant and also revealing volatility in price behaviour. Price volatility brings instability in agricultural income and consequently debt trap to the farmers. One of the probable reasons for farmer suicides across India, including Kerala, is this volatility. From Table 7.17, it is seen that prices undergo fluctuations. There are some interesting evidences also. Even though the price of paddy was low in the early years, since 2010 there is an improvement. This is an indication to the farmers that there is scope for paddy cultivation particularly when the Keralites depend on imported rice because of non-availability of rice within the state. At the same time, the price of imported rice is going up. Similarly, the problem of food security can be achieved only by focusing our cultivation practices to food crops from non-food crops. In the case of coconut, the increase in the price over the last decade is only marginal. Even the productivity of coconut is not significant after elaborate efforts made by the commodity board. Another crop for which price changes and volatility are distributing is rubber. There are many reasons behind this trend for rubber such as behaviour of domestic prices, increase in international price of rubber, currency appreciation in the Asian countries, integration between domestic price and international price, external demand, imports, rubber policy of both Government of India and international agencies. More or similar issues are relevant for crops such as tea, coffee and cardamom. In a nutshell, the possible remedy

Table 7.17 *Agricultural Commodity Prices in Kerala (in ₹)*

Year	Paddy (qtl)	Coconut with Husk (00)	Areca Nut (00)	Cashew Nut (qtl)	Banana (qtl)	Tapioca (qtl)	Pepper (qtl)	Rubber (qtl)	Tea (kg)	Coffee (kg)	Cardamom (kg)
2002–2003	649	475	32	2730	971	394	7,692	3,919	47	28	561
2003–2004	694	582	34	2,831	1,165	389	6,802	5,040	45	32	361
2004–2005	651	635	40	3,533	1,112	404	6,032	5,224	52	53	330
2005–2006	610	494	43	2,899	1,247	432	5,979	6,699	54	62	217
2006–2007	681	473	52	2,463	1,333	469	10,730	8,325	68	65	312
2007–2008	788	485	52	3,000	1,467	520	12,901	9,390	67	67	463
2008–2009	915	544	48	3,665	1,565	555	11,475	8,915	110	53	506
2009–2010	990	463	46	3,871	1,952	587	13,482	12,489	107	38	800
2010–2011	918	487	47	3,741	2,018	602	14,210	12,578	109	39	826
2011–2012	897	520	49	3,854	1,987	589	13,874	11,547	116	42	732
2012–2013	908	506	46	4,102	2,017	638	12,874	12,687	137	51	698

Source: Government of Kerala, Department of Economics and Statistics (various years).

for price stability in the case of plantation/cash/commercial crops is improving agro processing/value addition and also making agricultural operations globally competitive. This is highlighted in all recent agreements in agriculture such as Doha Agreement, ASEAN agreement, etc.

AGRICULTURAL COMMODITY TRADE

A detailed discussion on agricultural commodity trade is difficult mainly due to two reasons. First, difficulties in getting recent data indicate the direction and magnitude of agricultural commodity exports from the state and imports to the state. Second, state trade is regulated by export-import policy of the central government and about 10 agricultural commodity trade agreements between India and other countries. These agreements are country specific but not very much state specific. Still, some of the important trends in the agricultural commodity trade of Kerala state can be listed.

1. During the last 15 years, the share of Indian agricultural commodities has come down quantity-wise. Kerala state is also not an exception to this.
2. There are clear changes in the trade partners of Kerala's agriculture commodity exports. We are gradually losing our European market, Russian market, etc.
3. There are shifts in the commodity composition also. In earlier decades, Kerala had virtual monopoly in the trade of coffee, tea and cardamom. Now these commodities are traded more by other countries.
4. One of the reasons leading to this situation is the deteriorating quality of our agricultural commodities. We could not maintain the quality standards prescribed by the WTO, listed as 'Sanitary and phytosanitary conditions'.
5. Sanitary and phytosanitary conditions insist on many quality parameters such as quality of the product, hygiene, minimisation of toxic components, etc.
6. These quality parameters can be ensured only if appropriate technology is identified and used. Related to this, the probable issues are availability of technology, appropriateness of technology to local

environment, farmer's acceptability, sustainability and cost effectiveness of technology. This necessitates location-specific research and development in agriculture.

7. International market can be better ensured if agricultural commodities are processed or if value added products are made. Thus, the future of agriculture in Kerala very much depends on value addition and processing.

8. The aforementioned alternatives are possible only if appropriate policy regulations are legalised. The national agricultural policy framework is not completely adopted by the state governments since agriculture is a state subject. Still the scopes for compromises are many.

CHALLENGES

The major challenges are given as follows:

1. The share of agriculture in the SDP is consistently coming down. This raises doubts about the sustainability of state development experienced in recent years exclusively based on the service sector growth and foreign remittances.

2. A fall in the area under paddy is the greatest challenge. This happens in a state where we are producing only 16 per cent of our rice requirement of the state.

3. A priori, it is felt that a shift in favour of commercial/cash/planation crops is a welcome step under the agenda of reforms. But an excessive shift in favour of these crops in the state generates serious issues such as (a) suitability of crop conditions, (b) mismatch between demand and supply, (c) high volatility in commodity prices, (d) non-availability of steady market for the output and (e) the facilities for processing and value addition.

4. Low productivity of food and non-food crops in the state is another basic problem. This raises concerns about issues related to existing technology such as its suitability, adaptability, reachability to farmers, cost effectiveness, environment friendliness, etc.

5. Availability of credits for investment in agricultural infrastructure and production is crucial in agricultural growth. Reduction in the

supply of cooperative credit changes in credit policy of commercial banks giving low priority to agricultural credit, disbursal of agricultural loans in the name of gold loans and widespread utilisation of agricultural loans for non-agricultural purposes have resulted in substantial fall in credit used for actual agricultural purposes.

6. Non-scientific application of fertilisers (NPK) is another issue. Soil testing is the primary step in this direction. Only about 10 per cent of the farmers are using soil testing before application of fertilisers.

7. The share of irrigated land in the gross cropped area of the state has remained almost stagnant in the recent past indicating inadequate irrigation facilities.

8. In a state dominated by cash/commercial/plantation crops, one of the quick remedies to volatility of prices is processing and value addition.

9. The share of the state in the export of agricultural commodities can be improved only if the state agriculture is made 'globally competitive'.

10. From the previous discussion, it is clear that even though the state is experiencing a stagnant, unpleasant agriculture scenario, the prospects are still bright provided appropriate, timely, effective strategies are formulated, implemented and monitored by the state.

REFERENCES AND SELECT BIBLIOGRAPHY

Corea, G. (1992). *Taming commodity markets; the integrated programme and the common fund in UNCTAD.* New Delhi: Vistaar Publications.

Evas, H., & Goodwin, J. W. (eds). (2006). *Agricultural economics* (2nd ed.). New Delhi: Pearson Education.

George, K. T. (1999). The natural rubber sector: Emerging issues in 1990s. In B. A. Prakash (ed), *Kerala's economic development: Issues and problems* (pp. 186–199). New Delhi: SAGE Publications.

Government of India. Ministry of Finance Economic Survey (various years).

Government of Kerala. Department of Economics and Agricultural Statistics (various years).

Kerala Agricultural University. (2005). *Concurrent Evaluation of schemes under macro management in agriculture.* Thrissur: Department of Agriculture, Government of Kerala.

Mani, K. P. (2005). Dynamics of rice production in Kerala: A cobweb approach. In B. B. Battacharya & Arup Misra (eds), *Macro economics and welfare* (283–292). New Delhi: Academic Foundation.

Mani, K. P. (2006). Performance of agricultural sector in Kerala. In R. Sanathana Moorthy (ed), *Kerala economy: Achievements and challenges*. Hyderabad: ICFA Press.

————. (2008). Investment credit in Indian agriculture. In A. Vinaka Reddy & M. Yadagira Charuyulu (eds), *Indian agriculture challenges and globalization* (pp. 288–302). New Delhi: New Centaury Publications.

————. (2009). Cropping pattern in Kerala: Spatial intertemporal analysis. In K. Rajan (ed), *Kerala economy trends during the post reforms period*. New Delhi: Serials Publications.

Mathew, P. M. (1999). Industrial stagnation of Kerala: Some alternative explanations. In B. A. Prakash (ed), *Kerala's economic development: Issues and problems*. New Delhi: SAGE Publications.

Tharamangalam, J. (2006). Understanding Kerala's paradoxes: The problematic of the Kerala model. In Joseph Tharamangalam (ed), *Kerala the paradoxes of public action and development*. New Delhi: Orient Longman.

Thomas, T. A., & Thomas, J. A. (1999). Changing agrarian relations: A study with special reference to Kuttanad. In M. A. Oommen (ed), *Kerala's development experience II*. New Delhi: Institute of Social Sciences.

Chapter 8

Lagging Sector in a Leading Economy
Case of Plantation Agriculture in Kerala

K. J. Joseph and Brigit Joseph

INTRODUCTION

Viewed in terms of the conventional understanding of growth and structural change, Kerala holds a leading position among the states in India. Apart from its much acclaimed achievements in human development indicators, even comparable to some of the developed countries, Kerala has been able to record a GDP growth rate of 8.1 per cent (at 2011–2012 constant prices) as compared to 7.5 per cent at the national level. Kerala's leading position among the Indian states is further evident from the asset holding and consumption expenditure. The average rural asset holding in Kerala (₹40 lakh) is almost the twice the national average and is way above that in Punjab (₹26 lakh) and Haryana (₹37 lakh) and slightly below that in Maharashtra (₹43 lakh). Along with asset holding, the monthly per capita consumer expenditure in rural Kerala (₹2,669) is the highest for any state and 86 per cent higher than the national average. The urban monthly per capita consumer expenditure at ₹3,408 in Kerala is about 10 per cent lower than that in Haryana but is about 30 per cent higher than the national average (Government of Kerala, 2016).

In terms of the relative share of the primary, secondary and tertiary sectors, the state recorded the highest degree of structural change with the share of primary sector being one of the lowest in the country (11.6 per cent) and that of the tertiary sector the highest (77.27 per cent; construction included). To be more specific, in 2015–2016, while the share of the primary, secondary and tertiary sectors at the national level has been at 16.2 per cent, 22.4 per cent and 61.3 per cent, respectively, with a corresponding share of 11.6 per cent, 11 per cent and 77.4 per cent per cent, respectively, in Kerala. The share of agriculture in Kerala has been declining over time, with negative growth rates during the last three years in succession. Within agriculture, the share of commercial crops has been increasing and that today they account for over 80 per cent of the net sown area in the state. To the extent that within commercial crops, plantation crops like natural rubber (NR) have increased significantly over time, the performance of the agriculture in Kerala is closely linked with plantation crops.

Apart from the favourable agro–climatic conditions, the development of plantation sector in the state was facilitated by a host of factors. This included the protected environment from external competition through tariff barriers and considerable state support on account of its significant role in ensuring the livelihood for the small holders and the workers engaged therein. However, during the last two and half decades, there has been a shift in the policy pendulum from protection to open competition under globalisation, brought about by WTO and Free Trade Agreements (FTAs) along with the withdrawal of the state and greater play of market forces. As a result, the sector got integrated with the world economy and exposed to heightened international competition from low-cost producers. This in turn has had its implications on the plight of plantation sector in general and the livelihood of the million small growers and workers in particular. In this context, this chapter deals with the growth performance of plantation crops during the last two and a half decades of economic liberalisation.

In view of this perspective, the remainder of this chapter is organised as follows. First, we examine the landscape of Kerala's plantation agriculture and the institutional architecture that evolved over time to help facilitate its development. Then, we present the performance of these crops under globalisation and highlight certain emerging challenges.

In the end, we present concluding observations along with a plausible way forward.

KERALA IN THE LANDSCAPE OF INDIA'S PLANTATION SECTOR

Kerala is historically known for the cultivation of plantation crops. Plantations in Kerala started with the conversion of cardamom into plantation-type agriculture along with coffee, then moved into tea and rubber. Development of plantation sector in the state was facilitated by the state government in a number of ways that included provision of enormous surplus land and levying a very low or negligible land tax along with maintaining a very low wage rate (George & Tharakan, 1985). From Table 8.1, it is evident that the share of commercial crops in the net sown area in the state increased from about 57 per cent in 1970–1971 to about 83 per cent in 2000–2001 and declined marginally thereafter to reach the present level of over 80 per cent.

Table 8.1 also reveals while the share of most of the crops showed an increasing trend during 1970–1994, after mid-1990s, when the WTO agreement was signed, there has been a decline in their share. Here the plausible exception has been NR and coffee. During the last three and a half decades, the share of area under rubber increased from a little over 9 per cent to more than 27 per cent. It is also important to note that increase in the area under cultivation of planation crops such as rubber, coffee and cardamom was mainly on account of the growth of smallholdings (Joseph & George, 2010). With the increase in the area under plantation crops in the state, the regional economy has come to play a leading role in the plantation sector in the country as a whole (see Table 8.2). Kerala has near monopoly in the cultivation of rubber, cardamom and black pepper accounting for 87.6 per cent, 81 per cent and 76 per cent of the national production, respectively.

One of the important characteristics of commercial crops, as distinct from the food crops, is that they are perennial crops. They have long gestation period, ranging from three to four years for pepper, cardamom and tea to about seven to eight years for rubber and coconut. Further, once the gestation period is over, the production could continue for even decades. Second, very often, the specific agro-climatic conditions in which they are grown is such that other crops cannot be

Table 8.1 *Trend in Area (ha) Under Important Commercial Crops in Kerala*

Crop	1970–1971		1994–1995		2000–2001		2015–2016	
	Area	Share	Area	Share	Area	Share	Area	Share
Tea	37,422	1.73	34,745	1.55	36,847	1.65	30,205	1.49
Coffee	30,183	1.39	82,348	3.68	84,735	3.78	84,987	4.20
Cardamom	48,000	2.22	44,237	1.97	41,288	1.84	39,730	1.96
Cashew nut	98,960	4.57	103,451	4.62	86,232	3.85	43,090	2.13
Black pepper	117,540	5.43	186,720	8.33	199,368	8.90	85,431	4.22
Coconut	719,140	33.20	910,963	40.67	936,293	41.81	790,223	39.06
Rubber	198,424	9.16	443,300	19.79	472,900	21.11	550,840	27.23
Total	1,249,674	57.69	1,805,764	80.61	1,857,663	82.95	1,624,506	80.30
Net sown area	2,165,902		2,239,405		2,239,363		2,023,073	

Source: Government of Kerala, Economic Review, various years.

Table 8.2 *Distribution of Area and Production of Major Plantation Crops Across States in India in 2013–2014*

	Kerala	Tamil Nadu	Karnataka	West Bengal	Assam	Others	All India ('000 ha/'000 MT)
				Relative Share (%)			
Area (%)							
Tea	6.21	12.34	0.39	24.9	53.97	2.19	563.98
Coffee	20.37	7.53	54.98	–	–	17.12	418.98
Rubber	71.95	2.74	5.93	0.09	5.72	13.57	757.52
Cardamom	56.76	7.38	35.85	–	–	–	69.87
Black pepper	68.51	3.47	22.85	–	–	5.08	123.88
Production (%)							
Tea	5.25	14.45	0.46	25.82	52.04	1.98	1,208.78
Coffee	15.91	4.48	50.38	–	–	29.23	304.50
Rubber	87.56	2.77	3.42	–	1.28	4.97	913.70
Cardamom	81.10	6.10	13.00	–	–	–	14.00
Black pepper	76.03	1.76	15.71	–	–	6.50	50.90

Source: Estimates based on the data from Tea Board, Coffee Board, Rubber Board and Spices Board.

grown in their place. For example, cardamom is grown mainly under the shades of evergreen forests and that hardly any other crops can be raised there. Similarly, in the case of tea and coffee, the land suited for their cultivation is hardly fit for the cultivation of other crops. Hence, unlike the short duration crops such as wheat, rice and cotton, where the farmers have the option to periodically shift to other crops in line with the market situation, plantation crop cultivators will have to necessarily continue with the same crop over a long period (Joseph & Joseph, 2005). Hence, when it comes to commercial crops, a sustained institutional support is important for their long-term development.

After the Independence, development of the plantation sector in India has been mainly at the instance of national government. This has been on account of its important role as a foreign exchange earner for the country. Manmohan Singh (1964) observed that in 1950–1951, plantation crops such as tea, coffee and spices together accounted for as high as 20.8 per cent of India's total export earnings. Moreover, the plantation sector has been considered as a means of achieving development. As argued by Hayami and Damodaran (2004), the development of estate-based plantations called for clearing of large area of virgin land for cultivations and the building-up of needed physical infrastructures such as roads, irrigation systems, housing, along with facilities for education and health.

The active role played by the state in the development of plantation sector got manifested in inter alia the establishment of Commodity Boards and legislations empowering these Boards to undertake various activities needed for plantation development. Thus, the Coffee Board was established in 1942, Rubber Board in 1947, Tea Board in 1954 and Cardamom Board in 1964 backed by the respective Acts of Parliament. Later, by an amalgamation of Cardamom Board with the Spices Export Promotion Council, the Spices Board was formed in 1986 and all the 52 major and minor spices were brought under its purview. Although the agriculture is a state subject under the Indian Constitution, on account of its role in export earnings (and import substitution in case of NR), these Commodity Boards were put under the Ministry of Commerce of the central government.

Various activities were undertaken by these Boards for the long-term development of plantation sector and international competitiveness related to production, marketing (including trade promotion) along with R&D and extension. Interventions in the sphere of production included, among others, replanting/new planting schemes, certified nursery scheme, water harvesting and irrigation schemes along with institutional arrangements for financing these innovations (Joseph & George, 2010). In addition, research institutes have been established under the respective Commodity Boards for undertaking R&D on all aspects of the crops of their concern along with an elaborate extension network for the diffusion of R&D outcomes among the growers. Various rules and laws for the regulation of marketing, and the behaviour of different actors involved in processing, and trade, along with elaborate export promotion measures, also came into being in time. Given the instability associated with the price of most of the commodities, the government made interventions in the market aimed at ensuring stability in prices and income for farmers apart from ensuring a fair share for the producers in consumers' rupee. To protect the interest of labour engaged in plantations, the most important intervention relates to the Plantations Labour Act (PLA) of 1951. As per the PLA (amended in 1981), all the holdings with a size above 5 hectares or more and employing 15 or more workers on any day of the preceding year are expected to provide workers with housing, education, health, drinking water and other amenities needed for decent living.

With the initiation of economic reforms in the country in 1991, the approach of the state towards the plantation sector also underwent a major change. Perhaps the most important aspect of this change related to trading environment. Though the trade liberalisation measures in India during the early years of reform was with respect to industrial sector, after WTO, trade liberalisation measures got extended to agriculture including plantation sector. Studies have shown that immediately after WTO, there has been a simultaneous decline in the price of all the plantation commodities (Joseph & Joseph, 2005). Trade liberalisation-induced import competition got further accentuated with the signing of India–Sri Lanka FTA in 1999 and Association of Southeast Asian Nations (ASEAN)–India FTA in 2009. Harilal and Joseph (1999) had highlighted the adverse implications of India–Sri Lanka FTA on plantation sector of Kerala. ASEAN–India Vision 2020 had the provision for cooperation for supply chain management in plantation crops inter alia through the formation of India–ASEAN commodity boards. It also had provisions for interactive learning among

different actors, especially growers, in these countries through experience sharing and competence building (Research and Information
System for Developing Countries, 2004). However, the ASEAN–India
FTA without implementing such measures has had the effect of heightened competition (Joseph, 2009; Veeramani & Saini, 2011). Along
with trade liberalisation, the state has been increasingly withdrawing
from its interventions from the domestic market. Further, there has
been a significant reduction in the plan expenditure for the commodity
boards (see Figure 8.1), which in turn would have adversely affected
their flagship programmes such as subsidised replanting/new planting
and R&D and extension activities.

The Performance and Emerging Challenges

Growth in Area, Production and Yield

Table 8.3 presents indicators of performance of major plantation crops
such as growth in area, production, productivity in Kerala vis-à-vis all
India since liberalisation. It is evident from Table 8.3 that rate of growth

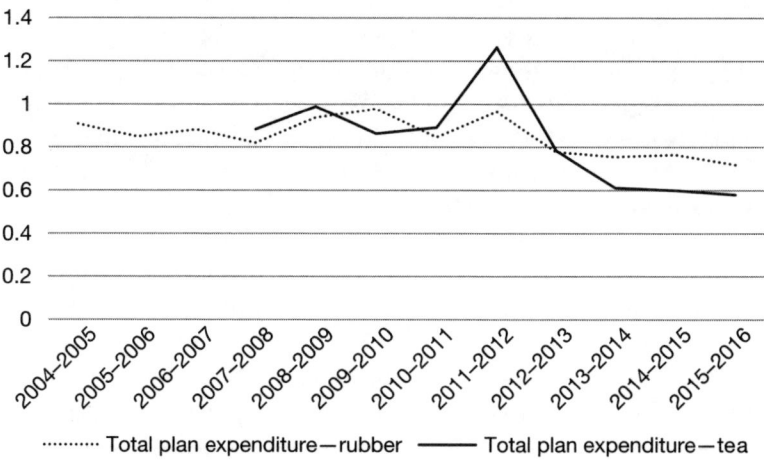

Figure 8.1 *Plan Expenditure of Rubber Board and Tea Board (2004–2005 Prices)*
Source: Estimates based on the data obtained from the annual reports of Tea Board
and Rubber Board.

Table 8.3 *Annual Average Growth Rates in Area, Production and Yield of Major Plantation Crops in Kerala and India*

Year	1990–1991 to 2000–2001	2001–2002 to 2010–2011	2011–2012 to 2014–2015	1990–1991 to 2014–2015
Tea				
Area	0.62	0.05	–4.56	–0.48
	(1.97)	(1.42)	(–0.57)	(1.32)
Production (in thousand kg)	1.29	–1.23	3.33	0.58
	(1.74)	(1.34)	(5.62)	(2.22)
Yield (kg per ha)	0.71	–1.32	9.43	1.32
	(–0.14)	(–0.06)	(6.20)	(0.95)
Natural Rubber				
Area	2.18	1.20	0.73	1.53
	(2.71)	(1.79)	(–1.35)	(1.65)
Production (in thousand kg)	6.60	2.98	–9.21	2.46
	(6.74)	(3.27)	(–6.50)	(3.09)
Yield (kg per ha)	4.36	1.77	–9.89	0.91
	(3.92)	(1.43)	(–5.29)	(1.35)
Coffee				
Area	1.39	0.03	0.13	0.61
	(3.53)	(1.40)	(1.74)	(2.34)
Production (in thousand kg)	10.78	–0.12	0.80	4.58
	(6.68)	(0.18)	(2.10)	(3.21)
Yield (kg per ha)	9.79	–0.17	0.67	4.12
	(3.03)	(–1.20)	(0.35)	(0.82)
Cardamom				
Area	–3.93	0.05	–0.91	–1.77
	(–1.12)	(–0.11)	(–0.36)	(–0.57)
Production (in thousand kg)	11.57	1.01	20.02	8.58
	(10.08)	(0.38)	(16.16)	(7.05)
Yield (kg per ha)	16.41	0.97	21.43	10.81
	(11.13)	(0.40)	(16.45)	(7.54)

Source: Government of Kerala, Economic Review (various years) and relevant Commodity Board Statistics.

Note: Figures in brackets correspond to all-India growth rates.

in the area under cultivation in Kerala has been declining over time in case of all the crops. This tends to suggest the expansion of plantations in the country to hitherto uncultivated areas. The observed trend in Kerala cannot be delinked from the withdrawal of the state along with the fact that cost of land in Kerala is much higher as compared to other regions. However, yield growth in Kerala for the whole period, except for tea, has been higher in comparison with national average. On the whole, the rate of growth in production and productivity has been declining or stagnating over time. To illustrate, in case of NR, production and productivity growth rates were as high as 6.1 per cent and 4.5 per cent, respectively, during the 1990s. As we move to the next decade, the recorded growth in production and productivity declined to 2.9 and 1.7 per cent. During the period since 2010, NR production and productivity declined with a negative growth rate of −9.2 per cent and −9.7 per cent, respectively. Such a drastic decline in either production or productivity was unheard of in the history of Kerala's rubber plantation sector leading to crisis-like conditions.

In case of perennial crops such as rubber, the age profile of the existing stock of trees affects yield per hectare and thus total output in any given period. The yield cycle of rubber involves broadly four phases. There is an initial pre-bearing phase of about seven years, followed by an early harvesting phase of about one to three years wherein yield is positive and increasing with high variability. Then comes the third phase, which can be termed as peak-bearing phase, and it lasts for about four to 13 years wherein the yield reaches the highest level. In the last phase, there is a decline in yield (Joseph & George, 2010). Since the age of the plant, inter alia, has a crucial bearing on the yield, timely replanting of the plants is required. Keeping this in mind, replanting scheme has been undertaken by the Rubber Board and the basic objective of this scheme is to induce the growers to undertake timely replanting such that the shares of old-age plants are reduced to minimum level (George, Haridasan, & Sreekumar, 1988). However, a preliminary enquiry of the age distribution of NR suggests that there has not been any marked decline in the share of old-aged plants; instead their share has increased significantly over time (Figure 8.2). The observed trend cannot be delinked from declining state support and ineffectiveness of the subsidised replanting scheme.

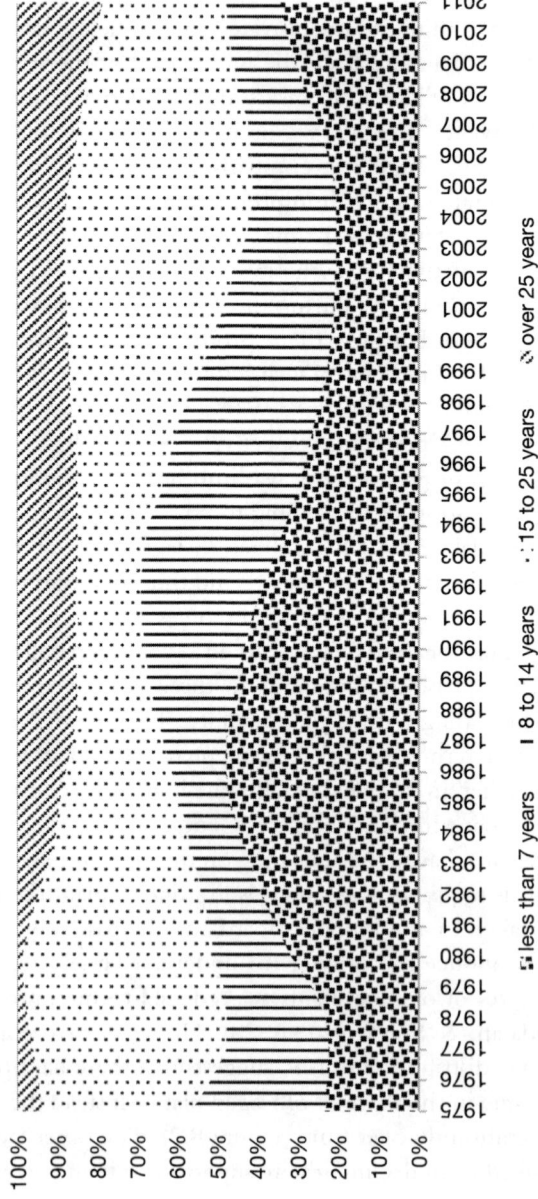

Figure 8.2 *Distribution of Area under NR According to the Age Structure*

Source: Calculated from various issues of Indian Rubber Statistics, Rubber Board of India.

Emerging Challenges

Varied infirmities that plague the planation sector have been subjected to earlier inquiries (Joseph & George, 2010). These infirmities emerge broadly from the institutional framework at the regional, national and international level wherein the planation sector operates. More specifically, the structural rigidities emerge from the existing administrative structures and legal framework that govern the varied operations in the plantation sector such as production, processing, marketing and trade along with the generation and diffusion of knowledge through R&D and extension. It has been argued that there are multiple spaces of exclusion in the institutional architecture governing the development of the plantation sector. These are manifested inter alia in the composition of commodity boards, provision of subsidy schemes and organisation of research and extension (Joseph, 2014). Moreover, there is limited inter-board collaboration even in spheres with much scope for collaboration like the promotion of marketing and R&D to reap economies of scale and scope and to learn from mutual experience. Yet another issue relates to the existing laws governing land utilisation, significant interstate variation in various taxes levied by the state governments, severe infrastructure deficit that in turn adversely affect the growth and competitiveness of the sector. In a context wherein such structural infirmities remain unaddressed, the sector has been integrated with the world market leading to heightened international competition. In what follows, we shall deal with some of the emerging challenges with crucial bearing on the development of this sector.

Declining International Competitiveness

If the available evidence is any indication, international competitiveness of India's plantation sector in general and that of Kerala in particular is on the decline. Studies have shown that over the years India has lost much of the markets of Russian federation. With establishment of Common Market for Eastern and Southern Africa (COMESA) in 1993, India lost markets of Egypt to Kenya for its tea (Nagoor, 2010). FTA between ASEAN and India could have both trade creation and trade diversion effects. In case of plantation crops, the FTA has had contributed to heightened import competition from low-cost producers of these crops from ASEAN with hardly any domestic market (Joseph, 2009; Veeramani & Saini, 2011). Analysing competitiveness in terms of the ratio of India's unit value with that of its competitors, Deepika (2015) observed that on an average the ratio for Indian coffee and pepper is less than one but is fairly above one for tea. Despite the price advantage, there has been a steady decline in India's share in the world tea market indicating the role of non-price factors. In 1950, India accounted for as high as 50 per cent of the world export of tea, and its share in the world market steadily declined to reach only about 11 per cent in 2014–2015.

Locked up in Low End of Value Chain

Plantation crops produced in the state could be divided into two categories. The first group (black pepper, cardamom, tea and coffee) caters to the needs of the consumers outside the country and outside the state. The second category (NR is an industrial raw material) is supplied mostly to large tyre manufacturing units outside the country. Historically, plantations were established as suppliers of industrial raw materials and consumption goods for the developed world. This essentially meant that the producers in the developing countries were at the low end of the value chain and their share in the consumers' dollar/rupee was negligible. The situation seems to have not changed significantly as the success of the planation sector to move up the value chain was, at best, modest (George & Joseph, 2005). In case of tea, for example, it has been estimated that average auction prices in producing countries are only 8 per cent of average retail prices for tea sold in Western Europe (Van der Wal, 2008). The vast majority of the final retail price is accounted for by non-producer interests including shippers, blenders, packagers, owners of brands and point-of-sale functionaries (Neilson & Pritchard, 2011). In case of NR, which is used as raw material in tyre and non-tyre manufacturing industries, it is observed that compared to other states, Kerala[1] has experienced

---

[1] Traditionally, cultivation of NR has been concentrated in Kerala. Kerala accounts for 78 per cent of the area under rubber in the country (Government of Kerala, 2010). Its share in total NR production in the country was around 91 per cent in 2010–2011.

increase in the share of NR consumption over the years. While the share almost doubled during 1970–1990 period (from 7.7 per cent to 15.2 per cent), it remained almost stagnant thereafter despite remarkable increase in the production of NR in the state (Mohanakumar, 2014). The state remained as a raw material supplier to the tyre manufactures outside the state (George & Joseph, 1992). This indicates the failure of the state to establish forward linkage within the state for the NR sector (Joseph, Thapa, & Wicken, 2014). With hardly any large tyre manufacturing units in the state, the observed increase in the NR consumption is mostly on account of the small-scale units operating in the non-tyre manufacturing sector. The future of NR to a great extent depends on the extent to which the state is able to build forward linkage by establishing a vibrant rubber-based manufacturing sector.

Increasing Import Competition

Though globalisation has led to increased import of all the plantation crops, its intensity was felt severely in the case of NR. Given the heavy dependence on imported NR on account of the demand from the growing automotive and other rubber-based industries, increasing domestic availability through domestic production has been the prime agenda of the Rubber Board since its inception (Joseph & George, 2016). Towards this end, supply-enhancing measures were initiated by the Rubber Board to increase the production and productivity of NR. These supply-enhancing measures initiated in a period wherein NR had protection from import competition that ensured remunerative prices to the growers. The domestic price used to be about 20–25 per cent above the international price. During the pre-WTO period, NR had an import duty of about 85 per cent. But under the WTO, NR has been treated as an industrial raw material with a bound tariff of only 25 per cent. The growers had to compete with their counterparts from other countries like Thailand which receive much higher level of production subsidy[2] (Viswanathan, 2008).

---

[2] While the planting grants in Thailand was around US$722 per ha, in India it was around US$444 per ha for area up to 5 ha and around US$355 per ha for areas above 5 to 20 ha.

Table 8.4 *Import Intensity of Natural Rubber*

Year	Production (MT)	Import (MT)	Import as a Percentage of Production
1990–1991	329,615	49,013	14.87
2000–2001	630,405	8,970	1.42
2010–2011	861,950	190,692	22.12
2011–2012	903,700	214,433	23.73
2012–2013	913,700	262,753	28.76
2013–2014	774,000	360,263	46.55
2014–2015	645,000	442,130	68.55
2015–2016	562,000	458,374	81.56

Source: Estimates based on the data obtained from the Indian Rubber Statistics, Rubber Board of India.

As the sector got exposed to open competition without adequate measures to enable them to withstand international competition, import intensity (import as a proportion of production) of NR crossed all the limits during the recent years to reach nearly 70 per cent at present (see Table 8.4). It is also important to note that nearly 60 per cent of the NR imports consists of block rubber and its price is about ₹50 lower than that of rubber sheets (Joseph & George, 2016). The preference of the manufacturers for block rubber also needs to be viewed in the context of perennial compliant by the manufacturers about the lack of uniformity in the quality of rubber sheets produced by NR growers (Government of India, 2015). Given the narrow focus on rubber research on increasing productivity, issues relating to latex processing and related aspects seem to have not received the attention that they deserve. It is evident that the practice followed in processing of latex into rubber sheet has hardly undergone any change for many decades. Further, there has been hardly any change in the machinery (rubber roller) used for sheet processing for many decades.

Trend in Prices

Financialisation of the commodity markets is shown to have contributed towards increased volatility in the prices of commodities in the world markets. Greater integration with such world market has led to the instantaneous transmission of price in the world markets to the domestic markets leading to greater volatility in prices (Anoopkumar, 2012; George & Joseph, 2005; Joseph & Joseph, 2005; Varkey & Kumar, 2013). Along with price fluctuations, from Figure 8.3, it is evident that the prices of all the major plantation crops have shown an absolute decline since 2010. It has been shown that along with increase in the cost of cultivation, on account of rise in the price of raw materials and increased wages, cultivation of plantation crops has become un-remunerative (Joseph & Ajithkumar, 2016). The price crash has usually brought about notable changes in agro-management practices with farmers resorting to cost-saving measures such as reduction in the application of chemical, organic and bio fertilisers, curtailment of weeding practices in rubber holdings and near stoppage of other cultural practices such as spraying fungicides and pesticides, and rain guarding (Mohanakumar & Chandy, 2005) leading to decline in productivity. The recent price crash, despite the state government's intervention to ensure a minimum price of ₹150/kg under the Rubber Production Incentive Scheme, has forced many farmers to keep away from tapping their rubber trees.

For the year 2015–2016, price of tea was calculated from the month-wise auction price data from the Tea Board of India, while for the other three crops, it corresponds to the average daily price reported by the respective commodity boards.

Plantations Labour Act and Labour Shortage

Being a highly labour-intensive sector, its sustenance depends on adequate supply of labour force. In the early stage of the development of the plantation sector, a major challenge for the planters was to retain the labour force in the highly backward and environmentally hostile context wherein plantations were located. This in turn has induced planters in the colonial era to resort to practices like depot marriages and other measures to entice the migrant labour (Mansingh & Johnson, 2012). PLA was a landmark legislation to ensure adequate supply of labour force while ensuring decent living and working conditions.

Over the years, however, PLA appears to have emerged as a double-edged sword for the planters. On the one hand, they have to incur the

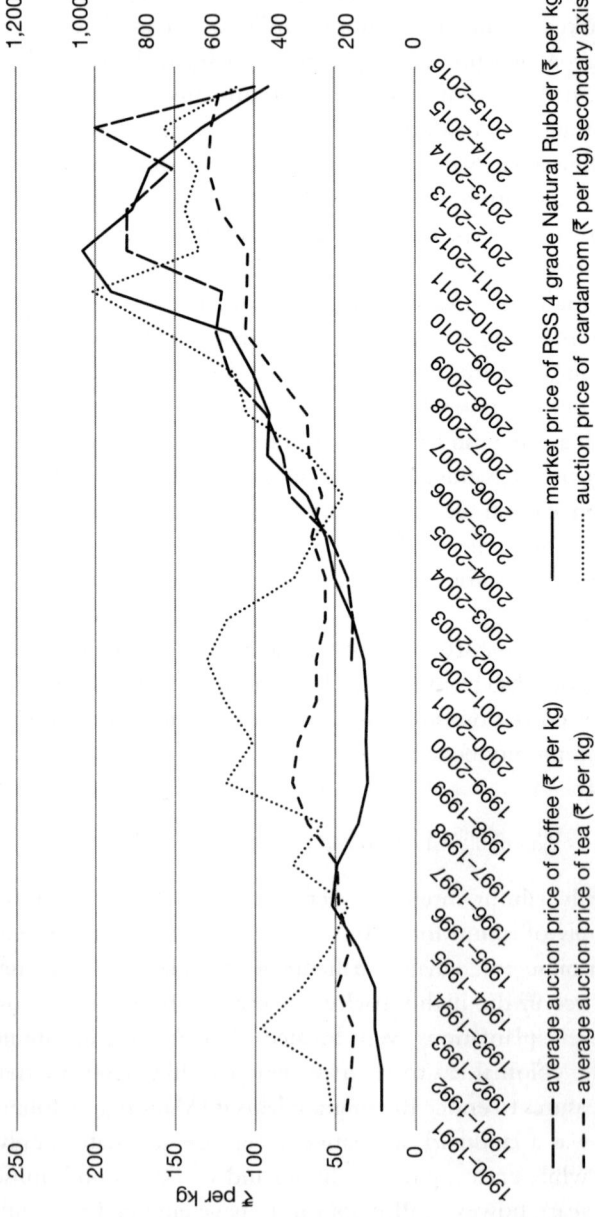

Figure 8.3 *Trend in the Price of Plantation Crops (₹ per kg)*

Source: Based on the data obtained from the respective commodity boards.

additional cost of social welfare undermining their profits. On the other hand, the welfare provisions of education, health and other facilities would capacitate the workers and their families such that these workers and their next generation may not be ready to continue as plantation workers. Hence, this provision may act as a deterrent to continuous labour supply and even deplete the existing stock of labour as well. Further, the decline in the prices and productivity of plantation crops undermined the ability of planters to adhere to the various provisions of PLA as they had to resort to cost-cutting measures in the wake of heightened international competition.

Empirical evidence tends to suggest poor compliance levels by the estates to the provisions of PLA. Though the total number of estates registered under PLA increased from 3,814 in 1999 to 4,039 in 2010, the percentage of estates submitting returns as per PLA at the national level during the same period declined from 55 per cent to 38.5 per cent with significant variation across states (Joseph & Viswanathan, 2016). It is interesting to note that compliance with PLA in Kerala has been much above the national average and the decline was from 77.6 per cent to 64.6 per cent during the period under consideration.

The results of a survey (Government of India, 2009) of 132 estates (47 from tea, 34 from coffee, 33 from rubber and 18 from cardamom) out of 1,655 estates submitting returns regarding the compliance of PLA by the estates shows that only less than 50 per cent of the estates are providing medical and educational facilities. The study further provides evidence for the poor compliance with other welfare facilities specified in PLA. However, when it comes to housing and maternity benefits the compliance level is higher at 77 and 73.5 per cent, respectively.

It appears that the history is repeating itself. Plantation sector in general is confronted with an acute shortage of labour (Joseph & George, 2010; Upendranadh & Subbaiah, 2016; Viswanathan, 2013). It is shown that rise in area under smallholders along with a corresponding rise in area, the inertia among younger generations to take up plantation work, ageing of the existing labour force engaged, the manner in which MNREGA has been implemented are some of the reasons for the labour shortage. The key issue of concern for most planters is to retain the available labour force at any cost—a situation similar to what prevailed when the PLA was enacted. In such a situation, it appears that the move to amend the PLA to relieve the planters from the social cost burden might have the effect of accentuating the labour shortage and could be perilous to the plantation sector (Joseph & Viswanathan, 2016).

The proposed amendments to relieve the planters from the commitments under PLA by offering those provisions through the flagship programmes of the central and state governments may be dissented by the labour. This is because the amendments will have the effect of depriving them of the entitlements with legal support and replacing them with claim on central/state government schemes for which there is no legal support. At the same time, to the extent that the planters are not able to bear the additional cost on account of PLA, it is important that this issue is addressed sooner than later.

Towards a Plausible Way Forward

The central message that emerges from our discussion is that the poor state of plantation sector is on account of a host of factors that include varied structural rigidities and spaces of exclusion in the different spheres of plantation sector such as production, processing, marketing and trade along with the generation and diffusion of knowledge. In a context wherein such structural infirmities remained unaddressed, the sector has been exposed to heightened international competition. This in turn has led to added challenges such as increasing price volatility, heightened import competition and more importantly unprecedented decline in prices. Yet another challenge is the shortage of labour force.

For the planation sector to survive and be a catalyst in the development process, it is imperative that the structural infirmities and challenges are addressed sooner than later. Given the heterogeneity of the crops, regions and classes concerned, evolving a single development strategy may be neither possible nor desirable. However, in what follows, we shall locate the broad contours of certain important tasks that shall attract the attention of different stakeholders.

In the 21st century, there is no sphere of economic activity wherein science and technology, especially information technology, could not have its profound influence. In such a context, a section of population need not be poor because they are engaged in plantation sector but because they fail to harness science, technology and innovation. For the plantation sector to become internationally competitive on a sustained basis, it needs to become more innovative. This calls for enhanced investment in R&D and extension along with harnessing informational technology for addressing issues in the sphere production, marketing and trade. The key objective shall be to facilitate learning, innovation and competence building of individuals and organisations. The system of innovation and production shall be one wherein a transition from factor-intensive to knowledge-intensive production at all levels takes place through investment in plantation infrastructure (physical, human and knowledge) such that the sector is made competitive, inclusive and sustainable.

The plight of plantation labour is much to be desired. Their marginalisation is evident not only from the low wages but also from the inferior social status and low human development indicators. At the same time, there is acute labour shortage and the coping strategies of growers tend to have adverse impact on labour. In the event of declining international competitiveness under globalisation, the planters in general consider the social cost associated with PLA as further worsening their international competitiveness. In such a context, a proposal has been made to abolish PLA and provide its various provisions under the central and state government schemes. Unlike PLA, none of the schemes under the central and state governments offer statutory rights to the workers. In this context, it would be desirable to establish a professionally managed and socially accountable national plantation labour welfare board by pooling resources from all stakeholders—the respective commodity boards, state governments, planters—and the national flagship programmes targeted towards health, sanitation, social protection and women empowerment (Joseph & Viswanathan, 2016).

Perhaps, the most debilitating structural infirmity of the sector is that it operates at the low end of the value chain without any role in the governance of such chains. While the prices of plantation crops remain low and are subjected to violent fluctuations at the farm gate level, the share of producers in the consumers' rupee/dollar is negligible. Moreover, the profitability of the producers of final products using plantation crops keeps a steady upward trend. The issue could be addressed if and only if the plantation sector moves up the value chain and plays an active role in the governance of such chains. This calls for bringing together all the planters' associations, representing both large and small growers, wherein the Ministry of Commerce and the state governments concerned have an important role. Perhaps it may be appropriate to establish plantation product–processing zones by harnessing the Make in India programme focusing on specific crops at the instance of the centre and state governments (where such initiatives are already made on a smaller scale, there is the need for scaling up). Thus viewed, it is high time for the planters and planters' associations to reflect on how long they can afford to play the subservient role in the commodity value chain.

REFERENCES AND SELECT BIBLIOGRAPHY

Anoopkumar, M. (2012). *Commodity price instability under globalisation: A study of India's plantation crops* (NRPPD Discussion Paper No. 13). Thiruvananthapuram: Centre for Development Studies.

Deepika, M. G. (2015). *Export performance and factors affecting competitiveness of plantation commodities in India* (NRPPD Discussion Paper No. 45). Thiruvananthapuram: Centre for Development Studies.

George, K. T., & Joseph, T. (1992). Rubber-based industrialization in Kerala: An assessment of missed linkages. *Economic and Political Weekly, 27*(1/2), 47–56.

George, K. T., Haridasan, V., & Sreekumar, B. (1988). Role of government and structural changes in rubber plantation industry. *Economic and Political Weekly, 23*(48), M158–M166.

George, K. T., & Joseph, J. (2005). Value addition or value acquisition? Travails of the plantation sector in the era of globalisation. *Economic and Political Weekly, 40*(26), 2681–2687.

George, T., & Tharakan, M. (1985, May). *Development of tea plantations in Kerala* (Working Paper No. 204). Thiruvananthapuram: Centre for Development Studies.

Government of India. (2009). *Report on the working of the Plantation Labour Act, 1951 during the year 2009*. Shimla: Labour Bureau of India.

————. (2015). Parliamentary Standing Committee Report on Rubber Industry in India, Parliament of India, Rajya Sabha, New Delhi. Retrieved on 9 May 2018, from http://164.100.47.5/newcommittee/reports/EnglishCommittees/Committee%20on%20Commerce/119.pdf

Government of Kerala. (2010). *Economic review*. Thiruvananthapuram: State Planning Board.

————. (2016). *Economic review*. Thiruvananthapuram: State Planning Board.

Harilal, K. N., & Joseph, K. J. (1999, 27 March). India–Sri Lanka free trade accord. *Economic and Political Weekly, 34*(13), 750–753.

Hayami, Y., & Damodaran, A. (2004). Towards an alternative agrarian reform: Tea plantations in South India. *Economic and Political Weekly, 39*(36), 3992–3997.

Joseph, B., & Joseph, K. J. (2005). Commercial agriculture in Kerala after the WTO. *South Asia Economic Journal, 6*(1), 37–57.

Joseph, K. J. (2009). ASEAN–India pact and plantation: Realities and myths. *Economic and Political Weekly, 44*(44), 14–18.

———. (2014). Exploring exclusion in innovation systems: Case of plantation agriculture in India. *Innovation and Development, 4*(1), 73–90.

Joseph, K. J., & George, P. S. (2010). *Structural infirmities in India's plantation sector, natural rubber and spices* (Report submitted to the Ministry of Commerce). Thiruvananthapuram: Centre for Development Studies.

Joseph, J., & George, K. T. (2016). India's liberalization initiatives and trends in balance of trade under the regional trade agreements: The case of rubber and rubber products. Paper submitted for India LICS conference. Trivandrum: Centre for Development Studies.

Joseph, K. J., & Viswanathan, P. K. (eds). (2016). *Globalisation, development and plantation labour in India.* New Delhi: Routledge.

Joseph, K. J., Thapa, N., & Wicken, O. (2014). *Bypassing the resource curse: Case of learning, innovation and competence building in natural rubber, Kerala, India* (NRPPD Discussion Paper No. 34). Thiruvananthapuram: Centre for Development Studies.

Mansingh, P., & Johnson, L. (2012). *Comparative analysis of existing models of small tea growers in tea value chain in the Nilgiris* (NRPPD Discussion Paper No. 20). Thiruvananthapuram: Centre for Development Studies.

Mohanakumar, S. (2014). *Indian rubber goods industry (non-tyre sector) under globalised market regime.* Paper presented at National Research Programme on Plantation Development Workshop, Emerging Issues in India's Plantation Sector, 31st March and 1st April 2014.

Mohanakumar, S., & Chandy, B. (2005). Investment and employment in rubber small holdings: Impact of market uncertainty in the reforms phase. *Economic and Political Weekly, 40*(6), 4850–4856.

Nagoor, B. H. (2010). *Trade aspect of plantation sector of India* (NRPPD Discussion Paper No. 8). Thiruvananthapuram: Centre for Development Studies.

Neilson, J., & Pritchard, B. (2011). *Value chain struggles: Institutions and governance in the plantation districts of South India* (Vol. 93). West Sussex: John Wiley & Sons.

Research and Information System for Developing Countries (RIS). (2004) *ASEAN India vision 2020: Working together for shared prosperity.* New Delhi: Research and Information System for Developing Countries.

Singh, M. (1964). *India's export trends and the prospects for self-sustained growth.* Oxford: Clarendon Press.

Upendranadh, C., & Subbaiah, C. A. (2016). Labour shortage in coffee plantation areas. In K. J. Joseph & P. K. Viswanathan (eds), *Globalisation, development and plantation labour in India* (pp. 167–196). New Delhi: Routledge.

Van der Wal, S. (2008). *Sustainability issues in the tea sector: A comparative analysis of six leading producing countries.* Amsterdam: SOMO (Centre for Research on Multinational Corporations).

Varkey, L., & Kumar, P. (2013). Price risk management and access to finance for rubber growers: The case of price stabilisation fund in Kerala. *Indian Journal of Agricultural Economics, 68*(1), 67–88.

Veeramani, C., & Saini, G. K. (2011). Impact of ASEAN–India preferential trade agreement on plantation commodities: A simulation analysis. *Economic and Political Weekly, 46*(10), 83–92.

Viswanathan, P. K. (2008). Emerging smallholder rubber farming systems in India and Thailand: A comparative economic analysis. *Asian Journal of Agriculture and Development, 5*(2), 1–20.

———. (2013). Regional dimensions of emerging labour shortage in rubber plantation sector in Kerala: An exploratory analysis. In K. J. Joseph & P. K. Viswanathan (eds), *Globalisation, development and plantation labour in India.* New Delhi: Routledge.

Chapter 9

Agrarian Change and Marginalisation of Agricultural Households
The Case of Kerala

P. Aravindh and S. Harikumar

The economy of Kerala, over the past 60 years, has undergone numerous changes. One of the biggest such changes is the shift from being a typical agrarian economy to one which is centred around the tertiary sector. In the beginning of the 1970s, the primary sector accounted for nearly 50 per cent of Kerala's gross state domestic product (GSDP), compared to roughly 34 per cent of the tertiary sector. Today, however, the share of agriculture in the state's GSDP has steeply declined to just around 14 per cent, while the tertiary sector contributes to nearly 61 per cent of the GSDP (George, 2011).

Land reforms implemented in Kerala by various governments sought to bring about an equitable redistribution of land. This process led to fragmentation of landholdings in the state. Over the years, the agricultural sector of Kerala has witnessed a massive decline in the cropped area and the production of various crops. The production of food crops such as paddy has steeply declined, and it can be seen that wetland crops like paddy have been replaced by garden crops such as coconut and plantain, as well as cash crops like rubber (Kumar, 2005; Unni, 1983).

One of the primary reasons for falling agricultural production can be identified as declining profit from the activity. This has led to a shift in the rural labour force in Kerala from agricultural to non-agricultural activities. The 1990s also saw the liberalisation policies being implemented in India. The post-liberalisation period has seen indebtedness of farmers increasing substantially, thus resulting in marginalisation of small farmers, and, in extreme cases, farmer suicides as well.

The chapter attempts to examine multiple facets of agrarian change in Kerala from the 1970s to the present. The analysis is arranged in four sections. The first section deals with the nature of landholdings in Kerala. The second section looks into the decline of agriculture since the 1970s and a possible shift of the rural labour force from agriculture to non-agricultural activities. The third section focuses on the level of indebtedness among cultivators in Kerala and how in the post-liberalisation period their survival is under grave threat. The last section summarises the entire study and brings out the concluding observations.

NATURE OF LANDHOLDINGS IN KERALA

The state of Kerala is characterised by large-scale fragmentation of operational landholdings. Recent statistics show that approximately 85 per cent of operational landholdings in Kerala are marginal or small, that is, less than 2 hectares in size (Rawal, 2013). The fragmentation has steadily increased from the formation of the state. A comparison of the data before and after the formation of the state of Kerala shows this fragmentation. Table 9.1 shows the nature of landholdings in Travancore–Cochin and Malabar in 1956, prior to the formation of Kerala.

It can be said that land fragmentation was greater in the Travancore–Cochin region than in Malabar. With regard to marginal or small farmers (less than 5 acres/2 hectares of land), 94.84 per cent of landholdings in erstwhile Travancore–Cochin were in this category, while in Malabar, the number was a smaller figure, at 69.55 per cent. Only 3.51 per cent of landholdings in Travancore–Cochin and 14.24 per cent of landholdings in Malabar were in the semi-medium category (5–10 acres/2–4 hectares). With regard to medium or large

Table 9.1 *Nature of Landholdings in Travancore–Cochin and Malabar*

Grade of Holding	Travancore–Cochin	Malabar
<1 acre	66.72	28.91
1–2.5 acres	19.75	22.61
2.5–5 acres	8.37	18.03
5–10 acres	3.51	14.24
10–20 acres	1.15	10.12
20–40 acres	0.36	3.97
>40 acres	0.14	2.12
Total	100.00	100.00

Source: Kerala Economic Review (1959).

holdings (above 4 hectares/10 acres in size), only 1.65 per cent land-holdings in Travancore–Cochin fell in this category. In Malabar, this figure was nearly 10 times this figure at 16.21 per cent, indicating a greater presence of feudal landlords in the northern parts of Kerala.

The crucial legislations that changed the nature of landholdings in Kerala were the Land Reform Ordinance passed in 1957 and subsequent legislations in 1960, 1963, 1964 and 1969. The Land Reforms (Amendment) Act, 1969 which came into force on 1 January 1970 abolished the Janmi system prevalent in Kerala, thus bringing about sweeping changes in the land relations and tenancy systems of the state. The land reforms led to the break-up of large holdings as ownership passed onto the cultivators (Radhakrishnan, 1981). The nature of landholdings in the state in the post-land reform period (Tables 9.2 and 9.3) shows that the fragmentation of operational landholdings has accelerated tremendously.

The data in Table 9.2 shows that 40 years after the implementation of the land reforms, the fragmentation of landholdings has increased substantially with regard to number of landowners. However, the distribution of area has not been fragmented to such an extent. Whether it is due to the inefficiency in the reform process is debateable, but nevertheless the fact remains that the overall agricultural land has seen substantial levels of fragmentation.

Table 9.2 *Distribution of Operational Landholdings in Kerala in the Post-Land Reform Period (Percentage of Holdings)*

Landholding Class	1970–1971	1980–1981	1990–1991	2000–2001	2010–2011
Marginal (<1 ha)	85.0	89.2	92.6	95.2	96.32
Small (1–2 ha)	9.5	7.0	5.2	3.4	2.64
Semi-medium (2–4 ha)	4.5	2.9	1.8	1.1	0.83
Medium (4–10 ha)	0.8	0.8	0.4	0.2	0.18
Large (>10 ha)	0.2	0.1	0	0.1	0.03
Total	100.0	100.0	100.0	100.0	100.0

Sources: George (1986), Devi and Kumar (2011) and GoI Agricultural Census (2010).

Table 9.3 *Distribution of Operational Landholdings in Kerala in the Post-Land Reform Period (Percentage of Area)*

Landholding Class	1970–1971	1980–1981	1990–1991	2000–2001	2010–2011
Marginal (<1 ha)	34.3	41.6	48.2	53.2	58.63
Small (1–2 ha)	22.8	22.1	21.3	20.5	18.67
Semi-medium (2–4 ha)	21.1	18.3	14.2	14.2	10.52
Medium (4–10 ha)	9.3	10.8	6.4	6.1	4.24
Large (>10 ha)	12.5	7.2	9.9	6.0	7.94
Total	100.0	100.0	100.0	100.0	100.0

Sources: George (1986), Devi and Kumar (2011) and GOI Agricultural Census (2010).

DECLINE OF THE AGRICULTURAL SECTOR IN KERALA POST-1970S

The decline of the agriculture sector in Kerala can be seen from the changing land use pattern of the state. The changing land use pattern in Kerala is shown in Table 9.4.

It can be seen from Table 9.4 that the total area under agriculture has declined over the reference period. Area under permanent pastures as well as barren land has also seen its share of fall. At the same time, the area which has been left fallow has increased. The share of

Table 9.4 *Changing Land Use Pattern in Kerala (Percentage Share)*

Category	1970–1971	1980–1981	1990–1991	·2000–2001	2010–2011
Forests	27.3	27.83	27.83	27.83	28.61
Area under non-agricultural uses	7.13	6.94	7.65	9.82	10.16
Barren and uncultivable land	1.86	2.21	1.50	0.75	0.52
Permanent pastures and grazing lands	0.73	0.14	0.04	0.004	0.00
Miscellaneous tree crops	3.42	1.64	0.80	0.40	0.10
Cultivable wastelands	2.04	3.32	2.43	1.52	2.42
Fallow other than current fallow	0.60	0.69	0.68	0.87	1.37
Current fallow	0.62	1.12	1.13	2.00	2.01
Net area sown	56.30	56.10	57.82	56.80	54.80
Net area sown more than once	19.70	18.15	20.49	20.98	15.23
Total area	100.00	100.00	100.00	100.00	100.00

Source: GOK, Economic Review (various).

cultivable wastelands, which reduced in the 1980–2000 period, has also increased in the last 20–25 years. The increasing usage of land for non-agricultural purposes points to an overall decline in agriculture in the state. Increasing population pressure and higher demand for constructing houses seem to have contributed to the large increase in land used for non-agricultural purposes (Devi & Kumar, 2011; Mahesh, 1999, p. 56). Another observation regarding the changing perception of Keralites towards land has been noted by Harilal and Eswaran (2016) who have stated that it is often viewed as a valuable asset due to an assured appreciation in its value, rather than as a means of production in the economy.

The agricultural sector in Kerala has also seen a shift in the cropping pattern during the last 40 years. The shift has seen the area under wetland crops such as paddy go down and heavily substituted by the likes of garden crops such as coconut and plantain. The area under commercial crops such as rubber has also increased during this period. The shift in cropping pattern in Kerala between 1970 and 2010 is shown in Table 9.5.

As can be seen from Table 9.5, the area under rice production has fallen by around 75.63 per cent in the reference period. The fall of

Table 9.5. *Area under Major Crops 1970–2010 ('000 ha) and Production[+] ('000 Tonnes)*

Crop	1970–1971	2000–2001	2010–2011	2014–2015
Paddy	874.93	347.45	213.19	198.16
	(1,298)	(751.33)	(522.74)	(562.1)
Plantain	48.8	99.41	107.8	118.7
	(369)	(731.65)	(837.44)	(893.69)
Tapioca	293.6	114.61	72.28	75.5
	(4,617)	(2,586.9)	(2,408.96)	(2,943.92)
Rubber	179.3	474.37	534.23	549.95
	(79)	(579.87)	(770.58)	(507.7)
Tea	37.6	36.8	36.97	30.2
	(41)	(69.13)	(57.29)	(65.17)
Coffee	31.6	84.7	84.93	85.36
	(13.6)	(70.55)	(65.65)	(67.7)
Cardamom	47.5	41.23	41.24	39.73
	(1.25)	(7.58)	(7.93)	(16)
Coconut*	719.1	925.78	770.47	793.86
	(3,981)	(5,536)	(5,287)	(5,947)
Areca nut**	85.8	87.36	99.83	96.69
	(12,738)	(84.68)	(99.91)	(125.93)
Cashew	102.7	92.12	43.85	45.44
	(115)	(66.18)	(34.75)	(29.72)
Pepper	11.75	202.13	172.18	85.43
	(25)	(60.93)	(85.33)	(40.69)

Source: Economic Review (various).

Notes: [+]Production is shown in brackets. *Production of coconut is measured in million nuts. **Production of areca nut is measured in million nuts till 1995–1996 and in '000 tonnes since 2000–2001.

tapioca, another food crop, is also similar at 75.38 per cent. At the same time, crops such as banana and other plantain (120.9 per cent) areca nut (16.3 per cent) and coconut (7.14 per cent) have shown a steady increase in the area cropped. In the case of commercial crops, the growth in cropped area is even more staggering, with pepper (1,359.3 per cent), rubber (198 per cent) and coffee (168.7 per cent) showing phenomenal growth. From Table 9.5, it can be assessed that the area under paddy cultivation has been replaced steadily by other crops such as banana, coconut and commercial crops. The change in cropping pattern with regard to production of the major crops is depicted in Table 9.6.

It can be seen from Table 9.5 that the production of paddy in Kerala has been on a steep decline throughout the reference period. The production of paddy declined by 56.7 per cent between 1970–1971 and 2010–2011. Tapioca also shows a falling trend, with overall decline in production to the tune of 36.24 per cent during the reference period. In the case of both paddy and tapioca, there was an increasing trend in the five years immediately after 1970, but since then, the trend has been continuously declining. Compared to paddy and tapioca, other crops such as banana (142.19 per cent), rubber (542.66 per cent), coconut (49.38 per cent) and pepper (62.76 per cent) have increased their total production during the reference period.

With regard to coconut, it can be seen that production has fluctuated throughout the reference period. The production declined in the first 10 years, before picking up steam between 1981 and 2001. However, since 2001, it has once again went into a general decline, with only a marginal increase of around 3 per cent observed between 2011 and 2015. Unni (1983) has reported that the substitution of paddy

Table 9.6 *Changing Average Daily Wages for Paddy Field Labourers in Kerala (in ₹)*

Category	1980–1981	1985–1986	1990–1991	1995–1996	2000–2001	2005–2006	2010–2011
Male labourer	11.13	26.06	35.77	77.17	125.76	174.67	312.82
Female labourer	7.91	15.1	21.11	51.17	85.41	119.8	228.48

Source: Government of Kerala, Economic Review (various).

with coconut happened in all topographical conditions of Kerala. Coconut was initially planted either along the bunds of the paddy fields or as mounds within the field itself. The coconut crop slowly expanded before it gradually took over the entire agricultural land. The downward spiral of coconut since the turn of the 21st century could be due to the fact that small farmers would grow coconut primarily for the value of the nuts, and the comparatively lower price of nuts may have made them shift their attention to other cash crops.

Commercial crops such as rubber and pepper have generally prospered on the back of the ruin of food crops. The total area under the cultivation of these crops has continuously increased as has their production. However, there is a catch with the case of rubber and pepper in that since 2010, their production has seen a steep fall. Between 1971 and 2011, the production of rubber had seen a steady rise to the tune of 875.42 per cent with no fluctuations. Since 2010–2011, the production of rubber has fallen by a whopping 338.85 per cent. The case is similar for pepper, in case of which the production increased by 241.32 per cent between 1971 and 2011. In the last five years, however, pepper production has also taken a hit, registering a decline of 109.71 per cent.

The decline of food crops and subsequent importance gained by commercial crops in Kerala can be explained by the question of profitability of agriculture. The rationalisation of the cultivator by factoring in the profitability of agricultural production can be identified as one of the major driving forces behind the agrarian shift, starting from the late 1970s (Viswanathan, 2014). Farmers who think rationally tend to deviate towards crops that provide a higher price in the market, which explains why the like of rice and tapioca have fallen by the wayside, while commercial crops like rubber have enjoyed increasing patronage from the cultivators. This is evident when one observes the trend of commodity prices in Kerala for the major crops in the reference period. Figure 9.1 compares the price trend of six major crops, namely, paddy, coconut, tapioca, banana, rubber and pepper.

The prices of food crops such as paddy and tapioca have been much lower than that of commercial crops (rubber and pepper) during the entire reference period. Juxtaposing Table 9.4 with Figure 9.1 reveals that the relatively low prices and price increase of paddy and tapioca have coincided with their reduction in the cropped area. Coconut in Kerala

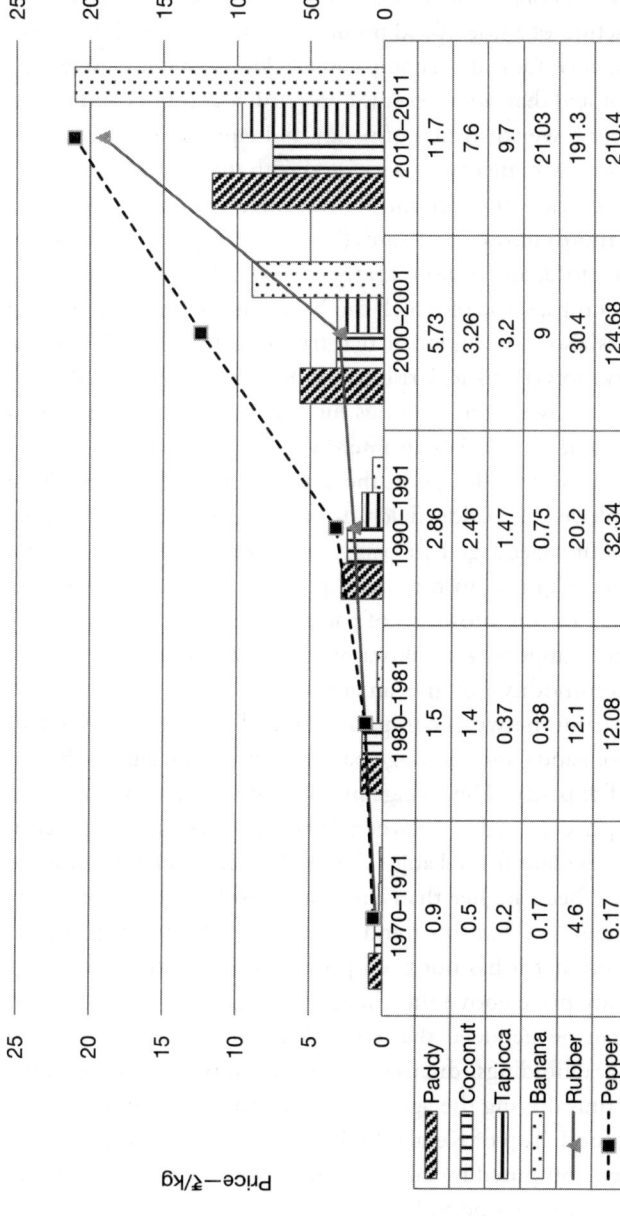

	1970–1971	1980–1981	1990–1991	2000–2001	2010–2011
Paddy	0.9	1.5	2.86	5.73	11.7
Coconut	0.5	1.4	2.46	3.26	7.6
Tapioca	0.2	0.37	1.47	3.2	9.7
Banana	0.17	0.38	0.75	9	21.03
Rubber	4.6	12.1	20.2	30.4	191.3
Pepper	6.17	12.08	32.34	124.68	210.4

Figure 9.1 *Farm Price Trend of Major Crops, 1970–2009*

Sources: Government of Kerala, Economic Review (Various) and Viswanathan (2014).

Note: ★Price of coconut is expressed in ₹/nut.

is largely cultivated in smaller holdings and it may be considered to have more value than that of just the nuts since the husk, shells, etc., can be used in the manufacture of value added products (Kannan & Pushpangadan, 1990). Besides, coconut is also a comparatively less labour-intensive crop.

It must be noted that labour cost for crops such as rubber and pepper is comparatively lower than that of paddy and tapioca. This combined with the consistently higher value associated with the two crops and their perpetual rise in prices throughout the reference period can be said to have attracted more cultivators towards them at the expense of crops such as paddy and tapioca, and more recently coconut. The export potential of commercial crops, some of which can be further processed into value added goods, is also a strong factor that has contributed to the decline of paddy cultivation (Panikar, Krishnan, & Krishnaji, 1980). Paddy can be considered to have taken a serious hit mainly due to rising costs of production since it is more labour intensive than other crops.

Table 9.6 shows the change in the wages of unskilled agricultural labourers employed in paddy fields. It can be seen that the average wages for labourers engaged in paddy cultivation has been steadily rising in Kerala. Coming to the main question of whether the rising labour cost has hurt the prospects of paddy cultivators, superimposing the percentage change in agricultural wages with the increase in farm price of the commodity can give an answer.

The comparison between compound annual growth rate (CAGR) of farm price of paddy and the wage paid to agricultural labour shows a high degree of disparity. The change in wage rate of paddy field labourers and farm price of paddy between 1980 and 2010 is compared in Table 9.7. It is evident from Table 9.7 that the annual change in wages has consistently been higher than the change in farm price of paddy. Only on one instance has this trend been reversed, but even then, it can be observed that it has not been possible to consistently keep the change in paddy price above the change in wage rate. In this kind of situation, it can be deduced that cultivators, particularly those with marginal or smallholdings, discovered paddy cultivation to be highly unprofitable, thus driving the agrarian population away from cultivating the staple food crop of Kerala. In Table 9.7, change in agricultural wages has been computed by taking average of the wages of male and female labourers in each period.

Table 9.7 *Compound Growth Rates of Paddy Price and Average Wages of Agricultural Labourers*

Period	CAGR Paddy Price (%)	CAGR Male Wages (%)	CAGR Female Wages (%)	CAGR Average Wages (%)
1980–1985	8.92	16.22	8.49	13.26
1985–1990	6.61	5.02	5.39	5.15
1990–1995	11.60	12.87	14.71	13.57
1995–2000	4.57	9.03	9.02	9.03
2000–2005	0.12	6.08	7.04	6.47
2005–2010	10.16	9.35	11.37	10.16
Overall	6.50	11.08	11.09	11.08

Source: Computed from Kerala Economic Review (various).

Decline in the Agrarian Workforce of Kerala

It can be hypothesised that the decline of agriculture in Kerala was accentuated by individuals' loss of interest in the activity. An examination of the Census data pertaining to the agricultural workforce of Kerala post the 1970s can help validate this assumption. Table 9.8 shows the declining trend of agrarian population in Kerala according to the various Census reports.

The number of agricultural workers in Kerala's workforce has been steadily declining since the 1960s. Cultivators and agricultural labour together constituted 38.29 per cent of the total workforce according to the 1961 Census. Immediately after the implementation of the land reforms in 1970, this number jumped to 48.5 per cent, but since then, it has been declining. The 1981 Census shows that 41.28 per cent of the workforce is engaged in agriculture. Ten years down the lane, this figure shrunk to 37.78 per cent, before plummeting to 23.3 per cent in the 2001 Census and just 17.16 per cent in the 2011 Census.

The number of individuals engaged in agriculture grew by 39.84 per cent between 1961 and 1971. In the next 10 years, this growth nosedived to −7 per cent before registering an 11.8 per cent growth from 1981 to 1991. The post-liberalisation period, however, witnessed a negative growth of 23.76 per cent before the growth rate became −16.61 per cent in the 2001–2011 period. The trend in the

Table 9.8 *Declining Agrarian Workforce in Kerala, 1961–2011 (No. in Lakhs)*

Category		Cultivators	Agricultural Labourers	Other Workers	Total
1961	No.	11.78	9.78	34.74	56.3
	Percentage	20.92	17.37	61.71	100
1971	No.	11.07	19.08	32.01	62.16
	Percentage	17.81	30.69	51.5	100
1981	No.	8.87	19.17	39.87	67.91
	Percentage	13.06	28.22	58.72	100
1991	No.	10.15	21.2	51.66	83.01
	Percentage	12.24	25.54	62.22	100
2001	No.	7.4	16.5	78.97	102.87
	Percentage	7.2	16.1	76.7	100
2011	No.	6.7	13.23	96.26	116.19
	Percentage	5.77	11.39	82.84	100

Sources: Databook on Agriculture, State Planning Board, Kerala (2000) and Census of India (various).

growth of total number of agricultural workers (including cultivators and labourers) between 1961 and 2011 is shown in Figure 9.2.

Data from NSSO surveys have shown that corresponding to the fall in agricultural workforce, the number of persons employed in construction rose from 2 per cent of rural males and 0.2 per cent of rural females in 1971 to 20.9 per cent and 13 per cent, respectively, in 2011–2012. In the case of major occupations in the service sector, the number of individuals engaged in trade, commerce and hotels rose from 9.3 per cent rural males and 1.4 per cent rural females in 1971 to 17 per cent and 6.1 per cent, respectively, in 2011–2012. A steady growth in these figures also happened in the cases of transport and communication jobs (3.5 per cent and 0.8 per cent in 1971 to 12.1 per cent and 0.9 per cent, respectively, in 2011–2012), and banking and finance (0.7 per cent and 0.1 per cent in 1971 to 1.2 per cent and 3.1 per cent, respectively, in 2011–2012).[1]

---

[1] Data for 1971 sourced from Eapen (1994, p. 1228), and data for 2011–2012 from NSSO (2014).

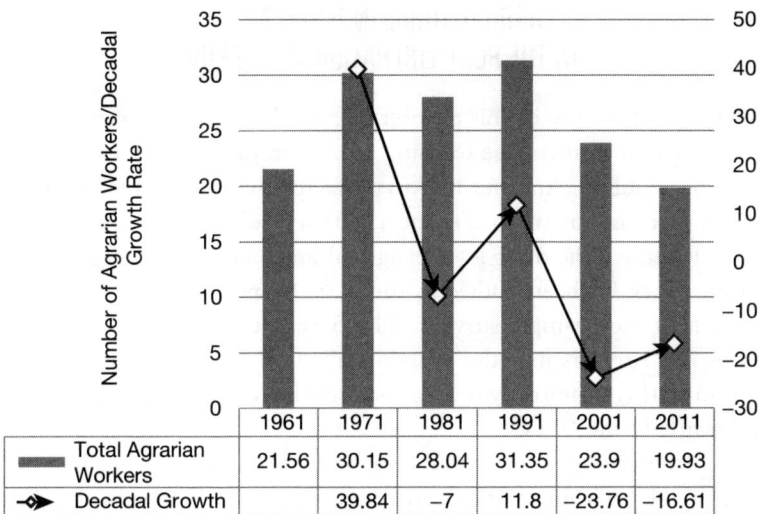

Figure 9.2 *Decadal Growth Rate of Agricultural Workforce in Kerala, 1961–2011*
Sources: Databook on Agriculture, State Planning Board, Kerala (2000); Ministry of Agriculture (2008); Ministry of Agriculture and Farmers Welfare (2016).

The period starting with the 1970s saw widespread changes come about in the socio-economic fabric of Kerala. Literacy rate of the population increased, and individuals became more informed about changes happening elsewhere in the world. The education level of Keralites registered a steady rise, and it can be hypothesised that with a rise in the level of education, individuals became more attracted towards white-collar jobs which seemingly had a greater prestige associated with them. In rural areas, individuals were simply not willing to take up agriculture, even though agricultural wages rose steadily (Nair, 1997).

Another reason for the shift of the workforce from agriculture could be the large-scale international migration from Kerala to the Gulf economies, beginning in the 1970s. The discovery of oil in the nations of the Persian Gulf led to an economic boom in the Middle East, with the construction sector in particular requiring large amounts of manual labour (Prakash, 1998). Despite being blue-collar jobs, it can be said that the higher wages available in the Gulf acted as a magnet which drew large swathes of the Kerala workforce towards it.

AGRICULTURAL INDEBTEDNESS
IN THE POST-LIBERALISATION PERIOD

The second section of this chapter discussed the possible marginalisation of paddy farmers due to rising cost of production and its apparent non-profitability. Another important factor that plays a major role in the marginalisation of small farmers and their subsequent abandonment of agriculture is the rising level of agricultural indebtedness. Agricultural indebtedness has been studied by the NSSO as part of the 59th and 70th rounds of their sample surveys. The 59th round (2003) corresponds to nearly 10 years into the post-liberalisation period, while the 70th round (2014) is almost two decades from the opening up of the Indian economy to the WTO.

The percentage of indebted agrarian households in Kerala has risen from 64.4 per cent in the 59th round to 77.7 per cent in the 70th round of the NSSO survey. The percentage rise in number of indebted agrarian households between the two estimates (as in Table 9.9) is 20.65 per cent. The rise in indebtedness is more evident when one considers the rising debt for farmers with different landholding sizes. This rise in total debt is shown in Table 9.10.

It can be seen from Table 9.10 that between the two rounds of the NSSO surveys, the average amount of debt has risen substantially for households in each landholding class. When the total average debt is taken for all categories, the rise amounts to 529.96 per cent, going up from ₹33,907 in 2003 to ₹213,600 in 2014. The data for Table 9.10 was sourced from the reports of the 59th and 70th rounds of the NSSO sample surveys.

Two aspects of indebtedness can explain why marginalisation has been happening in Kerala's agrarian sector. One is the percentage share of indebted households according to their operational landholding size, and the other is the cause for their indebtedness. These are shown in the following two pie charts, the former in Figure 9.3 and the latter in Figure 9.4.

A look at the percentage of agrarian households who were indebted in 2003 according to their landholding size (Figure 9.3) reveals that 87.7 per cent of indebted households were marginal farmers. Among the indebted households, 9.1 per cent had smallholdings, 2.6 per cent

Table 9.9 *Percentage of Indebted Agrarian Households in Kerala*

Year	Percentage of Indebted Households
2003	64.4
2014	77.7

Source: NSSO (2005, 2014).

Table 9.10 *Average Debt (in ₹) of Agrarian Households in Different Landholding Classes (Area in Hectare)*

	Area in Hectare			
	<0.01	0.01–0.4	0.41–1	1.01–2
2003	2,077	24,910	42,458	61,122
2014	169,000	159,200	194,400	346,700
Percentage change	8,036.74	539.10	357.86	467.23
	2.01–4	4.01–10	10+	All
2003	86,029	156,858	24,860	33,907
2014	607,000	750,500	1,572,600	213,600
Percentage change	605.58	378.46	6,225.82	529.96

Source: NSSO (2005, 2014).

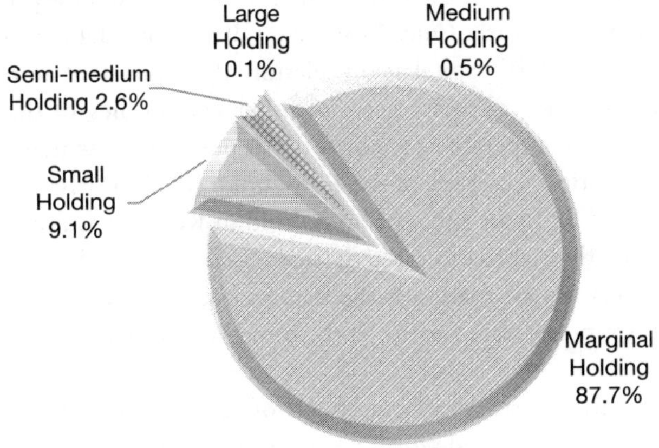

Figure 9.3 *Distribution of Indebted Households by Landholding Size, 2003*
Source: NSSO 59th Round (2005).

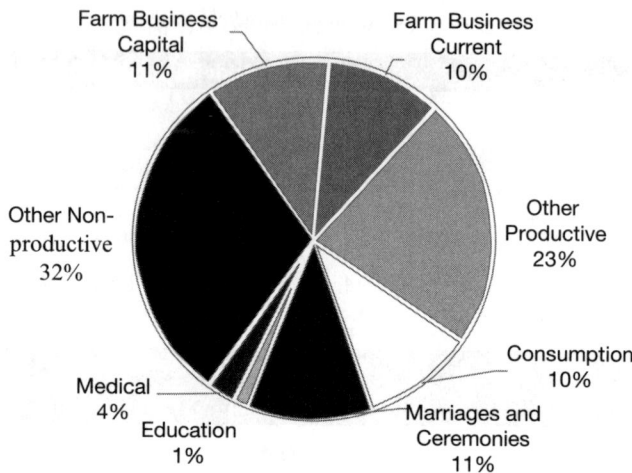

Figure 9.4 *Proportion of Debt Used for Various Purposes in Agrarian Households, 2003*

Source: NSSO 70th Round (2014).

had semi-medium holdings and 0.5 per cent had medium-sized land-holdings, while only 0.1 per cent of all indebted agrarian households had large landholdings above 10 hectares in size.

A look at the proportion of debt used for different purposes shows that only 44 per cent of the total debt amount was used for productive activities in agriculture. Only 11 per cent of the total debt amount was found to be used for capital accumulation. An equivalent amount was spent for conducting marriages and other ceremonies in the house-hold, while a comparable proportion (10 per cent) was used to meet the consumption expenses of the household. In all, nearly 56 per cent of the total debt in an agrarian household in Kerala was used for pur-poses other than agricultural activities. A comparison between 2003 and 2014 cannot be made for the data in both Figures 9.3 and 9.4 as the corresponding data for the 70th round is unavailable as of writing this chapter.

One of the most disturbing effects of agricultural indebtedness in Kerala in the post-liberalisation period is that it has increasingly led to farmer suicides in the state. The second section of this chapter discussed the changes in the production of crops, and it showed that commercial crops such as rubber, pepper, tea and coffee saw their area under cultivation and total production gain at the expense of food crops such as paddy and tapioca. One of the biggest blows to the commercial agriculture sector in Kerala was the opening up of the Indian economy to trade liberalisation in the 1990s. Joseph and Joseph (2005) have noted that 'in the event of increasing cost and declining income, it is obvious that the fortunes of commercial cultivators, a majority of them being smallholders, have been undermined during the post-WTO period'.

Farmer suicides in Kerala are most rampant in agricultural districts such as Wayanad and Idukki. In Wayanad especially, the number of farmers committing suicide has been rising throughout the post-liberalisation era. The neoliberal policies have contributed immensely to this situation, especially in areas that grow heavily export-oriented crops such as pepper and coffee (Jeromi, 2007; Mohanakumar & Sharma, 2006).

A high degree of vulnerability to price fluctuations and crop failure and a subsequent inability to pay back loans has broken the backs of small and marginal farmers in Wayanad. Almost a quarter of such farmers had to resort to selling their agricultural land to somehow clear the accumulated debt, thus making them even more marginalised (Mohanakumar & Sharma, 2006). Jeromi (2007) reports that nearly 39 per cent of farmer suicides in Wayanad were due to agrarian crisis and most of them had landholdings less than one acre in size. The inability of the small farmers to pay back the debts can be considered the proximate reason for committing suicide.

SUMMARY AND CONCLUDING OBSERVATIONS

It can be seen that throughout the reference period (1970–2010) since the land reforms were implemented in Kerala by way of the Kerala Land Reforms (Amendment) Act, 1969, the agricultural sector has been on a continuous downslide. The total area under cultivation has come down steadily as a result of mounting population pressure and declining profitability from agriculture. Among the major crops cultivated in Kerala, paddy cultivation has declined drastically and replaced by commercial crops such as coconut, rubber, pepper, etc., which gave higher returns to the farmers at significantly lower costs.

The rise in farm price of paddy was unable to consistently keep up with the rising labour cost in its cultivation, which ultimately sounded the death knell for the principal food crop of Kerala. Also, the socio-economic transformation of Kerala society beginning with the 1970s saw educated youngsters increasingly turn towards non-agricultural professions. This process was aided further by the escalating migration to foreign nations, especially those of the Persian Gulf (Eapen, 1994).

The fact that majority of agricultural landholdings in Kerala are marginal or small meant that the interplay of all these factors heavily marginalised the agrarian households. The marginalisation was further aggravated by rising level of indebtedness, which forced the abandonment of agriculture on a large scale in Kerala. The fact that the indebted amount is used more for non-agricultural purposes does very little to improve the state of agriculture in the indebted households. In the case of commercial crops which gained ground at the expense of food crops, the liberalisation era beginning in the 1990s brought about the kind of ruin which forced the cultivators to either sell off their agricultural land or commit suicide in extreme cases.

The changing agricultural scenario cannot be considered good for Kerala's economy. The state is heavily dependent on other states for meeting its consumption needs of agricultural commodities, while the commercial agricultural sector is virtually the backbone of many rich districts such as Kottayam, Wayanad and Idukki. Unless serious measures are taken to revive the agrarian sector at both micro level (with cultivators) and the macro level (state policies), it will continue to be in doldrums, falling further into a state of total ruin.

REFERENCES AND SELECT BIBLIOGRAPHY

Databook on Agriculture, State Planning Board, Kerala. (2000). Available at www.Indiastat.com, accessed on 7 May 2018.

Devi, D. R., & Kumar, N. A. (2011). *Population pressure on land in Kerala* (Vol. 24; Working Paper No. 24). Kochi: Centre for Socio-economic and Environmental Studies.

Eapen, M. (1994). Rural non-agricultural employment in Kerala: Some emerging tendencies. *Economic and Political Weekly*, *29*(21), 1285–1296.

George, K. K. (2011). *Kerala economy: Growth, structure, strength and weakness*. Kochi: Centre for Socio-economic and Environmental Studies.

George, P. S. (1986). Emerging trends in size distribution of operational holdings in Kerala. *Economic and Political Weekly, 21*(5), 198–200.

Harilal, K. N., & Eswaran, K. K. (2016). Agrarian question and democratic decentralization in Kerala. *Agrarian South: Journal of Political Economy, 5*(2–3), 292–324.

Jeromi, P. D. (2007, 4 August). 'Farmers' indebtedness and suicides impact of agricultural trade liberalisation in Kerala. *Economic and Political Weekly, 42*(31), 3241–3247.

Joseph, B., & Joseph, K. J. (2005). Commercial agriculture in Kerala after the WTO. *South Asia Economic Journal, 6*(1), 37–57.

Kannan, K. P., & Pushpangadan, K. (1990). *Dissecting agricultural stagnation in Kerala: An analysis across crops, seasons and regions* (Working Paper No. 238). Thiruvananthapuram: Centre for Development Studies.

Kumar, B. M. (2005). Land use in Kerala: Changing scenarios and shifting paradigms. *Journal of Tropical Agriculture, 42*(1–2), 1–12.

Mahesh, R. (1999). Causes and consequences of change in cropping pattern: A location-specific study. Thiruvananthapuram: Kerala Research Programme on Local Level Development, Centre for Development Studies.

Ministry of Agriculture. (2008). *Agricultural statistics at a glance 2008*. New Delhi: Directorate of Economics and Statistics, Government of India.

Ministry of Agriculture and Farmers Welfare. (2016). *Agricultural statistics at a glance 2016*. New Delhi: Directorate of Economics and Statistics, Government of India.

Ministry of Finance. (2007). *Report of the expert group on agricultural indebtedness*. New Delhi: Government of India.

Mohanakumar, S., & Sharma, R. K. (2006). Analysis of farmer suicides in Kerala. *Economic and Political Weekly, 41*(16), 1553–1558.

Nair, M. K. S. (1997). Rural labour market in Kerala: Small holder agriculture and labour market dynamics. *Economic and Political Weekly, 32*(35), L-45–L-52.

NSSO. (2005). *Situation assessment survey of farmers—Indebtedness of farmer households, NSS 59th round (January–December 2003)*. Report No. 498 (58/33/1). New Delhi: Government of India.

————. (2014). *Key Indicators of situation of agricultural households in India, NSS 70th round (January–December 2013)*. New Delhi: Government of India.

Panikar, P. G. K., Krishnan, T. N., & Krishnaji, N. (1980). Population growth and agricultural development: A case study of Kerala. In J. Cairncross (ed), *Population growth and agriculture in developing countries*. Rome: Food and Agricultural Organization.

Prakash, B. A. (1998). Gulf migration and its economic impact: The Kerala experience. *Economic and Political Weekly, 33*(50), 3209–3213.

Radhakrishnan, P. (1981). Land reforms in theory and practice: The Kerala experience. *Economic and Political Weekly, 16*(52), A129–A137.

Rawal, V. (2013). Changes in the distribution of operational landholdings in rural India: A study of National Sample Survey data. *Review of Agrarian Studies, 3*(2), 73–104.

Unni, J. (1983). Changes in the cropping pattern in Kerala: Some evidence on substitution of coconut for rice, 1960–61 to 1978–79. *Economic and Political Weekly,* A100–A107.

Viswanathan, P. K. (2014). The rationalization of agriculture in Kerala: Implications for the natural environment, agro-ecosystems and livelihoods. *Agrarian South: Journal of Political Economy, 3*(1), 63–107.

PART IV

Industry and Infrastructure

Chapter 10

Emerging Trends in the Information Technology Services Sector in Kerala

Tomy Joseph

INTRODUCTION

One of the industries that showed vibrant growth in India after liberalisation has been the information technology (IT) services. It is of academic interest to analyse the causes and pattern of growth of this industry in various regions of the country as each state has been competing to grab a big share of the pie. The spatial growth of the industry especially in South India as 'the Silicon Valley of India' and the share of Kerala as the southernmost part is the special focus of this chapter. It is a partial attempt to fill the gap that Ahluwalia (2000) pointed out that the performance of individual states in the post-reform period has received less attention than it deserves in public debates on economic policy. Much of the debate in academic circles was focused on national performance. Liberalisation has reduced the degree of control exercised by the centre in many areas leaving much greater scope for state-level initiatives.

The IT and information technology-enabled services (ITES) industry has become one of the growth catalyst for India. India continues to maintain a leadership position in global sourcing, accounting for above

55 per cent of the global sourcing market. IT–business process management (IT–BPM) service has grown from $59.9 billion to 76.3 billion in 2010–2011 to $95.2 billion in 2012–2013 to $105 billion in 2013–2014 to around $120 billion in 2014–2015 (National Association of Software and Services Companies [NASSCOM]). Employment in this sector has increased from 2.2 million in 2008–2009 to over 3 million by 2014–2015 and an indirect employment of over 10 million. More than 83 per cent of the revenue in this sector is from exports. The National Policy on Information Technology envisages revenues of IT and ITES industry expanding to US$300 billion by 2020 and exports to US$200 billion by 2020. However, India's capacity for innovation according to the Global Competitiveness Report 2013–2014 is lower than other BRICS (Brazil, Russia, India, China and South Africa) countries except Russia. This is exhibited in its poor score on university–industry collaboration, on the number of patents, company spending on research and development (R&D), etc.

Technology is considered as an important source of economic growth. This conclusion followed from the neoclassical growth model of Solow (1957), further established by Arrow (1962), Mansfield (1968), Grilliches (1957) and many others.

Of the many technologies, information and communication technology (ICT) is believed to be a revolution with profound influence on economic development. The rapid advancement in ICT is making it economically feasible to collect, process, store and transit information at breathtaking speed, reduce cost, raise productivity and increase economic welfare. The technology is making great strides and growing at a very fast pace both in the developed and developing countries.

CERTAIN FACETS OF THE IT INDUSTRY IN INDIA

The software industry in India is located mainly around a few major cities. Software industry is a 20th-century phenomenon. The academic interest in the software sector started with the liberalisation programmes. A number of studies highlighted the export potential of the industry as a catalyst for economic development (Narasimhan, 1985; Schware, 1987; World Bank, 1999). Schware (1992) pointed out the fallacy of following the strategy of concentrating on the export sector only which would be like 'walking on the one leg' and suggested 'walking on two legs'—the proposition of simultaneous growth of domestic and export sectors. Nagesh Kumar (2001) evaluated the capability of the Indian software industry and pointed out the various challenges in the form of growing scarcity of talent, rising wage cost and emerging competition from other countries. He cautioned that to maintain its position, Indian IT industry has to consolidate its strength by improving the value chain, making substantial investments in R&D and creating linkages. Arora, Arunachalam, Asundi and Fernandes (2001) pointed out that though there is a great deal of excitement about its rapid growth and its export success, the kind of work that they perform is typically and fairly mundane. There is little evidence of any attempt to 'learning to walk on two legs proposition'.

Some studies also looked at the labour dynamics of the industry (Vijaybhaskar, Rothbeck, & Gayathri, 2001). Kumar (2001) pointed out the predominance of the low-skilled tasks in projects. They highlighted the issues of the labour market in a post-Fordist organisational model, the wage setting being linked to performance and it is highly individualised. Porter (1990) observed that unless there is an appropriate improvement at the microeconomic level, political and macroeconomic reforms will not bear full fruit. He pointed out that successful firms are frequently concentrated in particular cities or states within a nation. Joseph (2008) tried to study the dynamics of the software industry in South India. The study concluded that one of the major factors was the cosmopolitan and industrial culture of the location in each state. Second discerning factor was the infrastructural facilities, both physical and social.

This chapter tries to explore whether the initiatives by the various governments in Kerala over the years have tried to overcome the various hassles in the state becoming an IT destination. It is an attempt to find out some of the drawbacks and, at the same time, to pinpoint the successes especially after 2000.

EMERGING TRENDS IN THE IT–BUSINESS PROCESS OUTSOURCING SECTOR

The challenges and prospects for the IT–Business Process Outsourcing (IT–BPO) sector in any state can be visualised only against the recent developments in the global market, the technological trends as well as the macroeconomic changes in the country. It is a challenge for each country and state to overcome the challenges and make a niche market for itself. While admitting that cost effectiveness is a decisive factor in location choice, the future of the sector depends on acquiring new skills, talents and new growth models to be sustainable (NASSCOM, 2017).

The industry added US$11 billion in revenue in 2016. The major changes brought about recently include emphasis on digitisation, new focus on skills in demand, search for new business models, expanding opportunities in new markets including continental Europe, Japan, China and Africa along with a new wave of acquisitions and partnerships.

The challenges seen are increased rhetoric on protectionism, Brexit and visa issues along with macroeconomic uncertainties and focus on cost minimisation as well as currency volatility.

To state as a case of sustained growth, IT and services, the largest exports sector, grew by 7.6 per cent, while merchandise exports grew only by 3.1 per cent and invisibles by 2.1 per cent. Export revenue from the industry was equivalent to 20 per cent of forex reserves, and foreign direct investment (FDI) share of the sector was more than 7 per cent of total FDI inflows. While the export revenues increased from $69 billion in 2012 to $108 billion in 2016, new trends are visible from a deeper perspective.

Table 10.1 shows increasing signs of fixed-price contracts, onshore activity, which means software technicians are sent abroad and the work is done as joint investment and joint innovation with clients. Mergers and acquisitions (M&As) intend to enhance competencies in terms of design, cloud, artificial intelligence (AI) solutions, etc. The top firms have taken efforts to train more than 50 per cent of their employees (almost 350,000) employees. Wipro has trained 40,000, Tata Consultancy Services (TCS) 1 lakh and Infosys 1.4 lakh employees; 37 per cent of them being trained on analytics, 26 per cent on mobility, 24 per cent on cloud and 13 per cent on others. A promising note is that over 8,000 firms are offering digital solutions, while over 2,000 are digitally focused start-ups. India ranks third in global start-up ecosystem.

There is an urgent need for re-skilling which is a new challenge to sustain. New talents are required with subject matter experts and hybrid professionals with domain, technical and soft skills. New jobs have to be

Table 10.1 *Recent Changes in the IT Sector*

Variables	2012	2016	Interpretation
Fixed price contract	42%	55%	Rising trend of joint investment with clients
Million-dollar clients	48%	46%	Smaller deal values—digital driving
Onshore revenues	48%	59%	Co-innovation with customers—digital projects
Digital mergers and acquisitions (nos.)	39	64	To enhance digital competencies
Digital revenue (as % of exports)	4%	15–20%	Digitisation drive

Source: NASSCOM (2017).

assumed with cyber security, mobile app development, new user interfaces, social media, data scientists and platform engineering. Mamath R. Nath of International Business Machines (IBM) Corporation Asia Pacific stated, 'the speed at which the technology, market trend and client requirement is constantly transforming demands all of us keep ourselves upgraded with new skills, its back to school for IT workers' (*Business Line*, 3 August 2017). According to NASSCOM, at least 60 per cent of the 3.7 million workforce of the IT industry needs to re-skill itself or lose jobs. New skills are required in big data analytics, cloud and cyber security, robotics, AI, etc. Various subject experts will be required especially for the knowledge process outsourcing (KPO) sector including graphic designing, humanities, sociology, finance, payments, etc.

The digital economy drive is a boosting factor with the push towards $1 trillion digital economy by 2020. Mobile business transactions have increased by 40 per cent in the last three years. E-commerce is estimated at $33 billion. The number of Internet subscribers has crossed 432 million, next only to China. The number of smartphone users has passed 300 million which is expected to cross 800 million by 2020.

While cost and talent are the major factors, industry expertise and innovation are the future sourcing drive. From 2010, growth of sales of tablets and smartphones outpaced the shipment of desktop and laptop market which has led to the development of consumer apps, enterprise apps and enterprise mobility solutions and building technology platforms.

Digital revolution is seen as a catalyst for the growth of the sector. The following pathways will enhance the capabilities of the sector.

1. Build India as the digital innovation hub
2. Accelerate the technology skilling and re-skilling platform
3. Centres of excellence initiatives
4. Digital ecosystems (start-ups)
5. Partner for domestic technology adoption
6. Outreach to new markets—Germany, Japan, Middle East, Africa and China

A look at the broad verticals and the prospects and challenges will help us in understanding the same for the Indian IT services industry (NASSCOM, 2012). The major verticals were as follows: banking, financial services and insurance (BFSI): 41.2 per cent; telecom: 19 per cent; retail, health and media: 32.5 per cent. BFSI is the most mature IT market with $247 billion in 2012. The Indian share was $28 billion, 11.5 per cent of the global share. In the banking and finance sector, there is new scope for customer service solutions through the cloud, smarter analytics, business intelligence and m-commerce. The scope includes biometrics and smart cards, web- and mobile-based solutions, security, authentication, risk management, data mining, data warehousing and financial inclusion.

Health care is another emerging IT market worth $56.4 billion in the global market but Indian share is just $2.6 billion. There are new possibilities with automation, decision support system–remote patient monitoring, telemedicine, clinical data repository, etc. It requires data security systems, m-health, smartphone applications, hospital information systems, enterprise resource planning (ERP), customer relationship management (CRM), big data and analytics. Development of nationwide health records in the United States, Europe, China as well as aging population in developed nations and the potential of IT for health care inclusion are areas in which the sector can find new avenues.

IT in retail globally was worth $123.3 billion but the Indian share was just 6.6 billion. Master data management, Mobile shopping/

payments, supply chain, inventory management systems, e-commerce and m-commerce platforms, point-of-sales software, digital marketing and demand forecasting are new developments in this sector. Customer application development and management (CADM) is also fast-growing with US$21 billion. Maintenance software and application software along with mobility, social, cloud and analytics are future of this segment.

Despite slowdown, India's KPO market is growing at a compound annual growth rate (CAGR) of about 30 per cent annually and may touch $30 billion by 2015 from the current level of $20 billion, according to The Associated Chambers of Commerce & Industry of India (ASSOCHAM) Report (ASSOCHAM, 2013). The rising demand for profession-based services is expected to drive the growth in the industry in areas of research for capital and financial markets, legal works, editing jobs for international publishing houses among many others, reveals the ASSOCHAM Secretary General Mr D. S. Rawat. He also said that presently, domestic KPO industry is facing stiff competition from countries such as the Philippines, Russia, China, Poland and Hungary as these are emerging strong contenders for KPO business in view of qualified KPO professionals, low-cost advantages, domain expertise, location advantage, sales and marketing capabilities and data compliance.

While releasing the paper, Mr Rawat added that it is difficult for KPO companies to always find a qualified, experienced and talented workforce in India (ASSOCHAM, 2017). Considering the situation that there is no dearth of engineers, doctors, MBAs, lawyers, etc., in India, the KPO industry is banking on availability of this talented pool to fill up its seats, but now they are facing the supply crunch.

The potential solution is expanding into tier-2 and tier-3 cities. There is sufficient untapped potential in these smaller cities but the questions on how to leverage on these opportunities without adversely affecting organisational and logistical effectiveness is a challenge. This approach of distributed working looks more promising for the KPO companies than traditional IT or BPO companies. Lot of work that is part of KPO can be done by individuals or small teams—remote work is also possible. The KPO work is knowledge intensive and it should be possible hence for these companies to come up with working models that can tap into the isolated resources pools available in smaller towns across India, adds the ASSOCHAM.

The second way is to partner with educational institutes to ensure that students passing out of universities have the right skill set. Both the approaches are being followed by Indian IT companies to certain extent so there is opportunity for KPO companies to learn from already existing partnerships and grow the scale to address their own requirement, reveals the paper. The KPO sector deals with confidential data, including financial data, treasury and cash management functions and investment portfolio decisions and needs to address the issue of data security raised by international clients, said Mr Rawat.

Small and Medium Enterprises (SMEs) are likely to be the major growth drivers for the KPO sector. According to estimates, out of the 20 million SMEs in the United States and Europe, about 15 per cent can benefit from KPO services due to reduced complexity, ability to compete effectively with small and large competitors, shorter time to market, higher flexibility, overall lower costs and potentially higher quality for the same costs.

The IT and services sector is currently facing a number of challenges. These will have its repercussions on the industry in the country and in the state. The global IT market was $650 billion in 2015, the growth rate being −0.2 per cent. *The Economic Times* estimates the IT sector growth to fall to 5.3 per cent in 2017. This will be the second successive year of a sharp drop in the growth rate of India's biggest export industry. The major IT companies are expected to slow down from 12.3 per cent in 2015 to 8.7 per cent in 2016 to 5.3 per cent in 2017. The pessimistic estimates are a reflection of widespread impact of digital disruption on the sector along with political factors such as Brexit and US protectionism. Shift to cloud and automation is forcing companies rework their model that depended on building customer software using mass of engineers. Cyclical impacts on BFSI, health care, retail, revenue compression on existing deals, share shifts with the existing clients are also the reasons for this pessimistic approach.

A major challenge for the IT sector in India is to rework the existing business model by taking up 'innovation as an agenda'. Some of the IT firms are making new strides to cope with the new times. For example, Accenture has launched its innovation hub in Bangalore with 4.45 lakh sq. feet space with an investment of $900 million.

IT firms are finding it difficult to increase their workforce in the fundamental change in the business model that Indian IT companies are wrestling with. The world has become digital, and they haven't. Cloud technology for example is moving away from a people-led model to fewer employees model. While NASSCOM projected an intake of 15,000 employees in the current year, large IT firms are planning the largest retrenchment drive. Seven biggest firms are planning to fire at least 56,000 employees. Between March and June 2017, staff strength of TCS reduced by 1,414, Infosys by 1,811, Tech Mahindra by 1,713 are some indications of the trend (Sood, 2017). Karnataka IT minister Vinod Kharge has accepted that there are 'lay-offs in software industry'. Announcements by Wipro, Infosys and Cognizant have sent alarms with the workers in the industry.

Dataquest (2015) is also rather pessimistic in the performance of major companies. It states that the Indian IT industry has reached an inflection point where it is playing with lot of trends.

Table 10.2 shows that the growth trends are not so promising. The recession of 2008 has hard-hit the industry.

Table 10.2 *Growth Rates in Revenues of Major IT Companies*

Company	2013–2014 (₹ Cr)	2014–2015 (₹ Cr)	Percentage Growth
TCS	81,809	94,648	16
Cognizant	55,894	65,779	18
Infosys	50,133	53,319	6
Wipro	43,763	47,318	8
HP India	36,697	37,985	4
Tech Mahindra	18,831	22,621	20
IBM India	18,754	20,442	9
Oracle India	11,437	12,440	9
SAP India	9,520	9,890	4
IGATE	6,734	7,879	17

Source: Dataquest (2015).

IT SERVICES INDUSTRY IN KERALA

Studies on industrialisation of Kerala mainly looked into reasons for the industrial backwardness of the state. The lopsided nature of industrial structure concentrated in a few traditional and resource-based industries was a reason for backwardness. A policy prescription that followed from the diagnosis is an industrial restructuring with focus on modern and skill-based industries such as electronics and software (Subrahmanian & Pillai, 1985). The ecological imperatives of the state and its dense population dictate the use of relatively non-polluting as well as energy- and material-efficient industries. It was suggested that the areas that should be tapped are the knowledge-based industries for which personnel can be trained in the Kerala context (Mohan, 1995).

IT industry being knowledge intensive has been viewed as most suited to the state of Kerala considering the high density and shortage of land and less pollution. Kerala has the best bandwidth connectivity, highly skilled human resource base and very high quality of life. Dissemination of IT through various schemes such as Akshayaa, IT@ School, e-governance initiatives provide good potential for creating a domestic market base. Another advantage is the low attrition rate among the software workers of Kerala as compared to other South Indian states.

There were institutional and policy initiatives conducive to the development of the industry in the state. Technopark was one of the pioneers established in 1990. A number of policy initiatives have been taken to remove many of the hassles and to provide a number of incentives for the development of the industry in the state. Transparency in policy environment and a single-window clearance system as regard imports and other licenses were introduced.

Kerala ranks high among various states in social and human development. However, study by the Confederation of Indian Industry (CII) ranked Kerala 13th among 18 states on the basis of investment climate, and investment ranking by *India Today* (September 2006) also put Kerala 16th among 20 Indian states. A look at the growth in the number of firms, employment and revenues will tell us whether the impressions have changed after 10 years. We will just look at the various initiatives by the state government for the development of the industry.

POLICY INITIATIVES FOR THE IT INDUSTRY IN KERALA

A number of policy initiatives have been taken by the state government to leverage the benefits of the IT boom starting with the IT Policy of 1998. It introduced various labour policy exemptions to the IT industry. Various concessions and incentives were also announced. It was followed by the policies of 2001, 2007, 2012 and latest IT draft policy of 2017. The major drive of these policies was basically to make Kerala an IT destination. A second aspect of these policies was to make digital technology for overall development of the state and to ensure quick and efficient delivery of all essential services to bridge the digital divide. The major initiative was to develop world-class infrastructure of international standards. Another policy prescription included a number of tax and duty exemptions and financial incentives as well as concessional rates of tariffs.

The IT policy of 2012 has given special emphasis to promote human resource development by strengthening Indian Institute of Information Technology and Management-Kerala (IIITM-K), Thiruvananthapuram, an ICT academy, an innovation zone, 'host' institutes of technology and changes in the curriculum of engineering colleges (Government of Kerala, 2013). Kerala Technology Startup policy 2014 is also rather highly optimistic in 'reversing the brain drain'. Further, it states the vision of developing a world-class scientific and technology ecosystem that would empower and enable its youth to pursue their dreams within the state. The major objective of the policy is to build an entrepreneurial society in Kerala. Technopark Business Incubation Centre was started in 2006 and 150 start-ups have been established in the last six years.

The draft policy (2017) also envisages creation of 1 crore sq. feet of space for IT and services, and to create 2.5 lakh employment.

It also proposes to make the state 100 per cent e-literate and use ICT in all walks of life and ensure inclusive development of society. Further, it intends to consolidate the activities of all IT parks (Technopark, InfoPark and Cyberpark) under brand 'Kerala IT'.

While the policies sound good, it has to be read along with the IT policy announcement of other states including Bihar to make the state an IT destination. The various states are competing with each other to woo the IT firms to come to their state and most of the states are providing similar kind of concessions, tax holidays and investment incentives. The targets fixed in terms of employment and revenues are often not realistic.

PERFORMANCE OF THE IT AND SERVICES SECTOR IN KERALA

Technopark was one of the first IT parks in the country established in 1990. It is an autonomous organisation fully owned by the Government of Kerala. It is Capability Maturity Model Integration (CMMI) Level 4; ISO9001:2008 (specifies requirements for a quality management system where an organisation); ISO 14001; 2004 and Occupational Health and Safety Assessment Series (OHSAS) 18001; 2007 certified. There are over 350 companies employing 50,000 professionals. The policy initiative in providing infrastructure has been successful with 9.33 million sq. feet built-up space completed and 3.5 million sq. feet in progress in 760 acres of land. Another notable achievement has been the growth of Infopark, Kochi, which was established in 2004 with 4 million sq. feet built-up space in 100 acres. Phase 2 expects to provide 8 million sq. feet in 160 acres of land. There has also been the positive note of growth of private parks of Infosys, the Leela Group, Lulu and Cognizant Techno parks, which fosters coexistence of public and private IT parks.

A major lacuna in the 1990s in IT sector in the state was the absence of market leaders. This has been overcome by the entry of leaders in the sector including Wipro, Infosys, Cognizant, Oracle and US software to mention a few. Now it has to be seen whether these large IT firms see Kerala as a spillover to tier-2 and tier-3 cities just to overcome the crowding and congestion problems faced in other cities or are they expanding with a restructured model of growth with disruptive technologies.

In terms of number of firms, we don't find a major growth from 2001 to 2016 as the number of firms increased from 229 to 350 during the period.

It is also important to look at the growth of revenues compared to other states.

Table 10.3 shows that Karnataka still holds its pre-eminent position followed by Maharashtra. Telangana (former Andhra Pradesh) followed

Table 10.3 *Statewise Software Exports Made by Registered Units Through Software Technology Parks of India*

State	2007–2008	2008–2009	2009–2010	2010–2011	2012–2013	2014–2015
Delhi	5,264	1,762	1,892	1,776	1,900	2,217
Haryana	10,960	12,410	14,795	13,650	15,363	17,857
Karnataka	–	–	–	70,240	95,048	109,797
Kerala	1,201	1,803	1,956	2,071	2,240	2,867
Maharashtra	35,374	42,360	45,709	49,873	49,796	61,314
Tamil Nadu	38,295	38,355	41,363	42,100	29,182	35,000
Telangana	26,122	31,039	27,665	28,674	34,492	39,185
Uttar Pradesh	10,695	10,264	10,590	10,281	13,194	13,740
West Bengal	4,500	5,129	5,441	5,665	6,030	7,015
All India	–	–	–	228,646	251,497	293,796

Source: STPI reports.

by Tamil Nadu comes second and third. The position of the five states has not changed ever since 2001. Compared with 2001, all the three South Indian states have grown more than 10 times in revenue by 2015. But Kerala has lagged behind all other states as the revenue increased from 300 crores in 2001–2002 to 2,867 crores in 2015. Again looking at the annual growth rates, though there was a 50 per cent increase in 2007 to 2008, it decelerated to 8 per cent and 5.9 per cent in the following years. The global recession from 2008 has a negative influence on all the major states.

It will be of interest to see whether the relative positions of the states have changed in the last 15 years.

The four South Indian states together account for 62 per cent of total revenue (Table 10.4). Of this, Kerala's contribution was less than 1 per cent. In terms of the acres of land allotted, square feet of space built, investment in terms of crores of rupees, one has to assess the benefits against the costs. The PC-based, people-based growth of industry and physical capital may not provide the competitive edge but more investment in human capital that will be required.

Table 10.4 *Share of Various States in IT Revenues (2014–2015)*

State	Percentage Share
Delhi	0.75
Haryana	6.0
Karnataka	37.3
Kerala	0.97
Maharashtra	20.86
Tamil Nadu	11.91
Telangana	13.33
Uttar Pradesh	4.4
West Bengal	2.3

Source: STPI reports.

CONCLUSION

The IT industry in Kerala has not been able to compete with the neighbouring states of Karnataka, Tamil Nadu and Telangana. On the policy front, the various announcements made look very charming but the state still remains in a state of infancy in terms of employment and revenues. The IT sector is facing challenges globally especially due to the recessionary trend, cutting down costs and profits along with local employment issues. The central and state governments have to be proactive in supporting this industry. The various announcements in the last two budgets of the central government were generally welcomed by the sector. R. Chandrasekhar, president of NASSCOM, welcomed the union budget for 2015 as it was 'comprehensive' and appreciated the government's focus on start-ups and technology. Bhaskar Pramanik, Chairman, Microsoft India, remarked that the budget reiterated the major programmes and initiatives that had been announced—Make in India, Skill India, Swachh Bharat and Digital India.

The need of the hour seems to be shifting to a remodelled IT growth based on innovation and technology, and on the other hand the boost of digitisation drives in all spheres to give fillip to the domestic market. Along with IT development, the focus also should lie on the BPO and KPO segments which offer great potential for the state. As mentioned in the ASSOCHAM report, the potential solution is expanding into tier-2 and tier-3 cities. There is sufficient untapped potential in these smaller cities but the question is how to leverage on these opportunities without adversely affecting organisational and logistical effectiveness. The digitisation drives as well as an ICT dissemination initiative of the Kerala government is promising. The emphasis on start-ups and incubators is a welcome move. Promotion of private IT parks is also a good initiative. The future of IT depends on championing the innovation and technology mode and remodelling the IT growth path investing human capital based on cloud, AI, big data analytics and KPO.

REFERENCES AND SELECT BIBLIOGRAPHY

Ahluwalia, M. (2000, 6 May). Economic performance of states in post reforms period. *Economic and Political Weekly, 35*(19), 1637–1648.

Arora, A., Arunachalam, V. S., Asundi, J., & Fernandes, R. (2001). The Indian software services industry. *Research Policy, 30*(8), 1267–1287.

Arrow, K. J. (1962). Economic welfare and the allocation of resources to invention. In Richard R. Nelson (ed), *The rate and direction of inventive activity: Economic and social factors* (pp. 609–626). New Jersey: Princeton University Press.

ASSOCHAM. (2013, 2 April). Current scenario of Indian KPO industry. Discussion Paper.

———. (2017). *IT, ITES research plateau in job creation; real estate, retail may drive employment.* ASSOCHAM-Thought Arbitrage Research Institute (TARI) Paper. June 3, 2017. Retrieved on 9 May 2018, from http://www.assocham.org/newsdetail.php?id=6310

Business Line. (2017). News item published on 3 August 2017. Retrieved on 9 May 2018, from https://www.thehindubusinessline.com/todays-paper/tp-others/its-back-to-school-for-it-workers/article9799325.ece

Dataquest. (2015, 5 August). *DQ top 20: Meet India's top 100 IT companies.* Retrieved 29 March 2018, from http://www.dqindia.com/dq-top20-meet-indias-top-100-it-companies/

Grilliches, Z. (1957). Hybrid zone: An exploration in the economics of technological change. *Econometrica, 25*(4), 501–522.

Government of Kerala. (2013). *Kerala IT policy 2012.* Thiruvananthapuram: Department of Information Technology.

Joseph, T. (2008). *Software industry in South India* (Unpublished PhD thesis). University of Kerala.

Kumar, N. (2001). Indian software industry development, international and national perspective. *Economic and Political Weekly, 36*(45), 4278–4290.

Mansfield, E. (1968). *Industrial research and technological innovation.* New York, NY: WW Norton.

Mohan, S. (1995). Global competitivity for Kerala industries. In Proceedings of the 7th Kerala Science Congress, Thiruvananthapuram: Kerala State Council for Science, Technology and Environment (KSCSTE).

Narasimhan, R. (1985). *Guidelines for software development in developing countries* (Report No. UNIDO/IS.439). Vienna: UNIDO.

NASSCOM. (2012). The IT–BPO sector in India—Strategic review. New Delhi, 8 February 2012, pp. 1–19. Retrieved on 9 May 2018, from https://www.net/nasscom/itbposector-in-Indiastrategicreview2012

———. (2017, 22 June). *IT–BPM industry in India: Sustaining growth and investing for the future.* Retrieved on 29 March 2018, from http://www.nasscom.in/sites/default/files/NASSCOM_Annual_Guidance_Final_22062017.pdf

NASSCOM. (Various years). www.nasscom.org

Porter, M. (1990). *The competitive advantage of nations.* New York, NY: The Free Press.

Saxenian, A. (1994). *Regional advantage; culture and competition in Silicon Valley and Route 128.* Cambridge, MA: Harvard University Press.

Schware, R. (1987). Software industry in the third world: Policy guidelines, institutional options and constraints. *World Development, 15*(10/11), 1249–1394.

———. (1992). Software industry entry strategy for developing countries: A walking on two legs proposition. *World Development, 20*(2), 143–164.

Solow, R. (1957). Technical change and the aggregate production function. *Review of Economics and Statistics, 39*(3), 313–320.

Sood, V. (2017, 1 August). *Infosys, TCS, Tech Mahindra see workforce shrink for the first time.* Retrieved on 29 March 2018, from https://www.livemint.com/Industry/UbruIMQLdE5tzyuUR1f8CO/Infosys-TCS–Tech-Mahindra-see-workforce-shrink-for-the-fi.html

STPI. (Various years). STPI reports. Retrieved on 20 May 2018, from http://www.blr.stpi.in/stpi-online-reporting.html

Subrahmanian, K. K., & Pillai, M. (1985). Kerala's industrial backwardness: Exploration of alternative hypotheses. *Economic and Political Weekly, 25*(21), 557–592.

Vijaybhaskar, M., Rothboeck, S., & Gayathri, V. (2001). Labour in the new economy: Case of the Indian software industry. *The Indian Journal of Labour Economics, 44*(1), 39–54.

World Bank. (1999). *Knowledge for development* (World Development Report, 1998–99). New York: Oxford University Press.

World Economic Forum. (2013–2014). *Global competitiveness report.* Geneva: World Economic Forum.

Chapter 11

Development of Power Sector in Kerala

N. Vijayamohanan Pillai

INTRODUCTION

There has been a universal unanimity in recognising the operational and financial inefficiency of the Indian power sector as the causative and promotional strains in the background of (power sector) reforms. Though the State Electricity Boards (SEBs) were statutorily required to function as autonomous service-cum-commercial corporations, they were required, in line with the letters sans spirit of the Venkataraman Committee Report of 1964, to subserve the socio-economic policies of the state and hence not to view power development exclusively from the perspectives of profits or return, as also not to put a heavy tariff burden on the consumers for purposes of replacement of assets and loan redemption. Thus, there was no need whatsoever on the part of the SEBs, at least till late 1970s, to earn a return on their capital and to contribute internal resources to capacity expansion. This unaccountability culture in turn led to gross inefficiency at all levels—technical, institutional and organisational, as well as financial, which in turn got reflected in avoidable cost escalations. This in the face of an irrational and uncompensated subsidised pricing practice left the SEBs in general with negative internal resources. At the same time, the traditional sources of investment funds—government loans and subventions—were fast draining, and the so-called 'fiscal crisis' at the turn of the 1990s facilitated the ushering in of the ideologies of restructuring. Funds had now begun to flow into the Indian power sector from a number of leading international financial institutions (FIs) on stringent conditionalities of restructuring. Though Kerala had remained, to a good extent, impervious to the incursions of such agencies upon the structure of the SEB, finally it had to follow suit and restructure itself as a company.

This chapter in this context discusses these issues, especially since 2000. It should be stressed at the outset that we have already shown that the problems confronting the SEBs are just internal to them, and hence what the system requires is not any market-oriented restructuring, but an essence-specific reform that can remove the impediments that stand in the way of the SEBs' improved performance (Kannan & Pillai, 2002). What follows essentially flows from this fact. The next section gives the Kerala scenario, its plight over time in growth and performance, in terms especially of a lack of planning, up to 2000, as a background for the study. The third section discusses its experiences since 2000, and the concluding section presents some alternatives to the so-called power sector reforms.

THE KERALA POWER SECTOR: GROWTH, PERFORMANCE AND REFORM BEFORE 2000

Electrification in Kerala began with its first hydroelectric generator of 200 kW run in a private tea estate (the Kanan Devan Hills Plantations Company) at Munnar in the high ranges in the then Travancore area in 1906. It took more than two decades after that for the government to come to the scene by commissioning (on 25 February 1929) a 5 MW thermal station in Trivandrum exclusively for the royal and administrative uses. The first public sector power project, designed on a large scale for commercial uses, in Kerala came on line in March 1940 with the first unit of 5 MW of Pallivasal hydroelectric power station. Within the next decade, five more units were added to the project to increase its installed capacity (IC) to 37.5 MW. Sabarigiri hydropower station of 340 MW of IC, commissioned in 1966–1967, was the first (of the two) major power project in Kerala. Idukki, with 780 MW of IC and commissioned in 1976 (I Stage) and in 1985 and 1986 (II Stage), is the largest hydropower station in Kerala. These two stations together constitute about 55 per cent of the total state sector hydropower IC of the 34 stations (2046.15 MW as in 2015–2016) in Kerala even today.

The Kerala State Electricity Board (KSEB), the second SEB to be set up on 31 March 1957 under the Electricity (Supply) Act, 1948, with the prime objective of rationalisation of power development at the state level, inherited an IC of 93.5 MW that rose to 1,995 MW (excluding the National Thermal Power Project [NTPC] and private projects) by 1999–2000, as against an estimated requirement of about 3,160 MW, as per the 14th Annual Power Survey (APS). However, the growth of the dependable, firm, power capacity of this hydro-dominant system was from 58.2 MW to 1,000.19 MW during the same period. That this represents an average annual compound growth rate of only 6.68 per cent against a minimum possible growth rate of 10 per cent of demand speaks volumes, though very generally, for the history of inadequacy of the system.

Failures in Planning

Facts do corroborate that the system growth in Kerala has never been up to the mark of potential requirement. Till 1966, the KSEB had been restricting new connections. The low accessibility (the system being open to the few rich only) along with these restrictions had rendered the system a much smaller one involving, in turn, slow and low growth. In fact, at the start of the Third Five-Year Plan (FYP, 1961–1966), Kerala system, even though small, experienced a shortage of 6 MW in firm power capacity (FPC), and at the end of the period, as much as 75 MW, resulting in major power cuts, despite energy import from Tamil Nadu (Government of Kerala, 1984, p. 22). The commissioning of the Sabarigiri Project in 1966 and 1967 eased the situation to such an incredible extent that the KSEB and the government suddenly found the system a power surplus one. Thence started the much-praised energy export era, and the KSEB also became liberal in giving new connections. Conveniently forgotten here were the dimensional realities of the system pregnant with threatening consequences—that the suddenly discovered surplus was the apparent result of the time-relative smallness of the consumption parameters capable of fast growth.

After four years, in 1972, Kuttiadi Project added 28 MW to the FPC, which, it can be seen, was not enough to contain the actual demand. However, the surplus euphoria continued, and export of energy picked up momentum, but at the cost of internal consumption, which continued to increase at a decreasing and low rate. Thus, in spite of the claims of being liberal in giving connections, electricity consumption in the state remained low and the system was painted rosy of surplus.

The inflated complacency reached its ne plus ultra with the commissioning of the Idukki (Stage I) Project in 1976, and the authorities now came down completely to rest on their oars, leaving the system seized by an export frenzy. Even with an average-designed generation potential of 4,730 million units (MU) (i.e., FPC of 540 MW) only, Kerala generated more than 5,000 MU annually during the four years from 1978–1979

> by slightly over-burdening of the generators, cutting short or even skipping the maintenance shutdowns of machines at the scheduled intervals and not keeping a stand-by or reserve generating capacity to meet an emergency due to pressing power demand in the Southern region, which would definitely tell on the life of the plants in the long run. (Government of Kerala, 1984, p. 25)

The state consumption still remained pathetically low, in spite of impressive growth in connections and connected load.

It should be noted that the 'monsoon betrayal' of the 1980s was, in fact, a blessing in disguise to some extent to the power consumption trajectory in the state. As the export frenzy subsided, internal consumption, put under leash during the export era, broke loose gradually and picked up an increasing momentum. It is evidenced in the time path of the power consumption in Kerala, which, after the 1980s, began to increase at an increasing rate much higher than during the previous period. Thus, after 1966, when the KSEB became somewhat liberal in providing connections, the number of electricity customers increased at an average annual compound growth rate of nearly 11 per cent and the connected load, at 8.5 per cent till 1980, but the power consumption grew at a rate of nearly 6 per cent only.

Planning per se has been absent for the long run also. What is technically more relevant and essentially significant for a hydropower system is its FPC, not just its IC. Then comparing the demand to be met by the system with the FPC would be more reasonably and reliably appropriate. Wide gap between IC and FPC is sheer waste of investment, unless timely FPC augmentation is carried out, and sadly this is the Kerala experience. By 1976 (with the commissioning of the Idukki Stage I project), FPC was 425 MW (42 per cent of the IC) only, equivalent to 3,723 MU of energy generation potential. On the other hand, the total storage capacity of all the commissioned hydel reservoirs was equivalent to only 3,365 MU, the difference being accounted for by the run-of-the-river-flow of water during the monsoons. The average generation potential was just enough, ceteris paribus, for at the most two normal years against a state (internal) average load growing at 10 per cent per annum.

Inordinate investment inertia reigned not only in IC expansion programmes but also in FPC augmentation programmes, such that the wasteful wide gap between the two persisted. Of the two large hydro-projects, Sabarigiri and Idukki, the former has at present a FPC of 153 MW (just 51 per cent of the IC, even after more than 20 years of its existence), and the latter, of 280 MW (a meagre 36 per cent of the IC). Sabarigiri augmentation of FPC (from 138.5 MW in 1967 to 153 MW) took about 15 years to be materialised! So did Idukki Stage III augmentation (by about 43 MW) also. As far back as in 1981, the Economic Review (Government of Kerala, 1982, pp. 75–76; 1983, p. 72) accused 'labour problems, contract failures, rehabilitation problems due to the enactment of the Forest Conservation Act, 1980 and the resultant physical obstruction caused by the local settlers, etc.', of contributing to 'the slippage of the earlier completion schedule'. Other four diversion projects (namely, Azhutha, Vazhikkadavu, Kuttiar and Vadakkeppuzha), works on which started during 1987 to 1991 also are entangled even at present in such dangerous time overrun. Thus, the KSEB as well as the government as its controller has functionally failed in effecting a development-based perspective planning not only for IC expansion in correspondence with growing demand but also for FPC augmentation to an adequate extent of the available IC itself (a detailed analysis of the time- and cost-overrun of the power projects in Kerala is given in the study of Kannan & Pillai [2001]).

The hydropower potential of Kerala is estimated at 2,301 MW at 60 per cent load factor. That about 76 per cent of this has already been harnessed might be taken as a surprising feat. But wait and consider the case of Tamil Nadu with a hydropower potential of a mere 1,206 MW (at 60 per cent load factor) against an actual hydropower IC of nearly 2,000 MW (as in 1997–1998)! While Kerala has remained utterly apathetic to the wasteful flowing away of its hydro resources, Tamil Nadu has successfully managed to make full use even of the interstate hydro resources available to it.

The price paid by Kerala for such failure or absence itself of a perspective planning mechanism has been immense in terms of power shortage for quite a long time. Most distressing is the fact that even during this pinching period of power famine, both the KSEB and the government have continued to be negligent, and the public at large indifferent. During the 20 years since 1976–1977 (when Idukki Stage I was commissioned), Kerala had added to its IC only a meagre 482 MW. And in the later 10 years (since 1986–1987, after commissioning Idukki II Stage and Idamalayar), a paltry 17 MW! Since the commissioning of the Idukki project, Kerala has been too unfortunate to launch another major power project. Moreover, a large number of (about 16) power projects, with a generation potential of nearly 2,000 MU (i.e., about 353 MW, at 60 per cent load factor, roughly equivalent to the state's then power deficit), have remained locked in at various points of unwarranted time overrun due mainly to labour militancy and contractual corruption; both the KSEB and the government have failed to rise to the occasion of obligations by strictly and discreetly dealing with the problems with a firm political will for common good.

A Shrinking Coffer

Thus, both investment inertia and prolonged lag in investment fruition have come to stay, standing in the way of the timely required capacity expansion. Funds scarcity in financing power development has been explicitly recognised as responsible for this sorry state of affairs. The unwarranted drying-up of the conventional source of funds, namely, the state, is generally accused of having led in part to the crisis. Though the plan outlay for power development was on the rise in money terms, from ₹118.5 million in First FYP to ₹26,710 million in Ninth FYP, its share in total outlay was on the decline, from 39.5 per cent to 26.5 per cent, respectively. In Fourth FYP, it was only 10.5 per cent and in Sixth and Seventh Plans, a little less than 20 per cent. However, there is another facet in this regard that merits serious account, but has been left unaccounted for, that is, even this allegedly inadequate outlay was not utilised fully for all but four FYP periods. Actually the expenditure far exceeded the plan outlay in these four FYP periods, the Third, Fourth and Eighth FYP having an expenditure ratio of around 140 per cent of plan outlay and the Sixth FYP, about 115 per cent. This specifically shows that funds scarcity was not the exclusive cause of the problem, though it was a significant one.

A Cash-strapped KSEB

While on the one hand, the government has been consistently shirking its power development obligations on the excuse of an apparently shrinking coffer, the only alternative (or contributing) source of funds available, namely, the internal resources of the KSEB itself, on the other hand, has remained weak, though the surplus of revenue over expenditure of the KSEB did remain positive for all but five years (in the late 1980s and early 1990s) after 1957–1958. The financial morbidity of the KSEB, like most of other SEBs, has often called for huge sums of subventions from the government even for financing its normal activities. Informed opinions in pursuit of the culprits behind the financial sickness of the SEBs have unanimously converged onto a single point of inadequate tariff levels and required continuously monitored upward revisions of the tariff. We have refuted such flimsy argument, at the same time maintaining the valid criticism against the unscientific pricing practice prevalent at present. We have shown that there do exist sufficient scopes for efficiency improvement at various points of operation in the power system that could potentially reduce the supply cost substantially (Kannan & Pillai, 2002). Thus, for instance, it has been shown that with some, quite reasonably achievable, improvement in the operational, transmission and distribution (T&D) and manpower deployment efficiencies, as well as with 1:1 debt–equity capital structure, the KSEB's unit cost of electricity supply in 1997–1998 could have been reduced by about 43.3 per cent. This along with the given average revenue realised in that year would have yielded a unit commercial profit of about 16 paise per unit of energy sold, instead of the reported loss of about 68 paise per unit! And still there remain resourceful rooms for efficiency improvement at all other levels of functioning. This plainly points to the poignant fact that if the power system had performed efficiently, it could have, along with a scientific tariff structure, generated internal resources sufficient for financing capacity expansion programmes, thus also dispensing with the avoidable leaning on the state exchequer. Again our analysis there suggests to question the logic and ethics of the widespread demand for tariff rate rises, proposed to be required to contain the increasing supply costs and thus to save the SEBs from the crunch, in the background of the continuously accumulating revenue arrears on the other side, that in turn utterly defeats the very purpose of the tariff revision. The revenue arrears of the KSEB in 1997–1998 was about 41 per cent of the annual sales turnover (nearly five months' sales revenue thus being locked up with the consumers). Regular and timely collection of all receivables could increase the KSEB's liquidity and avert the excessive dependency on loan or subsidy.

This financial mis-(or non-)management also has been a legacy for the KSEB. As far back as in 1967, the Government of Kerala appointed a Finances Enquiry Commission 'to enquire into the financial position of the Board' upon the suggestion of the Central Public Accounts Committee (1966–1967) that criticised 'the financial discipline in the working of the Kerala State Electricity Board' as 'somewhat slack', in their 67th Report (para 9.96). A number of recommendations to revamp and thus to rejuvenate the financial management of the KSEB proposed by the Commission fell, unheeded and unheard, to dust. Commissions after Commissions, in no dearth and in real earnest, have come and gone, and recommendations followed suit to dust in the sheer force of habit.

And All Leading to Reforms!

Against this gloomy, but apparently complicated, background should one discuss the implications of the imposition of power sector reforms. Things had come to such a pass that reforms were looked upon as the sole sure cure-all. However, the waves of power sector reforms that had swept the world over and many parts of India as well had left only moderate imprints till recently in Kerala's power sector. It was acknowledged in the then state government's electric power policy of 1998 (the first of its kind in Kerala!) that the huge capital investment required in the power sector imposes heavy burden on the KSEB with its weaker financial standing, leading to heavy reliance on the FIs. If tariffs were not regularly revised or arrears in revenue collections built up, the borrowings would have to be more. Given the financial status of the KSEB and its track record, it was found doubtful if external loans of this order could be raised. The situation was thus made ripe for some attempts on reforms.

The E. Balanandan Committee to study the development of electricity in Kerala (1997) recommended to set up a government-owned company, namely, The Kerala Power Development and Finance Corporation Ltd., to develop, finance and manage generation of electricity, construction and installation of power stations and transmission lines in Kerala. The Task Force on Policy Issues Relating to Power Sector and Power Sector Reforms (1997) and the Expert (under K. P. Rao) Committee to review the tariff structure of the KSEB (1998), both constituted by the State Planning Board, provided detailed discussion on reforms processes that to a great extent reflect the (then Marxist Party-led) government's ideological prejudice and political compulsions.

In the state's electric power policy, it was clearly stated that the (then Marxist Party-led) government had no intention of unbundling or of privatising the SEB. The suggestion to corporatise the three divisions of generation, T&D was also rejected. However, it was acknowledged that there should be significant changes in the structure and approach of the KSEB. The Task Force had, inter alia, stressed that a major change in the work culture in KSEB be required to eliminate the inefficiency inherent in it at present and recommended that as a first step in this direction, the three operations under its control, namely, generation, T&D, be compartmentalised and made as profit centres, fully accountable for the results.

The then government accordingly initiated necessary steps to restructure the functioning of the KSEB in terms of 'profit centres' at the levels of generation, T&D; three regional profit centres with headquarters at Thiruvananthapuram, Ernakulam and Kozhikode also were established. These regional centres would have the control over the electricity supply in the state. The profit centres would have wide autonomous powers in decision-making in several areas including capital investment, resource generation, appointments of personnel and so on.

Though the government promised all the help and cooperation to the independent power producers, only one project (one mini hydropower project of 12 MW at Maniyar owned by Tata Tea Estate, commissioned in 1994) came up in the private sector before 2000. In 1997, the then government proposed some ambitious plans to set up power projects in the private and public sectors within five years, with a total IC of 5,041 MW (including the Bombay Suburban Electricity Supply [BSES], NTPC and the KSEB's own thermal projects, works on which had already started that time). However, the fate of many of these projects is still not known. Despite the professed commitments and colourful plans, the required firm political will and sense of responsibility to value common good above everything else is conspicuously missing in our governments.

THE KERALA POWER SECTOR: GROWTH, PERFORMANCE AND REFORM AFTER 2000

The dawn of the new century had nothing to offer, despite the usual rosy slogans; and the Kerala power sector has continued on its lethargic linear trajectory. However, the period is marked by a number of significant, though cosmetic, changes in the name of power sector reforms.

The then (Congress Party-led) state government decided to swim along with the current, by joining the group of other 15 states in the country already engaged in radical power sector reforms at the terms and conditions of the central government; in August 2001, Kerala signed a memorandum of understanding (MoU) with the Union Power Ministry, expressing its willingness to undertake power sector reforms. As per the MoU, the KSEB was to be run on commercial lines and also to securitise all its dues to the central public sector undertakings (CPSUs). Such securitisation implies that the KSEB ensure that CPSU outstandings never cross the limit of two months' billing. And in return for its commitments, the state would be provided by the central government with funds from the Accelerated Power Development Programme (APDP) for renovation and modernisation of thermal and hydro plants of the state and for improvement of sub-T&D and metering in the identified circles in the state. The MoU required the state government to 'desegregate' the KSEB to make it accountable in respect of its functions of generation, T&D; accordingly, the KSEB was divided into three 'independent profit centres' having separate administrative set-up and accounts in April 2002.

A major development during this period was the establishment of the Kerala State Electricity Regulatory Commission (KSERC), a statutory organisation of quasi-judicial nature, in 2002, designed to bring in an effective and efficient regulatory process in the power sector in the state. The Commission was constituted under Subsection (1) of Section 17 of the Electricity Regulatory Commissions Act, 1998 and came under the purview of the Electricity Act, 2003, with effect from 10 June 2003 when Electricity Regulatory Commissions Act, 1998 was repealed.

In September 2008, the government went ahead by transferring all assets and liabilities of KSEB to be vested with the state government in line with the provisions of Electricity Act, 2003 and the central government directives. Subsequently, on 14 January 2011, the assets and liabilities were re-vested with a fully owned government company, KSEB Limited (KSEBL) under the Companies Act, 1956. It should be stressed that these seemingly structural changes have had nothing to do with the fundamentals of the functioning of the power sector such that the same miserable state of affairs has continued intact. Tables 11.1 and 11.2 show some snapshots of this fact.

As already explained, IC, after accounting for the per cent reserve margin, has never been adequate to meet an ever-surging peak load on the system; as Table 11.1 shows, the recent years have experienced a maximum demand much higher than the IC itself! Moreover, what matters for a hydropower system is FPC that has always been in shortage compared with the demand. Coupled with continuous monsoon failures, this keeps the system trapped in a low level performance. This is very much evident in the high dependence on energy import. Power purchase constituted 80 per cent of the own generation in 2000–2001, and the dependence went up to such an extent that power import was 2.4 times the own generation in 2015–2016.

Table 11.1 *Performance of the Kerala Power System*

	Unit	1960–1961	1990–1991	2000–2001	2004–2005	2009–2010	2015–2016
IC	MW	132.5	1,477	2,420.68	2,623.86	2,752.96	2,880.18
Maximum demand (restricted)	MW	116.3	1,147.8	2,316	2,420	2,998	3,860
Own generation (gross)	MU	591	5,491	6,967.00	6,328.98	7,189.51	6,739.25
Power purchase (gross)	MU	56.8	1,303.83	5,543.00	6,390.79	10,204.21	16,448.36
Energy sale to other states	MU	11.6	4.726	0	0	53.90	53.48
Energy sale (within the state)	MU	505.6	5,331.86	10,319	9,384.40	13,971.09	19,460.32
Total sale including export	MU	517.2	5,336.726	10,319	9,384.40	14,024.99	19,513.80
Energy loss	MU	130.60	1,458.10	2,191.00	3,335.37	3,368.73	3,673.81
Per capita consumption	kWh	30	185	311.67	289	420	565
Number of consumers	Lakh	1.74994	34.49888	64.46	77.99	97.43	116.68
Connected load	MW	311.343	4,642.68	8,551.00	10,333.51	15,866.55	20,980.53
Street lights	No.	82,645	521,297	763,912	908,016	1,148,220	1,407,024
Irrigation pump sets	No.	4,615	218,446	392,295	412,602	437,877	500,082
Total revenue from sale of power	₹ Crore	2.996	280.468	1,811.13	2,917.36	4,747.17	10,914.44
Average realisation	Ps/kwh	8.64	53	169.41	311.17	338.03	541.20
Cost per unit sent out	Ps	35.81	70.34	223.75	289	438	587

Source: KSEB, Power System Statistics, Different Issues.

Table 11.2 *Growth Rates of the Kerala Power System*

	Average Annual Growth Rates (%)					
	1960s	1970s	1980s	1990s	2000s	Since 2010– 2011
IC	15.66	7.08	4.29	3.71	1.44	0.07
Maximum demand	10.87	8.83	5.09	6.55	2.91	4.36
Generation	13.25	9.62	−0.10	3.03	0.35	−1.75
Sales (internal)	10.60	6.57	6.95	7.04	3.42	5.99
Sales (total)	12.90	10.04	1.44	7.04	3.47	5.86
Energy loss	11.03	7.94	6.14	3.67	3.84	3.19
Energy import	−10.50	37.39	42.56	12.93	7.02	9.37
Total revenue	19.01	20.95	10.18	24.98	11.30	15.99
Average revenue	5.41	9.91	8.62	16.50	7.98	8.85
Average cost	6.81	9.25	13.08	14.44	7.75	4.73
Per capita consumption	8.34	4.76	5.62	5.53	3.37	5.32
No. of consumers	11.83	10.52	7.37	6.28	4.70	2.87
Connected load	11.42	7.68	7.81	4.97	7.11	4.69

Source: KSEB, Power System Statistics, Different Issues.

Note: The last column is up to 2015–2016.

Kerala has at present 34 hydropower projects with an IC of 2,046.15 MW (equivalent to an annual generation capacity of 7,148.28 MU) and two state-owned thermal projects of 234 MW (Brahmapuram and Kozhikode) and a thermal project of NTPC at Kayamkulam of 350 MW; a wind farm (Kanjikode) of 2 MW and three solar projects of 1.156 MW also add to the power sector capacity in Kerala, along with three private wind farms of 41.25 MW, eight private sector hydro-electric projects of 58.16 MW, four private sector thermal projects of 198.90 MW and one private solar project of 13 MW.

The total IC in March 2016 was thus 2,880.20 MW, with a hydel capacity of 2,104.3 MW (73 per cent), thermal capacity of 718.46 MW (25 per cent), wind capacity of 43.27 MW (1.5 per cent) and solar capacity of 14.15 MW (0.5 per cent). As of 2015–2016, generation from the KSEBL's own plants provided only 34.5 per cent (6,739.25 MU) of the total energy requirement of 19,513.8 MU. Import from central generating stations, independent power producers and others accounted for the rest (16,448.36 MU) of the total requirement of energy, that is, about 84 per cent of the energy sale.

It is a relieving fact that Kerala is endowed with a vast small hydro-power potential, estimated to the tune of about 700 MW. With the objective of inducing private investment to harness green energy from these natural resources, the state government has issued a number of guidelines, especially under the umbrella of the Electricity Act of 2003, the National Electricity Policy of 2005 and the Tariff Policy of 2006. In 2012, the state government formulated the Kerala Small Hydro Power Policy, applicable to projects of IC up to 25 MW, with a view to harnessing green and clean natural resource in the state for environmental benefits and energy security. There are as many as 20 small hydro-projects in the state sector with a total capacity of 132.4 MW and eight projects in the private sector with a capacity of 58.16 MW as of March 2016. It is worth noting that out of the 20 small hydro-projects, only six (with an IC of 33.75 MW) have come up in the state sector since 2012, the year of the Kerala Small Hydro Power Policy, and only four (with a capacity of 13.66 MW) out of the eight in the private sector.

A distressing fact in this respect is the growing energy loss; for example, in 2015–2016, the total loss amounted to 22.34 per cent of the power purchased! It should be noted that the Indian power sector now uses a new concept of aggregate technical and commercial losses (AT&C), which captures technical and commercial losses in the network and is a true indicator of total losses in the system, instead of the old term of T&D loss. T&D loss in the Kerala system is reported to have come down to 14.37 per cent in 2015–2016 and AT&C loss to 15.71 per cent, the latter compared with 23.04 per cent (2013–2014) for all India. The KSEBL claims that since 2003–2004 onwards, AT&C loss has been considerably reduced by way of replacement of faulty meters, intensification of theft detection, installation of new substations and lines, and upgradation and modernisation of sub-T&D network through Accelerated Power Development Reforms Programme (APDRP; Government of Kerala, 2016, p. 302).

An indirect offshoot of such large-scale energy loss is the very small electricity consumption profile of the state, as rightly identified and pointed out by the state government itself as back as in 1967 (Government of Kerala, 1967, p. 62 [Annexure No. 1]). The smallness of the system gets reflected in the low per capita electricity consumption that has always remained much lower. For instance, in 1960–1961, the domestic and the industrial per capita electricity consumptions in Kerala were only 3 units and 23.5 units, while in Tamil Nadu, these were 4.5 and 27 units, and in Karnataka, 3.2 and 31 units, respectively. In 1970–1971, these were—Kerala: 4.8 and 60.3; Tamil Nadu: 8.3 and 74.9; Karnataka: 7.9 and 83.4 (CMIE, 1988). In 2015–2016, the per capita electricity consumption in Kerala was only 565 units (Government of Kerala, 2016, p. 300) as against an all-India average of 1,075 units (Government of India, 2017, p. 31). The very low industrial load in the state might also partly explain this low consumption profile; during the 1990s, industrial energy consumption increased by just 2.92 per cent per year, and in the 2000s, by 1.9 per cent per year; since then it has grown by only 2.4 per cent per year (till 2015–2016). The increased incidence of outages (interruptions) might have also affected the state consumption.

Kerala power sector is now predominantly domestic-consumer-based; in 1970–1971, domestic consumption accounted for only 4.34 per cent of the total consumption; but by the start of the 2000s, the share grew to 76.4 per cent, and it reached 78.2 per cent in 2015–2016 (Table 11.3).

In terms of the number of the consumers, the predominance has always been outstanding, though it decreased from about 71 per cent in 1970–1971 to 51.3 per cent in 2015–2016. It is highly significant that this, in fact, has helped Kerala achieve the distinction of being a fully electrified state, as declared on 29 May 2017 by the government. However, it is worth noting that the sales revenue from the domestic consumers is still only 36 per cent of the total revenue.

Where supply side constraints are stronger, as in the case of the Kerala power system, demand side management assumes much significance. However, here also the record has not been encouraging. Almost all the expert committees on the power sector have unequivocally underlined the significance of the adoption of energy auditing

Table 11.3 *Pattern of Electricity Consumption*

	Percentage Share		
	Consumption	No. of Consumers	Revenue
1970–1971			
Domestic	4.34	70.99	18.78
Commercial	3.53	22.18	16.59
Industrial light and medium (L&M)	5.99	3.08	13.09
Industrial high tension (HT) & extra high tension (EHT)	59.94	0.04	25.40
Public lighting	1.08	0.22	4.39
Railway traction	0.00	0.00	0.00
Agricultural pumping	2.20	3.45	3.03
Others	22.92	0.04	18.73
Total	100.00	100.00	100.00
2000–2001			
Domestic	76.41	45.43	21.74
Commercial	15.79	8.02	20.90
Industrial L&M	1.72	6.28	9.86
Industrial HT & EHT	0.03	30.39	39.82
Public lighting	0.02	1.75	1.25
Railway traction	0.000047	0.38	0.44
Agricultural pumping	5.99	3.39	1.35
Others	0.03	4.35	4.64
Total	100.00	100.00	100.00
2015–2016			
Domestic	78.20	51.31	35.70
Commercial	16.48	14.12	23.35
Industrial L&M	1.17	5.69	7.12
Industrial HT & EHT	0.04	21.19	26.86
Public lighting	0.04	1.89	1.49
Railway traction	0.00008	1.10	1.15
Agricultural pumping	4.06	1.44	0.63
Others	0.00	3.26	3.71
Total	100.00	100.00	100.00

Source: KSEB, Power System Statistics, Different Issues.

on a regular basis in the entire system, but to no avail. An Energy Audit Cell was formed in 2007 for taking steps as per provisions of the Energy Conservation Act, 2001, but its activities have been largely confined only to conducting a few workshops! Another important programme recently implemented by the KSEBL was Labha Prabha, aiming to implement Domestic Efficient Lighting Programme (DELP) to promote energy conservation by replacing filament lamps and old fluorescent lamps with energy-efficient LED bulbs in households. It is expected that 75 lakh domestic consumers would be provided with two numbers of 9 W LED bulb during 2016–2017, which would result in about 350 MW reduction in the peak demand and 400 MW savings in energy consumption.

CONCLUSION

There is no gainsaying the fact that the Indian power sector badly needs reform; but an informed opinion would seldom equate reform with restructuring. And this is the message of the analysis in this chapter of the experiences of the Kerala power system. However, political manoeuvres are on in many of the states including Kerala to effect a semblance of some restructuring of the power sector. It is generally recognised that distribution is the weakest link in the whole structure of power supply system. The massive leakage from this inefficient outlet in the form of subsidised sales and distribution loss, including technical loss and theft, illegal drawal, etc., under protective patronage, have been steadily sapping the SEBs, thus taking them to a no-return point of forced reforms. Thus, plugging such leakage constitutes the urgent remedy for all the problems. And a general perception in the informed circle endorses immediate privatisation of the distribution sector projected as the only way out (e.g., see Morris, 2000). Tackling such leakage in many rural/suburban areas involves 'a law and order dimension as well' (Government of India, 1996, p. 59), and a populist government, so far in the habit of winking at (if not abetting) such criminal errancy, finds it difficult to come out on the front. The government saves its face by leaving everything to the private sector. Thus, the private distribution company in Odisha, 'the AES of USA is having to employ goon gangs to install meters' and to collect the dues (*The Hindu Business Line*, 31 March 2000). See how easy the problem is solved! A blatant sell-out of governmental obligations!

It is not that there is no alternative to such suicidal sell-out. There have been some informed suggestions on setting up cooperatives at local levels and entrusting them or the local bodies themselves with distribution responsibilities. For example, the Task Force constituted by the Kerala State Planning Board on policy issues relating to power sector and power sector reforms cites the good examples of Hukkeri Cooperative in Karnataka and Trissur Municipality in Kerala. The former is one among the 38 cooperatives in the country set up as conceived by the Rural Electrification Corporation. Power is supplied to these cooperatives at tariffs below the standard bulk rates such as to enable them to operate with a surplus. In Trissur Municipality area, a licencee under the control of the Municipality is engaged in electricity distribution in a very satisfactory manner. A number of countries have such alternative arrangements functioning efficiently.

All this should not be misconstrued, let us reiterate, as an unreasonable justification for the persistence of avoidable inefficiency in the performance of the SEBs. As we have already noted, the inefficiency problems are only internal to the system. There do remain rooms for remedial exercises meant to remove these problems inhibiting the SEBs' improved performance, that is, what the system requires is only an essence-specific (internal) reform—a reformed work culture under the leadership of an enlightened, committed, professional management, and the government should flourish and further—not a disastrous structural reform, as is fetishistically made out now.

REFERENCES AND SELECT BIBLIOGRAPHY

CMIE. (1988, September). *Basic statistics relating to the Indian economy* (Vol. 2: States). Bombay: CMIE.

Government of India. (1996). *The India infrastructure report* (Vol. III, Sector Reports). Report submitted by the Expert Group on the Commercialisation of Infrastructure Projects for Ministry of Finance. New Delhi: NCAER.

———. (2017). *Power sector—January 2017.* New Delhi: Central Electricity Authority, Ministry of Power. Retrieved on 2 April 2018, from http://www.cea.nic.in/reports/monthly/executivesummary/2017/exe_summary-01.pdf

Government of Kerala. (1967, October). *Report of the Kerala State Electricity Board Finances Enquiry Commission (Single-Member Commission of P.S. Padmanabhan)*. Thiruvananthapuram: Government Press.

———. (1982). *Economic review: 1981*. Thiruvananthapuram: State Planning Board.

———. (1983). *Economic review: 1982*. Thiruvananthapuram: State Planning Board.

———. (1984, May). *Report of the High Level Committee on industry, trade and power* (Vol. III). Report on Power Development. Thiruvananthapuram: State Planning Board.

———. 2016. *Economic review (2016)*. Thiruvananthapuram: State Planning Board.

Kannan, K. P., & Pillai, N. V. (2001, June). *The political economy of public utilities—A study of the Indian power sector* (Working Paper No. 316). Thiruvananthapuram: Centre for Development Studies.

———. (2002). *Plight of the power sector in India: Inefficiency, reform and political economy*. Thiruvananthapuram: Centre for Development Studies.

The Hindu Business Line. (2000). Metering first step in reforms: Kumaramangalam. *The Hindu Business Line*, 31 March 2000, Chennai edition. Retrieved on 10 April 2018, from https://www.thehindubusinessline.com/2000/03/31/stories/143156mv.htm

Chapter 12

Development of Transport Sector in Kerala

Arun Shyamnath

The uniqueness of Kerala's geography and its development history have paved way for a transport system which consists of road transport, rail transport, air transport and water transport (inland and coastal). Currently, the transport system of Kerala consists of 2.05 lakh km of road, 1,588 km of railways, 1,687 km of inland waterways, 3 international airports and 18 ports. The transport sector in the state has witnessed steady and continuous growth post 2000, and certain trends and patterns are noticeable. The development of the transport sector during the recent years has been heavily in favour of roadways at the cost of other modes of transport. This has given rise to problems such as congestion, increasing pollution, increasing number of accidents and fatality, slow expansion and slow pace of transport.

This chapter tries to address the following objectives:

1. To study the growth and development of the transport sector in Kerala since 2000
2. To examine the constraints in development and the problems faced by different modes of transport
3. To analyse the emerging issues in the sector

The chapter has used the secondary data for analysis, and this includes government and private sources.

THE TRANSPORT SYSTEM AND ITS REGULATION

Transport helps in removing the distance barrier and plays a significant role in promoting national and global integration. An efficient transport system helps in increasing productivity and competitiveness of the economy and is considered indispensable for the social and economic development of any nation or region. The quality of life these days depends to a great extent on the quality of transport infrastructure. Hence, the demand for transport is derived demand—as income increases, demand for transport increases.

Kerala's transport sector has participation from public and private sectors. The public sector is involved in transport regulation, management and infrastructure creation. Private sector concentrates on providing transport services, consultancy and construction works. Recent years have seen increasing private participation with scope for more. Both central and state governments have played a key role in the development of the sector in the state, with contributions also from local governments. Policy is important for ensuring that the transport system meets social goals such as environmental sustainability, energy efficiency and social/economic inclusiveness (Planning Commission, 2014). Policy initiatives are undertaken in each of the modes by various levels of governments. Areas such as railways, national highways (NHs), shipping and navigation, major ports, airways fall within the jurisdiction of the central government. Items such as water, taxes (on the sale of petroleum products, on goods and passengers carried by road or on inland waterways or on vehicles) and tolls fall within the purview of state governments (Basu, 2011).

Kerala currently does not have a transport policy. A draft policy was submitted to the government in 2011 and further progress is awaited. The objective of the transport policy (as put forward by the draft) is to evolve a conducive transport regime for the state of Kerala, geared to meet requirements of faster mobility, safety, access to social and economic services and to minimise the impact of negative externalities.

ROADS

Road transport provides door-to-door connection and flexible movement of goods and passengers. Apart from being economical for short distances, it holds the capacity to provide personalised services, and its patronage by people in the state is on the rise. In Kerala, roads play a dominant role (for moving goods and passengers) over other modes of transportation owing to peculiarities of the state such as unique physiography, limited geographical area and widely scattered habitation with less rural–urban divide (Kerala State Planning Board, 2014). It also acts as the feeder service to the railways, airways, ports and inland waterways.

In Kerala, roads are maintained by various agencies such as Public Works Department (roads, bridges and NHs), local self-governments (LSG; such as panchayats, municipalities and corporations), irrigation, forests and railways. Roads in Kerala consist of three broad categories— NHs, state highways (SHs) and major district roads (MDRs) and village roads. Village roads are under the local bodies. There are two other types of roads—urban roads managed by urban bodies and project roads managed by respective authorities such as railway roads. Total road length in Kerala during 2015–2016 was 205,545.616 km (Table 12.1). This includes classified and non-classified roads as stipulated by the Indian Road Congress. Road density in the state is 528.8 km/100 sq. km and it is far ahead of the national average of 387 km/100 sq. km. The length of road per lakh population is 615.5 km.

Around 80,000 km of roads have been added in the state during the 15-year period post 2000–2001. In terms of absolute length, significant additions have been made in roads under panchayats which are village roads and they have benefitted due to generous funding from the centre through schemes such as Pradhan Mantri Gram Sadak Yojana (PMGSY) and Jawahar Rozgar Yojana (JRY). Over the 15-year period, only 221 km have been added to the NHs in the state which is very low considering progress made in other states.

In 2015–2016, the largest share (67 per cent) among roads in Kerala belonged to the panchayats (LSGs). But only about 54 per cent of these roads are pukka roads and upgrading the kaccha roads is one major requirement in road development in the state. Kerala has been a

Table 12.1 *Agency-wise Distribution of Roads in Kerala 2000–2001 and 2015–2016*

S. No.	Name of Department/ Agency	2000–2001		2015–2016		Percentage Change Since 2000–2001
		Length (km)	Percentage	Length (km)	Percentage	
1	Panchayats (LSGs)	87,094	69.2	139,380.410	67.81	60
2	PWD (R&B)	21,508	17.1	31,812.096	15.48	47
3	Municipalities	3,193.5	2.5	18,411.870	8.96	476
4	Corporations	4,776.84	3.7	6,644.000	3.23	39
5	Forests	3,633	2.9	4,575.770	2.23	26
6	Irrigation	3,787	3.0	2,611.900	1.27	−31
7	PWD (NH)	1,560	1.23	1,781.570	0.87	14
8	Others (railways, KSEB)	281.88	0.22	328.000	0.16	16
	Total	125,834.22	100.00	205,545.616	100.00	63

Source: Kerala State Planning Board (2002, 2017).

pioneer in building a rural road network. It is argued that a good rural road network has resulted in an urban sprawl, as people live in village with standard amenities and are still able to travel to work in major towns and cities. Urban sprawls typically lead to the 'car culture' and the state is no different.

Of the roads maintained by PWD (R&B), 4,342 km are SHs and 27,470 km are MDRs. SHs have seen an addition of only 12 per cent in length since 2000–2001. The district with greatest length of SHs is Idukki, and the district with least is Wayanad. In SHs, only 1,640 km is standard double lane and 2,404 km of roads is single lane. The rest is below standard single lane. Among MDRs, only 1,310 km are standard double lane and 26,160 km are standard single lane. For the state as a whole, almost 90 per cent of the road network is single lane and below standard. Increasing the width of roads to accommodate at least double lane traffic is a major hurdle. It needs to be highlighted that length added to existing roads has been miniscule during recent years. In 2015–2016, length added was nil.

There are nine NHs in the state, together constituting 1,781.57 km length. Of this, 1,339 km (76.6 per cent) are under various stages of development under the National Highways Authority of India (NHAI). Development of the remaining 408 km is under the control of the National Highway Wing of the state's PWD. It is developed mainly with the funds allocated by the Government of India (GoI) and is the responsibility of the state government. Upkeep of the highways, except 176 km, is being done by the state's PWD with fund allocated by the Ministry of Road Transport and Highways (MoRTH). The NHs, considered to be the primary network, carries 40 per cent of the total traffic; and the SHs and MDRs, the secondary road network, carry another 40 per cent of the road traffic. Thus, less than 10 per cent of the road network handles almost 80 per cent of the total traffic. Systematic upgradation of existing roads and formation of new roads has been slow in the state.

The major road network of Kerala, though well connected, faces severe constraints due to the urban sprawl and haphazard ribbon development along the routes. The existing traffic levels at most stretches are excessive and beyond the road capacity. The traffic on roads is increasing at a rate of 10 to 11 per cent a year, resulting in excessive pressure on roads in the state. Capacity augmentation of existing roads is beset with problems relating to limited right of way and land acquisition. Therefore, the main emphasis under road development in Kerala has been on improvement and upgradation of existing roads rather than construction of new ones. Investments have not kept pace with the requirements.

The quality and maintenance of bridges and culverts require greater attention. For example, as on 31 March 2016, the number of bridges on PWD roads was 1,806, of which 61 were found to be unsafe. Among the 51,400 culverts, 1,557 were found to be unsafe. Lack of well-defined criterion for selection of roads for improvement, poor vendor selection for awarding works and lack of coordination with other departments/agencies using roads such as Kerala State Electricity Board (KSEB), Kerala Water Authority, BSNL, etc., are also some additional challenges to be overcome (Kerala State Planning Board, 2012). Roads are adversely affected due to the fact that they are also used for providing large number of public services such as water, drainage, electricity and telecom, even from private sector.

Even though Kerala is comparatively better placed than most other states in the case of road length, the condition of many of these roads is very poor. Peculiar climatic conditions in the state, undulating geography of the state, soil conditions, lack of proper adherence to technical specifications/standards, poor drainage, bad geometry, poor workmanship and use of good quality material are put forward as some of the reasons for bad conditions of roads in Kerala. Inadequacy of funds, delay in implementation, poor work culture and lack of accountability, and lack of streamlined procedures for maintenance are issues on part of the implementing agencies (Kerala State Planning Board, 2013). The most important challenge in the road sector involves building durable all-weather roads of good quality.

ROAD TRANSPORT AND PUBLIC TRANSPORT

Road transport is considered the oldest form of transport. While most transport systems are made up of many modes—bicycle, bus, train, car, auto-rickshaws, boat, etc.—bus forms the backbone of most urban transport systems. In Kerala, road transport industry is dominated by private service providers. The major share of passenger transport operations on roadways is vested with private operators. Public transport in Kerala includes buses (both private and government), trains, rapid transit (like metro/mono rail) and ferries/boats (Dhanuraj & Madhu, 2014). The state government participates in the sector through the public–utility Kerala State Road Transport Corporation (KSRTC). Kerala has a total fleet of 25,449 buses; of which 19,145 are private buses (75 per cent) and 6,304 are KSRTC buses (25 per cent). Private buses dominate the bus transport in all districts of Kerala except Thiruvananthapuram. Owing to overcrowding, insufficient number of vehicles and terrible service conditions, public transport has been losing its market in many cities. It has led to a shift away from public transport towards individual motorised transport which has worsened situation in roads. Enlargement and improvement of public transport system is an urgent requirement.

The road freight services are wholly owned and operated by the private sector. Interstate goods movements are handled predominantly by road-based good carriers, followed by rail and waterways. As per a recent study by the National Transportation Planning and Research Centre (NATPAC), the share of road is 78 per cent, water transport 14 per cent and movement by rail is 8 per cent. A study by erstwhile Planning Commission (2008) revealed that road transport carried almost 88 per cent of total goods traffic, while railways handled about 10 per cent of total traffic and water transport carried less than 2 per cent of cargo movement. It is expected that once the National Waterway 3 (NW-3; Kottapuram–Kollam) becomes fully operational, about 20 per cent of the road-based cargo traffic can be shifted to water transport.

MOTOR VEHICLES

The motor vehicle population in Kerala, which was less than 2 lakh in 1980 increased to 19 lakh in 2000 and to 94 lakh in 2015 (Figure 12.1). During a decade between 2005 and 2015, the number of motor vehicles increased by 202 per cent.

Currently, more than 63 per cent of all registered vehicles are two-wheelers (either scooters or motorcycles) (Table 12.2). Commercial vehicles comprising goods vehicles, buses, taxis and

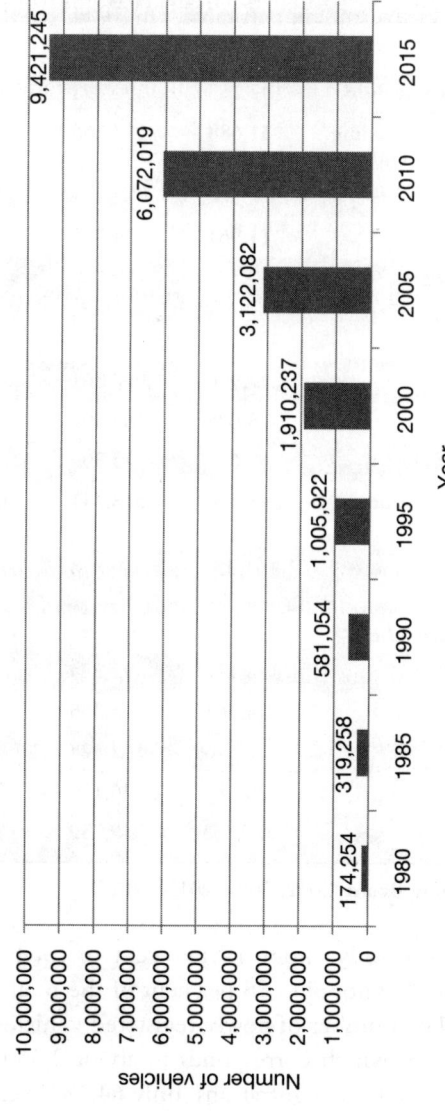

Figure 12.1 *Growth in the Number of Motor Vehicles in Kerala Since 1980*

Source: Kerala State Planning Board (2002, 2007, 2012c, 2017).

Table 12.2 *Growth in the Number of Vehicles with Valid Registration According to Classification of Vehicles*

S. No.	Type of Vehicle	2000–2001	2010–2011	2015–2016
1	Goods vehicles			
i.	Four-wheelers and above	142,168	294,395	419,813
ii.	Three-wheelers including tempos	31,688	117,266	136,938
2	Buses			
i.	Stage carriage	11,961	24,712	42,707
ii.	Contract carriage/ omnibuses	40,520	119,150	64,051
3	Four-wheelers			
i.	Cars	282,996	1,060,861	2,070,665
ii.	Taxis	75,628	163,407	107,567
iii.	Jeeps	69,621	73,700	
4	Three-wheelers—auto-rickshaws	248,350	518,741	610,235
5	Two-wheelers—scooter/ motorcycle	1,151,735	3,610,838	6,472,335
6	Tractors/trailers/others			
i.	Tractors	8,177	12,224	14,213
ii.	Tillers	4,763	5,335	187
iii.	Trailers	1,576	2,324	699
iv.	Others	28,680	46,106	232,403
	Total	2,097,863	6,049,059	10,171,813

Source: Kerala State Planning Board (2002, 2007, 2012c, 2017).

auto-rickshaws comprise only about 14 per cent of total vehicles with valid registration. A whopping 86 per cent of the total vehicles are for personal use. The number of newly registered vehicles during 2015–2016 was 861,323, which corresponds to about 2,360 vehicle registrations a day. Of the new registrations, only 64,136 were transport vehicles for commercial purposes. The rest 797,187 are vehicles for personal use.

The number of vehicles per 1,000 population for Kerala as in March 2016 was 305, which is higher than the national average and even those of some developed countries. There exists a mismatch between the growth in motor vehicles and the capacity augmentation of roads, which has led to traffic congestion and road accidents. Improvement in the economic condition of the people of the state in post-liberalisation period and the lack of a good system of public transport are often put forward as reasons for sharp rise in private vehicle ownership in the state.

Motor vehicles are considered one of the main sources of air pollution in India, and road transport is always held as the prime suspect. Automotive vehicles emit several pollutants including fugitive emissions of the fuel. Studies conducted by organisations such as TERI, UNEP/ WHO, World Bank, BARC/CESE/IIT, etc., in Mumbai and Delhi have shown that the transport sector contributes up to 92 per cent of carbon monoxide (CO), 74 per cent of nitrogen oxides (NO$_x$), 22 per cent of particulate matter (PM) and 12 per cent of sulphur oxide (SO$_2$) in air causing serious health issues to the population (Central Pollution Control Board, 2010).

ROAD SAFETY AND ROAD ACCIDENTS

Road accidents in Kerala have increased alarmingly since 1980–1981. Even bigger states such as Uttar Pradesh, Gujarat and Rajasthan report far less number of accidents compared to Kerala. However, the number of road accidents has shown only a marginal increase since 2001 in spite of the big jump in the number of registered vehicles. It means that the rate of accidents per lakh vehicle has decreased. Total injuries reported have declined (State Crime Records Bureau). However, death due to road accidents has increased by 60 per cent between 2001 and 2016 (Table 12.3). About 52 per cent of the total motor vehicles involved in accidents reported in the state are two-wheelers. The number of two-wheelers involved in accidents has increased during the recent years.

In our state, more than half of the road accident victims are in the age group of 20 to 55, the key wage earning and child raising age group. The main causes of the increasing death rates in the road accidents are mistake/fault of the driver, increasing number of new generation

Table 12.3 *Road Accidents Since 2001*

Year	No. of Accidents	Death	Total Injuries
2001	38,361	2,674	49,675
2006	41,647	3,589	49,881
2011	35,216	4,145	41,379
2016	39,420	4,287	44,108

Source: State Crime Records Bureau.

vehicles especially two–wheelers, bad condition of roads, absence of different lanes, unsafe conditions on roads, etc. (Kerala Road Safety Authority). Poor driving skills of the people and lack of vehicle fitness are also identified as causes for increasing accidents and fatality on roads.

RAILWAYS

Railways is considered one of the cheapest modes of transport for passengers and goods, more so for bulky goods and over longer distances. Energy efficiency of rail transport is over five times that of road transport. Indian railways, by increasingly moving to electric traction, is saving fuel and reducing environmental pollution. People in Kerala depend on railways for long distance transport needs. Kerala occupies a significant position on the Indian railway map with 1,046 route km and 1,588 km of total track that is spread over 13 railway routes. It includes 1,010 km of broad gauge and 36 km of meter gauge lines. The Southern Railway Zone, headquartered in Chennai, controls rail transportation in Kerala. Thiruvananthapuram, Palakkad and Madurai divisions of the Southern Railway zone are the administrative divisions having operations in Kerala. Palakkad division operates 76 express and 49 passenger trains and carries 2.16 lakh passengers daily. Thiruvananthapuram division operates 80 express trains and 60 passenger trains and carries 2.6 lakh passengers daily. It is significant to note that there is no rail connectivity to districts such as Idukki and Wayanad.

The rail transportation system in Kerala is passenger oriented. The commissioning of the Konkan Railway in 1998 has given a big boost to railway transport in the state (Planning Commission, 2008).

Development activities undertaken by the Indian Railways in Kerala post 2000 have covered the following:

1. Gauge conversion of tracks from narrow gauge and metre gauge to broad gauge
2. Doubling of tracks along significant rail routes
3. Electrification of tracks for movement from diesel to electric engines
4. Improvements and upgradation of railway stations including construction of new railway platforms, new waiting rooms including a/c rooms with toilet facilities, installation of escalators and lifts at main railway stations, new reservation counters, etc.
5. Introduction of new trains and increasing the service of existing trains, including special trains

Mainline Electrical Multiple Unit (MEMU) train between Kollam and Ernakulam was started in March 2012 and on the Kollam–Thiruvananthapuram–Nagercoil line was started in December 2012.

Over the years, the length of railway track has increased in the state with a total of 469 km of track length being added since 2000 (Table 12.4).

Experts point out that the use of the present rail transport system in the state has surpassed the installed capacity and there is excess demand

Table 12.4 *Increase in Railway Track Length in Kerala Since 2000*

S. No.	Year	Track Length (in km)
1	2000	1,119
2	2001	1,148
3	2005	1,148
4	2006	1,148
5	2009	1,148
6	2010	1,198
7	2011	1,257
8	2015	1,257
9	2016	1,588

Source: Kerala State Planning Board (2002, 2007, 2012c, 2017).

resulting in congestion and associated discomfort in travel. Lack of expansion of existing network and upgradation of existing facilities to cater to the rising demand are severe issues. Limited lines and congestion has meant that the trains run slowly and are late. The average speed of express trains running in the state is below 60 km/hr which is poor. Efficient road connectivity is also required in the state.

Railways are capital intensive, since investment has to cover the total system and its operation, whereas for most other modes of transport, public funds are needed only for construction of infrastructure (Prasad, 1999). High cost of railway projects is also one reason for slow growth of railway network in the state. Traditionally, the central government has contributed all funds for development of railways. However, the recent years have seen the central government requesting the state governments to make land available for projects. Difficulty in land acquisition is one of the biggest problems encountered in the development of railways in the state. The current efforts of the state in railway development are in the direction of developing railway transport within cities in order to create more public transport. The Kochi Metro, Light Metro (proposed for Trivandrum and Kozhikode) are efforts in this direction.

NEW TRANSPORT PROJECTS IN KERALA

Kochi Metro Rail Project (KMRP) was inaugurated on 17 June 2017. The project is implemented through the Kochi Metro Rail Ltd (KMRL) which is a special purpose vehicle jointly owned by the Government of Kerala and GoI with equity participation.

Light Metro Rail Project is a mass rapid transit system (MRTS) proposed to be implemented in the cities of Thiruvananthapuram and Kozhikode by a special purpose vehicle, Kerala Rapid Transit Corporation Limited (KRTL), and the detailed project report (DPR) has been prepared by the Delhi Metro Rail Corporation (DMRC). The approved DPR has been forwarded to the Ministry of Urban Development (MoUD), GoI, for 'in-principle' approval and for confirmation of GoI's participation and equity.

The Kochi Water Metro Project is proposed to be implemented by the KMRL at a cost of ₹741.28 crore with financial assistance from

German Financial Institution (Kfw) and state funding of ₹103 crore. This is being implemented as part of Unified Metropolitan Transport Authority (UMTA) project in Kochi. The project envisages the development of 76 km of inland canals in Kochi city.

AIR TRANSPORT

In an increasingly globalised world, air transport plays a major role in the movement of people and cargo across and within national borders, more so in a large country like India. It is the most modern and the quickest mode of transport. Air transport, previously considered the privilege of the rich, is now increasingly becoming affordable to the common man. It has played a key role in the development of the state especially in terms of migration and tourism. Kerala has three airports at Thiruvananthapuram, Kozhikode and Kochi. The Kochi airport is a joint venture and the other two are operated by the Airports Authority of India. All the three handle domestic as well as international flights. There is also a military airport in Kochi. The turn of the century saw the emergence of Kochi Airport as a landmark in the civil aviation history of India. Kerala developed the Kochi Airport on a public–private participation (PPP) basis during 1994–1999. It was the first state to do so.

Kerala has seen a huge jump in the air transport sector post 2000 (Tables 12.5 and 12.6). 'Open sky Policy' of the central government, migration and greater participation from the private sector are significant reasons for the growth. Not only have the number of flight operators/airline companies increased, there has been greater private participation for the development and management of new airports. Passenger and freight growth has been resilient in the state since 2000, in spite of the financial crisis due to tourism and migration. The biggest reason for growth is the reduction in airfare due to high competition. Air journey became affordable to larger sections of population, also because of the increasing incomes of the people. Airfare became comparable vis-a-vis other modes of transport like first-class A/C train. It is significant to note that during recent years, the number of international flights is more than that of domestic flights.

The number of passengers using air transport has also increased. Though the number of international passengers has increased, the number of domestic passengers has shown a greater increase.

Table 12.5 *Number of Flights Operated Since 2000*

Airport	2000–2001		2005–2006	
	Dom.	Int.	Dom.	Int.
Thiruvananthapuram	3,656	5,423	3,701	7,659
Cochin	7,847	2,454	9,331	11,444
Kozhikode	3,205	3,006	4,807	6,452
Total	14,708	10,883	17,839	25,555
	2010–2011		2015–2016	
Airport	Dom.	Int.	Dom.	Int.
Thiruvananthapuram	8,269	22,860	5,221	14,867
Cochin	22,600	17,827	27,901	29,861
Kozhikode	1,414	14,835	4,337	12,757
Total	32,283	55,522	37,459	57,485

Source: Kerala State Planning Board (2002, 2007, 2012c, 2017).

Table 12.6 *Number of Passengers Carried Since 2000*

Airport	2000–2001		2005–2006	
	Dom.	Int.	Dom.	Int.
Thiruvananthapuram	250,721	745,931	322,525	1,002,647
Cochin	455,316	296,258	696,822	1,154,717
Kozhikode	197,919	283,350	182,035	752,004
Total	903,956	1,325,539	1,201,382	2,909,368
	2010–11		2015–2016	
Airport	Dom.	Int.	Dom.	Int.
Thiruvananthapuram	686,834	1,846,404	1,008,691	2,058,714
Cochin	1,985,242	2,369,537	3,129,658	4,641,127
Kozhikode	129,532	1,908,196	871,107	2,262,436
Total	2,801,608	6,124,137	5,009,456	8,962,277

Source: Kerala State Planning Board (2002, 2007, 2012c, 2017).

During the year 2015–2016, Cochin International Airport handled more than 50 per cent of all flights and passengers in airports in Kerala. In spite of lesser number of flights than Thiruvananthapuram, the Kozhikode International Airport handled higher number of passengers due to a much higher number of international travellers. About a lakh tonne of export and import cargo are also handled by these airports every year, and it is bound to rise.

The state is building its fourth international airport at Kannur. Kannur International Airport Limited (KIAL) has been set up by the Government of Kerala to build and operate Kannur International Airport. It is a green-field airport being set up in 2,000 acres and is expected to give a boost to the economic development of North Malabar region.

Airport development works in the state are often slow due to issues associated with land acquisition. The efforts to construct a new airport at Aranmula in Pathanamthitta district had to be dropped in the face of stiff opposition from local population. In order to provide boost to tourism industry and enhance greater local connectivity, the state had started seaplane services, with aircrafts which could take-off and land in water (including the seas). However, they are also held up due to the concerns of the fishing community.

WATER TRANSPORT

Water transport including sea/ocean transport and inland water transport (IWT) is a fuel-efficient and environment-friendly mode of transportation for passenger and freight movement. It possesses high load-carrying capacity and plays an important role in international trade. It involves lower operating costs and environmental pollution than road, rail or air options. Due to its ability to carry in bulk, it could relieve pressure on the other modes of transport and reduce congestion in them.

IWT was the main form of transport in Kerala in the past and has played a significant role in its development. Important centres of trade and commerce were situated along the banks of the state's network of inland water bodies. Though Kerala is considered to be richly endowed with navigable waterways, the share of IWT in total transport is very low. In Kerala, water transport is used to a small extent for freight transport. Though they offer tremendous scope for transport of passengers, they are not utilised. The state has enormous potential for growth in water transport.

The IWT network in Kerala includes rivers, canals and backwaters. Kerala has 44 rivers (41 flowing to the west and 3 to the east) and numerous backwaters. The inland canals connecting rivers and backwaters are also significant. The West Coast Canal (WCC) system which has a length of about 560 km starts from Kovalam in Thiruvananthapuram district in the south and extends up to Hosdurg in Kasaragod district in the north. Of this, the Kollam–Kottapuram stretch (168 km) was declared as NW-3 in 1993. Kollam–Kottappuram stretch of WCC along with Champakkara (14 km) and Udyogmandal (23 km) canals for length of 205 km is the NW-3 now and is almost fully functional. In April 2016, apart from the existing five national waterways, the GoI has declared another 106 waterways spread all over the country as national waterways. It consisted of four canals in Kerala including Alappuzha–Changanassery (28 km), Alappuzha–Kottayam–Athirampuzha (38 km), Kottayam–Vaikom (42 km) and Anantha Victoria Marthandam Canal (AVM canal; 11 km). Recently, the central government has declared the extension of NW-3 between Kottapuram and Kozhikode (160 km) as national waterway.

There are about 1,687 km of IWT route network in the state consisting of the NW-3 from Kollam to Kottapuram which is maintained by the Inland Waterways Authority of India (IWAI) and other feeder canals maintained by the Coastal Shipping & Inland Navigation Department (CSIND)/state irrigation departments. Cargo transportation through mechanised barrages exists in NW-3.

Government agencies engaged in the development of IWT in the state are CSIND, State Water Transport Department (SWTD) and Kerala Shipping and Inland Navigation Corporation Ltd. (KSINC). The SWTD caters to the transport needs of people in the districts of Alappuzha, Kottayam, Kollam, Ernakulam, Kannur and Kasaragod, transporting about 150 lakhs of passengers per annum. Much of the cargo movement in waterways is done through the KSINC. It transports around 3 lakh tonnes of cargo annually.

Water transport plays and can play a much greater role in the tourism sector of the state. Backwater tourism and houseboats have become distinguished symbols of Kerala tourism. There is enormous scope to expand them. However, apprehensions regarding safety and pollution have to be addressed properly.

The three basic IWT-related infrastructure required for development of waterways are fairway or navigational channel with desired width and depth, navigational aids for safe navigation and modern terminals for berthing of vessels, loading/unloading of cargo and for providing interface with road and rail. These basic requirements are found wanting in Kerala. Issues such as conflict of interest and hostility between traditional fishermen and navigation operators, encroachment of water bodies, insufficient navigation lock/bridge clearance, apprehensions about water pollution (as highlighted in the case of Alappuzha and Kuttanad) exist. Water has competing uses from various sectors such as for drinking, fisheries, irrigation, etc. Under conditions of scarcity, the use of water has to be prioritised, and it works unfavourably for transport. Lack of maintenance of navigation system, accelerated growth of water hyacinth, delay in demarcation of canal land, need for more bank protection and objection from public are also some of the issues hindering progress in this sector (Kerala State Planning Board, 2012).

Making all of the designated waterways fully operational/fit for transport through movement of crafts and removal of impediments is the need of the hour. The deficiency of crafts, failure to implement standardisation of cargo handling and lack of development of feeder canals providing integration with the ports are limitations.

During recent years, the state has focused on the development of potential stretches of WCC and its feeder routes to increase the volume of passenger/cargo traffic and achieving a modal shift in inland cargo to the water transport sector coupled with related boost in tourism sector. State government has tried to mandate the transfer of hazardous/volatile materials through waterways and incentivised cargo movement through this mode.

PORTS

Globalisation of world economy has brought about tremendous increase in exchange of goods across the world. Ports play a critical and important role in handling the ever-increasing world trade. They play a pivotal role in stimulating economic activity in their surroundings and hinterland. The volume of seaborne cargo traffic handled by ports is mainly shaped by the levels and changes in both the global and domestic activity.

Kerala with a coastal line of 585 km has one major port at Cochin and 17 non-major ports. Out of 17 minor ports in Kerala, four are considered as intermediate ports based on berthing, cargo handling and storage facilities available in them. They are Vizhinjam, Beypore, Azheekal and Kollam ports. The remaining 13 minor ports in the state are Neendakara, Alappuzha, Valiyathura, Kayamkulam, Manakkodam, Munambam, Ponnani, Vadakara, Thalassery, Manjeswaram, Neeleswaram, Kannur and Kasaragod. Beypore also handles passenger traffic to Lakshadweep Islands.

Cochin Port has shown growth since 2000 where both import and export cargo has increased (Table 12.7). Among the cargo handled at Cochin Port, petroleum, oil and lubricants (POL) has the highest share of 62.33 per cent followed by container (26.17 per cent), other cargo (9.95 per cent) fertiliser and raw materials (1.15 per cent) and coal (0.40 per cent; Cochin Port Trust, 2016). The share of overseas/foreign cargo has consistently remained much higher than that for coastal shipping for both imports and exports.

Among the non-major ports, it is found that cargo handling was confined mainly to the intermediate ports such as Kozhikode, Kollam, Vizhinjam and Azhikkal. While the number of vessels calling in at ports have decreased, the tonnage has increased, meaning size of ships have increased. On the whole, the total cargo handled by then has come down over the years with a slight increase recorded in 2015–2016. Coastal cargo has increased and foreign cargo has decreased. Total import cargo has increased on the whole and export cargo has fallen drastically.

New cargo port facilities have been created at Thangassery (Kollam) utilising the calm fishery harbour basin. The Government of Kerala has recently decided to develop five non-major ports including Azheekal, Beypore, Ponnani, Alappuzha and Kollam through PPP mode. The Vizhinjam Deepwater Container Transshipment Terminal is under

Table 12.7 *Cargo Traffic at the Cochin Port Trust Since 2000 (in '000 Tonnes)*

S. No.	Year	Import	Export	Total
1	2000–2001	11,037	2,080	13,117
2	2005–2006	10,844	3,094	13,938
3	2010–2011	14,468	3,405	17,873
4	2015–2016	18,184	3,914	22,099

Source: Kerala State Planning Board (2002, 2007, 2012c, 2017).

construction and holds the potential to bring big benefits to the state. It is the first project in the state and first port in the country to receive viability gap funding (VGF) assistance from the central government.

Supporting infrastructure is deficient at ports in Kerala. The experience of operating berths through PPPs at some major ports in India has been quite successful (Kerala State Planning Board, 2012). Accordingly, the state has also tried to develop minor ports in the PPP mode, but the experiment is yet to bring about the desired success. Lack of maintenance and modernisation of port facilities and infrastructure have meant that they are not functional throughout the year. Lack of technical solutions to fix the problem of siltation and meagre policy support in terms of incentives for shifting to water transport via ports are also constraints.

Transportation by coastal shipping is the cheapest mode especially for bulk commodities and for long haulage traffic. Kerala has advantage of 585 km coastline through which bulk cargos can be transported if multi-modal transshipment logistics is built up at intermittent points along the coastline. However, the development in port sector in the state has been stymied by the constraints of port and logistic capacity, customs procedure and labour problems. The state lacks integration between the ports and IWT. In the present scenario, very little coastal shipping is taking place in the state.

CONCLUSION

The transport sector in Kerala has made considerable progress since 2000. However, the focus of such development has been primarily on roads and roadways. There are hurdles in the expansion of road transport. Other modes of transport such as waterways and railways hold opportunities and potential for growth but are not utilised properly. Poor maintenance of existing transport infrastructure, lack of coordination between various departments and stakeholders, scarcity of finance and difficulty in land acquisition are major problems in the sector. The development of an intermodal transport network integrating various modes of transport, tapping the advantages and potential of each mode can revolutionise transport in Kerala.

REFERENCES AND SELECT BIBLIOGRAPHY

Basu, D. D. (2011). *An introduction to the Constitution of India* Nagpur: Lexisnexis Publishers.

Central Pollution Control Board. (2010). *Status of the vehicular pollution control programme in India, program objective series.* New Delhi: Central Pollution Control Board.

Cochin Port Trust. (2016). *Administrative report and annual accounts 2015–16.* Cochin: Cochin Port Trust.

Dhanuraj, D., & Madhu, S. (2014). An evaluation of the public transport system in Kerala. In V Mathew Kurian & Raju John (eds), *Kerala economy and its emerging issues* (p. 352). Kottayam: Sahithya Pravarthaka Co-operative Society.

Kerala Road Safety Authority (KRSA). *Road accidents.* Retrieved 31 March 2018, from http://roadsafety.kerala.gov.in/index.php/road-accidents

Kerala State Planning Board. (2002). *Economic review 2001.* Thiruvananthapuram: Government of Kerala.

———. (2007). *Economic review 2006.* Thiruvananthapuram: Government of Kerala.

———. (2012a). *Report of the working group on inland waterways—Twelfth Five Year Plan 2012–17.* Thiruvananthapuram: Kerala State Planning Board.

———. (2012b). *Working group report on port and light house—Twelfth Five Year Plan 2012–17.* Thiruvananthapuram: Kerala State Planning Board.

———. (2012c). *Economic review 2011.* Thiruvananthapuram: Government of Kerala.

———. (2012d). *Working group report on roads, bridges and transport—Twelfth Five Year Plan 2012–17.* Thiruvananthapuram: Kerala State Planning Board.

———. (2013). *Report of the technical committee on roads and road safety.* Thiruvananthapuram: Kerala State Planning Board.

———. (2014). *Kerala perspective plan 2030* (Vol. 3). Thiruvananthapuram: Government of Kerala.

———. (2017). *Economic review 2016.* Thiruvananthapuram: Government of Kerala.

Planning Commission. (2008). *Kerala development report.* New Delhi: Academic Foundation.

———. (2014). *India transport report—Moving India to 2032* (Vol. 1). New Delhi: Routledge.

Prasad, M. N. (1999). An objective approach to transport development in Kerala. In M. A. Oommen (ed), *Kerala's development experience II* (p. 471). New Delhi: Concept Publishing Company.

State Crime Records Bureau (SCRB). *Road accidents in Kerala.* Retrieved 1 April 2017, from http://keralapolice.org/public-information/crime-statistics/road-accident

PART V

Tourism and Banking

Chapter 13

Tourism Development in Kerala
Issues, Problems and Prospects

Rony Thomas Rajan and Shijo Philip

PRELUDE

Kerala has emerged as a prominent tourism destination in the global tourism map. The state has been recognised as one of the world's fastest growing tourist destinations. The unprecedented importance gained by this sector since the last half of the 1980s, in the state as well as globally, is mainly because of its ability to generate income, employment and regional development in addition to the development in economic, social and cultural arenas. The influence of tourism on such varied areas ordained this sector as one of the prime pillars of the state economy. Since natural and cultural heritage are regarded as the pre-eminent capital for tourism, Kerala, with an abundance of these factors, considers itself as a region with immense potential for the development of tourism. The present chapter is an attempt to study the growth and development of the tourism sector in the state since the year 2000. The chapter also examines the policies associated with tourism development, the various constraints in its growth and the emerging issues associated with it, as well as the prospects of the sector. Since any sector has its positive and negative impacts on the economy, the chapter also makes an attempt to visualise these effects. For the analysis, we have used the World Travel and Tourism Council (WTTC), UNWTO (World Tourism Organization) and central and state governments in India.

TOURISM: AN INTRODUCTION

Tourism as an industry gained prominence since the Second World War. Growing urbanisation, mechanisation, availability of higher disposable income, better standards of living, search for authenticity, demand for leisure and recreation, etc., have immensely contributed to the development of this industry. For long, tourism was considered as a leisure activity of the rich and an unnecessary distraction for the poor.

Due to its very strong forward and backward linkages, this dynamic industry has occupied a prime place in the development paradigms of all countries. Since the tourism industry is highly dependent on the economic, social, political, historical, environmental and cultural fabric of the location, the growth potential of this industry is influenced by the level of interaction and correlation with each of these factors. Though they are aligned with each other, each supporting sector operates as an independent industry, focused on generating economic value, and competes with other sectors. Tourism being an evolutionary entity, it is not eternally sustainable on its own. Thus, the growth potential of other sectors directly or indirectly impacts tourism, which is, in fact, a product of conditioning.

In its potential to act as a catharsis for economic and social development, countries both rich and poor embraced this industry with the aim of achieving overall growth. The strong linkages this industry has generates multiplier effects which contribute to job creation, income generation, infrastructure creation and forex earnings as well as opportunities for the transfer of capital and knowledge.

According to UNWTO, over the past six decades, tourism has experienced continued expansion and diversification to become one of the largest and fastest growing economic sectors in the world. Travel and tourism is now a strategic priority of both developed as well as less developed economies. International tourist arrivals have increased from 25 million globally in 1950 to 278 million in 1980, 674 million in 2000 and 1,186 million in 2015. Likewise, international tourism receipts earned by destinations worldwide have surged from

US$2 billion in 1950 to US$104 billion in 1980, and US$495 billion in 2000 to 1,260 billion in 2015. As per WTTC, in 2016, this sector has contributed around 3.1 per cent of the direct GDP of global economy and has created 6 million net additional jobs. In total, travel and tourism generated 292 million jobs in 2016, which means 1 in 10 jobs in the global economy. This sector now accounts for 7 per cent of the total global exports and 30 per cent of the global service exports.

TOURISM: A CONCEPTUAL BACKGROUND

Definitions

Tourism as a phenomenon is not easy to define, though several attempts have been made to define it. It is the existence of the word 'tour' which forms the base of the word tourism. Tourism consists of all trades which together satisfy the varied needs of the travellers. Travel may be considered as touristic if it satisfies the following conditions, namely, temporary, voluntary and not aimed at remunerative employment.

The WTO recommends the following categories as characterising the main purpose of visit for tourists, namely, leisure, recreation and holidays, visiting friends and relatives, business and professional (including for study), health treatment, religion and pilgrimage, and others (e.g., airline or ship crews, transit travellers, etc.).

Definitions Followed in India

Foreign Tourist

A foreign tourist is a person visiting India on a foreign passport, staying at least 24 hours in the country and the purpose of whose visit can be classified as one of the following: (a) leisure (recreation, holiday, health, study, religion and sport), (b) business, family and mission meeting. The following persons are not regarded as foreign tourists: (a) persons arriving with or without a contract to take up an occupation or to engage in activities remunerated within the country, (b) persons coming to establish residence in the country and (c) 'same day visitors' (including travellers on cruise ships).

Domestic Tourist

A domestic tourist is a person who travels within the country to a place other than his usual place of residence and stays at hotels or other accommodation establishments run on commercial basis or charitable basis for a duration of not less than 24 hours or one night, and for not more than 12 months at a time (Government of Kerala, 2016).

Evolving Concepts and Theories in Tourism

Though very few early accepted theories are available on tourism, it was only during the 1970s and the 1980s that researchers began to focus on the outcomes of tourism development and the context for such development. The two approaches that dominated during this period include the dependency perspective (Britton, 1982) and the life cycle model (Butler, 1980). Both are based on the shared premise that industry's mass variant represents its crowning height (Milne & Ateljevic, 2001). To these theories, as a new region is incorporated into the global tourism map, the emerging industry is characterised by a relatively high level of local involvement. As the tourist number rises, incorporation into the global tourism network increases, then local industry structures soon become characterised by oversees or local elite ownerships. Locals end up receiving few economic benefits while having to carry the inevitable cost of rapidly increasing tourist numbers.

Another approach that emerged in the 1980s focused on the local agency or community participation. This approach highlighted the capability of locals to control the outcome of the industry (Murphy, 1985; Taylor, 1995). During the latter half of the 1980s, a new approach, namely, regulation theory, was more popular among the researchers on tourism. This approach is based on the objective of achieving flexibility, both internally and externally. Internally, firms must be able to produce a greater variety of specialised products and to change product configuration rapidly in response to variations in market tastes. Externally, these shifts are associated with vertical and horizontal disintegration and the emergence of downsized specialised firms often organised into spatially proximate networks (Tiague, 1990). In fact, the emergence of 'best practices' in tourism can be seen as an outcome of flexible specialisation (Poon, 1989). Profitability and competitiveness in tourism depend more on the economies of scope, systems gains, segmented markets, and designed and customised holidays (Milne & Ateljevic, 2001). Thus, regulation and flexible specialisation approach could be used to explain the emergence of less developed regions and their ability to achieve greater degree of self-determination in tourism than they have managed in the past (Poon, 1993).

The approach of mass production or Fordism can also be used to analyse the prevailing practices in tourism. While there is rapid rise in the small tourism centres, mass tourism firms continue to prosper and thrive. Mass tourism's convenience, price and travel style remain attractive to consumers, making it an important mainstay for the tourism industry (Williams & Montanari, 1995). Though different approaches are there, most sectorial research has focused on the manufacturing arena with little attention paid to services, particularly to tourism.

TOURISM IN INDIA

India is a relative newcomer in the global tourism business. Though we receive less than 2 per cent of global tourism receipts (US$21,071) and less than 1 per cent of the tourist arrivals (8.03 million), tourism has evolved to be a vibrant sector of our economy. International tourist arrivals in India increased from 1.6 million in 1991 to 8.03 million in 2015 (Table 13.1). During the same period, domestic tourist visits to all states increased from 6.6 million to 1431.97 million. The foreign exchange earnings from this sector has increased from US$1.86 billion in 1991 to US$21.07 billion in 2015, registering a growth of 11.33 per cent (Table 13.2). The sector has emerged as a prominent one, with the contribution to national GDP being estimated to be 6.3 per cent in 2015, and it has created around 8.7 per cent of the total employment in India (Government of Kerala, 2016). In 2015, according to the World Travel and Tourism Report, India occupied the 12th position in the world ranking in travel and tourism's total contribution to GDP. In terms of employment contribution, the country was positioned next to China holding the second rank at the global level. The report envisages that India's strong growth forecast will propel it into the top 10 travel and tourism economies by 2026. The WTTC has identified India as one

Table 13.1 *India's Share in Global Foreign Tourist Arrivals (in Million)*

Year	International Tourist Arrivals (Number)			Percentage Share and Rank of India			
	World	Asia Pacific	India	World	Rank	Asia Pacific	Rank
2000	683.3	109.3	2.65	0.39	50th	2.42	11th
2005	803.4	154.6	3.92	0.49	43rd	2.53	11th
2010	948	204.9	5.78	0.61	42nd	2.82	11th
2015	1,184	278.6	8.03	0.68	40th	2.88	11th

Source: World Travel and Tourism Council, various reports.

Table 13.2 *International Tourism Receipts (in US$ Billion)*

Year	International Tourism Receipts (in US$ Billion)		FEEs in India (in US$ Million)	Share of India and Rank in World		Share of India and Rank in Asia Pacific	
	World	Asia Pacific		% Share	Rank	% Share	Rank
2000	475.3	85.3	3,460	0.73	36th	4.06	10th
2005	679.6	135.0	7,493	1.10	22th	5.55	7th
2010	931.0	255.3	14,193	1.52	17th	5.56	7th
2015	1,232.0	418.9	21,071	1.71	14th	5.03	7th

Source: World Travel and Tourism Council, various reports.

of the foremost tourist growth centres in the coming decade. WTTC estimates that the likely contribution by travel and tourism to economic activity in the country will have the fastest rate of growth at around 9.7 per cent over the next 10 years.

Though tourism plays quite a significant role in moulding India's economic variables, this sector received very little attention during the first three decades of planning. It was only in 1982 that the country came out with a policy exclusively for the tourism sector. This reflects the slow pace of organised support for this sector. Even during the initial decades with a dedicated policy, the focus was confined to a sectorial growth strategy rather than integrating tourism into the overall scheme of development (Bezbaruah, 1999).

India, though has in it all the ingredients to be one of the most sought after destinations in the world tourism map, still has very few globally popular tourist centres. Among those centres, Agra, Jaipur and Kashmir as well as the states of Goa and Kerala stand out. Kerala came into the global tourist map only in the 1990s, but since then, it has carved out a niche of its own.

TOURISM IN KERALA

For centuries, the tiny piece of land sandwiched between the Arabian Sea and the hill ranges of Western Ghats in the south of Indian peninsula was the centre of the worlds' attraction. This land was one of the key centres of trade between the Red Sea and the Indian Ocean. For years, this fabled land mesmerised Babylonians, Assyrians, Egyptians, Arabs, Chinese, Romans and Greeks. Traders around the world looked for a chance to engage with this land of spices. But centuries down the line, more than trade, this land was fancied by travellers for its tourist potentials.

Until the 1980s, Kerala was rather an unknown destination in the Indian tourist map. Identifying the potential of tourism to elevate the economy to a higher growth path, the Kerala Tourism Development Corporation (KTDC) has launched aggressive marketing campaigns. These campaigns brought before the world Kerala's uniqueness through the tag line—'God's own country'—which later became a global super brand. In the decades that followed, Kerala tourism was able to transform itself to one of the niche holiday destinations of India. The National Geographic *Traveler* rated Kerala in the 'Paradise Found' category among the 50 must see destinations of lifetime (National Geographic, 2009). Also *Travel and Leisure* magazine rated Kerala's breakfast as 'one of the best in the world'. Quite recently, in 2016, a tiny island Kakkathuruthu has been listed in the 'around the world in 24 hours', a photographic tour of travel worthy spots in the world. The state has in it an abundance of beaches, backwaters, hill stations, wildlife, waterfalls, festivals, health holidays, monuments, art forms and every other tourist attractions, all of which can be covered in 20 hours.

These natural endowments along with aggressive marketing took Kerala possibly into all available international tourist brochures. Kerala now is regarded as one of the destinations with the highest brand recall.

Though among states in India Kerala maintains one of the highest positions in human development indicators, it ranks poor in many economic indicators such as employment, economic growth, infrastructural development, revenue generation, etc., It is at this juncture that tourism reflects its potential. In fact, there is hardly any other economic activity which is capable of generating as much added value, employment and hard currency and that too at a low cost as tourism. Tourism being a service industry, it is highly labour intensive and, especially in a state like Kerala, it can contribute to economic development of the area, create huge employment opportunities, provide equitable distribution of wealth, help to acquire the much needed foreign exchange, eradicate regional imbalances, improve the standard of living of the local people, boost up local and cottage industries, promote international understanding by bringing diverse people face to face and, above all, help in achieving social, cultural, political and educational understanding among the people. The existence of such outcomes affecting various sectors, the government of Kerala declared tourism as an industry in 1986. This notification entitled tourism establishments in the state for the concessions and privileges enjoyed by other industries.

With the abysmally low performance of the primary and secondary sector, the Kerala economy has been riding on the vibrant service sector as well as on the remittances of its expatriates in West Asia. In the midst of unpredictable fluctuations in agriculture and the tendency of falling expatriate earnings, tourism emerged as the major potential earner for the state economy as well as the provider of employment. It is no longer possible to ignore the vital role this sector is destined to play in the economy of Kerala. Tourism has been identified as the powerful engine that can move the Kerala economy. Nevertheless, a careful management of this sector is essential as mass tourism has resulted in adverse consequences to society, culture and environment (Sreekumar & Parayil, 2002). The consequence of such an impact would be more on the tourism sector itself, as this industry thrives on these factors. Thus, a critical evaluation of the tourism industry is very essential in order to get a correct picture of this engine of growth.

TOURIST ARRIVALS: FOREIGN AND DOMESTIC

Foreign Tourists

Foreign tourists to India and Kerala have been growing remarkably during 2002–2015 (Table 13.3). Foreign tourists to India have nearly tripled while that to Kerala has quadrupled during this time period. Kerala has been maintaining a share of around 10 per cent of the total foreign tourists who visited the country without much wide difference over the period (except during 2005). The country as well as the state has been experiencing consistent growth, except during the global economic recession of 2008–2009. The period also witnessed heightened terrorist activities as well as the H1N1 influenza pandemic (GoI, 2011).

Table 13.3 *Foreign Tourist Arrival in India and Kerala*

Year	Tourists in India	Rate of Growth	Tourists in Kerala	Rate of Growth	% Share of the State
2000	2,649,378	6.7	209,933	3.80	7.92
2001	2,537,282	–4.2	208,830	–0.53	8.23
2002	2,384,364	–6.0	232,564	11.37	9.75
2003	2,726,214	14.3	294,621	26.68	10.81
2004	3,457,477	26.8	345,546	17.28	9.99
2005	3,918,610	13.3	346,499	0.28	8.84
2006	4,447,167	13.5	428,534	23.68	9.63
2007	5,081,504	14.3	515,808	20.37	10.15
2008	5,282,603	4.0	598,929	16.11	11.34
2009	5,167,699	–2.2	557,258	–6.96	10.78
2010	5,775,692	11.8	659,265	18.31	11.42
2011	6,309,222	9.2	732,985	11.18	11.62
2012	6,577,745	4.3	793,696	8.28	12.07
2013	6,967,601	5.9	858,143	8.12	12.32
2014	7,679,099	10.2	923,366	7.60	12.02
2015	7,713,658	4.5	977,479	5.86	12.67

Source: Various annual reports of the Kerala and the Indian Ministry of Tourism.

Domestic Tourists

Domestic tourist arrival is also as important as foreign tourist arrivals. Domestic tourism demand is characterised by three factors, namely, knowledge about the destination, proximity of destinations and cost of transport (Government of Kerala, 2016). On the domestic tourism front, the state achieved double digit growth during 2008, but it dropped to 4.25 per cent during 2009 and gathered momentum in the succeeding years (Table 13.4). In fact, domestic tourists constituted the majority among those who visited Kerala. The domestic tourist flow was consistently lower than the national average growth during the decade under consideration.

Table 13.4 *Domestic Tourist Visits in Kerala*

Year	No. of Domestic Tourists	Growth Rate
2000	5,013,221	2.55
2001	5,239,692	4.52
2002	5,568,256	6.27
2003	5,871,228	5.44
2004	5,972,182	1.72
2005	5,946,423	−0.43
2006	6,271,724	5.47
2007	6,642,941	5.92
2008	7,591,250	14.28
2009	7,913,537	4.25
2010	8,595,075	8.61
2011	9,381,455	9.15
2012	10,076,854	7.41
2013	10,857,811	7.75
2014	11,695,411	7.71
2015	12,465,571	6.59

Source: Various annual reports of the Kerala Tourism Department.

FOREIGN EXCHANGE EARNINGS FROM TOURISM

Tourism can be considered as an important export industry because of its ability to earn foreign exchange without actually exporting any material goods. This revenue inflow creates household income, business turnover, employment and government revenue, and above all, a portion is ploughed back within the destination economy, thereby creating further rounds of economic activity. In fact, the relationship between the tourist arrival and foreign exchange earnings from tourism is not a function of the number of tourists visiting a tourist destination but depends on the spending pattern of the tourist. The state's foreign exchange earnings from tourism has increased from ₹12.67 billion as on 2005 to ₹69.5 billion by 2015 (which is the second highest after remittances), registering a compound annual growth rate of 14.6 per cent (Table 13.5). The forex earnings showed a steady increase over the years, except for the year 2009 when the global financial crisis affected the flow of foreign tourists. The share of the state tourism contribution in the national economy's foreign exchange has been hovering around 5 per cent. Even during 2009, when the overall tourist flow to India was dull, the share of the state remained stable around 5 per cent.

The total revenue (including direct and indirect) generated from tourism during the last decade registered a compound annual growth rate of 11.33 per cent (Table 13.6). It grew from ₹45 billion in 2001 to ₹77.38 billion in 2005 and to ₹266.8963 billion by 2015. Between 2013 and 2015, a declining tendency of growth rate is visible, from 12.22 per cent in 2013 to 7.25 per cent in 2015. Currently, this revenue accounts for 12 per cent of the Gross State Domestic Product (GSDP).

SPENDING ON TOURISM

Since the Second Five-Year Plan, tourism was brought under the purview of planning. The Sixth Plan (1980–1985) gave due emphasis for increasing the state's share in international tourist traffic to India. The plan envisaged the pooling of resources not only from the central and state governments but also from the private sector for achieving the plan objectives. Though the overall plan outlay to the sector has been increasing over the years, the share of the tourism sector in the

Table 13.5 *Foreign Exchange Earnings from Tourism (in ₹ Crore)*

Year	Forex Earning in India	Forex Earning in Kerala	Share of Kerala (%)
2001	15,083	535	3.5
2002	15,064	706	4.6
2003	20,729	983	4.7
2004	27,944	1,267	4.5
2005	33,123	1,552	4.68
2006	39,025	1,988	5.09
2007	44,360	2,641	5.95
2008	51,294	3,067	5.98
2009	53,700	2,853	5.31
2010	64,889	3,797	5.85
2011	77,591	4,222	5.44
2012	94,487	4,572	4.84
2013	107,671	5,561	5.16
2014	123,320	6,399	5.19
2015	135,193	6,950	5.14

Source: Various annual reports of Ministry of Tourism, GoI.

total state plan outlay has been negligible. The allocation to the tourism sector has not been above 1 per cent, except during the Ninth Plan period where the share was around 1.22 per cent. The outlay was quite less during the 10th and 11th Plan periods, while an increase was witnessed during the 12th Plan period.

In addition to plan allocation, the tourism sector has been receiving supplementary funds over and above the budget allocation from the state as well as the central fund for specific tourism projects. A major portion of the government spending has been on infrastructural projects as well as for marketing, while the allotment for human resources has been meagre. Though the sector depends a lot on quality human capital, the shortage of which is challenging the development of tourism in the region, the emphasis of the state on this area is still less than sufficient.

Table 13.6 *Earnings from Tourism in Kerala (in ₹ Crore)*

Year	Foreign Exchange Earnings	Percentage of Increase	Total Revenue Generated from Tourism (Direct & Indirect)	Percentage of Increase
2001	535.00	1.85	4,500.00	9.58
2002	705.67	31.90	4,931.00	20.42
2003	983.37	39.35	5,938.00	12.83
2004	1,266.77	28.82	6,829.00	15.01
2005	1,552.77	22.54	7,738.00	13.31
2006	1,988.40	28.09	9,126.00	17.94
2007	2,640.94	32.82	11,433.00	25.28
2008	3,066.52	16.11	13,130.00	14.84
2009	2,853.16	−6.96	13,231.00	0.77
2010	3,797.37	33.09	17,348.00	31.12
2011	4,221.99	11.18	19,037.00	9.74
2012	4,571.69	8.28	20,430.00	7.32
2013	5,560.77	21.63	22,926.55	12.22
2014	6,398.93	15.07	24,885.44	12.11
2015	6,949.88	8.61	26,689.63	7.25

Source: Various reports of the Kerala Tourism Department.

EMPLOYMENT AND TOURISM

Tourism being a labour-intensive industry, its potential for creating employment for the skilled, semi-skilled and unskilled surpasses any other industry. With its high backward and forward linkages, the sector can generate direct, indirect or induced employment, thereby providing a solution to the issue of unemployment to both the advanced as well as less advanced countries. The jobs created are spread across the economy, from the modern highly sophisticated industry to the most traditional ones. The importance of tourism as creator of job opportunities can be understood by the fact that in India, every one million invested in tourism creates 47.5 jobs directly and around 85–90 jobs indirectly. In contrast, agriculture creates only 44.6 jobs and manufacturing a mere 12.6 jobs (Agarwal, 2016). Though no empirical data is available regarding the total number of jobs created by this sector in the state, independent studies identified that the share of this sector as a percentage of the total employment in Kerala between 2009 and 2012 is around 23.52 per cent (NCAER, 2010). This contribution to employment is quite significant even with a less than 1 per cent share for this sector in the state's plan spending, of which only a miniscule is being spend on human resource development. Thus, carefully planned investment in this sector can help in mitigating unemployment, which still remains as the biggest social and economic ailment of the state.

SOURCE MARKET FOR FOREIGN TOURISTS

For the last two decades, Europe remains the major source market for foreign tourist arrivals to Kerala (Table 13.7). Tourism in Kerala can be described as Euro-centric with UK leading the list of countries from where bulk of the tourists comes to Kerala, while France and Germany occupy prime positions. Quite recently, there has been an increase in the flow of tourists from the USA and Saudi Arabia, and a fall in the share of UK tourists from 23.36 per cent in 2007 to 17.1 per cent by 2015.

Table 13.7 *Trend in the Share of Foreign Tourists Arrivals (in %)*

Year	U.K.	France	Germany	USA	Saudi Arabia
2005	20.32	8.02	6.59	7.92	1.38
2010	23.70	9.79	7.62	10.8	1.38
2015	17.06	9.37	7.86	7.75	5.23

Year	Australia	Russia	Malaysia	Canada	Switzerland
2005	2.87	1.24	0.08	2.17	2.52
2010	5.59	1.56	2.85	2.77	2.07
2015	3.61	3.35	2.87	2.68	2.67

Source: Report of the Ministry of Tourism (various years), Government of Kerala.

REGION-WISE PREFERENCE OF TOURISTS

Regarding the region-wise preference of foreign tourists, central Kerala which is comprised of four districts, namely, Kottayam, Ernakulum, Idukki and Thrissur, tops the list of favourite destinations for both foreign as well as domestic tourists (Table 13.8). More than half of the tourists visiting Kerala prefer the central Kerala region. Among the four districts, Idukki and Ernakulam are the ones which are preferred by travellers. Even though due importance has been given to tourism by the successive governments, the northern districts are yet to gain a dominant position in the tourism map of Kerala, especially among the foreign tourists.

SWOT ANALYSIS

SWOT is an acronym that stands for strength, weakness, opportunities and threats. It is an accepted approach used to evaluate any sector or organisation. In this approach, both internal and external factors are reviewed according to their influence on the sector under consideration. Strength and weakness are attributes occurring inside an organisation, while opportunities and threats are usually external (Bader, 2010). Tourism is a double-edged sword since even while this sector provides considerable economic benefits, it can also bring in adverse environmental as well as sociocultural impacts.

Strength

The uniqueness of Kerala tourism is its ability to position itself as a major player in the different forms of tourism other than the one based on the environmental advantage. The state can be considered as a destination for different forms of tourism such as cultural, heritage, medical, hill station, rural, wildlife, religious, Ayurveda, dental, yoga, forest, etc. In addition to the rich cultural heritage which is the source of many exclusive art forms, the availability of greenery and water sources makes the state an avian and wildlife paradise which is home to many endangered species.

Table 13.8 *Region-wise Visit of Foreign and Domestic Tourists*

	2005		2010		2015	
	Number	Share (%)	Number	Share (%)	Number	Share (%)
South Kerala						
Foreign	157,376	45.42	255,066	38.69	389,822	39.88
Domestic	1,168,392	19.65	1,623,299	18.89	2,535,218	20.34
Central Kerala						
Foreign	170,589	49.23	362,857	55.04	525,387	53.75
Domestic	2,992,481	50.32	4,627,676	53.84	6,684,429	53.62
North Kerala						
Foreign	18,534	5.35	41,342	6.27	62,264	6.37
Domestic	1,785,550	30.03	2,344,100	27.27	3,245,924	26.04
Total						
Foreign	346,499	100.00	659,265	100.00	977,473	100.00
Domestic	5,946,423	100.00	8,595,075	100.00	12,465,571	100.00

Source: Report of the Ministry of Tourism (various years), Government of Kerala.

The availability of a friendly and English-speaking population along with skilled manpower, civil society organisations, strong governmental policies, responsible media, multitude of micro enterprises and an active private sector provides the state with an ideal setting for the tourism industry to flourish. The advancement of the state in the health care sector along with the existence of a peaceful atmosphere with relatively good transport and communication infrastructure, and above all a distinctive cuisine which reveals the eventful history and richness of the state's culture, is the biggest highlight of the state tourism potential.

Ayurveda care, the health tourism product, is the Unique Selling Proposition (USP) of Kerala. The natural abundance of forests with herbs and medicinal plants along with an equable climate with monsoons helps to bring out the best in Ayurvedic curative and rejuvenation packages.

The state also has many unique art forms. The performing arts of the state such as Kathakali, Koodiyattam, Mohiniyattam and Ottam Thullal; ritual arts such as Theyyam, Tholpavakkoothu Padayani and Kavadiyattom; and martial art forms such as Kalaripayattu are unique in their style and form. Of these, Koodiyattam, one of the oldest art forms of Kerala and the only surviving form of the ancient Sanskrit drama, has been declared as a world heritage by the United Nations Educational, Scientific and Cultural Organization (UNESCO, 2010). Traditional festivals such as Thrissur Pooram and Snake Boat Races are events which are witnessed only in this part of the world.

Weakness

For a place to have tourism potential, it is not enough to have some resources; their identification as tourism resources and the effective utilisation of these resources are equally important (Formica & Uysal, 2006). The major weakness of Kerala tourism lies in the ineffective utilisation of the available resources. Tourists prefer a destination based on its natural beauty, cultural richness, availability of recreational opportunities, food and accommodation, peacefulness and other amenities. The weak coordination among the tourist entities and the resulting poor management of destinations has become an issue to be tackled. The poor management of waste has led the state to become a hub for several contagious diseases such as H1N1, dengue, chicken guinea, rat fever, etc. The stray dogs menace which has become a crucial issue in the state is an aftermath of the poor management of waste.

The existence of political over-activism leading to frequent strikes and 'bandhs' resulting in the sudden closure of economic activities is an important factor that drives away potential and actual tourists from the destination. The increase in crime rate, especially towards women, makes tourism a rather painful experience. Frequent damaging of roads due to rains makes commuting through roads a not-so-enjoyable experience.

Tourism is a labour-intensive industry with tourists always expecting certain standards of professionalism. This requires trained professionals as guides, managers, drivers, care givers, chefs, etc. Unfortunately, the state has only very few institutes that train individuals in the professional way of managing tourists. The human resource training for tourism gets only a small pie in the overall spending for tourism by the exchequer.

Though the state of Kerala has been a pioneer in coming up with many tourism-related policies and efficient marketing strategies, the share of Kerala in Indian tourism has been hovering around 10–12 per cent and has not shown an increasing trend over the years. The state is still not very popular among domestic tourists as it is still not listed among the 10 best states in India for domestic tourist arrivals. In fact, the state lags behind all the three south Indian states, namely, Andhra Pradesh, Tamil Nadu and Karnataka.

The tourism industry is closely integrated with several other industries and sectors such as accommodation, aviation, railways, roadways, health care, entertainment, hygiene, social order, pollution, etc. Thus, any weakness on any of those sectors makes the tourism a vulnerable one.

Opportunities

Foreign tourist arrival to Kerala is mostly Euro-centric, with the bulk of the tourist coming from five European countries. Since brand Kerala has wide acceptance globally, there exists a huge potential especially from other European nations, the USA, West Asia, Southeast Asia, etc. Better marketing in the countries of these regions can result in better acceptance of the state as a potential tourism destination. The growing acceptance of Kerala among Russian tourists evidences this aspect.

The growing acceptance of Ayurveda as an alternative form of medicine has been attracting many towards the state, especially for rejuvenation treatments. As this treatment is most effective during the monsoon season, combining both can attract domestic as well as foreign tourists. The attempts by the tourism department to present Kerala as a destination for sustainable tourism can bring the consumers who look for 'guilt-free' holidays as well as those affluent consumers who look forward to better quality products.

With a view to stimulate domestic and international investment in the tourism sector, the government has permitted 100 per cent FDI in the automatic route. FDI is also permitted in all construction and development projects including hotels, resorts, recreational facilities, and city- and regional-level infrastructure. Also a five-year tax holiday has been provided to organisations that set up hotels resorts and convention centres at specific locations. Availing this opportunity can bring in the much-needed capital for fine tuning the potentials in the sector.

Though the state has in its valet many unique art forms, with the economic progress, much of these are on the verge of vanishing. Tourism can play a major role in sustaining the culture, art forms, festivals and even cuisine, though much of these may lose their authenticity as a consequence of the commodification.

Threats

Though tourism can be considered as an engine of growth, uncontrolled tourism can aggravate poverty. In many parts of the world, due to tourism, small-scale farmers continue to be driven out from their farm land and fisher-flock are being denied access to beaches, mangroves, forests and marine resources (Haseena & Mohammed, 2014). As tourism develops, the property market becomes highly volatile, with prices sky rocketing when developers use legal and illegal methods to appropriate land. This might lead to frequent land conflicts affecting the traditional livelihoods.

Mass tourism can negatively affect the fragile ecology of the state. Already tourism has turned out as a source of pollution in Kerala's backwaters with sewage discharge from hotels, resorts and houseboats (Rajan et al., 2011); beaches such as Kovalam and Varkala are being littered with garbage (Tatjana 2016); hill stations like Munnar are being cleansed of its forest cover. Also the increasing demand for infrastructural facilities such as roads, electricity, water and accommodation can disturb the natural ecosystem. Tourism can also pollute the society and culture. The alcohol addiction and drug abuse can come out as an inevitable consequence of tourism if left unchecked.

Climate change looms as the greatest threat to tourism in the state. The fall in the rainfall and the drying up of water sources has resulted in the rise in the average temperature. This can make the state less attractive to tourists who look forward to the state as a cool and green location. The increasing crime rate, especially towards women, can act as deterrence for women to prefer the state. Since females constitute the majority among the international tourists to Kerala (Rajasenan, Varghese & Bijith, 2012), their preference for a destination will mostly be based on the safety and peacefulness that the location can offer. Also, increasing religious intolerance and frequent strikes can give a different image to the prospective visitors.

CONCLUSION

Tourism is looked upon as one of the few options left to uplift the Kerala economy to a growth phase. With its strong forward and backward linkages, this sector can play a crucial role in ameliorating the economic ills of the state such as unemployment, low revenue, etc., and can bring in the much needed vitality to the economy. Though the contribution of this sector to the state GDP is only around 1 per cent to 6 per cent, because of its high potential to act as a catalyst for economic development, the sector draws much attention from policy formulators. Though Kerala is looked as a forerunner in coming up with innovative initiatives and policies on tourism, the state's share in the national pie has been hovering around 10 per cent, especially for foreign tourist visits. In case of domestic tourists also, the state is not rated among the top 10 prominent tourist destinations. The state has come up with many policies dedicated to tourism since the first policy. Each of these policies focussed on developing tourism infrastructure and tourism products as well as tourism marketing and promotion. With the objective of making tourism an engine of economic growth, the government has come up with a Vision 2025 document. Even after three decades of visions, policy formulations and implementations, the plan fund allocation to tourism is less than 1 per cent of the total plan fund.

If a region has to develop through tourism, tourism should be able to strengthen the economic variables of the destination. For this, careful interaction of tourism with different sectors of the state needs to be promoted. Building interactions with sub-sectors such as art and craft, cuisine, transportation, accommodation, environment, etc., tourism will be able to strengthen these sectors. For any such development, effective and proactive social and political action is essential. By ensuring the active participation of local administrations, NGOs, the private sector and above all the local population, the state can be built as a quality tourist destination.

REFERENCES AND SELECT BIBLIOGRAPHY

Agrawal, V. (2016). A review of Indian Tourism Industry with SWOT analysis. *Journal of Tourism Hospitality*, 5(1), 1–4.

Bader, A. (2010). Tourism business environment analysis conducted for Kerala/India (Thesis). Saimaa University of Applied Sciences, South Karelia, Finland.

Bezbaruah, M. P. (1999). *Indian tourism beyond the millennium*. Delhi: Gyan Publishing House.

Britton, S. G. (1982). The political economy of tourism in the Third World. *Annals of Tourism Research*, 9(3), 331–358.

Butler, R. W. (1980). The concept of a tourist area cycle of evolution and implications for management of resources. *The Canadian Geographer*, 24(1), 5–12.

Government of India. (2011). *Annual report of Ministry of Tourism 2010–11*. New Delhi: Ministry of Tourism.

———. (2016). *India tourism statistics 2015*. New Delhi: Ministry of Tourism.

Government of Kerala. (2016). *Economic review*. Thiruvananthapuram: State Planning Board.

Formica, S., & Uysal, M. (2006). Destination attractiveness based on supply and demand evaluation: An analytical framework. *Journal of Travel Research*, 44, 418–430.

Haseena, V. A., & Mohammed, A. P. (2014). Sustainable tourism strategy development in Kerala as a tool of growth. *Asian Journal of Science and Technology*, 5(3, March), 192–197.

Milne, S., & Ateljevic, I. (2001). Tourism economic development and the global-local nexus: Theory embracing complexity. *Tourism Geographies*, *3*(4), 369–393.

Mowforth, M., & Munt, I. (1998). *Tourism and sustainability, new tourism in the Third World*. London: Routledge.

Murphy, P. E. (1985). *Tourism: A community approach*. New York, NY: Methuen.

National Council for Applied Economic Research (NCAER). (2010). *Regional tourism satellite account for Kerala and Madhya Pradesh 2009–10*. New Delhi: NCAER.

National Geographic. (2009). *National Geographic traveller: 50 places of a life time*, 25th Anniversary edition, September. Retrieved on 25 April 2018, from http://intelligenttravel.nationalgeographic.com/2009/09/17/50_places_of_a_lifetime_1/

Poon, A. (1989). Competitive strategies for a new tourism. In C. P. Cooper (ed), *Progress in tourism, recreation and hospitality management* (pp. 91–102). London: Belhaven Press.

———. (1993). *Tourism, technology and competitive strategies*. Wallingford: C. A. B. International.

Rajasenan, D., Varghese, M., & Bijith, G. A. (2012). Tourist profiles and characteristics vis-à-vis market segmentation of ecotourism destinations in Kerala. *Journal of Economics and Sustainable Development*, *3*(4), 134–144.

Rajan, B., Varghese, V. M., & Pradeepkumar, A. P. (2011). *Recreational boat carrying capacity of Vembanad Lake ecosystem*. Kerala, South India. *Environmental Research Engineering and Management*, *2*(56), 11–19.

Singh, R. (1998). *Dynamics of modern tourism*. New Delhi: Karishka Publishers and Distributors.

Sreekumar, T. T., & Parayil, G. (2002). Contentions and contradictions of tourism as development options: The case of Kerala, India. *Third World Quarterly*, *23*(3), 529–548.

Taylor, G. (1995). The community approach: Does it really work? *Tourism Management*, *16*(7), 487–489.

Tatjana, T. (2016, March). *The Kerala tourism model: An Indian state on the road to sustainable development*. John Wiley & Sons online library.

Teague, P. (1990). The political economy of regulation school and the flexible specialization scenario. *Journal of Economic Studies*, *17*(5), 32–54.

UNESCO (United Nations Educational Scientific and Cultural Organization). (2010). *Cultural, India*. UNESCO. Retrieved on 25 April 2018, from https://ich.unesco.org/en/RL/kutiyattam-sanskrit-theatre-00010

Willams, A. M., & Montanari, A. (1995). Tourism regions and spaces in a changing social framework. *Tijdschrift voor Economische en Sociale Geografie*, *86*(1), 3–12.

Chapter 14

Development of Banking in Kerala

Jerry Alwin

Kerala has a long history of banking tradition even before the Independence of India. At the time of Independence, there were about 190 banks in Travancore and Cochin, and most of them were unit banks. The post-Independence era saw the growth of many private banks in the state. The nationalisation of Indian banks in 1969 led to branch expansion of major banks in the state. The large-scale emigration of Keralite workers to Gulf countries since the mid-1970s, inflow of foreign remittances and growth of non-resident deposits (NRD) helped the growth of the banking sector. The implementation of market-oriented liberalisation policies in India since 1991 increased the demand for more investment and credit and led to expansion of banking sector in Kerala. The global recession in 2008 adversely affected the growth of deposits and advances during the period 2008–2012. One of the major features of the banking sector in Kerala is the higher mobilisation of deposits and the comparatively lower credit disbursement. Another feature of the banking sector of Kerala is the concentration of bank branches in urban and semi-urban areas, and poor coverage in rural areas.

OBJECTIVES, HYPOTHESES AND SOURCE OF DATA

The aim of the study is to examine the growth of the banking sector in Kerala since 2000, discuss the trends in deposits, advances and credit deposit ratio (CDR), to analyse the trends and pattern of NRD, and location-wise distribution of bank branches, deposits and CDR.

We present the following hypotheses to explain the development of banking sector in Kerala: (a) The major factor which contributed to the growth of banking in Kerala since the mid-1970s has been migration of Keralite workers to foreign countries and the receipt of foreign remittances. (b) CDR is low in Kerala due to a number of reasons such as low credit absorption in productive sectors, low rate of private investment, higher labour cost and associated labour issues, higher production cost compared to other states, lack of entrepreneurial skills of the people, strong preference of youth for public sector jobs, stringent norms followed by banks to give credit for investment, etc. (c) Bank branches, deposits and advances in Kerala are largely concentrated in urban and semi-urban areas due to concentration of non-primary economic activities and demand for credit.

The major indicators used for examining the growth of banking sector are the following: (a) growth rate of deposits and advances, (b) CDR, (c) NRD as percentage of total deposits and (d) region-wise concentration of bank branches, deposits and credit. The study is based on secondary sources of data published by the Reserve Bank of India (RBI) such as Basic Statistical Returns of Scheduled Commercial Banks in India, Report of Trends and Progress of Banking in India and other reports. Other data sources include State Level Bankers Committee data published by Canara Bank annually and *Economic Review* published by the State Planning Board.

The chapter is divided into four sections. The first part gives the introduction, objectives, hypotheses and source of data, the second part deals with the development of banking in Kerala up to 2000, the third part of the study examines the developments of banking sector since 2000 and the last part gives the conclusions of the study.

BANKING DEVELOPMENT UP TO 2000: A REVIEW
History

The evolution of banking in India was linked with the development of foreign trade and commerce. The banks in Kerala first originated in Travancore in places such as Thiruvalla, Thalavady, Ambalapuzha and Chenganoor. Modern commercial banks in Kerala are said to have emerged along with capitalist form of business organisation and production (Oommen, 1976). Traditional financial institutions in Kerala, such as chit funds and kuris, and indigenous banks were considered as forerunners of commercial banks. Kerala's first commercial bank was the Travancore Bank which was formed in 1893, which was a partnership bank with a paid up capital of ₹15,000. Another important bank which was started in 1919 was the Quilon bank with a paid up capital of ₹56,000. When the RBI was established in 1935, the banks Travancore National and Quilon bank were classified as scheduled banks. These two banks were amalgamated in 1937 with the approval and credit support of RBI under the new name Travancore National and Quilon Bank (TNQB). The TNQB was ranked first in the number of branch offices in India and third in the total volume of business. But the TNQB was liquidated through a deliberate strategy by the Diwan of Travancore Sir C. P. Ramaswamy Iyer in 1938.

Before 1936, all the bank branches were concentrated in towns such as Cochin, Ernakulam and Thrissur. In 1936, out of 31 banks, 29 were in towns. It was only during the 1940s that banks came up in rural and semi-urban areas. At the time of Independence, there were 190 banks in Travancore and Cochin, and most of them were unit banks. The State Bank of Travancore (SBT) was established in 1945 as the Travancore Bank Ltd at the initiative of Diwan Sir C. P. Ramaswamy Iyer. Although the Travancore government put up only 25 per cent of the capital, the bank undertook government treasury work and foreign exchange business apart from its general banking business. The head office of the bank was in Thiruvananthapuram. In 1960, it became a subsidiary of the State Bank of India (SBI) under SBI Subsidiary Banks Act of 1959 enacted by the Indian parliament, and thus achieved the name SBT. As on March 2016, SBT had 852 branches in Kerala. In

February 2017, the Government of India accepted a proposal to merge SBT and other associate banks with SBI. It was merged with SBI on 1 April 2017.

The major trends in the banking sector of Kerala after the formation of the state up to 2000 is examined in the following. As on June 1969, Kerala had only 601 bank branches (DES, 2001). But the number of bank branches in Kerala had increased to 2,838 in 1990 and 3,233 in the year 2000. One of the important factors that led to an increased demand for branch expansion is the migration of Keralites to Gulf countries which started during the second half of the 1970s. Another factor which contributed to the increase in the number of bank branches is the growth of public sector banks. It should also be noted that majority of bank branches are situated in urban districts such as Ernakulam, Thrissur and Thiruvananthapuram. The factors such as urbanisation and emigration led to concentration of bank branches in these districts. The lowest number of bank branches is in districts such as Wayanad and Idduki, which have a low share of emigrants and urban population.

Trends in Deposits and Advances

The banking sector of Kerala up to the year 2000 comprised of public sector banks, private sector banks and foreign banks. The implementation of market-oriented liberalisation policies in India since 1991 increased the demand for more investment and credit, and led to expansion of the banking sector in Kerala. The state's economy also achieved higher growth during the post-liberalisation period. There was a robust growth rate of bank deposits during the 1990s. There was also a substantial increase in the advances of the banks during the 1990s. One of the major factors which contributed to the development of banking in Kerala since the 1970s has been the growth of NRDs. NRD to total deposits increased from 29.02 per cent in 1990 to 48.48 per cent in 2000 due to an increase in remittances sent by Keralite emigrants from Gulf countries.

An indicator of the performance of the banking sector is the CDR. During the period 1970–1992, there was a fall in the CDR, which was in tune with the declining trend at the national level (Jeromi, 2008). This was due to rise in statutory reserve requirements of banks as it reduced the loanable funds of banks. During this period, cash reserve ratio (CRR) increased from 3 per cent to 15 per cent, and statutory liquidity ratio (SLR) from 27 per cent to 38.5 per cent. Higher growth of NRD was also cited as one of the reasons for low CDR according to the study. During the period 1990 to 2000, CDR decreased from 62 per cent in 1990 to 41.3 per cent in 2000.

When compared to the all-India average, the CDR of Kerala was much lower for the period 1990 to 2000. Due to low CDR in Kerala, the RBI constituted a task force on CDR in 1993 to examine the issue and offer suggestions. The task force noted that the banking system in Kerala did not cater to the developmental needs of the commodity-producing sectors due to some important institutional and organisational constraints which are peculiar to Kerala. The low credit absorption capacity of Kerala's industrial sector due to lack of private investment was cited as an important reason for low CDR.

BANKING DEVELOPMENT SINCE 2000

There has been a faster expansion of commercial banks in Kerala over the recent years. At the end of March 2015, Kerala accounted for 4.76 per cent of the total number of bank branches, 3.6 per cent of deposits and 3.36 per cent of the credit disbursed by commercial banks in the country. It should be noted that despite Kerala having a high density of population, the average population per bank branch is significantly lower at 5,583 as against 10,300 at all-India level, indicating the development of banking system in the state (RBI, 2015).

Bank-wise Deposits and Advances

Kerala's banking sector comprises of public sector banks, private banks, cooperative banks and foreign banks. An analysis of the total deposits, total advances, its growth rate and CDR of Kerala's banking sector is given in Table 14.1. There was a substantial increase in the growth rate of deposits from ₹448.5015 billion in 2001 to ₹4.2132742 trillion in 2016. The lowest growth rate of deposits was recorded for the year 2005. This may be due to the problem of return emigration from

Table 14.1 *Total Deposit, Advances and CDR for Kerala (in ₹ Crore)*

Year	Total Deposits	Growth Rate	Total Advances	Growth Rate	CD Ratio
2001	44,850.15	–	19,180.27	–	42.77
2002	51,655.78	15.17	22,061.94	15.02	42.71
2003	59,399.36	14.99	27,006.53	22.41	45.47
2004	65,961.11	11.05	31,867.31	17.99	48.31
2005	71,860.48	8.94	43,997.23	38.06	61.23
2006	80,515.29	12.04	55,314.09	25.72	68.70
2007	94,510.00	17.38	68,298.00	23.47	72.26
2008	109,236.29	15.58	79,312.28	16.13	72.61
2009	135,034.10	23.62	87,059.68	9.77	64.47
2010	150,052.77	11.12	101,009.76	16.02	67.32
2011	16,6767.20	11.14	126,896.48	25.63	76.09
2012	225,692.90	35.33	172,605.97	36.02	76.48
2013	259,785.51	15.11	202,086.80	17.08	77.79
2014	319,883.72	23.13	220,964.42	9.34	69.08
2015	366,030.75	14.23	252,220.20	14.15	68.91
2016	421,327.42	15.11	269,201.33	6.73	63.89

Source: State Level Bankers Committee, various years.

the Gulf countries and decline in the flow of remittances. The highest growth rate of deposits (35.33 per cent) was recorded for the year 2012. This may be due to the recovery of the state economy after the severe shock of global recession. The total advances of Kerala's banking sector grew from ₹191.8027 billion to ₹2.6920133 trillion in 2016. The highest growth rate of advances was for the years 2005 and 2012. The lowest growth rate of advances was recorded for the year 2016.

The CDR, which was 42.77 per cent in 2001, increased to 77.79 per cent in 2013. This may be due to the slow growth of deposits when compared to credit. But the ratio declined to 63.29 per cent in 2016 due to faster growth of deposits. CDR is low in Kerala due to a number of reasons such as low credit absorption in productive sectors, low rate of private investment, higher labour cost and associated labour issues, higher production cost compared to other states, lack of entre-preneurial skills of the people, the strong preference of youth for public sector jobs, the stringent norms followed by banks to give credit for investment, etc. Certain other factors such as scarcity of land available for large-scale industries, high population density, lack of agro-based industries and export of agricultural raw materials, and reluctance of banks to provide credit even for viable projects due to stringent norms also contributed to low CDR.

Public sector banks comprise all nationalised banks and regional rural banks. There are 28 public sector banks operating in Kerala as on March 2016. The total deposits, advances and CDR of public sector banks are given in Table 14.2.

Table 14.2 *Total Deposit, Advances and CDR for Public Sector Banks (in ₹ Crore)*

Year	Total Deposit	Growth Rate	Total Advance	Growth Rate	CD Ratio
2001	30,635.91	–	13,344.22	–	43.56
2002	34,975.84	14.17	15,719.84	17.80	44.94
2003	40,726.58	16.44	18,986.67	20.78	46.62
2004	44,697.53	9.75	22,717.36	19.65	50.82
2005	47,151.69	5.49	28,053.84	23.49	59.50
2006	52,218.31	10.75	35,037.86	24.90	67.10
2007	62,148.00	19.02	42,942.00	22.56	69.10
2008	71,328.60	14.77	50,426.64	17.43	70.70
2009	89,063.97	24.86	56,595.86	12.23	63.55
2010	98,031.14	10.07	68,562.30	21.14	69.94
2011	109,860.03	12.07	85,168.41	24.22	77.52
2012	131,612.72	19.80	105,078.89	23.28	79.84
2013	149,395.66	13.51	122,645.50	16.71	82.09
2014	177,412.45	18.75	132,171.35	7.77	74.50
2015	204,347.03	15.18	148,376.06	12.26	72.61
2016	227,211.29	11.19	152,170.96	2.56	66.97

Source: State Level Bankers Committee, various years.

The total deposits of public sector banks increased from ₹306.3591 billion in 2001 to ₹2.2721129 trillion in 2016. The highest annual growth rate of deposits was for the year 2009 and the lowest was for the year 2005. The total deposits of public sector banks increased from ₹133.4422 billion in 2001 to ₹1.5217096 trillion in 2016. The highest growth rate of advances was recorded for the year 2006 and the lowest for the year 2016. The highest CDR of public sector banks was recorded for the year 2013 (82.09 per cent). The CDR of public sector banks is comparatively higher than private banks. This is because Keralites are relying more on public sector banks for credit needs such as housing loans, vehicle loans and educational loans. Another reason for high CDR is that salary of central and state government employees is disbursed through public sector banks. Moreover, the public sector banks are also giving a proportion of credit to priority sectors such as agriculture, micro, small and medium enterprises, etc.

The total deposits, advances and CDR for private banks are given in Table 14.3. There are 16 private banks in Kerala with 2,043 branches and 31.89 per cent of total share of deposits as on March 2016. The total deposits of private banks increased from ₹138.4815 billion in 2001 to ₹1.3438187 trillion in 2016. The annual growth rate of deposits was highest for the year 2014 and lowest for the year 2005.

The total advances of the private banks grew from ₹57.415 billion in 2001 to ₹802.4666 billion in 2016. The lowest annual growth rate of advances for private banks was registered for the year 2009 (4.45 per cent). This may be due to the slowing down of economic activities in the state due to global recession. The CDR of private banks was lower compared to public sector and cooperative banks.

The total deposits, advances and CDR of cooperative banks from 2005 to 2016 is given in Table 14.4. The data for cooperative banks is available only from 2005 onwards. It should be noted that CDR of cooperative banks is higher than all the other categories of banks. This is because of the fact that the account holders in the cooperative banks require more credit, and the surety requirements for credit is simple compared to public sector banks. The cooperative banks are more accessible for the general public, and have higher rate of interest for deposits and speedy availability of credit, especially for informal and agricultural activities.

Table 14.3 *Total Deposits, Advances and CDR for Private Banks (in ₹ Crore)*

Year	Total Deposits	Growth Rate	Total Advance	Growth Rate	CD Ratio
2001	13,848.15	–	5,741.50	–	41.46
2002	16,302.23	17.72	6,248.91	8.84	38.33
2003	18,293.05	12.21	7,875.67	26.03	43.05
2004	20,891.72	14.21	8,981.31	14.04	42.99
2005	22,037.99	5.49	12,670.78	41.08	57.50
2006	25,012.45	13.50	16,641.75	31.34	66.53
2007	29,039.00	16.10	21,055.00	26.52	72.51
2008	33,617.98	15.77	24,547.72	16.59	73.02
2009	40,528.73	20.56	25,641.30	4.45	63.27
2010	44,555.41	9.94	27,885.03	8.75	62.59
2011	51,701.72	16.04	36,813.45	32.02	71.20
2012	65,944.19	27.55	44,214.16	20.10	67.05
2013	79,752.81	20.94	52,441.82	18.61	65.76
2014	102,242.41	28.20	59,838.84	14.11	58.53
2015	115,542.87	13.01	70,330.02	17.53	60.87
2016	134,381.87	16.30	80,246.66	14.10	59.72

Source: State Level Bankers Committee, various years.

Table 14.5 gives the share of total deposits and advances in different categories of banks. From the data, we can infer that a major share of deposits and advances are in the public sector banks. The deposits of public sector banks ranged between 54 per cent and 68 per cent of total deposits and advances ranged between 57 per cent and 70 per cent of total advances. The deposits of private sector banks ranged between 29 per cent and 32 per cent of total deposits and advances formed 27 per cent to 30 per cent of total advances. The deposits of cooperative banks formed 3 per cent to 14 per cent of total deposits, and advances formed 6 per cent to 14 per cent. The share of deposits and advances of foreign banks is less than 1 per cent.

Table 14.4 *Total Deposit, Advances and CDR for Cooperative Banks (in ₹ Crore)*

Year	Total Deposit	Growth Rate	Total Advance	Growth Rate	CD Ratio
2005	2,276.84	–	3,048.94	–	133.91
2006	2,838.22	24.66	3,395.58	10.21	119.64
2007	2,813.00	−0.89	4,024.00	18.51	143.05
2008	3,748.04	33.24	4,007.54	−0.41	106.92
2009	4,684.25	24.98	4,241.13	5.83	90.54
2010	6,649.21	41.95	4,022.84	−5.15	60.50
2011	5,205.45	−21.71	4,914.62	22.17	94.41
2012	28,136.01	440.51	23,312.90	374.36	82.86
2013	30,637.04	8.89	26,999.48	15.81	88.13
2014	40,228.86	31.31	28,954.23	7.24	71.97
2015	46,140.85	14.70	33,514.13	15.75	72.63
2016	59,734.27	29.46	36,783.81	9.76	61.58

Source: State Level Bankers Committee, various years.

Table 14.5 *Bank-wise Share of Deposits and Advances (in %)*

Year	Total Public Sector	Cooperative Banks	Private Sector	Foreign Banks	Total
Deposits Percentage					
2001	68.31	–	30.88	0.81	100
2005	65.62	3.17	30.67	0.54	100
2010	65.33	4.43	29.69	0.55	100
2016	53.93	14.18	31.89	–	100
Advances Percentage					
2001	69.57	–	29.93	0.50	100
2005	53.76	6.93	28.80	0.51	100
2010	67.88	3.98	27.61	0.53	100
2016	56.93	13.66	29.81	–	100

Source: State Level Bankers Committee, various years.

Trend and Pattern of NRD

One of the major factors which led to the growth of the banking sector in Kerala is the large-scale emigration of Keralite workers to the Gulf countries. The state of Kerala received ₹136.52 billion as remittances in 1998, which increased to ₹711.42 billion in 2014 (Zachariah & Rajan, 2016). The increased flow of remittances has led to the growth of NRD (Table 14.6).

The NRD increased from ₹214.3083 billion in 2001 to ₹1.3560906 trillion in 2016. Though the NRD increased in absolute terms, the share of NRD in total deposits decreased from 47.78 per cent in 2001 to 32.19 per cent in 2016. The decline in the share of NRD to total deposits can be attributed to fall in remittances due to the global economic crisis and subsequent return emigration from Gulf countries.

Table 14.6 *Non-resident Deposits (in ₹ Crore)*

Year	NRD	Growth Rate	Share in Total Deposit
2001	21,430.83	–	47.78
2002	24,533.71	14.48	47.49
2003	28,695.57	16.96	48.31
2004	30,100.39	4.90	45.63
2005	29,121.40	−3.25	40.52
2006	30,672.65	5.33	38.10
2007	33,304.00	8.58	35.24
2008	29,889.81	−10.25	27.36
2009	37,019.48	23.85	27.42
2010	36,885.90	−0.36	24.58
2011	37,689.94	2.20	22.60
2012	48,454.40	28.56	21.47
2013	66,190.31	36.60	25.48
2014	93,883.52	41.84	29.35
2015	109,603.95	16.74	29.94
2016	135,609.06	23.73	32.19

Source: State Level Bankers Committee, various years.

Another factor which led to decline in the share was the fall in the interest rate of NRD resulting in the shifting of their savings to other avenues of investment.

The share of NRD to total deposits in different categories of banks is given in Table 14.7. From the data, we can infer that NRD formed a major share of public sector and private sector banks during the period 2001 to 2016. A noticeable development during the last few years is the increasing share of NRD in private banks.

Location-wise Distribution of Branches, Deposits and Advances

The growth of bank branches of different categories of banks in Kerala from 2004 to 2016 is given in Table 14.8. The bank branches in Kerala increased from 3,614 in 2004 to 7,122 in 2016. As on 2016,

Table 14.7 *Share NRD to Total Deposits of Each Category of Banks for Kerala (in %)*

Year	Public Sector Banks	Private Sector Banks	Cooperative Banks	Foreign Banks
2001	50.30	41.82	–	66.30
2005	42.41	40.51	0.074	49.45
2010	26.84	23.67	0.005	3.53
2016	33.97	43.48	0.001	–

Source: State Level Bankers Committee, various years.

Table 14.8 *Number of Bank Branches in Kerala*

Year	Public Sector Banks	Cooperative Banks	Private Banks	Foreign Banks	Total
2004	1,920	123	1,121	5	3,617
2010	2,878	123	1,427	5	4,433
2016	4,143	936	2,043	–	7,122

Source: State Level Bankers Committee, various years.

public sector banks had 4,143 branches, private sector banks had 2,043 branches and cooperative banks had 936 branches.

Based on the size of population, a centre where the bank branch is located is classified either into rural, semi-urban or urban. A centre is defined as the revenue unit (and not just the locality) classified and delineated by the respective state government, that is, a revenue village/city/town/municipality/municipal corporation, etc., as the case may be, in which the branch is situated—(a) Rural: Population less than 10,000; (b) Semi-urban: Population of 10,000 and above, but less than 1 million; and (c) Urban: Population of 100,000 and above, but less than 1 million. Location-wise bank branches, deposits, credit and CDR for Kerala for the years 2010 and 2016 are given in Table 14.9. From the data, we can infer that the share of rural and semi-urban branches, deposits and advances have declined from 2010 to 2016. But the share of urban branches, deposits and credit have increased during the period. Bank branches, deposits and credit in Kerala are largely concentrated in urban and semi-urban areas due to concentration of non-primary economic activities and demand for credit. It should be noted that in 2016, only 8.59 per cent of branches, 4.9 per cent of deposits and 6.39 per cent of advances were in rural areas. The lack of banking services in rural areas has led to the growth of non-banking financial institutions (NBFIs) in rural Kerala.

District-wise Distribution of Banks

In this section, an attempt is made to examine the district-wise growth of bank branches, deposits, advances and CDRs of scheduled commercial banks in Kerala for the year 2016. A review of the number of bank branches shows that the highest number of bank branches is located in urban districts such as Ernakulam, Thrissur and Thiruvananthapuram (Table 14.10). A similar trend is also observed in the case of deposits, credits and CDR. Banks and banking activities are concentrated in urbanised districts having a higher share of urban population and having non-primary sector economic activities compared to non-urbanised districts.

Table 14.9 *Location of Bank Branches, Deposits, Credit and CDR of Kerala*

Year	Rural	Semi-urban	Urban	Total
Bank Branches				
2010	539	2,904	990	4,433
2016	612	4,284	2,226	7,122
% Share				
2010	12.16	65.51	22.33	100
2016	8.59	60.15	31.26	100
Deposits (₹ Crore)				
2010	9,226.45	82,129.02	58,697.30	150,052.77
2016	20,624.85	208,285.89	192,416.68	421,327.42
% Share				
2010	6.15	54.73	39.12	100
2016	4.9	49.4	45.7	100
Advances (₹ Crore)				
2010	7,614.56	47,123.62	46,271.58	101,009.76
2016	17,188.51	114,333.99	137,678.82	269,201.33
% Share				
2010	7.54	46.65	45.81	100
2016	6.39	42.47	51.14	100
Credit Deposit Ratio				
2010	82.53	57.38	78.83	67.32
2016	83.34	54.89	71.55	63.89

Source: State Level Bankers Committee, various years.

CONCLUSIONS

The major factor which contributed to the development of banking in Kerala has been the emigration of Keralites to Gulf countries since the mid-1970s and the receipt of large amount of foreign remittances. The major share of deposits and advances in the banking sector of Kerala are in public sector banks, followed by private sector, cooperative and foreign banks. The low CDR of Kerala may be attributed to low credit absorption in productive sectors, low rate of private

Table 14.10 *District-wise Branches, Deposits, Credit and CDR of Scheduled Commercial Banks in Kerala (in ₹ Crore)*

District	Branches 2016	% Share	Deposits 2016	% Share	Credit 2016	% Share	CD Ratio 2016
Thiruvananthapuram	706	11.45	56,014	15.41	35,717	15.89	63.76
Kollam	380	6.16	24,370	6.70	14,764	6.57	60.58
Alappuzha	371	6.02	21,978	6.05	10,334	4.60	47.02
Kottayam	487	7.90	27,681	7.61	14,811	6.59	53.51
Ernakulam	965	15.65	73,629	20.25	59,654	26.54	81.02
Thrissur	715	11.60	41,948	11.54	22,484	10.00	53.60
Palakkad	410	6.65	16,900	4.65	10,900	4.85	64.50
Idduki	173	2.81	4,073	1.12	4,932	2.19	121.09
Pathanamthitta	380	6.16	30,918	8.51	7,964	3.54	25.76
Kozhikode	437	7.09	20,838	5.73	14,623	6.50	70.17
Malappuram	433	7.02	17,096	4.70	10,238	4.55	59.89
Kannur	374	6.06	19,418	5.34	10,250	4.56	52.79
Wayanad	119	1.93	2,437	0.67	2,969	1.32	121.83
Kasargod	216	3.50	6,213	1.72	5,160	2.30	83.05
Total	6,166	100.00	363,513	100.00	224,800	100.00	61.84

Source: Government of Kerala (2016).

investment, poor infrastructural facilities, etc. Though there has been an increase in growth of NRD, its share in total deposit has been showing a decline in the recent years. The bank branches, deposits and credits are concentrated in urban and semi-urban areas. District-wise distribution of scheduled commercial banks reveals that bank branches, deposits and CDRs are higher in urban districts such as Ernakulam, Thiruvananthapuram and Thrissur.

REFERENCES AND SELECT BIBLIOGRAPHY

Canara Bank. (1994). *Report of the committee on credit deposit ratio in Kerala*. Bangalore: Canara Bank.

———. (2001–2016). *Report of the State Level Bankers Committee, Kerala*, various issues. Thiruvananthapuram: Canara Bank.

Department of Economics and Statistics (DES). (2001). *Statistics for planning*. Thiruvananthapuram: Department of Economics and Statistics.

Jeromi, P. D. (2003). What ails Kerala economy: A sectoral exploration. *Economic and Political Weekly, 38*(16), 1584–1600.

———. (2004). Development of commercial banking in Kerala. In B. A. Prakash (ed), *Kerala's economic development: Performance and problems in the post liberalization period*. New Delhi: SAGE.

———. (2008). Credit deposit ratio in Kerala: Myth and reality. In B. A. Prakash & V. R. Prabhakaran Nair (eds), *Kerala's economic development: Issues in the new millennium*. New Delhi: Serials Publications.

Oommen, M. A. (1976). Rise and growth of banking in Kerala. *Social Scientist, 5*(43), 24–46.

RBI (Reserve Bank of India). (2005). *Basic statistical returns of scheduled commercial banks in India*. Mumbai: RBI.

———. (2015). *Report of the trend and progress of banking in India*. Mumbai: RBI.

Zachariah, K. C., & Rajan, S. I. (2016). Kerala migration study 2014. *Economic and Political Weekly, 51*(6), 66–71.

PART VI

Education and Health

Chapter 15

Higher Education for Kerala's Development
A Focus on Expansion and Equity

A. Abdul Salim

INTRODUCTION

The state of Kerala has been termed as the most literate state in India and the model of education that is being rendered is taken as a role model by others. In terms of the Human Development Index (HDI), the state ranks fairly well in comparison with some of the advanced countries of the world. The state has achieved all the Millennium Development Goals set for education, much ahead of time. A number of historical, social and political factors contributed to this. The progressive outlook of the princely states during the pre-Independence period and the involvement of the missionaries created the basis of the educational development in the state. The committed efforts of the social organisations and the farsightedness of the elected governments in the state after Independence provided the impetus for the present-day achievement. The current system is the result of a complex interplay of national and state aims, plans and execution, intermingled with desires for individual and collective economic and social development, and layered with concerns of equity and access (Sharma, 2013).

Even after leading in many of the indicators, the state of Kerala could not transform itself into a developed state. The lack of importance given to higher education is the main cause of this scenario. In 2015, gross enrolment ratio (GER) of higher education in Kerala was less than that of the national GER. In some districts, the GER is below 12 per cent. The College Population Index is miserably less in the northern districts of Kerala. The GER of marginalised communities seems to be lower than that of well-off sections. The spirit of competition among the students in the higher education sector has been strangely declining. The number of students from Kerala qualifying for national entrance examinations is quite low compared to the students of other states. The higher education sector had not been rooted in the economy of Kerala. There seems to be very little interaction between education and industry. The capacity of Kerala's formal education system to respond to qualitative changes taking place in job markets in India and abroad has been declining at an alarming rate.

Since 1991, a large number of new higher education institutions mostly in the self-financing sector have come up in Kerala. Even these institutions seem to give importance to traditional/conventional courses. The courses are not re-oriented taking into account either the developments in the disciplines or the changes in the job markets. Generally, courses are started not by considering the academic interests or their relevance to the state. They are started by extraneous pressures of groups such as college managements and teachers. There is very little coordination among the universities and with the government.

The Kerala State Higher Education Council in its report (2012) discusses the major areas of concern such as the over-commercialisation of education in private professional institutions and lowering down of standards of teaching facilities and laboratories in a number of private institutions. It identifies the major reason for this as the absence of a national as well as a regional linkage and monitoring mechanism. The study also focused on issues such as access to women and disadvantaged groups, and quality maintenance. The committee viewed with great concern as to why the state of Kerala is not a preferred destination to students from other states and the international community, while most of the other states attract students from across the country. There are also studies by Kunhaman (2000), Abdul Salim and Gopinath Nair

(2002), Abdul Salim (2004), Nair and Gopinath Nair (2008), Ajith Kumar and George (2009) and George (2014). While these studies no doubt shed light on certain important issues of higher education in Kerala, their implications for the sector are limited by the absence of a more general mapping and comprehensive analysis of the issues. The present chapter examines the problems of higher education in Kerala with the following objectives.

1. To examine the nature and extent of expansion of higher education between the Travancore–Cochin and Malabar regions.
2. To examine the equity in access to higher education between the regions, various socio-economic groups and between genders.

EXPANSION OF INSTITUTIONS AND COURSES IN KERALA

Higher education in Kerala has witnessed rapid expansion since the formation of the state in 1956. However, the role of the government in college education is limited, as government colleges are small in number. Of the total of 210 government and private-aided arts and science colleges in Kerala, the number of private-aided colleges was 152 in 2015–16 (72 per cent) (GoK 2016). The expansion of higher education took further momentum since 1995, mainly due to the starting of self-financing colleges for engineering, medical, para-medical, management and computer science courses. There was also an increase in the number of self-financing arts and science colleges offering courses in the non-conventional subjects. Besides, a number of government and aided colleges themselves started conventional and non-conventional self-financing courses. Further, there is a rapid increase in the number of 'non-formal' educational institutions which offer job-oriented courses and are run purely on commercial lines (Ajith Kumar & George, 2009).

Table 15.1 shows the growth of higher education institutions in Kerala during 1991–2014/2015. Right from the early years, the presence of government colleges is less in number compared to private colleges. Interestingly, only government and aided private colleges were present till 2005. In 2005/2006, there occurred a tremendous increase from 186 colleges to 356, with the starting of 167 private self-financing engineering colleges in the state, which is a major attempt

Table 15.1 *Growth of Higher Education Institutions, 1991–2015*

Type of Institution	1991				2011				2015			
	Govt.	Aided	Unaided	Total	Govt.	Aided	Unaided	Total	Govt.	Aided	Unaided	Total
Arts and science college	40	132	0	172	40	150	160	350	58	152	234	444
Engineering colleges	5	3	0	8	9	3	130	142	9	3	163	175
Medical/nursing/dental/pharmacy/Ayurveda/homeo	21	11	1	33	25	18	139	182	–	–	–	247
BEd colleges	4	17	40	61	4	17	147	168	–	–	–	170
Polytechnics	26	6	0	32	43	6	9	58	–	–	–	66
Total	96	169	41	306	124	216	560	900	–	–	–	1,102

Source: Compiled from Anvar (2016), CEE official website of Technical Education (2016) and GoK (2016).

at privatising the higher education stream in Kerala. This shows the interest of the government to withdraw from the higher education sector in Kerala. During 1991–2014/2015, the number of arts and science colleges nearly trebled, while the number of engineering and medical colleges increased by 10 times. The number of institutions further increased from 900 in 2011 to 1,102 in 2015, an increase of 22 per cent within a period of four years. Over a period of 25 years from 1991, the state has gradually moved from a public-funded system to a private-funded one; the share of self-financing private colleges rose from 13 per cent to 62 per cent.

The dominant role of the government in financing the higher education sector has come to an end, and at present, the expansion of the sector does not rely heavily on public funds. The role reversal in financing higher education has taken place due to the reform measure of privatisation of public institutions and promotion of private institutions in the sector (Varghese, 2013). Over a period of time, since the introduction of reforms in 1991, there has been a fall in higher education expenditure by the government, which would adversely affect the expansion, equity and efficiency of higher education system in Kerala and other parts of India. In 2014, public expenditure on higher education out of the total allocation for education at all-India level was 10.88 per cent, and in Kerala, it was 15.89 per cent (MHRD, 2014). At present in Kerala, higher education institutions are under the control of a few community-based organisations. For instance, more than 51 per cent are under the control of Christian denominations; 32 per cent under Nair Service Society (NSS), Sree Narayana Trust, and other Hindu denominations; and the rest 17 per cent under the Muslim Educational Society (MES) and Muslims (Anvar, 2015, p. 91). These philanthropic institutions of yesteryears have now turned to be increasingly commercial, which has serious adverse implications on equity and access.

Region-wise and management-wise details of colleges and sanctioned intake are given in Table 15.2. There were 164 engineering colleges in the state with a total sanctioned intake of 52,802 in 2013. Out of these engineering colleges, almost 93 per cent were self-financing colleges while only 7 per cent are government/private-aided colleges. Regional disparity in the number of colleges and sanctioned

Table 15.2 *Region-wise Details of Engineering Colleges in Kerala 2013*

	No. of Colleges			Sanctioned Intake		
Region	Govt. & Aided	Unaided	Total	Govt. & Aided	Unaided	Total
Travancore–Cochin	7	116	124	3,209	37,955	41,164
Malabar	5	36	41	1,582	10,056	11,638
Kerala	12	152	164	4,791	48,011	52,802

Source: Compiled from GoK (2013).

intake is magnifying; Malabar region lags behind (three times in the number of colleges and nearly four times in the sanctioned intake) the Travancore–Cochin region.

Expansion of Higher Education Enrolment in Kerala

The GER in higher education in Kerala increased to 22.9 per cent in 2012–2013 from 9.0 per cent in 2000–2001 and 5.9 per cent in 1972–1973 (Varghese, 2015). It is interesting to find that in a pioneering state like Kerala, its position in 2002/2003, among the major states in India, was 6th, while in 2012/2013 it was relegated to 11th position (calculated from Varghese, 2015). It is found that the total number of students enrolled in various arts and science colleges (excluding unaided colleges) under the four general universities in Kerala during 2014–2015 is 227,000. Of this 156,000 (68.66 per cent) are girls. Interestingly, the representation of girl students for science courses is almost 73 per cent. Out of the total students enrolled for degree courses, 43.01 per cent are enrolled for BA degree courses, 40.19 per cent enrolled for BSc and 16.80 per cent enrolled for B.Com degree courses. Children from middle and poor families prefer to join courses which are more economical and suitable to their educational background. Children from such families lack strong academic capabilities, proficiency in language, soft skills, etc. Therefore, they prefer light degree courses. Twenty-seven subjects are offered for BA degree courses. Among the subjects, economics has the largest number of enrolment of students.

Thirty-one subjects are offered for BSc courses and mathematics has the largest number of student enrolment. The number of enrolment in arts and science courses has increased tremendously.

In the technical education sector in Kerala, 88 per cent of the seats were in conventional streams such as electronics and communication, mechanical, civil, computer science, and electricals and electronics (see Table 15.3). Seats for new-generation branches such as diary science and technology, agricultural engineering, food technology, printing technology, etc., are very few at less than 12 per cent, and that too in the self-financing sector. Most of these new-generation courses are given by the self-financing institutions, and the fees and other academic costs of these courses are heavy. The economically deprived students cannot afford the new-generation and job-oriented courses. Kerala, having 100 per cent literacy and higher GER, is still unable to offer its youth a wide variety of courses that the global and national economy demands. Despite the high demand, the courses with high employment opportunities are few, with most colleges offering only conventional ones. During the three-year period between 2013 and 2016, there was an increase in the number of seats from 52,820 to 58,237; the increase was mostly in the conventional stream. This shows the lack of any vision from the part of the government and the universities in sanctioning courses suited to the requirements of the modern economy.

Table 15.3 *Distribution of Seats in Engineering Colleges, 2015–2016*

Name of Course/Branch	Total Sanctioned Seats
Conventional engineering courses*	51,293
New-born engineering courses**	6,944
Total	58,237

Source: GoK (2015).

Notes: * Includes civil engineering, computer science and engineering, electronics and communication, electricals and electronics, and mechanical engineering.

** Includes agricultural engineering, biomedical engineering, biotechnology, chemical engineering, diary science and technology, industrial engineering, polymer engineering, printing technology and so on.

Regional Variations in Enrolment in Kerala

In Kerala, almost 92 per cent of the total enrolment is for degree courses. The share of postgraduation (PG) courses is nominal, which has important adverse implications for research and development of the state and the country. The state has very few research institutions, and a highly structured and well-developed PG education is essential to develop R&D of the state. There exist serious regional disparities in the distribution of institutions. Travancore–Cochin region dominates with 68 per cent of the total seats and enrolment, while Malabar region is lagging behind with only 32 per cent of the total enrolment in the state (see Table 15.4). Further, almost 81 per cent of the total enrolment for PG courses is concentrated in the former region. Both the number of institutions and the number of courses are less in Malabar region. Regional disparity is predominant in the case of new-generation courses. Therefore serious positive intervention measures from the part of the government is essential for bridging this gap in enrolment.

All the districts in Travancore–Cochin region have significantly higher GER (30.24) than the Malabar region (12.92). The whole Travancore–Cochin region stands well above the national average of 21.9 per cent (Table 15.5), while three districts, Kottayam,

Table 15.4 *Enrolment of Students in Arts & Science Colleges in Kerala by Regions, 2014–2015*

District	Govt. & Private Aided		Self-financing	
	UG	PG	UG	PG
Travancore–Cochin	380,970	35,808	99,870	13,594
Malabar	157,227	12,274	78,465	3,264
Kerala	538,197	48,082	178,335	16,858

District	Total		
	UG	PG	UG & PG
Travancore–Cochin	480,840	49,402	530,242
Malabar	235,692	15,538	251,230
Kerala	716,532	64,940	781,472

Source: Compiled from Anvar (2016).

Ernakulam and Pathanamthitta, stand above the global GER of 30 per cent. Surprisingly, Kottayam with the GER of 47 per cent is closer to that of the developed countries. High GER in Travancore–Cochin region is due to relatively higher interest given by the people of the area to higher education right from the British period. The role of the Christian missionaries and the social reform movements under various Hindu, Christian and Muslim organisations for initiating and running colleges is remarkable in this context (see Abdul Salim & Nair, 2002). Access to higher education differs widely across the districts. The more progressive southern districts have a higher GER as well as higher availability of educational institutions, whereas the districts in Malabar are characterised by the lack of adequate educational institutions and low GER.

A subject-wise distribution of degree and PG courses shows that even in 2015, there is a massification of conventional courses and the consequent enrolment (Table 15.6). New-generation courses which offer better employment opportunities are very few. There is no long-term vision in Kerala in sanctioning new courses in colleges. Courses are started not by considering the employability or requirements in the

Table 15.5 *Region-wise Breakup of GER in Kerala, 2012*

District	Population in the Age Group 18–23	Gross Enrolment	GER	Rank
Travancore–Cochin	1,643,279	496,978	30.24	4.5
Malabar	1,525,700	197,228	12.92	11.5
Total	3,168,979	694,206	21.91	

Source: Calculated by the author.

Table 15.6 *Enrolment in Arts & Science Colleges (Govt. & Aided), 2015*

Courses	BA	BSc	B.Com	MA	MSc	M.Com
Conventional	82,604	66,765	14,963	7,875	9,521	–
Non-conventional	14,784	11,975	3,712	1,042	1,806	5,453
Total	97,388	78,740	18,675	8,917	11,327	5,453

Source: Compiled from the Statistics by the Directorate of Collegiate Education, GoK (2015).

economy, but by considering the short-term interests of managements and other stakeholders. A look into the nature of courses allotted recently by the government reveals that most of them are still conventional, which have no value for the students and the economy. In the case of BSc course, 31 subjects are offered, and mathematics has the largest number of student enrolment, followed by physics and chemistry. In the case of commerce degree course, general B.Com has larger number of seats than B.Com with specialisations. On the whole, almost 84.4 per cent of the degree courses and 86 per cent of the PG courses are conventional.

Thus, the great expansion in college education in Kerala began in the 1960s when, in response to consistent demands from various organisations in the state, the government began to build or sanction the establishment of colleges. Since the 1990s, with the introduction of economic reforms, higher education in Kerala has been subjected to significant policy shifts. The major policy shift is the opening of the doors to self-financing colleges, which initiated full-fledged private participation in the sector. Previously private participation had been through private-aided colleges, which received public funds but were managed by private managements, mostly of the nature of voluntary or charitable trusts. In the year 2000, the government decided to 'grant "no objection certificates" to any private agency that approached it for permission to start an unaided professional college' (GoK, 2006). This decision evidently evoked a huge response from the private agencies, particularly for the development of professional and technical education in the state (GoK, 2013). The number of self-financing or unaided colleges are increasing tremendously in Kerala. Besides, a number of government and aided colleges themselves started conventional and non-conventional self-financing courses. Most of the courses in Kerala are irrelevant to the productive sectors of the economy. Even professional and technical courses are not different from this. Courses are increasingly irrelevant to the changing labour markets.

ACCESS AND EQUITY OF HIGHER EDUCATION IN KERALA

As noted earlier, higher education institutions are not equally distributed across the state; they are overcrowded in Travancore–Cochin region whereas Malabar region is lagging behind. This implies that the students of Travancore–Cochin region have easy access to higher education, while the access to students of Malabar region is a serious issue. Again, the number of courses and sanctioned strength of the students in the Malabar region are lesser, with very few new-generation courses. In terms of GER, all the districts in the Travancore–Cochin region are either closer to or better than the world average of 30 per cent. But Malabar region still has to travel a lot, and Malappuram district has the lowest GER of 8.4 per cent.

In terms of caste, the highest number of population in the age group 18–23 belongs to the OBC category (1.566 million). The second highest population under this age group is General (1.27 million) while that of SC/ST is the lowest. But GER for OBC is lower at 14 per cent than that of SC. The general category has a GER of almost 33 per cent (Table 15.7). The GER of SC and ST students in Kerala is much better than that of other states in India because of several positive discrimination policies such as mandatory reservation of seats in colleges, travel and fee concessions, and scholarships given by SC/ST development department and other agencies. Interestingly, most of the private institutions come under Christian managements. Therefore, students belonging to the Christian community are more privileged to get enrolled into such institutions due to the existence of a large number of management and community seats. This is the reason why the GER of Christians is much higher than the GER of Hindus and Muslims. Even though the population in the age group of 18–24 is lowest among Christians (601,000), the GER occupied by them is the highest (35.94 per cent). Hindus, with the highest population under this age group, have a GER of 23.3 per cent. But the GER of

Table 15.7 *Caste-wise Details of GER in Kerala*

	SC	ST	OBC	General	Total
Population in the age group 18–23 (in Lakh)	2.85	0.46	15.66	12.7	31.67
Gross enrolment	0.51	0.066	2.16	4.204	6.94
GER (%)	17.89	14.35	13.79	33.1	21.91

Source: Anvar (2016).

Muslims is the lowest at 8 per cent (Table 15.8). The new–generation courses started recently are in self-financing institutions which are not accessible to the low income groups and marginalised communities who have no community colleges of their own.

However, there is not much rural urban and gender disparities in GER. Compared to the all-India level, the share of female enrolment under all categories is high. There is a predominance of girls in arts and science colleges. Almost 75 per cent of the students in arts and science colleges in Kerala are females (Tables 15.9). In degree programmes, about 69 per cent of the students enrolled in Kerala are girls. In PG programmes, there is a virtual predominance of girl students. But their predominance is lesser in the case of non-conventional courses. In 2015/2016, girls dominate even the engineering and medical courses. Girls outnumber boys because a large number of boys prefer early jobs out of compulsion to look after their parents and family members, or they prefer blue collar jobs either in the state or outside at an early age rather than spending a huge amount of money and energy for higher

Table 15.8 *Religion-wise Details of GER in Kerala 2011–2012*

	Hindu	Muslim	Christian	Total
Population in the age group 18–23 (in Lakh)	17.81	7.85	6.01	31.67
Gross enrolment	4.15	0.63	2.16	6.94
GER (%)	23.30	8.03	35.94	21.91

Source: Anvar (2016).

Table 15.9 *Share of Girls in Arts and Science Colleges (Govt. and Aided), 2015 (in %)*

Courses	BA	BSc	B.Com	MA	MSc	M.Com
Conventional	67.06	75.57	62.76	83.45	86.96	–
Non-conventional	64.92	66.67	61.04	71.01	79.90	51.69
Total	66.73	74.21	62.41	81.83	85.83	51.69

Source: Compiled from the statistics by the Directorate of Collegiate Education, GoK (2015).

education. Moreover some boys lose interest in higher education faster than the girls. Some boys exercise their freedom to opt out of more higher education due to their dislike in the subject or the intensity of the waiting period for getting a white-collar job.

Recent studies (Abdul Salim, 2004; Ajith Kumar & George, 2009) reveal that access to professional and technical education is mostly limited to students coming from the middle and affluent classes. Entry of rural, Malayalam medium- and first-generation students is not significant. While the access of the rural poor to general education is high, the same for professional education is restricted. It appears that passports to unemployment are issued to everyone, while the same to employment opportunities are issued only to the elite groups, made on the basis of their financial and social background. The problem becomes more serious when we find that for the marginalised groups such as SC/ST, fisher folk and the bottom poor, the access to quality education is a prerequisite not only as a means for social liberation but also for seeking better economic opportunities. This is particularly so as these groups have very limited possessions of material means of production.

Privatisation of Higher Education and Equity in Kerala

Since the introduction of new economic reforms, higher education in Kerala has been subject to significant policy shifts. The major change was the emergence of large number of self-financing colleges catering to the requirements of middle- and upper-class parents. They charge very high fees and are run largely on commercial lines. Fees are not charged by any rational calculations of the institutional or parental costs. Recent cost estimates which can serve the basis of charging fees are not available in the state. 'What the traffic can bear' is the principle of charging the fees. The self-financing courses strengthen the already existing entry barriers to higher education.

Presently, in government/aided colleges, students pay fees of about ₹1,200 per year for degree arts and science courses; and ₹25,000, ₹5,500 and ₹6,000 respectively for MBBS, BTech and LLB courses. In private-aided and self-financing institutions, the average annual fees for pursuing general education, MBBS and LLB are ₹17,000, ₹500,000 and ₹30,000 respectively. The donations range from 30,000 to 50,000 for general education and 1 million to 5 million for professional education in self-financing institutions. In this context, the Ashok Mitra Commission found that the self-financing colleges are primarily commercial institutions working for increasing the profit rather than giving qualitative education. The dominance of these institutions which charge huge fees to cover both the recurrent costs and the capital costs effectively rule out the entry of the poor into higher education. In addition to the amount collected from the students, the management of many private-aided institutions collects a huge amount from the candidates appointed as teaching staff, and the government pays the salary and pension of these teaching staff. Thus, in private and self-financing colleges, even the teaching posts are reserved for the rich, which further widens the inequality in the education sector. Thus, as a result of neoliberal policies, higher education, particularly in the self-financing colleges, was found to be less affordable to a vast majority, and thus widening the inequalities.

To help the low caste groups from the cumulative effects of exclusion, the government of Kerala introduced several affirmative measures such as reservation for admission in their favour, stipends and scholarships. But the implementation of these measures has remained half-hearted. Even though the reservation system has benefitted the lower caste group students to an extent, it was not channelised to the needy. Several entry barriers have restricted the poorer sections of the low caste groups to access higher education (for details of entry barriers, see Abdul Salim, 2004). The situation is worse in the professional courses where entry barrier stands as monster for these sections. An individual study based on a sample survey of 1,934 students of 1999 admission and 2,048 students of 2006 admission reveals that during 1999–2006, the access of SC/ST, OEC and OBC in the regular colleges has improved, but not up to the level of their population proportion, while the access of SC/ST to self-financing colleges has not improved significantly (Table 15.10). Thus, even after 69 years of Independence, Kerala has only partially succeeded in ensuring equality of opportunity. The boom created in the higher education has, in fact, aggravated inequality.

Thus, we find that the regional, social and economic disparities are still predominant in Kerala. The students of Travancore–Cochin region

Table 15.10 *Caste/Community-wise Distribution of Students, 1999–2006 (%)*

Category	Degree			
	1999 Admission		2006 Admission	
	Regular	Self-financing	Regular	Self-financing
OBC	32.0	17.6	41.7	49.2
SC/ST	8.8	2.9	16.0	2.6
OEC	6.2	1.2	6.6	1.3
Others	53.0	78.3	35.7	46.9
Total	100.0	100.0	100.0	100.0

Category	Postgraduation			
	1999 Admission		2006 Admission	
	Regular	Self-financing	Regular	Self-financing
OBC	23.8	Nil	27.6	30.2
SC/ST	7.5	Nil	13.7	3.4
OEC	2.6	Nil	3.8	5.9
Others	66.1	Nil	54.9	60.5
Total	100.0	Nil	100.0	100.0

Source: Compiled from Zachariah (2010).

have easy access to higher education, while the access to students of Malabar region is a serious issue. Again the number of courses and sanctioned strength of the students in the Malabar region are lesser with very few new-generation courses.

The highest level of GER is attained by General category children. In general education, the GER of SC/ST and OBC students in Kerala is much better than that of other states in India because of several positive discrimination policies such as mandatory reservation of seats in colleges, travel and fee concessions, scholarships and stipends. But their situation is worse in the professional courses where entry barrier stands as monster for these sections. Moreover, self-financing courses are found to be gradually becoming less and less affordable by the majority of these people.

CONCLUSION

The study shows that the level of expansion in higher education is very impressive in Kerala compared to other parts of the country. But the institutions are not equally distributed across the state; they are overcrowded in Travancore–Cochin region, whereas Malabar region is lagging behind. Not only the number of colleges but also the number of courses and sanctioned seats in the Travancore–Cochin region are large. Thus, the students of Travancore–Cochin region have easy access to higher education, while the access to students of Malabar region is a big issue. But it is surprising to find that most of the courses offered in the colleges were conventional, and are not meeting the requirements of the fast-growing knowledge economy. A few new generation courses have come to Kerala only recently, and that too in the private self-financing colleges. Declining financial support provided by the government on higher education and the exorbitant fee structure of self-financing colleges have adversely affected the enrolment level of students belonging to the less-privileged class whose talent is also needed by the society for its comprehensive development.

Further, higher education, particularly professional and technical education in Kerala, is mostly private self-financing, which is not affordable for poor students. Interestingly, most of the private institutions are run by one minority community, and the students belonging to that community are more privileged to get enrolled into such institutions. This is the reason why the GER of Christians is much higher than the GER of Hindus and Muslims. The highest level of GER is attained by General category children while that of children belonging to OBC and SC/ST are very low. However, the GER of SC/ST students in Kerala is much better than the same in other states in India because of several positive discrimination policies like the mandatory reservation of seats in colleges. Gender equality is almost complete in the all types of colleges in Kerala. In fact, GER among genders favours women in Kerala.

REFERENCES AND SELECT BIBLIOGRAPHY

Abdul Salim, A. (2004). *Opportunities for higher education: An enquiry into entry barriers, Kerala research programme on local level development* (Discussion Paper No. 71). Thiruvananthapuram: Centre for Development Studies.

Abdul Salim, A. (2014). Economic reforms and inclusive growth of higher education. *Productivity*, *55*(3, October–December), 309–313.

Abdul Salim, A., & Nair, P. R. G. (2002). *Educational development in India: The experience of Kerala since 1800*. New Delhi: Anmol Publications.

Ajith Kumar, N., & George, K. K. (2009). Kerala's education system: From inclusion to exclusion. *Economic and Political Weekly*, *44*(41), 55–61.

Altbach, P. G. (2009, 6 June). The giants awake: Higher education systems in China and India. *Economic & Political Weekly*, *44*(23), 39–51.

Anvar, P. (2016). *World class state without word class higher education*. Thiruvananthapuram: Southern Books.

Basent, R., & Sen, G. (2010, 25 September). Who participates in higher education in India? Rethinking the role of affirmative action. *Economic & Political Weekly*, *45*(39), 62–70.

Borker, Hem. (2012, 5 April). Shutting the school door on the Muslim child. *The Hindu*, p. 11.

Controller of Entrance Examinations (CEE) official website of Technical Education. 2016. Retrieved on 25 April 2018, from www.cee-kerala.org/

George, A. (2014). Education of poor in Kerala: Achievements, aspirations and orientation, NEUPA. *Journal of Educational Planning and Administration*, *28*(3), 235–248.

GoK (Government of Kerala). (2006). *Economic review*. Thiruvananthapuram: Kerala State Planning Board.

———. (2013). *Economic review*. Thiruvananthapuram: Kerala State Planning Board.

———. (2015). *Economic review*. Thiruvananthapuram: Kerala State Planning Board.

———. (2016). *Economic review*. Thiruvananthapuram: Kerala State Planning Board.

Kamalakar, G., & Chakravarthy, A. S. (2014). *GATS and Indian higher education*. New Delhi: Commonwealth.

Kunhaman, M. (2000). *Higher education in Kerala: Access of the poor and marginalised*. Paper presented at the National Conference on 'Education in Kerala's Development, Institute of Social Science, New Delhi.

———. (2016, October). *Higher education in the context of development*. Paper presented at the National Seminar on Higher Education in a Developing Economy: Problems, Policies and Perspectives at the Inter University Centre for Alternative Economics, University of Kerala, Thiruvananthapuram.

Madan, A. (2015). Practice of caste in higher education. *Economic and Political Weekly*, *50*(3), 31–32.

MHRD (Ministry of Human Resource Development). (2014). *All-India survey of higher education 2013–2014*. New Delhi: Government of India.

Nair, K. N., & Nair, P. R. G. (eds). (2008). *Higher education in Kerala*. New Delhi: Danish Publications.

Nayak, D. (2013, 2 February). The pitfalls of privatisation of higher education. *Economic & Political Weekly*, *48*(5), 15–17.

Sharma, K. (2013). *Sixty years of the University Grants Commission.* New Delhi: UGC.

Tilak, J. B. G. (2014, 4 October). Private higher education in India. *Economic & Political Weekly, 49*(40), 32–38.

———. (2015a). *Higher education in India: In search of equality, quality and quantity.* New Delhi: Orient Blackswan.

———. (2015b). Higher education in South Asia: Crisis and challenges. *Social Scientist, 43*(1–2), 43–59.

Varghese, N. V. (2013). *Private higher education: The global surge and Indian concerns, in India Infrastructure Report 2012: Private sector in education.* New Delhi: Routledge.

———. (2015). *Challenges of massification of higher education in India, Centre for Policy Research in Higher Education.* New Delhi: NUEPA.

———. (2016). The changing landscape of higher education: An analysis of changes in developing and developed countries. Paper presented at National Seminar on Higher Education in a Developing Economy: Problems, Policies and Perspectives, Inter University Centre for Alternative Economics, University of Kerala, Thiruvananthapuram.

Zachariah, George. (2010). *Changing enrolment patterns in arts and science colleges in Kerala.* Report submitted to Kerala State Higher Education Council Government of Kerala, Centre for Socio-economic & Environmental Studies (CSES) Kochi.

Chapter 16

Health Care Development in Kerala
Current Status and Emerging Issues

K. Gangadharan

INTRODUCTION

Health care is the prevention, treatment and management of illness and the preservation of mental and physical well-being through the services offered by the medical and allied health professions. The purpose of health care services is to improve the health status of the population. The goals to be achieved was fixed in terms of reduction of mortality and morbidity, decrease in population growth rate, reducing health care expenditure and avoiding catastrophic ruin, improvements in nutritional status, provision of basic sanitation and health, requirements of manpower, development of resources, and certain other parameters such as food production, literacy rate, reduced level of poverty and providing equitable access to medicine to all citizens, etc. Studies have shown that the budgetary allocation to the health care sector in India shows more of supply side factors than demand side in the public sector, whereas health care expenditures represent more of demand side than supply side in the private health care sector (Bhat, 2004; Summut and Burns, 2011). The Planning Commission has reported that in the private health sector, incentives are tilted towards curative services and medical education (Srinivasan, 2012).

India's health care approach has been always oriented towards developing primary health care services. The provision of primary health care with basic health services was conceived in India much before the Alma Ata Declaration, as pursued by various committees commissioned for formulating health care development in the country (Ghosh, 2014).

Kerala has achieved remarkable progress in human development, as reflected in the high levels of education and health of its population. Kerala has achieved good health indicators compared to other Indian states. Government intervention in this sector is the main reason for these achievements. This has become even more important at a time when the state is facing the emergence and re- emergence of some the communicable diseases such as malaria, dengue, chicken guinea, etc., over the last few years along with problems resulting from epidemiological and population transition (Government of Kerala, 2013). The widely accepted health indicators, namely, death rate, infant mortality rate (IMR) and life expectancy at birth, etc., are far advanced than the rest of the states in India, and are even comparable with developed countries. In Kerala, the life expectancy has increased, IMR is very low and there is decline in death rate. Also, the health awareness among the citizens of the state remains at a very high level. The maternal mortality rate of Kerala is better than the all-India average. Most of the deliveries performed in Kerala take place in institutions, and the quality of obstetric care has to be improved. However, some issues such as maternal anaemia, malnutrition among children, early marriage and teenage pregnancy in some of the district and tribal areas are still continuing (Health and Family Welfare Department, 2013). Similarly, the dominant role of the private sector in the health care development is another emerging issue. The private sector in Kerala grew to meet the demand that was unmet when the government cut back its investment due to fiscal strain. Currently, the private sector accounts for more than 70 per cent of all the facilities. The types of ownership range from corporate to single proprietor. They vary in sophistication from single-doctor hospital to multi-specialty hospitals and have become the preferred providers for the affluent and the middle class. The health status of the tribal communities is worse in most parts of Kerala. Tribal communities suffer from diseases that result from lack of safe drinking water, sanitation, and lack of proper housing and medical care.

OBJECTIVE, DATA SOURCE AND CONCEPT OF THE STUDY

This chapter is an attempt to provide a profile of health care development and emerging issues in health care in Kerala in the new era. Since health is the core part of social sector development, it has very high relevance in the human development potential of the state. The policies and programmes undertaken by the government and the initiative of private sector have converted the state of Kerala to a health-friendly state in India, and health has become a vibrant segment of the economy, requiring much attention and capital. An attempt is made in this chapter to travel along the health care development of Kerala, especially since the year 2000, by picking up elements that are relevant to health care advancement of the state, and also those issues which has made Kerala a very high morbidity prevalent state in the country. The following are the specific objectives the study targets:

1. To examine the health care development in terms of infrastructure and human resources in Kerala.
2. To study the morbidity profile and health and nutrition transition path of Kerala, and also to focus on the problems of health in the tribal hamlets of Kerala.

The data source for the study is mainly secondary sources including the data from Directorate of Health Services, Government of Kerala; Ministry of Health, Government of Kerala; and State Planning Board. Similarly, health data collected by non-government organisations (NGOs) and other apex institutions in the health and social sector in the country such as NFHS, etc., are also used in the study. The basic concepts used and analysed in the study include social determinant of health, epidemiological transition, nutritional deprivation, health infrastructure and human resource development, tribal health issues, etc.

The chapter is divided into four sections. Section I deals with the profile of health care development in Kerala and Section II focuses on social determinants of health and the emerging issues in the health care sector of Kerala. Section III deals with the tribal health of Kerala and Section IV is the summary and conclusion.

SECTION I: HEALTH CARE DEVELOPMENT IN KERALA—A PROFILE

Kerala is a small state located in the southwestern tip of the Indian peninsula. It came into existence in its present form in November 1956 when state boundaries were demarcated on the basis of language. Kerala accounts for a mere 1.18 per cent of the total land of India. The state is divided into 14 districts. The total population of the state has increased from 16.9 million in 1961 to 33.8 million in 2011. This is a very densely populated and highly literate state with 859 persons per sq. km in 2011, with a female literacy rate of 91.02 per cent and a male literacy rate of 96.02 per cent.

It can be seen that in Kerala, in less than two decades, one in every five persons will be at least 60 years of age, leading to a new type of health problem for the state to face. Among the aged, a higher proportion will be females, of which the majority are likely to be widows. At the same time, the decline in the percentage share of children from 26 per cent to 18.8 per cent during the reference period should also be noted, which would necessitate a rethinking on the state's spending pattern, particularly in the health sector. Kerala's development experience is known to be characterised by a high level of social development that is disproportionate to the level of economic growth. In terms of all conventional physical quality of life indicators, Kerala is way ahead not only of other Indian states and middle-income countries but also some of the developed countries. The state is also ranked top on the basis of the Human Development Index. The India Social Development Report ranked Kerala as first in social development in the rural areas and second in the urban areas among the states in India. The state is often described as a land of 'good health at low cost' achieved by improving the access to health services, especially for the underprivileged people. The foundation for a medical care system accessible to all citizens was laid in the state much before Independence. Some of the hospitals in Kerala are more than 50 years old. Democratic decentralisation since 1994 in Kerala improved the infrastructure facilities and equipment in primary and secondary health care institutions, and widened health care delivery. Easy accessibility and coverage of medical care facilities has played a leading role in influencing the health status of Kerala. In Kerala, both allopathy and AYUSH systems play a crucial role in providing universal accessibility and availability even to the poorer sections of society.

Kerala has made significant gains in health indices such as IMR, birth rate, death rate and life expectancy at birth. The challenges before the state are to sustain the achievements in the health sector and to tackle the problems of lifestyle diseases such as diabetes, coronary heart disease, renal disease, cancer and geriatric problems. Communicable diseases such as chicken guinea, dengue, leptospirosis and swine flu are also major concerns. Other than these, there are new threats to the health scenario of the state, such as mental health problems, suicide, substance abuse and alcoholism, adolescent health issues and rising number of road traffic accidents. To tackle these, concerted and committed efforts with proper intersectoral coordination is essential.

Health Indicators of Kerala

The health indicators of the state are considerably superior to the national figures. The comparative figures of major health and demographic indicators at state and national levels are given in Tables 16.1 and 16.2.

Kerala has a long tradition of organised health care. Families of practitioners of indigenous systems like Ayurveda handed down their traditions from generation to generation, and the people of Kerala become very

Table 16.1 *Demographic, Socio-economic and Health Profile of Kerala and India-2011*

S. No.	Indicator	Kerala	India
1	Total population (in Crore)	3.34	121.08
2	Decadal growth	4.90	17.70
3	Sex ratio	1,084	943
4	Child sex ratio	964	919
5	Density	860	382

Source: Census Report (2011).

Table 16.2 *Socio-economic and Health Profile of Kerala and India*

S. No.	Indicator	Kerala	India
1	Birth rate	14.7	21.4
2	Death rate	6.9	7.0
3	Infant mortality rate	12.0	40.0
4	Neonatal mortality rate	7.0	5.0
5	Child mortality rate	2.0	5.0
6	Under 5 mortality rate	13.0	55.0
7	Maternal mortality ratio	66.0	178.0
8	Expectancy of life at birth (Male)	74.9	67.9
9	Total fertility rate	0.7	2.6

Source: Directorate of Health Services, Government of Kerala and Rural Health Statistics Report 2016.

much accustomed to approaching the healers when they are sick. From 1961 to 1986, the state greatly expanded its government health facilities. The number of beds and institutions increased sharply. The total number of beds in government hospitals in the Western medical sector increased from around 13,000 in 1960–1961 to 20,000 in 1970–1971 and 29,000 in 1980–1981. By 1986, the total number of beds was 36,000. Thus, the major growth phase of facilities in the government sector was before 1986, after which it slowed considerably (Ramankutty, 2008). The period from the mid-1970s to the early 1990s has been termed as a period of 'fiscal crisis' for the state government. Severe financial impact is perhaps surprising for some as the Kerala health system was once advocated as the ideal Good Health at Low Cost model. Fiscal crisis was due to economic stagnation, rising social expenditure and steep rise in health care costs, and this financial crisis of the government resulted in the default of millions of rupees as payment to medical companies related to the purchase of medicines and supplies to government hospitals. A new Kerala model started to arise in 1990s through decentralised administration, especially planning, uniting productive and environmental objectives, and cooperation between the state NGO and civic movements (Veron, 2001).

Decentralisation policy has strengthened the capacity of local bodies to manage scarce resources and necessitated a dialogue with the local people, and it seems to create inequity of a different kind between the panchayats. But decentralisation brought no significant change to the health sector both quantitatively and qualitatively, and the high morbidity reported from both urban and rural areas, and Kerala has been identified as the state with highest morbidity prevalence. This hike in morbidity culminated in declaring a health package for the state. Public sector hospitals have continued to annoy the common people by not filling the vacant posts of the doctors. Because of the private sector boom and also the tendency of specialised doctors refusing to join the government hospitals, there is a severe dearth of doctors in the rural hilly and tribal areas and even some urban centres and medical colleges, which reflects the anarchy in public hospitals, and no individual and personal attention is paid to the patients and to those who approach health care services (Table 16.3).

Access to hospitals in terms of distance was also considered as one of the major factors in the utilisation of the health care system. Table 16.4 shows the state-wise status of infrastructure in primary health centres (PHCs) in India in 2016.

Some of the reasons of unused/under-used potentials of many institutions are (a) lack of periodic or annual maintenance of buildings resulting in dilapidated conditions; (b) non-availability of building/ lack of proper electrification/lack of water and sanitation facilities, (c) lack of manpower (often building and equipment were con-structed and established but the lack of manpower results in idling

Table 16.3 *Doctor Availability at PHC in India During 2005–2015*

	2005		2015	
State	Doctors Required	Doctors Vacant	Doctors Required	Doctors Vacant
India	23,236	4,282	25,308	9,389
Kerala	911	396	827	
Andhra Pradesh	1,570	360	1,069	858
Haryana	408	0	461	146
Madhya Pradesh	1,192	439	1,171	659
Odisha	1,282	0	1,305	304

Source: https://nrhm-mis.nic.in, retrieved on 4 April 2018.

Table 16.4 *State-wise Status of Infrastructure in Primary Health Centers in India—2016*

Status of Infrastructure	Kerala	India
No. of PHC	824	25,354
Per cent having govt. building	95.8	91.5
Per cent without water facility	0	4.6
Per cent without electricity	0	6.6
Per cent having labour room	7.5	70.9
Per cent having telephone facility	99	54.7
Per cent having referal transport	6.6	45.5
Per cent having at least 4 bed	30.5	75.6

Source: Rural Health Statistics Report 2016.

of a facility); (d) lack of sufficient equipment and furniture, rusty and unrepaired cots, spoilt mattress and torn, and dirty bed sheets or their absence is a common sight in many of the government health care institutions; (e) majority of them may not even have basic clinical investigation facilities and may even lack life supporting facilities such as round the clock availability of oxygen, etc.; and (f) shortage of medicine due to the irregular supply of medicines and other materials, so patients seeking medical care from the government hospitals are forced to buy them from outside, mounting to high out-of-pocket expenditure coupled with curt attitudes of doctors and other staff members.

Child growth is the most widely used indicator of nutritional status in a community, and it is internationally recognised as an important public-health indicator for monitoring health in populations. Nutritional status of children is reflected in three generally used indices: (a) wasting, defined as an abnormally low weight for the child's height; (b) stunting, a situation where the children are too short for their age (an indicator of chronic malnutrition); and (c) underweight, which is low weight for their age due mainly to inadequate diet and infection.

The nutritional deprivation in Kerala is also comparatively high, and it is high among tribal populations. The proportion of children wasted (indicator of malnutrition) is higher in Kerala compared to north eastern states. The NRHM data reveals this (Table 16.5).

Table 16.5 *Nutritional Status of Children in India—2013*

States	Stunted Children Total	Stunted Children Rural	Stunted Children Urban	Wasted Children Total	Wasted Children Rural	Wasted Children Urban	Underweight Children Total	Underweight Children Rural	Underweight Children Urban
Kerala	22.8	25.4	20.7	24.2	22.3	25.9	21.0	22.6	19.5
Arunachal Pradesh	32.2	32.0	32.7	21.4	20.8	23.9	27.3	27.3	27.2
Manipur	37.4	39.1	32.6	15.8	16.3	14.5	27.5	28.2	25.4
Meghalaya	41.7	42.7	35.2	16.7	17.2	13.1	30.5	31.8	21.8
Mizoram	37.8	41.1	31.9	18.2	19.6	16.0	27.2	31.3	20.3
Nagaland	39.8	41.8	32.4	10.8	9.9	14.3	25.5	26.2	23.0
Sikkim	35.0	36.2	26.9	13.1	12.9	14.1	23.6	24.3	19.3

Source: https://nrhm-mis.nic.in, retrieved 4 April 2018.

SECTION II: SOCIAL DETERMINANTS OF HEALTH AND EMERGING ISSUES

Water Supply

Even though Kerala gets over 3,000 cm of rain in a year, poor management reduces the state to near-drought conditions in the period between January and May. Unless the state manages its environmental and water situation better, we are likely to witness outbreaks of water borne diseases such as cholera and hepatitis A.

Solid and Liquid Waste Management System

For last few years, this is the most burning issue with administrative, ecological and public health dimensions. It is a major problem in municipal corporations of Trivandrum, Ernakulam, Kozhikode and Thrissur. This is becoming a major threat to public health in urban areas and urban townships of the rural areas also. Accumulation of plastic waste and the issue of thin plastic carry bags which is still being used even after repeated legal measures further complicate the scenario. Ecological degradation and the contamination of the water bodies and ecosystem in general due to the unscientific use/misuse of pesticides pose a serious health hazard. Health problems due to occupational pollutants, asthma, allergy and chronic obstructive pulmonary diseases, especially in the context of raising urbanisation and increase in the automobile use, are other related issues to be addressed.

Climate Change and Public Health

The changing climate will inevitably affect the basic requirements for maintaining health, clean air and water, sufficient food and adequate shelter. Climate change also brings new challenges to the control of infectious diseases. Many of the major killers are highly climate sensitive as regards to temperature and rainfall, including cholera and the diarrheal diseases, as well as diseases including malaria, dengue and other infections carried by vectors. Also, the issues of reductions and seasonal changes in the availability of fresh water, regional drops in food production, and rising sea levels, etc. has the potential to force population displacement with negative health impacts. Climate change is a new challenge for the control of infectious diseases and public health. It leads to change in pattern of infection, emergence/resurgence/of diseases such as H1N1, H5N1, malaria, dengue, chicken guinea, and leptospirosis. In the year 2016, the number of patients treated for leptospirosis was 1,339 and death reported was 21, and the number of people who obtained treatment for chicken guinea was 106 and for viral fever was 2,040,667, and all these are slightly higher than previous years.

Managing the Emerging/Re-emerging Communicable Diseases

Waterborne diseases such as diarrhoea, hepatitis, typhoid fever and vector bone diseases such as dengue fever, malaria, etc., remain a major problem in Kerala. Leptospirosis, which was a problem for few southern districts in the last decade, has become a major communicable disease in the whole state, causing much morbidity and mortality throughout the year. These diseases follow a seasonal pattern. Outbreaks of waterborne diseases such as diarrhoea and cholera are always more in the monsoon season extending from May to August. Higher incidences of acute viral fevers along with diseases such as dengue, chicken guinea, leptospirosis, scrub typhus, etc., make this as the 'season of epidemics'. There is an apprehension that the presence of migrant labourers from different states might introduce/reintroduce diseases that are not prevalent here. A high level of epidemiological surveillance and outbreak management has to be maintained in the state.

Non-communicable Diseases

In Kerala, NCDs account for more than 50 per cent of total deaths occurring in the age group between 30 and 60. With 27 per cent of adult males and 19 per cent of adult females being diabetic, Kerala is considered to be the diabetic capital of India. The percentage of hypertension, cardiovascular diseases and cancer is also very high in the community across all sections of the society. Yet there was no organised programme to combat these problems. Similarly Kerala reports nearly 35,000 new cancer care registrations and around 100,000 patients' are under treatment every year. But treatment in the government sector is limited to the Regional Cancer Centres at Thiruvananthapuram and Malabar Cancer Centre at Thalassery, Kannur. Radiotherapy is available in five government medical colleges and GH Ernakulam, leaving the remaining seven districts with no facility for cancer treatment in the government sector. The focus has to be on elimination of risk factors, increased awareness, and early detection and prompt treatment.

Maternal Health

Though the maternal mortality rate of Kerala is better than the all-India average, it is unacceptably high compared to the international standards and has been relatively stagnant for the past few years (Tables 16.6 and 16.7).

Table 16.6 *Delivery Care (for Births in the Five Years Before the Survey)*

| Indicators | India | | Kerala | |
	NFHS-4 (2015–2016)	NFHS-3 (2005–2006)	NFHS-4 (2015–2016)	NFHS-3 (2005–2006)
Institutional births (%)	78.9	38.7	99.9	99.3
Institutional births in public facility (%)	52.1	18.0	38.4	35.6
Home delivery conducted by skilled health personnel (out of total deliveries) (%)	4.3	8.2	0.1	0.1
Births assisted by a doctor/ nurse/LHV/ANM/other health personnel (In %)	81.4	46.6	100.0	99.4
Births delivered by caesarean section (%)	17.2	8.5	35.8	30.1
Births in a private health facility delivered by caesarean section (%)	40.9	27.7	38.6	32.7
Births in a public health facility delivered by caesarean section (%)	11.9	15.2	31.4	26.0

Source: NFHS Report 2015–2016.

Table 16.7 *Maternity Care (for Last Birth in the Five Years Before the Survey)*

Indicators	India		Kerala	
	NFHS-4 (2015–2016)	NFHS-3 (2005–2006)	NFHS-4 (2015–2016)	NFHS-3 (2005–2006)
Mothers who had antenatal check-up in the first trimester (%)	58.6	43.9	95.1	91.9
Mothers who had at least four antenatal care visits (%)	51.2	37.0	90.2	93.0
Mothers whose last birth was protected against neonatal tetanus (%)	89.0	76.3	96.5	88.7
Mothers who consumed iron folic acid for 100 days or more when they were pregnant (%)	30.3	15.2	67.1	70.1
Mothers who had full antenatal care (%)	21.0	11.6	61.2	66.7
Registered pregnancies for which the mother received Mother and Child Protection (MCP) card (%)	89.3	na	84.2	na
Mothers who received postnatal care from a doctor/nurse/LHV/ANM/midwife/other health personnel within two days of delivery (%)	62.4	34.6	88.7	84.6
Mothers who received financial assistance under Janani Suraksha Yojana (JSY) for births delivered in an institution (%)	36.4	na	20.4	na
Average out of pocket expenditure per delivery in public health facility (₹)	3,198	na	6,901	na
Children born at home who were taken to a health facility for checkup within 24 hours of birth (%)	2.5	0.3	na	na
Children who received a health check after birth from a doctor/nurse/LHV/ANM/midwife/other health personnel within two days of birth (%)	24.3	na	49.1	na

Source: NFHS Report 2015–2016.

For the last one decade, both government and private sector hospitals are reporting a rising trend of caesarean section touching 40 per cent. Though some administrative and technical measures have been taken up at the state level, so far, it has not made any major impact. Other issues such as maternal anaemia, early marriage and teenage pregnancy in some of the districts and tribal areas also remain intractable.

Child Health

While the IMR of Kerala (6 per 1,000) is far better than most Indian states and NFHS data reveals that the state could sustain this target (Table 16.8), for further reducing the infant mortality, the Neonatal Intensive Care Unit (NICU), Special New Born Care Unit (SNCU) and New Born Care Corner (NBCC) and other new born care facilities attached to the delivery points has to be further strengthened (NFHS, 2016).

Health Problems of Elderly

At present, the percentage of population above 60 is 12 per cent and is expected to cross 25 per cent by the year 2050. As in many other areas, the capacity of the health sector has to be scaled up substantially

Table 16.8 *Maternal and Child Health Indicators During the Four NFHS Periods in Kerala*

Indicators	NFHS-1	NFHS-2	NFHS-3	NFHS-4
Fully immunised children (%)	54	80	75	82.1
Infant mortality rate	24	16	15	6
Underweight children (%)	27	27	29	16.1
Any antenatal care (%)	88	99	100	95.1
Institutional delivery (%)	89	93	100	99
Total fertility rate (TFR)	2	2	1.9	1.6
Women who are exposed to spouse's violence (%)			16.4	14.3

Sources: NFHS Reports (1993–1994, 1998–1999 and 2005–2006, 2015–2016).

to deal with the enormity of the problem. This has taken efforts to set up geriatric care wards with geriatric-friendly facilities at district- and taluk-level hospitals. However, a comprehensive geriatric health care programme is yet to be developed in the state.

SECTION III: TRIBAL HEALTH IN KERALA

Health problem of the tribals and tribal health infrastructure is an important weakness of Kerala's health care system. The geographical nature of the tribal hamlets and the cultural perceptions of the tribal people make the health care system inaccessible to many of them.

Improvement of health manpower in rural and tribal areas mainly depends on the availability of qualified and trained human resources. Currently, there has been a shortage of all key cadre including doctors, nurses and paramedics, particularly in tribal areas of Wayanad and Idukki districts. Irregular attendance/absenteeism in these remote areas, inadequate system of incentives for postings in difficult areas, lack of opportunities for continuing medical education (CME), skill upgradation, and lack of orientation to needs of rural and tribal areas are the main problems facing the health care systems of this areas. A significant proportion of position is vacant at various levels. The data reveals that out of 18 sanctioned posts of medical officers in the seven PHCs, seven sanctioned posts are vacant. The PHC is the first contact point between the tribal community and the medical officer. PHCs provide integrated curative and preventive health care to the tribal population, with an emphasis on the preventive and promotive aspects. The requirement of trained professionals becomes even more crucial in tribal areas, where, due to malnutrition and gaps in routine immunisation, even preventable diseases are rampant. In fact, there is a pressing need of well-trained specialists and experts for rural health services in the country. For the smooth functioning of a sub-centre in the remote area, the junior health inspectors' (JHIs) service is mandatory. As per the Indian public health standards, each sub-centre should have one JHI and one junior public health nurse (JPHN). Tribals hamlets lack these human resource facilities.

The health care infrastructure in the PHC and sub-centres in tribal areas of Wayanad and Idukki district shows that (Table 16.9) they are facing the problem of lack of infrastructure in health care institutions.

Table 16.9 *Health Care Infrastructure of Sub-centres in Tribal Hamlets of Wayanad and Idukki District*

		Wayanad (30)	Idukki (18)
Government Building		27	8
Rent free building		2	9
Society building		1	1
Building condition	Good/Satisfactory	17	7
Cleanliness	Good	23	7
Premises cleanliness	Good	24	7
Water supply	Piped	11	6
	Pucca well	17	3
	Neighbourhood well	12	5
Power supply	Regular	20	8
	No power supply	10	10
Attached quarters Staying JPHN	Yes	27	9
	No	24	4
Weighing machine (adult)	Yes	26	17
Weighing machine (child)	Yes	25	17
Nirodh	Yes	24	12
Oral pills	Yes	19	11

Source: Field data.

All PHCs in the tribal areas are semi-*pucca*, and all the building of these area need huge maintenance works. As we know, quarters are important for a PHC because doctor's availability is needed 24 hours in the tribal area for their health care. Six PHCs have medical officers' quarters, but only three of them are occupied by medical officers. Three PHC medical officers are not staying in the quarters because of poor condition and family outside the PHC locating area. The same situation exists in the case of staffs such as health inspector, staff nurse and pharmacist. It is seen in the field study that three PHC have no inpatient admission during the last six months because of the acute staff shortage. Due to this problem, tribes in these areas are not going to hospitals or depend on the private hospital or private clinic.

Safe delivery care means a baby born in medical institution or delivery attended by a skilled birth attendant. Childbirth-related problems, such as haemorrhage and prolonged labour, are difficult to predict for the untrained birth attendant. It is seen that (Table 16.10) home delivery performed in the case of tribes is very high. As in most cases, their settlements are in deep forest and hilly areas; the health facility is unreachable to this community. Another reason for the low institutional delivery is high superstitious traditions followed by the tribal community. The tribals during their pregnancy stage depend mostly on the nearest health facility such as PHCs and sub-centres. The influence of health workers has an important role for increasing the utilisation of any health service during pregnancy and post-delivery by the tribal women.

The main reason of this home delivery (Table 16.11) is the distance to health facility and lack of doctors. Many of the tribal hamlets are situated in the forest areas; the average distance to reach the hospital for their delivery care is 30 to 40 km. They need huge financial burden for one visit in this hospital.

Table 16.10 *Tribal Mothers Delivery Place in Different Tribal Community*

	Delivery Place			
Tribes	Govt. Hospital	Pvt. Hospital	Home Delivery	Total
Paniya	221 (48.9)	3 (0.7)	228 (50.4)	452 (100)
VettaKuruma	17 (85)	2 (10)	1 (5)	20 (100)
MullaKuruma	96 (92.3)	4 (3.8)	4 (3.8)	104 (100)
Kurichiya	94 (79)	24 (20.2)	1 (0.8)	119 (100)
Kattunaikka	33 (33.1)	3 (2.8)	70 (66)	106 (100)
Adiyan	30 (55.6)	4 (7.4)	20 (37)	54 (100)
Muthuvan	25 (24)	5 (4.8)	74 (71.2)	104 (100)
Mannan	39 (72.2)	2 (3.7)	13 (24.1)	54 (100)
Hill Pulaya	23 (48.9)	11 (23.4)	13 (27.7)	47 (100)

Source: Field data.
Note: Figures in brackets are percentage share.

Table 16.11 *Reason for Home Delivery*

Tribes	I	II	III	IV	V	VI	VII	Total
Paniya	23 (10.1)	88 (38.6)	46 (20.2)	6 (2.6)	33 (14.5)	18 (7.9)	14 (6.1)	228 (100)
VettaKuruma	—		1 (100)					1 (100)
MullaKuruma			3 (75)		1 (25)			4 (100)
Kurichiya			1 (100)					1 (100)
Kattunaikka	3 (4.5)	37 (52.9)	13 (18.6)	5 (7.1)	7 (10)	5 (7.1)		70 (100)
Adiyan		8 (40)	6 (30)	3 (15)	2 (10)	1 (5)		20 (100)
Muthuvan	2 (2.7)	50 (67.6)	6 (8.1)	5 (6.8)	11 (14.9)			74 (100)
Mannan	1 (7.7)	3 (23.1)	7 (53.8)		2 (15.4)			13 (100)
Hill Pulaya	1 (7.7)	7 (53.8)	1 (7.7)	2 (15.4)	2 (15.4)			13 (100)

Source: Field data.

Notes: I: Feel is not necessary; II: For distance; III: Doctors are not available; IV: Being costly; V: No vehicle; VI: Fear; VII: No by standards. Figures in brackets are percentage share.

Antenatal care is an important safety net for healthy motherhood and childbirth, where the well-being of both the future mother and her children can be protected. The antenatal care under the supervision of health care providers and delivery in medical institutions promotes child survival and reduces the risk of maternal mortality (Susuman, 2012). Mothers belonging to the various tribal communities visited the health care institutions for their pregnancy care only after second trimester. Lack of accessibility of health care infrastructure, unawareness of pregnancy confirmation, some superstitious beliefs among the tribal groups, socio-economic status, cultural beliefs, bad and poor perceptions, lack of knowledge, etc., are the main reasons behind the home delivery and poor antenatal care among tribal people in Wayanad and Idukki districts.

SECTION IV: CONCLUSION

Kerala has made significant gains in health indices such as IRM, birth rate, death rate and expectancy of life at birth. The challenges before the state are to sustain the achievements in the health sector and to tackle the problems of lifestyle diseases such as diabetes, coronary heart disease, renal disease, cancer and geriatric problems. Checking the spread of communicable diseases such as chicken guinea, dengue, leptospirosis and swine flu is emerging as a major challenge. The medical services provided by PHCs are poor or unsatisfactory due to a number of factors such as lack of periodic maintenance of buildings, sufficient equipment and furniture, and basic clinical investigation facilities; shortage of medicine; inadequate staff; etc. The percentage share of the delivery of a child at home in the case of tribal people was found very high mainly due to lack of accessibility of health institutions, facilities and poor medical services. The Kerala experiences of social progress and health with equity are under threat; there is a need to return to the earlier public health policy, giving priority to the access to health care of the weakest and poorer sections of the society.

REFERENCES AND SELECT BIBLIOGRAPHY

Bhatt, R. (2004). *Analysis of public expenditure on health, using state level data.* Ahmadabad: Indian Institute of Management.

Bhatt, T. N. (2014). Development of primary healthcare systems and MCH services in Karnataka. *Journal of Health Management, 16*(1), 113–131.

Government of Kerala. (2013). *Health policy of Kerala 2013, draft report.* Thiruvananthapuram: Health and Family Welfare Department.

Ghosh, S. (2014). Trends and differentials in healthcare utilization of pattern in India. *Journal of Health Management, 16*(3), 337–363.

Ministry of Health and Family Welfare. (2012). *Indian public health standards (IPHS) for primary health centers.* New Delhi: Ministry of Health and Family Welfare.

National Commission on Macroeconomics and Health. (2005). *Report of the National Commission on Macroeconomics and Health.* New Delhi: Ministry of Health and Family Welfare (MoHFW), Government of India.

National Family Health Survey (NFHS). (2016). *NFHS Report 2015–2016.* Fact Sheet on Kerala, Mumbai: International Institute of Population Science.

Ramankutty, V. (2008). Historical analysis of the development of healthcare facilities in Kerala state, India. *Health Policy and Planning, 15*(1), 103–109.

Summut, S. M., & Burns, L. R. (2011). Meeting the challenges of healthcare needs in India, Paths to innovation. *Insight,* Balance of Care, *9*(2), 5–9.

Srinivasan, R. (2012). *Healthcare in India—Vision 2020 Issues and Prospects.* New Delhi: Planning Commission, Government of India.

Susuman, A. S. (2012). Correlates of antenatal and postnatal care among tribal women in India. *Studies on Ethno-Medicine, 6*(1), 55–62.

Veron, R. (2001). The new Kerala model lessons from sustainable model. *World Development, 29*(4), 6001–6617.

PART VII

State Finance and Planning

Chapter 17

Kerala's Acute Fiscal Crisis
An Analysis of Causes

B. A. Prakash and Jerry Alwin

INTRODUCTION

The white paper on state finances published by the Left Democratic Front government which assumed office in May 2016 says that Kerala is facing an acute fiscal crisis. This is the third white paper; the earlier two were published in 2011 and 2001. The situation is so grave that after meeting the day-to-day expenditure on administration and other routine activities, hardly any resources are left for meeting the plan and capital expenditure. The crisis may be considered as the second-largest fiscal crisis in Kerala, the first being the fiscal crisis during the period 1998–2001. In this context, the chapter examines the nature, magnitude and causes of the fiscal crisis.

The chapter is presented in four sections: a review of studies on state finances of Kerala, the nature and magnitude of the crisis, trends in the total receipts and trends in total expenditure. The data sources used for the study are the publications of the Government of Kerala (GoK), the Comptroller and Auditor General (CAG) of India and the Reserve Bank of India. In order to explain the causes of the crisis, we present the following hypothesis:

[T]he successive governments in Kerala have been following fiscal policies neglecting resource mobilisation for political gains on the one side and resorting to fiscal extravagance to satisfy the demands of powerful vested interest and pressure groups on the other, leading to a vicious circle of persistent low revenue receipts, higher non-plan revenue expenditure (NPRE) and higher rate of revenue and fiscal deficits. Political considerations are the major factors behind lack of timely revision of taxes and non-taxes, poor collection, laxity in collection of arrears, fixing inflated annual plan outlays and fiscal extravagance.

REVIEW OF STUDIES

Kerala has been facing fiscal crisis since the early 1980s, and attempts were made by scholars and government committees to study the nature, magnitude, causes and consequences of the crisis. In one of the earlier studies, it was argued that Kerala's fiscal problems were the inevitable consequences of the success it achieved with respect to the social goals set by national planners with regard to public education, health and other social services. It was pointed out that Kerala's fiscal crisis and its economic crisis are reinforcing each other. Due to paucity of funds arising out of large non-plan expenditure in social welfare items, there had been a deceleration in state plan expenditure during the 1980s (George, 1990).

Reviewing the state finances between 1974–1975 and 1989–1990, another study argued that fiscal crisis faced by the state was not due to the slow growth of revenue receipts, but due to the faster growth in revenue expenditure, particularly non-plan spending on social services (Aiyar & Kurup, 1992). Another study attributed factors such as low cost recovery of economic and social services in the public sector, excessive financial burden imposed by large number of loss-making state-level public enterprises, increase in non-plan revenue expenditure (NPRE), the growth of staff expenditure on pay, dearness and other allowances, low realisation of small savings collection and debt liability for the fiscal crisis (Kurien & Abraham, 1999).

A survey of the trends in state finances during the second half of the 1990s indicated a steady deterioration in the finances of most of the states in India. Failure to contain wasteful expenditure and reluctance to raise additional resources on the part of the states are the main causes. Another reason was the pay revision of state employees consequent upon the implementation of the Central Fifth Pay Commission Report. Due to this, states were starved of funds to meet the essential investment needs in the social and infrastructure sectors, and were forced to resort to large borrowings to meet current expenditure (Kurien, 1999). These broad factors were also applicable in the case of Kerala's poor finances.

The white paper of 2001 on state finances gives a clear picture about the unprecedented and acute fiscal crisis faced by Kerala during 1998–2001. On the one hand, there was huge growth in revenue expenditure due to unsustainable salary and pension bill built up over time, commitments on debt servicing, liberal support given by using state funds to cover losses of public sector undertakings, fixing plan size with total disregard to resource availability, wasteful expenditure on many fronts, borrowing to meet the additional liability arising out of the pay and pension revision of 1997, financial liability due to implementation of the Plus Two School scheme, etc. On the other hand, the state's own tax and non-tax resources stagnated due to narrow tax base of the state with heavy dependence on sales tax, non-repayment of loans by public sector undertakings and agencies, seasonality of revenue inflow with minimum inflow during the first quarter, falling trend in resource transfer from the central government, the slow growth of the economy affecting revenue collection, etc. (GoK, 2001). In order to face the crisis, the state government effected a cut in expenditure in plan, social sector and capital items, and grants in-aid to local governments, and increased public borrowing. It is argued that the acute fiscal crisis has resulted in a substantial increase in public debt and interest liability (Alwin, 2014).

A study on the total tax potential of the general sales tax and the actual collection of tax between 1972–1973 and 2000–2001 came to the conclusion that almost 35 per cent of the total tax potential was not tapped in Kerala (Rakhe, 2003). Another study attributes the increase in establishment expenditure due to pay revisions, enhancement of plan outlay without adequate resources, slump in resource mobilisation and decline in sales tax collection, and the decline in central transfers as the major causes of the fiscal crisis (Abraham, 2004).

The white paper of 2011 on state finances presented the critical fiscal situation that prevailed in the state and the rapid rise in public debt, making Kerala a debt-stressed state (GoK, 2011). A study which examines the trends in state finances between 1991 and 2012 indicated that there had been a marginal improvement in the fiscal situation of Kerala in recent years. But the fiscal situation remains unstable, and the state's performance fares badly in comparison with the average of all states and many individual states (George & Krishnakumar, 2012).

The Kerala Public Expenditure Review Committees (KPERC), constituted as per the Kerala Fiscal Responsibility Act 2003 (KFR Act), reviewed the state finances and submitted reports for the financial years from 2004–2005 to 2013–2014. The Third Committee in its four reports had examined the state finances and given a number of recommendations on tax and non-tax revenue, capital and revenue expenditure, plan expenditure, debt management, etc. (KPERC). The committee had emphasised the need for curtailing the persistently high rate of increase in NPRE. The white paper of 2016 presents a clear picture about the nature and magnitude of the fiscal crisis of Kerala (GoK, 2016a). The other recent notable studies on state finances are that of Sen (2012) and Issac Thomas and Mohan (2016).

From the review, we may draw the following broad conclusions about the unstable fiscal situation that prevailed in Kerala since the early 1980s. On the one hand, the slump in resource mobilisation, slow growth in revenue collection of state taxes, non-tax revenue, decline in central transfers, the mounting losses of public sector undertakings and inadequate resources to meet unrealistic and inflated plan outlays have contributed to high fiscal deficit and unstable fiscal situation. On the other hand, the high rate of growth of NPRE on salaries, pension, interest, grant-in-aid to private educational institutions, administration, subsidies, etc., have contributed to high level of revenue and fiscal deficits, forcing the state government to resort to continuous borrowing and mounting debt.

NATURE AND MAGNITUDE OF CRISIS

To present the nature and magnitude of fiscal crisis, we have used revenue deficit (RD), fiscal deficit and debt–gross state domestic product (GSDP) ratio as the indicators. The RD is the difference between revenue receipts and revenue expenditure. The RD–GSDP ratio remained at high levels compared to the fiscal target stipulated by the KFR Act (Table 17.1). In spite of the RD grant of ₹46.4 billion awarded by the

Table 17.1 *Trends in Revenue Deficit*

Year	RD (₹ Crore)	RD as % of Revenue Expenditure	RD as % of GSDP	RD Target as per KFR Act (%)
2000–2001	3,147	26.5	4.3	–
2005–2006	3,129	17.0	2.3	–
2010–2011	3,674	10.6	1.4	–
2011–2012	8,035	17.4	2.6	1.4
2012–2013	9,352	17.5	2.7	0.9
2013–2014	11,309	18.7	2.9	0.5
2014–2015	13,796	19.2	3.1	0.0
2015–2016	9,657	12.3	1.6*	0.0

Source: CAG (2012, 2016a, 2017) and GoK (2011, 2016b, 2017a).

Note: * Based on provisional GSDP.

14th Finance Commission, the state was not able to achieve the RD target as per the fiscal responsibility targets in 2015–2016. Another measure, the RD as percentage of revenue expenditure, indicates an increasing trend except in 2015–2016. This suggests that the state failed to curtail the persistent rise in RD, indicating a deterioration in state finances since 2011–2012. The revised budget for 2016–2017 says that the entire borrowing of the state is not sufficient to meet the day-to-day revenue expenditure (GoK, 2016c).

The gross fiscal deficit (GFD), denoting the gap between total receipts (excluding borrowing) and total expenditure in the consolidated fund, indicates the borrowing required to meet the deficit. The GFD ranged between 4.1 per cent and 4.3 per cent of Kerala's GDP, much higher than the fiscal deficit target stipulated in the KFR Act, between 2011–2012 and 2014–2015 (Table 17.2). GFD accounts for nearly one-fourth of the total expenditure of the state during the stated four years. The high level of fiscal deficit and the spending of entire borrowing permitted by the KFR Act for NPRE have created a situation of extreme paucity of funds for capital expenditure such as construction of roads, bridges, major infrastructure projects, etc.

Table 17.2 *Trends in Gross Fiscal Deficit*

Year	GFD (₹ Crore)	GFD as % of Total Expenditure	GFD as % of GSDP	GFD Target as per KFR Act (%)
2000–2001	3,878	31.1	5.3	–
2005–2006	4,182	21.4	3.1	–
2010–2011	7,731	19.9	2.9	–
2011–2012	12,815	25.2	4.1	3.5
2012–2013	15,002	25.3	4.3	3.5
2013–2014	16,944	25.5	4.3	3.0
2014–2015	18,642	24.2	4.1	3.0
2015–2016	17,818	20.5	3.0★	3.0

Source: CAG (2012, 2016a, 2017) and GoK (2011, 2016b, 2017a).

Note: ★ Based on provisional GSDP.

The trend in public debt, growth rate of debt, debt–GSDP ratio and the target as per KFR Act are given in Table 17.3. The public debt or outstanding fiscal liabilities comprises of the internal debt of the state, loans and advances from the Government of India (GoI) and public account liabilities. The annual increase in public debt ranged from 12.2 per cent to 16.5 per cent during the last five years. Except in the years 2013–2014 and 2014–2015, the state was able to meet the KFR target on debt–GSDP ratio. But the debt has created a huge liability for repayment during the immediate future. An aspect is that the debt maturity profile of the state shows that 44.1 per cent of the debt has to be repaid within seven years. As the non-debt receipts of the state were insufficient, some portion of the borrowed funds was used for bridging the revenue gap. During 2014–2015, the total borrowed fund under public debt in the consolidated fund was ₹185.09 billion. After providing for interest and repayment of principal, the net availability was only ₹53.65 billion. Similarly, the accumulation in public account comprising small savings, provident fund, reserve fund, deposit account, etc., was ₹469.79 billion during 2014–2015. Under this sector, the net availability of funds after disbursement with interest was only ₹27.45 billion (CAG, 2016a). This indicates that the state is moving towards

Table 17.3 *Trends in Public Debt*

Year	Public Debt (₹ Crore)	Growth (%)	Debt/ GSDP (%)	Target as per KFR Act (Debt-GSDP Ratio)
2000–2001	23,919	–	32.9	–
2005–2006	45,929	–	33.5	–
2010–2011	82,420	–	31.2	–
2011–2012	93,132	13.00	29.8	32.20
2012–2013	108,477	16.48	31.2	31.70
2013–2014	124,081	14.38	31.3	30.70
2014–2015	141,947	14.40	31.4	29.80
2015–2016	160,539	13.10	27.3★	31.34

Source: CAG (2012, 2016a, 2017) and GoK (2011, 2016b, 2017a).

Note: ★ Based on provisional GSDP.

a debt trap in which the major share of borrowed funds is utilised for repayment of interest and principal.

TRENDS IN TOTAL RECEIPTS

Revenue and capital are the two streams of receipts that constitute the resources of the state government in the consolidated fund. Revenue receipts consist of tax revenue, non-tax revenue, state's share of union taxes and duties, and grants-in-aid from GoI. Capital receipts comprise of non-debt capital receipts such as miscellaneous capital receipts, recoveries of loans and advances, and public debt resources from internal sources (market loans and borrowings from other financial institutions/commercial banks), and loans and advances from GoI. The funds available in the public accounts, which are outside the consolidated fund, can also be utilised by the government to finance its deficit. Of the three items of receipts of the state, the share of non-debt capital receipts comprising miscellaneous capitals, and recoveries of loans and advances is negligible. The growth rate of total receipts also registered a fall in the years 2013–2014 and 2015–2016 (Table 17.4). A notable aspect is that the share of public debt receipts to total receipts ranged between 19 per cent and 24 per cent between 2010–2011 and 2015–2016.

Table 17.4 *Trends in Total Receipts in the Consolidated Fund* (in ₹ Crore)*

Year	Total Revenue Receipts	Non-debt Capital Receipts	Public Debt Receipts	Total Receipts	Total Receipts (Growth in Per Cent)
2000–2001	8,731	117	2,156	11,004	–
2005–2006	15,295	52	5,823	21,170	–
2010–2011	30,991	69	7,189	38,249	–
2011–2012	38,010	71	9,799	47,880	25.2
2012–2013	44,137	89	13,261	57,487	20.1
2013–2014	49,177	123	14,461	63,761	10.9
2014–2015	57,950	152	18,509	76,611	20.2
2015–2016	69,033	181	19,658	88,872	16.0

Source: CAG (2012, 2016a, 2017) and GoK (2011, 2016b, 2017a).

Note: *Excluding public account receipts.

The broad trend in the growth of total revenue receipts and its components between 2010–2011 and 2015–2016 are as follows (Table 17.5). First, the rate of growth of total revenue receipts registered a steep fall in 2013–2014 due to the fall in own tax revenue, but it witnessed a rise in the subsequent years. Second, the rate of increase of state own tax revenue was lower since 2013–2014 compared to earlier years. Third, there was a fall in the share of own resources of state comprising state taxes and non-tax receipts from 76.4 per cent in 2013–2014 to 68.7 per cent in 2015–2016. This indicates a structural shift in revenue receipts witnessing a fall in the share of state resources on the one hand, and a rise in the share of central funds on the other. Fourth, the huge increase of 60 per cent in the share of Central taxes in 2015–2016 has helped the state to a great extent from total collapse of the state finances.

State Tax and Non-tax Revenue

The fiscal policy pursued by the successive governments in the state generally does not favour timely upward revision of rate of taxes, fees

Table 17.5 *Total Revenue Receipt (in ₹ Crore)*

Year	Own Taxes	Non-tax Revenue	Central Tax Transfer	Grant-in-aid	Total Revenue Receipts	Revenue Receipts/ GSDP (%)
2000–2001	5,867	655	1,589	620	8,731	12.5
	–	–	–	–	–	
2005–2006	9,779	937	2,518	2,061	15,295	12.9
	–	–	–	–	–	
2010–2011	21,722	1,931	5,142	2,196	30,991	11.5
	–	–	–	–	–	
2011–2012	25,719	2,592	5,990	3,709	38,010	12.1
	(18.4)	(34.2)	(16.5)	(68.9)	(22.6)	
2012–2013	30,077	4,198	6,841	3,021	44,137	12.1
	(16.9)	(62.0)	(14.2)	(–18.5)	(16.1)	
2013–2014	31,995	5,575	7,469	4,138	49,177	12.4
	(6.4)	(32.8)	(9.2)	(37.0)	(11.4)	
2014–2015	35,232	7,284	7,926	7,508	57,950	12.8
	(10.1)	(30.7)	(6.1)	(81.4)	(17.8)	
2015–2016	38,995	8,426	12,691	8,921	69,033	12.1
	(10.7)	(15.7)	(60.1)	(18.8)	(19.1)	

Source: CAG (2012, 2016a, 2017) and GoK (2011, 2016b, 2017a).

Note: Figures in brackets are growth rate in per cent.

and user charges due to political factors. Frequent elections at one- or two-year intervals in state legislature or local governments or Parliament prompt the political leaders in power to postpone the revision of taxes. The revision of taxes will also invite strong protests and agitations from opposition political parties. Most of the political parties consider that an increase in rate of taxes, fees, user charges, etc., as anti-people. Therefore, the governments used to give very low priority for periodical revision of tax and non-tax rates. We have to examine mobilisation of state taxes and non-tax items in this context.

State tax comprises of sales tax and value added tax (VAT), stamps and registration, excise, taxes on vehicles and other taxes. The other taxes comprise of land revenue, taxes and duties on electricity, agricultural income, taxes on immovable property other than agricultural land, luxury tax and entertainment tax. The amount collected from other taxes account for less than 2 per cent of the total state's own tax revenue.

Among the taxes, sales tax and VAT is the major item accounting for 78 per cent of the total state tax revenue. The system of value added taxation was introduced in the state with effect from 1 April 2005. There was a steep fall in the growth rate of sales tax and VAT since 2012–2013 (Table 17.6). Two major reasons are attributed to the fall. One is the recessionary situation prevailing in the state's economy between 2013 and 2016 due to global as well as domestic factors. The steep fall in the price of rubber due to price fall in the international market, price fall of other commercial crops, stagnation of construction and real estate sectors, and fall in oil prices in the Gulf and its adverse impact on Keralite migrant workers have created a recessionary situation, affecting sales tax and VAT collection. The recession in construction and real estate has affected the sale of construction items which earn large amount of sales tax and VAT. Among the 21 items of commodities earning the largest revenue of sales tax and VAT, seven items, namely, cement, electrical goods, iron and steel, paint, timber, tiles and sanitary ware belonged to the construction sector in 2013–2014 (KPERC Fourth Report).

The second is the underperformance of the tax collection machinery, lack of sincere effort by the state government to mobilise tax revenue, and inefficient and poor collection of the tax. The CAG

Table 17.6 *Trend in State Own Tax Revenue (in ₹ Crore)*

Year	Sales Tax and VAT	Stamps and Registration	State Excise	Taxes on Vehicles	Other Taxes	Total
2000–2001	4,344	341	689	395	101	5,870
	–	–	–	–	–	–
2005–2006	7,038	1,101	841	629	170	9,779
	–	–	–	–	–	–
2010–2011	15,833	2,552	1,700	1,331	306	21,722
	–	–	–	–	–	–
2011–2012	18,939	2,987	1,883	1,587	323	25,719
	(19.6)	(17.0)	(10.8)	(19.2)	(5.6)	(18.4)
2012–2013	22,511	2,938	2,314	1,925	389	30,077
	(18.9)	(–1.6)	(22.9)	(21.3)	(20.4)	(16.9)
2013–2014	24,885	2,593	1,942	2,161	414	31,995
	(10.5)	(–11.7)	(–16.1)	(12.3)	(6.4)	(6.4)
2014–2015	27,908	2,659	1,777	2,365	523	35,232
	(12.1)	(2.5)	(–8.5)	(9.4)	(26.3)	(10.1)
2015–2016	30,737	2,878	1,964	2,814	602	38,995
	(10.1)	(8.2)	(10.5)	(19.0)	(15.1)	(10.7)

Source: CAG (2012, 2016a, 2017) and GoK (2011, 2016b, 2017a).

Note: Figures in brackets are growth rates in per cent.

of India has conducted a performance audit on VAT of the state for 2014–2015 and has pointed out the following: (a) failure to bring all eligible dealers under tax net and consequent escape of majority from VAT liability (though the Economic Census of 2013 reported that there were 1.341 million establishments, only 220,000 dealers were registered for VAT in the state); (b) the system of scrutiny of returns not properly defined in the Act or in any guidelines issued result in poor coverage of scrutiny; (c) lack of coordination with other departments, in terms of collection of data useful for the completion of assessment, resulted in non- or short levy; (d) no system in place for analysis and utilisation of data available in the Kerala VAT Information System (KVATIS);

and (e) internal control mechanism existing in the department was not sufficient (CAG, 2016b).

Among the other items of taxes of state government, the stamps and registration, and state excise registered a decline or negative growth rate in recent years (Table 17.6). During the last five years (2010–2011 to 2015–2016), there occurred a change in the composition of revenue in state taxes. While there has been an increase in the share of sales tax, VAT, taxes on vehicles and other taxes on the one hand, the share of duty on stamp and registration and state excise witnessed a decrease.

Non-tax Revenue

Non-tax revenue comprises of interest receipts of the loans issued by the government, dividends and profits of public sector undertakings of the state government, and income from lotteries, forestry and wildlife department and other non-tax receipts. The other non-tax receipts include fees, user charges, fines, etc., collected by various departments, public educational and health institutions, and other governmental agencies. Non-tax revenue accounts for about 13 per cent of the total revenue receipts of the state. Of the stated items, income from state lotteries and other non-tax receipts are the major items in terms of revenue earnings (Table 17.7). Though there is much scope for increasing the revenue from this source by periodical revision of rates, strengthening collection machinery and prompt collection of arrears, the successive governments in the state had not taken many steps in this regard. A small revision in fees and user charges invites agitation from opposition political parties. Due to this political economy, majority of fees and user charges levied by government departments remained very low or without revision for decades.

In the case of state lotteries, the total earnings from the sale of lottery tickets is taken as income. But if we deduct the cost of conducting lotteries, the net income will be about 18 to 22 per cent of the total earnings. In the case of items such as interest receipts, dividends and profits from public sector undertakings, and income from forestry and wild life department, the growth of earnings is either negative or the amount collected is very small. The KPERC, which examined the non-tax revenue of 30 government departments, came to the conclusion

Table 17.7 *Trends in Non-tax Revenue (in ₹ Crore)*

Year	Interest Receipts	Dividends and Profits	State Lotteries	Forestry and Wildlife	Other Non-tax Receipts	Grand Total
2000–2001	37	13	–	141	468	659
	–	–	–	–	–	–
2005–2006	46	18	–	190	683	937
	–	–	–	–	–	–
2010–2011	172	75	571	274	839	1,931
	–	–	–	–	–	–
2011–2012	136	67	1,283	221	885	2,592
	(–20.9)	(–10.7)	(124.7)	(–19.3)	(5.5)	(34.2)
2012–2013	172	48	2,674	237	1,067	4,198
	(26.5)	(–28.4)	(108.4)	(7.2)	(20.6)	(62.0)
2013–2014	149	101	3,796	330	1,199	5,575
	(–13.4)	(110.4)	(42.0)	(39.2)	(12.4)	(32.8)
2014–2015	102	74	5,445	300	1,363	7,284
	(–31.5)	(–26.7)	(43.4)	(–9.1)	(13.7)	(30.7)
2015–2016	105	90	6,271	283	1,677	8,426
	(2.9)	(21.6)	(15.1)	(–5.7)	(23.0)	(15.7)

Source: CAG (2012, 2016a, 2017) and GoK (2011, 2016b, 2017a).

Note: Figures in brackets are growth rate in per cent.

that the rate of fees, fines and user charges levied are very low and needs periodical revision.

Arrears of Revenue

An important issue in revenue mobilisation has been the accumulation of arrears of tax and non-tax due to various reasons. The amount of arrears outstanding is given in Table 17.8. Of the total amount of ₹104.36 billion of arrears as on March 2015, sales tax and VAT accounted for ₹63.98 billion (61 per cent; CAG, 2016b). Of the total arrears of sales tax and VAT, 57 per cent is pending due from individuals, private firms, private companies, etc.; 37 per cent from public sector undertakings of GoI; 3 per cent from public sector undertakings of GoK; and 2 per cent from other state governments. It is reported that due to the stays issued by the High Court, other judicial authorities and the government, the Commercial Taxes Department was not able to proceed recoveries involving an amount of ₹12.67 billion, accounting for 20 per cent of total arrears. It is disturbing to note that ₹13.75 billion arrears, accounting for 21.5 per cent of total arrears of sales tax and VAT, are pending for more than five years.

The other items having sizeable outstanding arrears are land revenue, tax on vehicles, income from forests and excise duty. The practice of giving indiscriminate stays on collection, the laxity on the part of successive governments to take prompt action on collection of arrears every year, acting at slow pace for revenue recovery, and legal action

Table 17.8 *Amount of Tax and Non-tax Arrears Outstanding (in ₹ Crore)*

Year (as on March)	Total Amount of Arrears	Amount of Arrears for More Than Five Years	Amount of Arrears for More Than Five Years (Per Cent)
2011	5,358	1,679	31.3
2012	10,273	3,768	36.7
2013	12,244	4,389	35.8
2015	10,436	1,872	17.9

Source: CAG (2016b).

in cases pending before courts and other judicial authorities have contributed to the accumulation of arrears.

TRENDS IN TOTAL EXPENDITURE

Expenditure is classified as revenue and capital. Revenue expenditure is incurred to meet expenses for the day–to-day running of the government. Capital expenditure is used to create permanent assets, or to enhance the utility of such assets or to reduce permanent liabilities. Expenditure under revenue and capital is further classified into two categories, namely, (a) plan and non-plan, and (b) general, social and economic services. The general services include administration of justice, police, jail, public works, pension, etc. The social services include education, health and family welfare, water supply, welfare of SC/ST, etc. The economic services include agriculture, rural development, irrigation, cooperation, energy, industries, transport, etc.

The trend in the total expenditure and the parameters of expenditure are given in Table 17.9. During the last five years (between 2010–2011 and 2015–2016), the annual average growth rate of total expenditure was 18.2 per cent, but there was a spurt in the growth of total expenditure during 2011–2012, mainly due to revision of salaries and pensions. The total expenditure-GSDP ratio also ranged between 15 per cent and 17 per cent during this period. A disturbing thing is that there was a revenue gap of about 25 per cent to meet the total expenditure since 2010–2011. The buoyancy of total expenditure with respect to GSDP, denoting rate of growth of total expenditure/rate of growth of GSDP, was more than one for most of the years, indicating a higher growth in expenditure compared to GSDP. Of the total expenditure, 41.1 per cent was spent for general services, 32 per cent for social services, 17.5 per cent for economic services, 8.4 per cent for giving grants-in-aid, and 1 per cent for loans and advances in 2014–2015.

Revenue Expenditure

The trends in revenue expenditure comprising non-plan and plan are shown in Table 17.10. The revenue expenditure registered a steep increase of 32.8 per cent in 2011–2012, mainly due to the

Table 17.9 *Total Expenditure: Basic Parameters*

Year	Total Expenditure (TE) (₹ Crore)	Rate of Growth (%)	TE/GSDP (%)	Revenue Receipts/ TE (%)	Buoyancy of TE with Respect to GSDP
2000–2001	12,726	–	18.2	68.6	0.8
2005–2006	19,528	–	16.4	78.3	0.6
2010–2011	38,791	–	14.4	79.9	1.0
2011–2012	50,896	31.2	16.1	74.7	1.7
2012–2013	59,228	16.4	16.3	74.5	1.5
2013–2014	66,244	11.8	16.7	74.2	0.8
2014–2015	76,744	15.9	17.0	75.5	1.1
2015–2016	87,032	13.4	14.9★	79.3	1.1★

Source: CAG (2012, 2016a, 2017) and GoK (2011, 2016b, 2017a).

Note: ★ Based on provisional GSDP.

Table 17.10 *Revenue Expenditure: Parameters (in ₹ Crore)*

Year	Revenue Expenditure (RE) (₹ Crore)	Growth Rate of RE (%)	RE to total Expenditure (%)	Buoyancy of RE with Respect to GSDP
2000–2001	11,878	–	93.3	0.5
2005–2006	18,424	–	94.3	0.5
2010–2011	34,665	–	89.4	0.8
2011–2012	46,045	32.8	90.5	1.8
2012–2013	53,489	16.2	90.3	1.4
2013–2014	60,486	13.1	91.3	0.9
2014–2015	71,746	18.6	93.5	1.3
2015–2016	78,690	9.7	90.4	0.8★

Source: CAG (2012, 2016a, 2017) and GoK (2011, 2016b, 2017a).

Note: ★ Based on provisional GSDP.

implementation of pay and pension revision. The revenue expenditure also accounts for 89.4 per cent to 93.5 per cent of total expenditure which is not a healthy way of spending from the point of view of development. Due to this spending pattern, a small share is spent as capital expenditure or for creating capital assets for infrastructural development. The buoyancy of revenue expenditure with respect to GSDP suggests that the revenue expenditure is on the higher side, showing an unhealthy trend in expenditure in majority of the years. On the whole, the parameters presented in the table do not give a healthy change in the trend in revenue expenditure.

Non-plan Revenue Expenditure

The NPRE denotes the expenditure incurred for meeting the day to day expenditure such as salaries, pension, interest, subsidies, establishment, administration, grants-in-aid, etc. This is the expenditure incurred for non-developmental items. The pattern of NPRE witnessed a similar trend as in the case of revenue and total expenditure (Table 17.11). A disturbing development was that the NPRE exceeds the total revenue

Table 17.11 *Non-plan Revenue Expenditure*

Year	NPRE (₹ Crore)	Rate of Growth (%)	NPRE/ GSDP Ratio	NPRE as Percentage of TE	NPRE as Percentage of Revenue Receipts
2005–2006	15,201	–	11.1	78.0	99.4
2010–2011	30,469	–	11.6	78.5	98.3
2011–2012	40,718	33.6	13.0	80.0	107.1
2012–2013	46,640	14.5	13.4	78.7	105.7
2013–2014	53,412	14.5	13.5	80.6	108.6
2014–2015	61,462	15.1	13.6	80.1	106.1
2015–2016	66,611	8.4	11.4*	76.5	96.5

Source: CAG (2012, 2016a, 2017) and GoK (2011, 2016b, 2017a).

Note: * Based on provisional GSDP.

receipts of the state for four years between 2011–2012 and 2014–2015. This suggests that the entire revenue receipts were not sufficient for meeting NPRE and a portion of the borrowed funds is also utilised for meeting the expenditure.

Rapid rise in NPRE is the root cause of the fiscal crisis in the state. Instead of curtailing the NPRE, the successive governments in the state have been following a policy to promote its growth. Without considering resource availability, capital requirement or recurring expenditure in future, a large number of new public institutions, projects and private-aided educational institutions were started, and populist schemes of benefit distribution were implemented. Though the state cannot afford revision of salaries and pensions once in five years, the successive governments revised it in every five years. Efforts were not made to abolish unnecessary establishments, institutions, public sector undertakings making huge losses on a sustained basis, and schemes which do not produce any social returns, reduce excess staff and curtail wasteful administrative expenditure. Here nobody is bothered about the huge financial liability of excessive wasteful expenditure and its negative consequences on infrastructure development, public services, public utilities and the overall development of the state. The successive governments promoted the growth of it mainly to satisfy powerful vested interest groups, trade unions, and social and communal organisations due to political considerations. This political economy is a basic factor which prevents the state from following a healthy fiscal policy of controlling the excessive growth in socially undesirable NPRE, leading to continuous instability of state finances.

Among the items of expenditure, the two major items which account for nearly half of the revenue expenditure are salaries and pensions. The state government is paying salaries and pensions at the same rate from treasury for government staff and for those belonging to private aided educational institutions such as schools, arts and science colleges and other educational institutions. Of the total staff of 508,000 in March 2016, 72 per cent are government staff and 28 per cent are in private-aided educational institutions. Similarly, the government is paying monthly pensions to 478,000 pensioners in March 2014 consisting of retired staff of government and private-aided educational institutions. The salaries and pensions are increased once in five years based on the recommendations of the State Pay Commission. This creates huge additional financial burden on the state government. As a result of the pay revision, the salary and pension expenditure increased by 47 per cent in 2011–2012, the year in which it was implemented (Table 17.12).

One of the major reasons for the acute fiscal crisis in 1998–2001 was due to pay and pension revisions. As the local governments, universities, semi-government institutions and public sector undertakings are following the salary pattern of the state government, they will also be forced to revise it once in five years. Due to the salary and pension revision once in five years, the annual average growth rate of the expenditure registered a steep increase every five years (Table 17.13). The scale of pay of staff also registered a spurt once in five years (Table 17.14). As the state cannot mobilise resources to meet the huge additional financial burden arising due to frequent salary and pension revisions, it is likely that the state will continue to remain in the fiscal crisis trap.

Similarly, efforts are not made to curtail the wasteful revenue expenditure on many items. The KPERC had found the following items of wasteful expenditure: (a) 33,061 temporary excess staff are retained in non-functional establishments created for implementing projects, in March 2014; (b) the committee found that in the case of 191 schools where the total strength was less than 10, the government

Table 17.12 *Salary and Pension Expenditure (In ₹ Crore)*

Year	Salaries and Wages	Pension	Total	Growth Rate (%)	Total as % of Revenue Expenditure	Total as % of Revenue Receipts
2000–2001	4,451	1,929	6,380	–	53.7	73.1
2005–2006	5,678	2,861	8,539	–	46.3	55.8
2010–2011	11,178	5,767	16,945	–	48.9	54.7
2011–2012	16,229	8,700	24,929	47.1	54.1	65.6
2012–2013	17,505	8,867	26,372	5.8	49.3	59.8
2013–2014	19,554	9,971	29,525	12.0	48.8	60.0
2014–2015	21,621	11,253	32,874	11.3	45.8	56.7
2015–2016	23,757	13,063	36,820	12.0	46.8	53.3

Source: CAG (2012, 2016a, 2017) and GoK (2011, 2016b, 2017a).

Table 17.13 *Annual Average Growth Rate of Salary and Pension Expenditure (in %)*

Period	Salary	Pension	Total
2000–2001 to 2005–2006	5.4	8.6	6.2
2005–2006 to 2010–2011	14.6	16.5	15.0
2010–2011 to 2015–2016	17.7	18.9	17.6

Source: Calculated based on CAG (2012, 2016a, 2017) and GoK (2011, 2016b, 2017a).

Table 17.14 *Pay Revisions: Lowest and Highest Scales of Pay*

Date of Implementation	Lowest Scale of Pay (₹)
1 July 1983	550 (10–15) 800
1 July 1988	750 (10–25) 1,025
1 March 1992	775 (12–20) 1,065
1 March 1997	2,610 (60–70) 3,680
1 July 2004	4,510 (120–150) 6,230
1 July 2009	8,500 (230–330) 13,210
1 July 2014★	16,500 (500–900) 35,700
	Highest Scale of Pay (₹)
1 July 1983	3,700 – 125 – 4,200
1 July 1988	4,435 – 170 – 5,785
1 March 1992	5,100 – 150 – 6,300
1 March 1997	16,300 – 450 – 19,900
1 July 2004	26,600 – 650 – 33,750
1 July 2009	48,640 (1,100–1,200) 59,840
1 July 2014★	93,000 (2,000–2,400) 120,000

Source: GoK, Budget for 2017–2018, Appendix I. Details of Staffs.

Note: ★Implemented on 20 January 2016 (increments are given in brackets).

spent an amount of ₹210 million every year to pay salaries to the teachers; (c) 3,531 schools where salaries of the staff are paid by government are uneconomic schools; (d) though nearly half of the total staff and salary expenditure of the government belonged to public education sector consisting of government and private-aided institutions, the successive governments follow a policy of starting new educational institutions in the public sector involving huge financial commitment instead of promoting private investment in the sector; and (e) in spite of the implementation of e-governance in most of the government departments, steps were not taken to reduce the staff strength (KPERC Third Report).

From the budgetary resources, the government is supporting a large number of loss-making commercial public sector undertakings which are not providing much social returns. Similarly, a lot of wasteful expenditure is incurred for distribution of subsidies for items such as conducting festival markets, widespread misuse of government vehicles, etc. Two examples will give an idea about the extent of wasteful expenditure that prevails in many areas of administration. While the Madhya Pradesh State Public Service Commission has three full-time members including the chairman, the Kerala Public Service Commission has 21 full-time members. A minister in the central government had 15 personal staff, but in Kerala, a minister had 32 personal staff on average in March 2016.

Capital Expenditure

The pattern of NPRE has resulted in a situation where the state finds it extremely difficult to find resources for capital and plan expenditure. A review of the capital expenditure indicates that there has been a negative growth rate in capital expenditure during the years 2013–2014 and 2014–2015 (Table 17.15).

This implies that the state has reached a stage of acute fiscal crisis where resources cannot be mobilised for capital expenditure on infrastructure, public services, public utilities, etc. It is disturbing to note that the plan expenditure comprising revenue and capital also registered a negative growth in 2014–2015. It is reported that the state was able to spend only 71 per cent of the budgeted plan outlay during 2014–2015. Thus, the failure of the successive governments to control the excessive spending of NPRE has contributed to the acute fiscal crisis in the revenue side.

FISCAL SITUATION: COMPARISON WITH OTHER STATES

An attempt is made to compare Kerala's fiscal situation with other states based on the Reserve Bank of India's study of state budgets for

Table 17.15 *Capital and Plan Expenditure*

Year	Capital Expenditure (₹ Crore)	Growth Rate (%)	Plan Expenditure (Revenue + Capital) (₹ Crore)	Growth Rate (%)
2000–2001	577	–	3,303	–
2005–2006	817	–	4,231	–
2010–2011	3,364	–	10,025	–
2011–2012	3,853	14.54	11,758	17.29
2012–2013	4,603	19.47	14,737	25.34
2013–2014	4,294	−6.71	14,901	1.11
2014–2015	4,255	−0.91	14,252	−4.36

Source: CAG (2012, 2016a, 2017) and GoK (2011, 2016b, 2017a).

2016–2017. Table 17.16 gives the RD GSDP ratio, GFD GSDP ratio and Debt GSDP ratio for 18 non-special category states for 2014–2015. While nearly half of the states had revenue surplus, Kerala had very high rate of RD (second rank). Kerala has the second-highest fiscal deficit among 18 states in India. But with regard to the debt GSDP ratio, Kerala's position is slightly different. Kerala ranks fifth with regard to debt ratio. Thus, the three fiscal indicators mentioned earlier give a very bad fiscal situation of Kerala compared to other states.

The major item which influences the growth of NPRE is the growth in expenditure of wages and salaries of government staff and other categories. First, Kerala had the highest growth in salaries and wages during the period 2009–2010 to 2014–2015 (118.4 per cent) compared to other states. Second, the total wage and salary expenditure in Kerala was lower than those of other bigger states such as Karnataka, Madhya Pradesh and Odisha in 2009–2010. But after five years, Kerala's salary expenditure was larger than these states. Third, the wage bill of Kerala was higher than the bigger states such as Bihar, Gujarat, Karnataka, Madhya Pradesh and Odisha during the year 2014–2015. These evidences suggest an excessive increase in expenditure of salaries and wages in Kerala compared to other states.

A review of the development expenditure (DEV) indicators also suggest that Kerala's position is at the bottom level with regard to DEV/GSDP ratio (RBI, 2017). Among the 18 states, Kerala's DEV/

Table 17.16 *Deficit Indicators of State Governments (in %)*

| S. No. | State | 2014–2015 | | |
		RD/ GSDP	GFD/ GSDP	Debt–GSDP Ratio
	Non-special Category	0.4	2.7	NA
1	Andhra Pradesh	4.6	6.0	23.3
2	Bihar	−1.6	3.0	26.6
3	Chhattisgarh	0.7	3.4	13.2
4	Goa	−0.7	2.3	34.7
5	Gujarat	−0.6	2.0	22.6
6	Haryana	1.9	2.9	21.2
7	Jharkhand	0.1	3.0	20.1
8	Karnataka	−0.1	2.1	17.2
9	Kerala	2.6	3.5	27.3
10	Madhya Pradesh	−1.3	2.4	22.6
11	Maharashtra	0.7	1.8	18.0
12	Odisha	−1.8	1.7	15.8
13	Punjab	2.1	2.9	30.5
14	Rajasthan	0.5	3.1	24.2
15	Tamil Nadu	0.6	2.5	17.0
16	Telangana	−0.1	1.8	14.2
17	Uttar Pradesh	−2.1	3.1	30.1
18	West Bengal	2.1	3.4	34.6
All States		0.4	2.6	21.7

Source: RBI, State Finances: A Study of Budgets 2016–2017.

Notes: RD: Revenue Deficit, GSDP: Gross State Domestic Product, GFD: Gross Fiscal Deficit.

Negative (−) sign indicates surplus.

GSDP ratio was the lowest (7.4 per cent) after Punjab, indicating very low rate of expenditure in 2014–2015. Regarding social sector expenditure GSDP ratio, Kerala's rank is 13. It is disturbing to note that capital outlay GSDP ratio is the lowest compared to all other states (0.8 per cent).

CONCLUSION

The analysis may be concluded with the following observations. The state has been facing acute fiscal crisis and heading towards a fiscal crisis trap. The revenue and fiscal deficits are at very high levels compared to other states in India. The reliance on borrowing to cover fiscal deficit is diminishing as the net availability of borrowing after adjusting payment of interest and repayment of debt is meagre. This has led to a situation where the state is forced to seek funds outside the budget for capital, plan and development projects. The causes of the current crisis are similar to that prevailed earlier. On the revenue side, slump in resource mobilisation, lack of periodical revision of rate of taxes and non-taxes, fall in the growth of tax revenue, under-performance of the Commercial Taxes Department in collection of sales tax and VAT, non-realisation of additional resource mobilisation targeted in the budget, inflated plan outlays, fall in dividends and profit from public sector undertakings, accumulation of arrears of revenue, and inefficient and poor collection of taxes and non-tax items have contributed to the crisis. The fiscal policy pursued by the successive governments in the state had not favoured timely revision of taxes and non-tax items, or given priority for resource mobilisation due to political considerations.

Rapid rise in NPRE and the failure of successive governments to curtail the expenditure is the root cause of the present crisis as well as earlier crises. Though the state does not have the resources to meet the additional expenditure required for salary and pension revision once in five years, the successive governments effect the revision to satisfy the powerful trade unions of government employees which are allied with political parties. Similarly, a large number of new public institutions, projects and private-aided educational institutions were started, and populist schemes of benefit distribution were implemented without considering the resource availability and due to political interests. Efforts are not made to abolish unnecessary establishments, institutions, public sector undertakings making huge losses on a sustained basis, excess staff and wasteful administrative expenditure due to political considerations. The diversion of resources for non-development purposes and non-availability of resources for development is emerging as the most serious fiscal issue of the state.

REFERENCES AND SELECT BIBLIOGRAPHY

Abraham, K. M. (2004). Kerala: The fiscal crisis and its aftermath. In B. A. Prakash (ed), *Kerala's economic development: Performance and problems in the post-liberalisation period* (pp. 359–417). New Delhi: SAGE.

Aiyar, R. R., & Kurup, K. N. (1992). State finances in Kerala. In A. Babchi et al. (eds), *State finances in India* (pp. 430–487). New Delhi: National Institute of Public Finance and Policy.

Alwin, J. (2014). *Recent trends in Kerala state finances.* New Delhi: Serials Publications.

CAG (Comptroller and Auditor General of India). (2012). *Report of the CAG of India on state finances for the year ended March 2011.* Thiruvananthapuram: GoK.

———. (2016a). *Report of the CAG of India on state finances for the year ended March 2015.* Thiruvananthapuram: GoK.

———. (2016b). *Report of the CAG of India on revenue sector for the year ended March 2015.* Thiruvananthapuram: GoK.

———. (2016c). *CAG report on public sector undertakings for the year ended March 2015.* Thiruvananthapuram: GoK.

———. (2017). *Report of the CAG of India on state finances for the year ended March 2016.* Thiruvananthapuram: GoK.

George, K. K. (1990). Kerala's fiscal crisis: A diagnosis. *Economic and Political Weekly, 25*(37), 2097–2105.

George, K. K., & Krishnakumar, K. K. (2012). *Trends in Kerala state finances—1991–1992 to 2012–2013: A study in the backdrop of economic reforms in India* (Working Paper No. 28). Kochi: Centre for Socio-economic and Environmental Studies.

GoK (Government of Kerala). (2001). *WHITE PAPER ON STATE FINANCES.* Thiruvananthapuram: GoK.

———. (2011). *White paper on state finances.* Thiruvananthapuram: GoK.

———. (2016a). *White paper on state finances.* Thiruvananthapuram: GoK.

———. (2016b). *Revised budget 2016–2017 At A Glance.* Thiruvananthapuram: GoK.

———. (2016c). *Revised budget speech 2016–2017.* Thiruvananthapuram: GoK.

———. (2017a). *Budget in brief 2017–2018.* Thiruvananthapuram: GoK.

———. (2017b). *Budget for 2017–2018,* Appendix I, Details of staff. Thiruvananthapuram: GoK.

Issac, T. T. M., & Mohan, R. (2016). *Sustainable fiscal consolidation: Suggesting the way ahead for Kerala* (Working Paper Series No. 469). Thiruvananthapuram: Centre for Development Studies.

KPERC (Kerala Public Expenditure Review Committee). (Third Committee): *Reports: First report (2010–2011), Second report (2011–2012), Third report (2012–2013), Fourth report (2013–2014)*. Thiruvananthapuram: GoK.

Kurian, N. J. (1999). State government finances: A survey of recent trends. *Economic and Political Weekly, 34*(19), 1115–1125.

Kurian, N. J., & Abraham, J. (1999). The financial crisis: An analysis. In B. A. Prakash (ed), *Kerala's economic development: Issues and problems* (pp. 327–346). New Delhi: SAGE.

Rakhe, P. B. (2003). *Estimation of tax leakage and its impact on fiscal health in Kerala* (Working Paper No. 347). Thiruvananthapuram: Centre for Development Studies.

RBI (Reserve Bank of India). (2017). *State finances: A study of budgets 2016–2017*. Mumbai: RBI.

Sen, T. K. (2012). *Recent development in Kerala state finances* (Working Paper Series No. 449). Thiruvananthapuram: Centre for Development Studies.

Chapter 18

India's Goods and Services Tax
An Overview

Jose Sebastian

INTRODUCTION

India has finally rolled out its much awaited Goods and Services Tax (GST) from 1 July 2017. This marks the culmination of the reform process of indirect tax system which began with the appointment of the Indirect Taxation Enquiry Committee in 1977. Though our GST is far removed from the ideal GST model, it is indeed an achievement for a country of India's size and diversity to have introduced this major tax reform. The objectives of this chapter are (a) to discuss the economic rationale and relevance of GST, (b) to outline its salient features, and (c) to analyse the impact of GST on India's economy in general and Kerala's economy in particular.

ECONOMIC RATIONALE AND RELEVANCE OF GST

GST is the system of indirect tax that prevails in over 160 countries of the world. Essentially, it is a value added tax (VAT) on both goods and services wherein the value added at each stage in a value chain is brought under the tax net with provision for set-off on the tax paid at earlier stages. In order to keep the tax system simple to administer and comply with, the number of rate categories is kept to a minimum. Accordingly, most countries have a two-rate system, a standard rate and a reduced rate for certain goods and services. With a few goods and services exempt from the tax net, international experience with GST shows that it is productive in terms of revenue, and it contributes to economic growth by avoiding the distortions and complexities associated with cascading-type sales taxes and excises. Though the country had planned to switch over to GST from March 2010, the negotiation between the centre and states took so long to arrive at a consensus. With the centre's assurances to compensate the losses that the states may incur in the coming five years, the stage was set for the rollout of the new levy. Basically, there are three specific circumstances that necessitated the introduction of GST in India. We may briefly outline each of them in some detail.

Narrow Tax Base

One of the basic problems plaguing India's fiscal federalism is the growing fiscal stresses both at the central and state levels. The mismatch between revenue and growing expenditure requirements has resulted in uncontrolled revenue and fiscal deficits over the years. While tax–GDP ratio of most developed countries hovers around 30 per cent, India's is as low as 16.4 per cent as on 2015–2016. The major factor behind this is that the indirect tax system of the country is heavily inclined towards taxation of goods. The seventh schedule of the Indian Constitution which delineates the taxing powers of the centre and states does not permit either of them to tax services along with goods. However, the constitution permits both the centre and states to bring under taxation certain services. The taxes thus levied by the centre are taxes on goods and passengers carried by railways, sea or air, taxes on railway fares and freights, and taxes on expenditure in hotels and restaurants. Comparable taxes in the case of states are taxes on consumption of electricity, taxes on advertisement other than those published in newspapers, taxes on goods and passengers carried by road and inland waterways, and taxes on entertainments, amusements, betting and gambling. These taxes, it may be noted, are neither levied as 'service tax' nor known so among tax payers and tax practitioners.

It has been pointed out that the total indirect taxes mobilised from these sources by the central and state governments together formed only 1 per cent of gross domestic product (GDP) or 6.6 per cent of total tax revenue during the period 1985–1986 to 1998–1999 (Rao, 2001, pp. 4000–4006).

Service taxation per se began in 1994 when the Government of India brought three services (telecommunications, non-life insurance and stock brokers) under the tax net, making use of the residuary powers under the Constitution. The centre has been widening the coverage of service tax over the years by bringing more and more services under the tax net. Now all services except those included in the negative list are brought under the service tax net. Service tax, which contributed just 0.44 per cent of the centre's total tax revenue in 1994–1995, contributed 14.52 per cent of the centre's gross tax revenue in 2015–2016. However, as a percentage of service sector which accounts for 61.5 per cent of GDP, service tax is only 1.86 per cent (Table 18.1).

This shows that without tapping the potential of service sector, it may not be easy for the country to raise its tax-GDP ratio. This is possible only by empowering the states also to levy service tax. The dichotomous treatment of goods and services should be replaced by a comprehensive GST that empowers both the centre and states to mobilise more resources from the fastest-growing segment of the

Table 18.1 *Contribution of Service Tax in India*

Year	Share of Service Sector in GDP (%)	Service Tax Revenue (₹ Crore)	Service Tax as a Percentage of GDP	Share of Service Tax in the Gross Tax Revenue of the Centre (%)
1994–1995	45.0	407	0.04	0.44
1999–2000	50.0	2,128	0.12	1.24
2004–2005	53.0	14,200	0.48	4.66
2009–2010	54.7	60,941	0.96	9.35
2015–2016	61.5	211,414	1.86	14.52

Source: Economic Survey, Government of India, various issues.

national economy. Introduction of GST is the logical conclusion of the tax reform process that India initiated with the introduction of VAT in 2005.

Cascading Effect of Complex Tax System

The indirect tax system of the country is characterised by multiplicity of taxes. There are mainly three central levies—excise at the manufacturing stage, central sales tax (CST) on interstate trade and service tax on services. The commodities which attract one or more of these levies are subjected to VAT at the state level. In the absence of any 'set-off' or credit to the taxes paid at the manufacturing and logistics stages, these taxes become part of the prices of commodities. Manufacturers and traders fix their profit margin on the price inclusive of these taxes. The resulting 'tax on tax', known as 'cascading', is one of the major reasons for the comparatively high prices of manufactured products in India.

Distortions and Complexities

India's resolve to go ahead with GST is also influenced by the need to address the distortions and complexities of a dichotomous indirect tax system that treats goods and services separately. This has given rise to a number of issues involving efficiency, equity and compliance. The present system of indirect taxation places a disproportionate burden on the goods-producing sectors at the expense of the service sector. This is adversely affecting the competitiveness of our manufactured products in the international market. This also has an equity dimension as the rich consumes more services than the poor. From the point of view of tax administration and compliance, the present system opens umpteen avenues of tax evasion and avoidance. As services form an inseparable part of manufacturing and trading activity, exclusion of services facilitates collusion of manufacturers and traders to evade and/or avoid tax (Rao, 2001, p. 4002). It should also be noted that in the present world of digital technology and e-commerce, the distinction between goods and services is increasingly getting blurred (Bagchi, 2004, pp. 1876–1878). Substantial revenue gets blocked in disputes and litigations relating to the definition of 'manufacturing', 'good' and 'service'.

SALIENT FEATURES OF INDIA'S GST

Following are the salient features of India's GST.

Conceptual Base of GST

GST marks a change in the concept of levy of tax. Till the implementation of GST, excise duty was levied on 'production', sales tax or VAT on 'sale' and service tax on 'provision' of service. Under GST, all these are replaced by the concept of 'supply' of goods or services. While these indirect taxes were origin-based taxes, GST is a destination-based tax. In an origin-based tax system, the manufacturing states are actually exporting tax burden to the consuming states. The concept of destination-based taxation underlying GST ensures that tax exportation is eliminated and the consuming states get revenue.

Dual GST Model

Like most federations, India has adopted the dual GST model. Accordingly, the centre will levy central GST (CGST) and states will levy state GST (SGST) on the same tax base. The interstate transactions and imports will be subjected to integrated GST (IGST) which is basically a mechanism for settling transactions between states. IGST is the sum of SGST and CGST. CGST will subsume the central taxes such as central excise duty (CENVAT), additional excise duty, excise duty on medicinal and toilet preparations, service tax, additional customs duty known as countervailing duty (CVD), special additional duty of customs (SAD), and surcharges and cesses. The state taxes which SGST would subsume are VAT, purchase tax, entertainment tax other than those levied by local bodies, luxury tax, taxes on lottery, betting and gambling, octroi and entry tax, and state cesses and surcharges. Alcoholic beverages and petroleum products are kept outside GST.[1]

---

[1] While implementing VAT in India, alcoholic beverages and petroleum products were kept outside VAT. These two items together contributed nearly 50 per cent of the total sales tax revenue of most states. The level of tax compliance in the case of these two items is comparatively higher as both are dealt by

GST Council

The GST Council constituted under Article 279-A of the Indian Constitution is the ultimate decision-making authority on all matters pertaining to GST. The Union finance minister is the chairman of the GST Council with state finance ministers as members. The decisions of the GST Council are made by three-fourths majority of the votes cast. The centre has one-third of the votes cast, and the states together have two-thirds of the votes cast. Irrespective of its size or population, each state has one vote.

Rate Structure

Considering the fact that GST will subsume these taxes at the state and central level, the challenge was to work out the rate of GST which will be revenue neutral (Table 18.2). After considerable deliberations, the GST Council resolved to adopt a rate structure with the following four rate categories.

India's GST exempts a wide range of goods and services from the tax net. Some of the major among them are fruits and vegetables, unpacked cereals, unbranded *atta* and *maida*, education and health services, local train travel and hotel rooms below ₹1,000. It is proposed to levy cesses at varying rates over and above the highest rate of 28 per cent on selected commodities to finance compensation to states in the event of revenue loss due to GST implementation.

Goods and Services Tax Network

One remarkable feature of India's GST is its high dependence on information and communication technology (IT). GST Network (GSTN) is the IT backbone of India's GST. GSTN facilitates the registration of tax payers, submission of returns and tax payment, and settlement

---

public sector enterprises in most states. While petroleum products are marketed by central public sector enterprises, wholesale and retail trade of alcoholic beverages is mostly handled of public sector marketing companies. It seems that by keeping these two assured sources of revenue outside GST, the risk of revenue loss due to the introduction of GST is reduced to some extent.

Table 18.2 *Rate Structure of GST*

Rate of Tax	Examples of Goods and Services	
	Goods	Services
5%	Packed and branded cereals, sugar, edible oils, footwear below ₹500, clothes below ₹1,000	Transportation services, air-conditioned train journey, air travel in economy class
12%	Ghee, dry fruits, jam, jelly, mobile phones, umbrellas, note books	Business class air travel, non-AC restaurant services, room rent between ₹1,000 and ₹2,500, state run lotteries
18%	Ice cream, hair oil, toothpaste, electronic toys, colour television, footwear above ₹500	AC restaurants serving liquor, telecom services, hotel rooms between ₹2,500 and ₹7,500
28%	Beedi, pan masala, washing machine, vacuum cleaner, private aircraft, motor cycles above 350 cc	Services in five star hotels, room rent above ₹7,500, private lotteries

Source: Compiled from various notifications issued by Ministry of Finance, Department of Revenue, Government of India in connection with GST.

of input tax credit (ITC) between tax payers across the country. This is expected to reduce compliance cost of tax payers besides eliminating the scope of corruption as the need for interaction between tax payers and officials is kept to the minimum.

Anti-profiteering Authority

India's GST Act contains an anti-profiteering clause. The Government of India is in the process of setting up an anti-profiteering authority. The five member authority will be chaired by a person retired at the level of secretary. The responsibility of the authority includes examining whether input tax credits availed by any registered taxable person or the reduction in the price on account of any reduction in the tax rate have actually resulted in a commensurate reduction in the price of the said goods or services supplied by him or her.

IMPACT OF GST

What will be the impact of GST on India's economy? This question has engaged the attention of scholars and policy-makers for quite some time. GST is expected to remove the distortions and complexities of India's indirect tax system which we have outlined earlier. This has its impact on revenue, economic growth and price level. We may briefly examine each of them in some detail.

Impact of GST on Revenue of Centre and States

As pointed out earlier, narrow tax base is one of the major reasons for implementing GST. GST will enable the centre to shift its tax base from the manufacturing point to the retail point. On an average, there is 20 per cent to 25 per cent value addition between the manufacturing point and retail point. This suggests that the centre may experience 20 per cent to 25 per cent broadening of its tax base. To a large extent, broadening of tax base in the case of states depends upon the composition of the underlying economies.

On the face of it, it may appear that the manufacturing states would be the losers and service-oriented states would be the gainers. A close look will reveal that it is extremely difficult to arrive at any firm conclusion. The subsuming of CST causes substantial revenue loss to manufacturing states. But these states will be in a better position to mobilise more revenue from services associated with manufacturing activity. This is evident from the fact that the manufacturing states of Andhra Pradesh, Gujarat, Karnataka, Maharashtra and Tamil Nadu account for 62.85 per cent of the central service tax collections in 2012–2013. The services associated with manufacturing activity such as legal services, patents and trademark, freight and forwarding, insurance, accounting and consultancy are the major sources of the central service tax revenue. GST will enable these states to levy tax on these services, and to that extent, their revenue loss on account of subsuming of CST will be made good. They can also hope to benefit from the boost that GST is going to provide to their manufacturing sector.

In the case of service-sector-oriented states, the potential of additional revenue from the service sector depends upon the presence of taxable services and size of the service providers. Thus, states with large number of small service providers, and exempted services such as education and health are unlikely to benefit significantly in the GST scenario.

Both for the centre and states, the principal source of additional revenue under GST will be the self-policing feature of GST. The Arvind Subramanian Committee observed:

> The first relates to the self-policing incentive inherent to a valued added tax. To claim input tax credit, each dealer has an incentive to request documentation from the dealer behind him in the value-added/tax chain. Provided, the chain is not broken through wide ranging exemptions, especially on intermediate goods, this self-policing feature can work very powerfully in the GST. (GoI, 2015, p. 3)

The information technology driven administrative architecture and dual monitoring structure at the central and state levels are likely to reduce tax evasion significantly. Several tax payers who at present remain outside the tax net fearing the rigors of the complex and cumbersome indirect tax system of the country are likely to become tax payers in the changed scenario. The consuming states are at present experiencing substantial revenue loss through e-commerce as the present tax system is origin-based. As we have already noted, the destination principle underlying GST will ensure that this revenue loss is brought down substantially.

Impact on Economic Growth

According to a study undertaken by the National Council of Applied Economic Research (NCAER), with the implementation of GST, economic growth would increase by 0.9–1.7 per cent of GDP, purely due to the elimination of the cascading of taxes on exports. Though the country unleashed the Make in India Campaign, its progress is hampered by several factors, one of the major among them being the current tax structure. To quote Arvind Subramanian Committee,

> The current tax structure unmakes India, by fragmenting Indian markets along state lines. This has the collateral consequence of also

undermining Make in India, by favouring imports and disfavouring domestic production. The GST would rectify it not by increasing protection but by eliminating the negative protection favouring imports and disfavouring domestic manufacturing. (GoI, 2015, p. 4)

Besides the cascading effect of various indirect taxes, the high logistic cost is also contributing to high manufacturing cost in India. Arvind Subramanian Committee pointed out that trucks in India drive just one third of the distance that trucks in the US cover. This raises direct costs like wages to drivers and indirect costs like requirement of firms to have larger inventory and location choices. Only 40 per cent of travel time is spent driving. Official stoppages and check-posts consume almost one quarter of the total travel time. With the introduction of GST, the check-posts could be eliminated and this would keep trucks moving almost six hours more per day, equivalent to 164 km per day. The resulting reduction in logistic cost will provide a boost to interstate trade and productivity growth within the country.

Another factor depriving Indian manufacturers a level playing field is the exemptions in countervailing duties (CVD) and special additional duties (SAD). In India, these are levied to offset the impact of excise duty levied on domestically manufactured goods. CVD/SAD exemptions tend to favour foreign products over domestically produced goods, and act as negative protection to Indian manufacturing. An exemption-free GST would ensure neutrality between imported products and domestically manufactured products.

The present tax structure of India discourages investment by not providing set-off or input tax credit on capital goods. This makes capital goods costly and reduces investment, which in turn reduces output and employment. The full set-off provision under GST to capital goods is expected to spur investment, employment and output.

Will GST Be Inflationary?

One lurking fear is that GST would lead to inflationary price rise. Most countries that implemented GST experienced inflation in the short run. India's GST rates are unlikely to cause inflationary price rise as the effective rates on many goods have actually come down. One possibility of marginal price rise is on account of higher tax burden on services.

Prices may increase in the short run as GST makes tax evasion and avoidance difficult. In the present system of indirect taxes, the level of tax evasion and avoidance is quite high and the benefits are shared between the trading community and consumers is in varying proportions depending upon the level of competition in the market. An evasion-proof GST may cause a price increase temporarily as the traders will be forced to pass on the tax to the consumers. But the inflationary price rise that GST may cause can be expected to subside once the benefits of GST such as reduced logistic cost and transaction cost start to flow in.

Impact of GST on India's Fiscal Federalism

While Indian states do not enjoy the kind of autonomy that states in federal countries like the USA enjoy, they do enjoy a fair degree of autonomy with respect to fiscal powers. There is a lurking fear among the states whether GST would eat into their fiscal autonomy. It is true that states will not be in a position to tinker with tax rates in the post-GST scenario. Any increase or decrease in tax rates will have to be taken collectively, and it should have the approval of the GST Council. So long as GST is providing states with the much needed fiscal space, the question of fiscal autonomy may not arise. It should also be remembered that the Indian Constitution has assigned several other tax handles to the states. GST has not touched on these sources.

Will GST strengthen India's fiscal federalism? It appears that the benefits of GST will not be uniform across the centre and states. The centre's tax base is likely to experience a widening to the tune of 20 per cent to 25 per cent as the point of levy gets shifted from manu-facturing to retail. The revenue impact of GST on states, however, will vary widely depending upon their economic circumstances. This would suggest that vertical and horizontal imbalances in India's fiscal federalism may widen in the post-GST scenario. The future union finance commissions have a major role to address this issue.

Impact of GST on Kerala Economy

GST has generated lot of expectations in Kerala. As a regional economy importing most of the manufactured commodities from other states, GST is likely to benefit Kerala immensely. At present, Kerala is at the receiving end of high manufacturing cost due to 'tax on tax' and transportation bottlenecks created by entry tax and check posts. GST is likely to bring down the manufacturing cost in the country. If this translates into lower prices, consuming public in Kerala will be the major beneficiary.

Will GST ease Kerala's persistent fiscal stress? There is a widely held view that as a service sector dominated economy, Kerala would benefit as the state will be able to tax services. However, available evidences question this view. As we have already seen, to a large extent, revenue from services depends upon the level of manufacturing activity. The industrially backward Kerala cannot expect much revenue from services associated with manufacturing activity. The fact that only 1.30 per cent of the country's service tax revenue was collected from Kerala in 2012–2013 proves this point. Kerala's service sector is dominated by small fry businessmen. The vast majority of them would come under the threshold limit of ₹2 million per annum (Sebastian & Kumari, 2015). Two fast-growing services of Kerala, namely, education and health, are outside GST.

The additional revenue that Kerala can count on in the GST scenario will be mostly from the goods sector. At present, the state is losing substantial revenue due to e-commerce. The destination principle underlying GST would arrest this revenue loss to a large extent. The surveillance by the centre and the state in the GST scenario is likely to arrest tax evasion and avoidance to a large extent.

GST offers a big opportunity for Kerala to kick-start its lost industrialisation opportunity. Cost of raw materials, intermediate products and machinery is likely to come down in the coming years. GST offers the hassle-free marketing of industrial products across the country.

CONCLUDING OBSERVATIONS

The vast diversity and complexity of the country and federal polity prevented India from keeping the GST very simple. The interests of various stakeholders have to be accommodated. While most developed countries have two GST rates, we have at least five rate categories. Petroleum and petroleum products are kept outside the GST. This means that those manufacturers who use these as intermediate products will not be eligible for input tax credit. All these rob our GST of much of its benefits, and render tax administration and compliance difficult. But these deficiencies can be rectified in course of time, and the country can look forward to a GST which is closer to the ideal. It should be remembered that GST alone cannot be expected to change the backwardness of our country. The progress of the country is hampered by several factors, and tax structure is only one of them. Unless physical infrastructure such as the power, road and rail network is improved, it may not be possible for the country to take full advantage of GST. The additional revenue that GST is going to bring will enable the central and state governments to invest in infrastructure, and this in turn will spur growth in output and employment.

REFERENCES AND SELECT BIBLIOGRAPHY

Bagchi, A. (2004). Taxing services: The way forward. *Economic and Political Weekly, 39*(19), 1876–1878.

GoI (Government of India). (2015, December). *Report on the revenue neutral rate and structure of rates for the goods and services tax (GST)*. New Delhi: Government of India.

Rao, M. G. (2001). Taxing services: Issues and strategy. *Economic and Political Weekly, 36*(42), 4000–4006.

Sebastian, J., & Kumari, L. A. (2015). *Goods and services tax: Will it be a panacea for Kerala's fiscal woes?* (Working Paper No. 1/2015). Thiruvananthapuram: Gulati Institute of Finance and Taxation.

Chapter 19

Eleventh Five-Year Plan
An Analysis of Plan Performance

Jerry Alwin

The successive governments which came to power in Kerala since the inception of the state in 1956 have been giving high priority to economic plans for the development of Kerala. The strategy pursued was to mobilise state resources, formulate five-year and annual plans, and implement it through departments and agencies of the state government. The projects and schemes of the annual plan are put in the plan head of budget. It is believed that through this planned effort, the state can be transformed from a backward to a developed economy. Greater emphasis was given to plan and public investment compared to private investment between 1956 and 1990. Though there was a shift in the policy approach due to the implementation of structural adjustment reforms by the central government since 1991, the emphasis given to planning continued in the state. The 11th Five-Year Plan was implemented in the state in this context. Though the state plan and its performance is a core issue in the state's development, not many attempts were made to study the issues related to plan formulation, financing, implementation, plan expenditure and achievement of physical targets except a few (GoK, 2012, 2013; Alwin, 2014). In this context, an attempt is made to study the 11th Five-Year Plan of Kerala.

THEORETICAL FRAMEWORK

According to W. Arthur Lewis, a development plan may contain any or all of the following parts, namely, survey of current economic conditions, list of proposed public expenditures, discussion of likely developments in the private sector, macroeconomic projection of the economy and a review of the government policies (Lewis, 1996). The plan normally begins by reviewing the recent progress of the important macroeconomic variables such as population, national output, investment, savings, consumption, government expenditure, taxation, balance of payments and major industries. The next step of the planning process is the review of public expenditure, and each government department or agency is asked to submit its proposals for expenditure over the period of the plan. A review of the likely developments in the private sector is also made because private and public sectors are interrelated, and government planning consists of establishing intelligent priorities for public investment programme and formulating a sensible and consistent set of public policies to encourage growth in private sector. A macroeconomic projection of the economy is made to understand the degree of interrelationship between private and public sectors. The quality of a plan depends upon the quality of its policies, rather than the quality or quantity of its arithmetic.

There are three types of plans, namely, short, medium and long term. The short is the annual plan or the operational plan which is to be implemented. An annual plan is an operational plan which consists of large number of expenditure projects/schemes implemented through government department and other public agencies. The annual plan indicates the sum total of development activities proposed and funded by the government through allocation in the state budget. Annual plans are usually prepared based on a medium-term plan. The medium plan ranges between three and seven years with five years as the most popular choice. Five-Year plans are medium-term plans and indicate medium-term goals for development. The long-term or perspective plan ranges from 10 to 20 years. The perspective plans can serve as guide to decision-makers for preparing medium-term plans.

Development plan is an instrument by which governments intervene in the economy through public investment projects and schemes to achieve certain socio-economic objectives. Preparation of financially, technically and economically feasible projects, finding resources, time-bound and efficient execution of projects, and achievements of physical targets are important elements in plan performance. The bureaucratic practices, rules and regulations relating to project formulation and execution, delays in the issue of administrative sanctions, inadequate allotment of resources, problems of land acquisition, lack of coordination among departments responsible for execution, lack of availability of competent contractors, incompetency of administrators, etc., lead to poor and inefficient execution of plan projects. In Kerala, a core development issue during the last six decades is the poor implementation of annual plan schemes. The achievements of financial and physical targets were far below the targets fixed.

OBJECTIVES, HYPOTHESIS AND SOURCE OF DATA

The objectives of the study are to examine the state component of the plan on the following: (a) strategies, objectives, plan financing and plan outlays of the 11th Plan; (b) priorities in plan allocation and sector-wise outlay and expenditure; and (c) execution of annual plans by government departments and plan performance. The focus of the study is to examine the state plan component of the plan formulated and implemented by the state government and exclude the plan of local governments.

We present the following hypothesis to explain the plan performance.

1. The practice of fixation of an unrealistic and inflated plan for political propaganda without adequate resource support, and introduction of supplementary projects and schemes subsequent to passing of the budget, led to incompletion of projects within the stipulated time, spillover of projects and poor achievement of plan targets.
2. The low priority given for infrastructure sectors such as irrigation and flood control, power, industry, transport and communication, urban infrastructure, scientific research, etc., in the plans led to the inadequate creation of infrastructure, resulting in serious development constraints.

3. The failure in passing the budget before the beginning of the financial year, the incapability of government departments to prepare sound projects in the annual plan, inadequate allocation of funds, inefficiency in the execution of projects, lack of accountability of officers, etc., led to persistent bunching of plan expenditure and poor achievement of financial and physical targets.

The major indicators for evaluation of plan performance are the following: (a) percentage of realisation of resources to total projected outlay; (b) percentage of plan expenditure to yearly outlay (aggregate and sector-wise/sub-sector-wise); (c) sector-wise plan expenditure and growth in the sectors; (d) physical targets and actual achievements; and (e) norms for utilisation of plan funds and actual spending. A plan expenditure of 90 per cent or above the annual plan outlay is used as an indicator for rating plan performance as good/satisfactory/better performance.

The study is based on secondary data from state plan documents and *Economic Review* published by Kerala State Planning Board; *Annual Plan Review* published by Central Plan Monitoring Unit (CPMU), Planning and Economic Affairs Department, Government of Kerala; reports of the Kerala Public Expenditure Review Committee (KPERC); and other secondary sources.

The chapter is divided into five sections. The first section examines the strategy, objectives and plan financing during the 11th Five-Year Plan, the second section gives the gross plan outlay and expenditure, the third section deals with sector-wise outlay and expenditure, and the fourth section deals with execution of state plans by government departments and the last section gives the conclusions of the study.

ELEVENTH PLAN: STRATEGY, OBJECTIVES AND PLAN FINANCING

Strategy

When compared to the earlier plans, the 11th Five-Year Plan (2007–2012) of Kerala envisaged three basic strategic shifts. The first was to break Kerala's excessive dependence on cash crops and essay a shift towards larger production of food grains, not necessary to make the state self-sufficient, but to provide a cushion against contingencies. The second strategic shift is to resurrect the role of public investment, which had been whittled down in the 10th Plan period. The third strategic shift, linked to the second has been the re-assertion of the role of the government as the guarantor of a minimum living for all. This required not just the provision of social services of a minimum quality and quality to all, but also support to the distressed petty producers, including peasants, fisher folks and artisans, the workers in the declining traditional industries who have been hit hard by globalisation.

Objectives

The 11th Five-Year Plan was formulated against the background of a profound crisis, which affected, among others, peasants, petty producers, agricultural labourers, rural workers and workers in traditional industries. The plan had to deal with massive unemployment, both among male and female, skilled and unskilled labourers, and rural and urban workforce. This crisis not only affected the backbone of the economy but also led to breaking the real structure of the economy. Therefore, the objective of the 11th Plan was to reverse this trend and take bold and positive steps to increase investment, and to provide immediate relief package to promote weaker sections, especially those affected by the crash in commodity prices in the world market. So the major objectives of the plan were to address the problem of an agrarian economy and, on the other hand, address the problem of educated unemployment and unemployment of Gulf returnees, preserve and extend magnificent achievements in the social sector, and expand the modern secondary and tertiary sectors, even while nurturing and making viable traditional industries and occupations. The other objectives are increasing the outlays in social sector and skill-imparting activities for the generation of educated employment, and creating a conducive atmosphere for private investment in industry and IT sectors.

Plan Financing

One of the major reasons for poor achievement of plan outlays is the fixation of unrealistic and inflated plan outlays for political propaganda without adequate resources. The fiscal health of the state government had also steadily deteriorated in the late 1990s. This has constrained the state in taking the plan activities, especially after the enactment of fiscal responsibility legislation, which restricted fiscal deficit relative to gross state domestic product (GSDP) to 2 per cent. The 12th Finance Commission enforced the State Level Fiscal Responsibility Legislation as a conditionality for states in obtaining debt relief. This has led to serious resource mobilisation problems.

Table 19.1 gives the projected as well as the realised financing pattern of the 11th Plan outlay of the state. The gross budgetary support (GBS) in the 11th Plan was projected at ₹247.5326 billion at 2006–2007 prices. This included ₹34.2153 billion of central assistance (CA) and ₹47.8 billion of resources of public sector enterprises (PSEs). The total resource projected for the state plan including the resources of local bodies was fixed at ₹404.22 billion. However, the state was

Table 19.1 *Projected vis-à-vis Realised Financing Pattern of the Eleventh Plan (2007–2012) Outlay (in ₹ Crore at 2006–2007 Prices)*

Item	Projection (2006–2007 Prices)	Realisation Total	% Realisation
A. State government (1+2+3)	24,753.26	21,645.08	87.44
1. State's own resources	–6,553.41	–14,663.86	–223.76
of which BCR	–8,662.43	–8,394.35	–103.14
2. Borrowings	27,885.14	29,689.41	106.47
3. Central assistance (grants)	3,421.53	6,619.53	193.47
B. Resources of public sector enterprises	4,780	1,240.61	25.95
C. Resources of local bodies	10,888.74	10,152.12	93.24
Total plan resources (A+B+C)	40,422	33,037.81	81.73
State plan outlay	40,422	33,037.81	81.73

Source: 12th Five-Year Plan, Government of Kerala.

able to realise only 82 per cent of total amount projected. This was mainly due to steep increase in revenue deficits resulting in utilisation of borrowed funds to cover the deficit. Though the projected resources from public sector for the plan were ₹47.8 billion, the actual realisation was only ₹12.4 billion or 26 per cent. In the case of resources of local bodies, the actual realisation was only 93 per cent. Thus, the deterioration of finances of the state and lack of profitability of public sector undertaking forced the government to attain only 82 per cent of the projected resources. The KPERC which examined the plan expenditure of government of Kerala has identified the introduction of a large number of schemes through supplementary demands after passing the budget as a reason for poor implementation of plan schemes (GoK, 2012). The committee says that it distorts the priorities and implementation of original plan projects of the state. The committee recommended that this practice may be discouraged and the plan proposals of the supplementary demands for grants may be limited to the declaration in the budget speech.

GROSS PLAN OUTLAY AND EXPENDITURE OF 11TH PLAN

A plan outlay consists of three components, namely, state plan, local body plan and special CA. The plan utilisation of 90 per cent and above to the outlay may be considered as a better performance. Table 19.2 gives the gross plan outlay, its components, plan expenditure and percentage of expenditure during the five-year period. A noticeable aspect is that the percentage of plan expenditure of state plan excluding the local bodies ranged between 82 per cent and 88 per cent during the period, indicating poor performance. Thus, the state plan component of the plan formulated and executed by the state government recorded poor performance in all the five years of the 11th plan.

We have also attempted an analysis about the item–wise outlay and expenditure of the state plan schemes. The state plan schemes comprises of six items, namely, state plan schemes including state share of other centrally sponsored schemes (OCSS), externally aided projects (EAP), funds provided in the 12th and 13th Finance Commission, rural infrastructure development fund (RIDF), one-time additional central assistance (ACA) and others. Table 19.3 gives the item–wise outlay,

Table 19.2 *Gross Plan Outlay, Expenditure and Expenditure as Percentage of Outlay of 11th Plan (in ₹ Crore)*

Category	2007–2008	2008–2009	2009–2010	2010–2011	2011–2012
I. Gross Plan Outlay (₹ Crore)					
Total state plan (excluding local body)	4,712.87	5,822.96	6,834.87	7,827.35	9,435.95
Local body plan	1,790.01	1,877.5	2,085.13	2,197.65	2,574.05
Total state plan	6,950	7,700.47	8,920	10,025	12,010
Special central assistance	995.53	922.17	882.9	1,240.86	1,406.28
Total plan outlay	7,534.78	8,641.14	9,811.9	11,280.86	13,428.28
II. Total Plan Expenditure					
Total state plan (excluding local body)	3,987.45	4,858.41	5,943.5	6,706.83	8,258.79
Local body plan	1,396.59	1,474.37	1,850.58	1,994.15	2,696.1
Total state plan	5,690.4	6,332.78	7,794.08	8,700.98	10,954.89
Special central assistance	782.42	1,140.62	1,041.14	1,073.43	1,281.04
Total plan expenditure	6,472.82	7,486.96	8,826.89	9,788.22	12,248.81
III. Percentage of Expenditure to Outlay					
Total state plan (excluding local body)	82	83	87	86	88
Local body plan	78	87	98	91	105
Total state plan	82	82	87	87	91
Special central assistance	79	80	118	87	91
Total expenditure	89	86	90	87	91

Source: Central Plan Monitoring Unit (CPMU), *Annual Plan Review*, various years.

Table 19.3 State Plan Outlay, Expenditure and Expenditure as Percentage of Outlay of 11th Plan (in ₹ Crore)

Category	2007–2008	2008–2009	2009–2010	2010–2011	2011–2012
State Plan Schemes (Outlay)					
1. State plan schemes (including state share of other centrally sponsored schemes [OCSS])	2,237.13	2,544.95	4,565.84	5,883.34	6,997.04
2. EAP (externally aided projects)	1,862.14	1,560.00	1,564.41	1,216.48	1,042.95
3. 12th and 13th FC (Finance Commission)	136.25	136.25	136.25	50.44	431.63
4. RIDF (Rural Infrastructural Development Fund)	344.5	452.01	136.25	454.8	554.64
5. One-time ACA (additional central assistance)	579.97	1,129.75	1,573.93	111.22	320
6. Others*			4.37	111.07	89.69
Total State Plan (excluding local body)	4,712.87	5,822.96	6,834.87	7,827.35	9,435.95
State Plan Schemes (Expenditure)					
1. State plan schemes (including state share of OCSS)	2,806.2	3,069.56	4,428.9	5,693.15	6,845.41
2. EAP	973.78	838.6	763.99	504.6	533.25
3. 12th and 13th FC	47.16	136.25	208.08	32.02	325.24
4. RIDF	160.31	167.91	4,454.59	330.39	318.9
5. One-time ACA	306.36	736.51	91.42	66.53	163.45

(Continued)

Table 19.3 (*Continued*)

Category	2007–2008	2008–2009	2009–2010	2010–2011	2011–2012
6. Others★	–	–	5.52	80.14	72.54
Total State Plan Expenditure (excluding local body)	3,987.45	4,858.41	5,943.5	6,706.83	8,258.79
State Plan Schemes (% Expenditure)					
1. State plan schemes (including state share of OCSS)	125	121	97	97	98
2. EAP	52	54	49	41	51
3. 12th and 13th FC	35	34	153	63	75
4. RIDF	47	39	98	73	57
5. One-time ACA	53	65	83	60	51
6. Others★	–	–	126	72	81
Total State Plan Expenditure as % of Outlay (excluding local body)	82	83	87	86	88

Source: Central Plan Monitoring Unit (CPMU), *Annual Plan Review*, Various years.

Note: ★Others include food security and public private partnership.

expenditure and percentage of expenditure. A review of the item-wise percentage of expenditure shows that the first item, state plan schemes including state share of OCSS, registered better utilisation in all the five years. On the other hand, the percentage of utilisation of EAP was only around half of the plan outlay during the entire plan period, indicating very poor utilisation. The utilisation of the funds provided by the Finance Commission and one-time ACA was poor except for one year. The percentage of expenditure of RIDF and others also indicate unsatisfactory spending. Thus, failure to use the plan funds other than the state plan component was the cause for poor plan performance.

SECTOR-WISE OUTLAY AND EXPENDITURE OF 11TH PLAN

A sector-wise outlay gives an idea about priority and allocation of outlays to different sections. The sector-wise allocation may be broadly classified into four, namely, agriculture and rural development, industry and power, tertiary sector activities and local bodies. Table 19.4 gives the yearly outlay of 4 broad sections and 12 sub-sectors. The share of sectoral composition of outlay is given in Table 19.5. A review of the sectoral outlay shows that the sub-sectors, agriculture and allied services, rural development, irrigation and flood control registered an increase in the share during the plan period. On the other hand, it is disturbing to note that the share of outlay of the power sector registered a decline. This indicates the low priority given to the power sector, the crucial infrastructure sector. Another infrastructure sector which witnessed a decline in its share was transport and communications. The low priority given for infrastructure sectors such as irrigation and flood control, power, transport and communication, urban infrastructure, scientific research, etc., in the plans led to inadequate creation of infrastructure resulting in serious development constraints. The sectors which registered an increase in share are industry and minerals, and social and community services. Though Kerala is considered a leader in the country with regard to decentralised planning, the share of plan outlay registered a steady decline.

Table 19.6 gives the percentage utilisation of plan outlay. For the sector agriculture and allied services, the plan utilisation was better except for the years 2007–2008 and 2010–2011. The plan utilisation

Table 19.4 *Sector-wise Plan Outlay★ of 11th Plan (in ₹ Lakhs)*

Category	2007–2008	2008–2009	2009–2010	2010–2011	2011–2012
Agriculture and allied service	36,849	40,331	44,404	70,555	99,500
Rural development	29,655	32,902	36,052	39,701	62,278
Cooperation	1,480	1,530	2,000	4,250	4,300
Irrigation and flood control	21,527	25,762	35,065	33,286	55,103
Power	99,793	93,435	97,506	104,700	112,300
Industry and minerals	15,104	29,900	37,551	56,387	63,967
Transport and communications	95,882	99,847	81,646	88,640	128,739
Scientific services and research	6,123	6,500	6,698	7,864	9,164
Social and community services	198,414	241,585	304,092	364,981	386,639
Economic services	9,338	8,073	35,506	8,724	9,951
General services	1,835	2,431	2,967	3,697	11,654
Local bodies plan	179,000	187,751	208,513	219,765	257,405
Total	695,000	770,047	892,000	1,002,500	1,201,000

Source: Central Plan Monitoring Unit (CPMU), *Annual Plan Review*, various years.

Note: ★Excluding central assistance.

Table 19.5 *Sector-wise Plan Outlay* as Percentage to Total of 11th Plan*

Category	2007– 2008	2008– 2009	2009– 2010	2010– 2011	2011– 2012
Agriculture and allied services	5.30	5.24	4.98	7.03	8.28
Rural development	4.27	4.27	4.04	3.96	5.19
Cooperation	0.22	0.20	0.22	0.42	0.36
Irrigation and flood control	3.09	3.35	3.93	3.32	4.59
Power	14.36	12.12	10.93	10.44	9.35
Industry and minerals	2.17	3.90	4.21	5.62	5.33
Transport and communications	13.80	12.97	9.15	8.84	10.72
Scientific services and research	0.88	0.84	0.75	0.78	0.76
Social and community services	28.55	31.37	34.09	36.42	32.19
Economic services	1.34	1.04	3.98	0.88	0.83
General services	0.26	0.30	0.34	0.37	0.97
Local bodies plan	25.76	24.40	23.38	21.92	21.43
Total	100.00	100.00	100.00	100.00	100.00

Source: Computed from Table 19.4.

Note: *Excluding central assistance.

was very poor for infrastructure sector power for all the years. The sector industry and minerals, transport and communication achieved better plan utilisation. The plan utilisation of the sector social and community sectors was very poor (below 80 per cent) during all the five years of the 11th Plan.

EXECUTION OF STATE PLANS

The State plan is executed by different government departments. Two major issues in the execution of annual plan are bunching of plan expenditure during the last quarter or last month of the financial year and poor plan fund utilisation. We are examining the time frame fixed by the government for spending the annual plan outlay in four quarters.

Table 19.6 *Expenditure as Percentage of Outlay*

Category	2007–2008	2008–2009	2009–2010	2010–2011	2011–2012
Agriculture and allied service	64	101	111	85	91
Rural development	99	75	105	110	88
Cooperation	52	62	160	78	77
Irrigation and flood control	91	70	62	67	29
Power	58	85	75	63	62
Industry and minerals	248	109	104	113	82
Transport and communications	95	77	147	187	172
Scientific services and research	36	63	76	85	84
Social and community services	77	78	69	60	73
Economic services	97	191	88	154	82
General services	305	183	215	205	177
Local bodies plan	78	79	98	97	105
Total	82	82	87	87	91

Source: Central Plan Monitoring Unit (CPMU), *Annual Plan Review*, various years.

The state government has fixed a quarter-wise target of plan expenditure for the four quarters in a financial year. According to this norm, a department has to spend 10 per cent of the plan outlay during the first quarter of the financial year between April to June, and 30 per cent during the second quarter from July to September. The target fixed for the third and fourth quarters is 30 per cent each. Table 19.7 gives a month-wise plan expenditure of all government departments in Kerala for the years 2010–2011 and 2011–2012. From the data, it is seen that the departments have not achieved the target of plan expenditure fixed by the government during the first three quarters in the two years. On the other hand, more than 50 per cent of expenditure was incurred during the last quarter of the financial year. Another notable thing is that about 34 per cent of plan expenditure was incurred during the month of

Table 19.7 *Month-wise Plan Expenditure of Government Departments (in ₹ Lakhs)*

Month	Total Plan Expenditure 2010–2011	% to Total Expenditure	Total Plan Expenditure 2011–2012	% to Total Expenditure
April	12,906.26	1.48	6,819.02	0.62
May	25,612.93	2.94	18,631.05	1.70
June	31,453.33	3.61	27,798.96	2.54
1st quarter	69,972.52	8.03	53,249.03	4.86
July	4,479.56	0.51	46,860.74	4.28
August	102,758.30	11.81	47,667.13	4.35
September	65,856.30	7.57	37,942.51	3.46
2nd quarter	173,094.16	19.89	132,470.38	12.09
October	20,150.79	2.32	75,364.73	6.88
November	108,990.00	12.53	98,988.92	9.00
December	56,992.26	6.55	121,557.77	11.10
3rd quarter	186,133.05	21.40	295,511.42	26.98
January	71,566.14	8.23	92,072.48	8.40
February	71,923.73	8.27	140,394.82	12.82
March	297,408.20	34.18	381,791.10	34.85
4th quarter	440,898.07	50.68	614,258.40	56.07
Total	870,097.80	100.00	1,095,489.23	100.00

Source: Report of Kerala Public Expenditure Review Committee, 2010–2011 and 2011–2012.

March, the last month of the financial year. Thus, the bunching of plan expenditure to the last quarter of the financial year was an important issue in plan execution and plan expenditure.

The Kerala Public Expenditure Committee, which examined the plan performance, has identified the following reasons for the inefficient implementation of plan schemes by government departments for the years 2010–2011 and 2011–2012.

1. Delay in passing the state budget before the month of April. Though, the financial year starts with 1 April, state budgets are usually passed after three to four months. The departments usually

wait till the passing of the budget to start the processing of schemes resulting in delayed administrative sanction and implementation.

2. After passing the budget, a large number of schemes are brought through supplementary demands, which change the priority of plan schemes initially planned, which leads to poor implementation of budgeted plan schemes.

3. The publication of head-wise plan schemes in the budget creates confusion about the plan schemes coming under each department. The head-wise summary of plan schemes makes it very difficult to identify which departments are responsible for which schemes.

4. Inadequate allocation of funds for major schemes results in long delays in execution and cost escalation.

5. Lack of accountability in project formulation, monitoring and implementation of projects in the departments. No person in the department is accountable for preparation, monitoring and implementation of plan schemes.

6. The annual plan document lacks completeness. The annual plan document gives brief details of plans/schemes of various sectors without sufficient details needed for getting administrative sanction later. Many departments prepare the detailed plan schemes incorporating physical and financial targets and achievements with timescales only after the annual plan document is approved by the state government. This leads to a delay in administrative sanction, and consequent delay in implementation of plan schemes.

7. Failure to prepare sound or financially, economically and technically viable projects by the departments is a major reason for poor plan implementation. The lack of quality of plan schemes also leads to the delay/non-sanctioning of administrative clearance and the consequent non-utilisation of plan funds. There is no professional body to scrutinise the physical and financial viability of schemes prepared by departments either at department level or at state level.

8. The delay in implementation of various plan schemes connected with land acquisition is longer. Such schemes not only lead to delay but also cost overrun in future.

9. One important factor identified for delaying the project implementation is delay in tender procedure and sanctioning. The present-tender process is very long and hurdled with a lot of formalities.

10. Lack of timely revision of the rate for materials and works also adversely affect the time-bound implementation of schemes.

11. Lack of availability of competent contractors with modern equipment and skilled labour to execute major public works in different categories of work (roads, bridges, electrical works, water supply, waste disposal and other items of infrastructure) is a major constraint of efficient, time-bound implementation of schemes.

12. The delay in physical movements of files and documents leads to delayed administrative sanctions and consequent implementation.

13. In many departments, the plan schemes are implemented through offshoot agencies. However, the parent department has less control over these offshoot agencies, and the former is not able to efficiently monitor the activities of the latter.

14. Many departments are not able to implement centrally sponsored schemes (CSS) fully. One of the reasons cited for non-implementation of centrally sponsored schemes is the insufficient matching grants from the state budget.

15. For major projects, there is a need for getting clearance from different departments such as finance, public works department (PWD), fire service, health, etc., which leads to delay in the issue of administrative sanction and consequent delay in the implementation of schemes.

CONCLUSIONS

The analysis may be concluded with the following observations.

The practice of fixation of unrealistic and inflated plan outlays without adequate resource support has led to poor achievement of targeted outlay in the 11th plan. Another problem with the state plan is the introduction of the supplementary projects and schemes subsequent to the passing of the budget, resulting in incompletion of projects in the budget within the stipulated time frame. The sector-wise outlay of infrastructure items such as irrigation and flood control, power, industry, transport and communications, urban infrastructure, scientific research, etc., shows that only a small amount is spent on these critical sectors, and the shares of expenditure to these sectors had been showing a decline.

The plan performance was poor for the sectors such as power and social and community services which are critical for development. Another major issue regarding plan execution by government departments is the bunching of plan expenditure during the last quarter of the financial year. The KPERC has identified the following major reasons for the inefficient implementation of plan schemes, namely, delay in passing the state budget, inadequate allocation of funds for major schemes resulting in delays and cost escalation, lack of accountability in project formulation, monitoring and implementation, failure to prepare financially viable projects, delay in physical movements of files and documents leading to delay in administrative sanctions, etc.

REFERENCES AND SELECT BIBLIOGRAPHY

Alwin, J. (2014). *Recent trends in Kerala state finances*. New Delhi: Serials Publications.

GoK (Government of Kerala). (2012). *Report of Kerala Public Expenditure Review Committee 2010–2011*. Thiruvananthapuram: Government of Kerala.

———. (2013). *Report of Kerala Public Expenditure Review Committee 2011–2012*. Thiruvananthapuram: Government of Kerala.

Lewis, W. A. (1966). *Development planning*. London and Harlow: George Allen and Unwin Ltd.

Planning and Economic Affairs Department. Annual Plan Review for various years from 2008–2009 to 2014–2015. Central Plan Monitoring Unit, Thiruvananthapuram: Government of Kerala.

State Planning Board. (2009). *Eleventh Five Year Plan (2007–2012): Mid-term appraisal*. Thiruvananthapuram: State Planning Board.

———. (2013). *Twelfth Five Year Plan (2012–2017)*. Thiruvananthapuram: State Planning Board.

———. (2014). *Eleventh Five Year Plan (2007–2012), outlay and expenditure*. Thiruvananthapuram: State Planning Board.

———. (2015a). *Economic review 2014*. Thiruvananthapuram: State Planning Board.

———. (2015b). *Perspective plan 2030* (Vols. I to IV). Thiruvananthapuram: State Planning Board.

Chapter 20

Decentralised Planning
A Study of Plan Performance of
Grama Panchayats in Kerala

B. A. Prakash

The 73rd and 74th amendments of the Constitution of India have given Constitutional status to rural and urban local governments (LGs) and assigned the responsibility for preparation of plans for economic development and social justice. In Kerala, the LGs consist of three-tier panchayats, namely, grama, block and district, and municipalities and municipal corporations began to implement development plans since 1995. In spite of the implementation of the plan for the last two decades, the majority of them were not able to achieve a satisfactory performance due to a number of factors. Poor plan performance on all fronts, namely, plan formulation, execution, monitoring, and achievement of physical and financial targets, is the basic problem faced by LGs at present (GoK, 2016). In this chapter, an attempt is made to study plan performance of grama panchayats (GPs) based on a sample survey of 12 GPs. In order to explain the poor plan performance, we present the following hypothesis:

[T]he major causes for the poor plan performance of LGs are irrational and irrelevant plan formulation guidelines giving too much emphasis for pre-project preparation activities, low priority for project preparation, delays in getting approvals, postponement of execution to later parts of the financial year, implementation of a large and unmanageable number of projects, execution of projects through beneficiaries committees, projects giving undue importance to wards and neglecting overall development of LG, inadequate staff and bunching of plan expenditure to last-quarter or last month of the financial year.

DECENTRALISED PLANNING: A REVIEW

In this section, we examine the broad objectives pursued during the last two decades, and the views of the Fourth State Finance Commission (SFC) on decentralised planning. Kerala has 1,200 LGs consisting 941 GPs, 152 block panchayats, 14 district panchayats, 87 municipalities and 6 municipal corporations.

The broad objectives of decentralised planning pursued during the last two decades are the following (GoK, 2009): (a) Promotion of local economic development by enhancing production and productivity of agriculture and allied sectors, and traditional and small-scale industries, with focus on employment and poverty reduction; (b) improving governance, especially in terms of transparency, people's participation and responsiveness; (c) bringing about an organic relationship between transferred departments and LGs, and bringing in role clarity; (d) achieving sustainable local-level development through preservation of ecology, environment and natural resources; (e) achieving integrated area development; (f) infrastructure development to achieve better quality of life for all (provision of housing, drinking water, electricity, better transport facilities, health services, clean environment for all and sanitation, including solid waste management); (g) improving the delivery of public services (hospitals, schools, anganwadis, etc.); (h) improving the welfare of marginalised and vulnerable sections of people (women, children, old-aged people, SC/ST categories, traditional fishermen and those employed in traditional industries); and (i) achieving reduction in gender disparities.

The Fourth SFC had examined the decentralised planning of LGs and identified certain serious issues in plan formulation and implementation (GoK, 2011). They are as follows: (a) tendency to divide the devolved funds ward-wise, leading to relatively small projects being taken up; (b) plans appear to emerge from negotiated priorities rather than from participatory situation analysis based on data and experience; (c) working groups and technical advisory groups, the instruments of the preparation of plans, are becoming perfunctory; (d) the planning and implementation of the Special Component Plan (SCP) and Tribal Sub-Plan (TSP) is far below the desired levels; (e) although 10 per cent of the general sector expenditure has to be spent as the Women Component Plan (WCP), the realisation of the desirable outcome is poor (the planning and implementation of WCP are below expectations); (f) significant improvement in the horizontal and vertical integration of plans is needed; (g) poor record of service delivery in public institutions; (h) the focus continues to lie on the LG-level plan and annual plan; (i) no significant achievement in the production sector and local economic development sector; (j) the absence of effective system of quality assurance for concurrent monitoring; (k) the weak role of intermediate panchayats; and (l) District Planning Committees (DPCs) still function as committees with emphasis on the project clearance of LGs.

A review of the annual plan expenditure for 2014–2015 of the LGs gives a dismal picture. During the financial year 2014–2015, the total plan outlay of LGs was ₹47 billion. But the actual expenditure incurred was only ₹20.85 billion, that is, 44 per cent (Table 20.1). It is disturbing to note that the utilisation of funds was very low in three-tier panchayats as well as municipalities and municipal corporations. A major reason for this was the large and unmanageable number of projects implemented by the LGs.

PLAN FORMULATION PROCEDURES

A development plan comprises of a list of economically, financially and technologically feasible projects and schemes. The preparation of a financially feasible and implementable type of project is the precondition of a good development plan. The plan should also be supported by adequate resources. Instead of following simple procedures taking into account the manpower, administrative capacity and ground realities of LGs, elaborate procedures are prescribed by the state government and state planning board from the inception of decentralised planning in Kerala since the mid-1990s. Insisting on

Table 20.1 *Annual Plan Expenditure of Local Governments 2014–2015*

LG	Outlay (₹ in Crore)	Expenditure (₹ in Crore)	% of Expenditure	Average Number of Projects per LG
Grama panchayat	2,595.59	1,185.05	46	116
Block panchayat	622.99	332.58	53	49
District panchayat	622.99	261.49	42	733
Municipalities	482.38	191.12	40	208
Corporations	376.05	114.85	31	1,051
Total LSG	4,700.00	2,085.09	44	–

Source: CPM Unit, Planning and Economic Affairs Department; Chief Engineer, LSGD.

implementation of elaborate, time-consuming and unnecessary procedures has resulted in exhausting a lot of time and effort of the LGs on initial activities of plan formulation process. Currently, the elaborate procedures prescribed for the various stages of plan formulation and execution can be classified into four phases (LSGD, 2013). The first is a project identification phase where appointment of a plan coordinator, constitution of working groups, stakeholder consultations, discussion on a project proposal, preparation of a draft development plan, development seminars, plan outlay finalisation and preparation of projects are done. The various steps in the project identification phase are shown in Table 20.2.

The second phase in the preparation of a development plan is scrutiny and approval of projects, especially construction type projects. In the case of projects of the GPs, the authorised officer to approve the projects is the assistant executive engineer of block panchayats. The third phase in the preparation is the issue of technical sanction by competent officers. In the case of projects of GPs, the assistant executive engineer of block panchayats is the competent authority to give technical sanction. The fourth phase is a project execution stage where projects are given to contractors or beneficiary committees for execution. This involves tendering, finalisation of tender, supervision of the work execution, verification of the completed work and payment of bills.

Table 20.2 *Project Identification Stage (Phase I)*

Step	Committee/Group Responsible
Appointment of plan coordinator, constitution of working groups under standing committees	Committee/Council of LGs
Preparation of status report	Standing Committees/Working Groups
Stakeholder consultations	Working Group/Standing Committees
Discussion of project proposals/issues of development	Grama/Ward Sabha
Finalisation of status report and project proposals	Standing Committees, Working Groups
Preparation of draft development plan/ annual plan	Standing Committee for Development, Working Groups
Development seminar	Committee/Council of LGs, Development SC
Plan outlay finalisation	Committee/Council of LGs
Preparation of projects	Working Groups

Source: LSGs (2013).

We may make the following observation about the plan formulation procedures. Elaborate, time-consuming and irrelevant plan formulation procedures are prescribed to identify the projects. At the same time, adequate importance is not given to actual preparation, scrutiny, approval and issue of technical sanction of projects. As a result, the execution of the projects, especially engineering type of projects, are delayed or executed at the fag end of the financial year.

PLAN PERFORMANCE OF SAMPLE GPS

Plan Formulation Stage

For the study, we have selected 12 GPs on a sample basis from four districts, namely, Thiruvananthapuram, Ernakulam, Thrissur and Kozhikode. Data was collected from them based on a detailed interview schedule. We have discussed the plan formulation and execution issues with the officials, engineers and office bearers of the GPs. The indicators used for the study, are date of approval and implementation of plan, category of projects implemented, percentage of projects completed, percentage of plan fund utilisation, quarter-wise plan spending, etc. The first stage in the plan formulation is the appointment of a plan coordinator, constitution of working groups, conducting stakeholder meetings, convening grama sabhas, preparation of a draft development plan and organising development seminars. The information supplied by GPs shows that except for three, the rest of them appointed by the plan coordinator during the month of October–November 2013 for the preparation of the annual plan of 2014–2015. All the 12 GPs constituted working groups, and their number ranged between 11 and 13. It is reported that the working groups met during the month of December 2013 and January 2014. Of the 12 GPs, five had not conducted any stakeholder meetings.

Discussion on the development requirements of wards and projects in the grama sabhas is an important step in the formulation of an annual plan. Table 20.3 gives the date of meeting the grama sabha and the date of development seminar. The grama sabhas were met either in the month of December 2013 or January or February 2014. The average number of participation range between 104 and 204. But it is pointed out that majority of the participants were women. In a good number of GPs, the average number of women participants ranged between 70 and 80 per cent. Majority of participants are persons connected with the activities of GPs such as MGNREGA workers, Kudambashree members, and beneficiaries of housing and other schemes meant for the poor. Usually the participants are concerned about only those issues from which benefits will accrue to them. Except a few, all the GPs reported that the grama sabhas are not contributing much to the projects and schemes to be included in the annual plan of the LG.

It is reported that all the sample GPs conducted development seminars. But in the case of three GPs, the development seminar was conducted in May and July. This shows that these panchayats were not able to complete the initial stage project identification prior to the beginning of financial year.

Another stage in plan formulation is getting approval of the panchayat committee, DPC, scrutiny of the projects by engineers, issue of

Table 20.3 *Grama Sabha and Development Seminar in GPs for 2014–2015*

S. No.	Name of GP/District	Month in Which Grama Sabha Met	Average No. of Participants	Date of Development Seminar	No. of Participants in Development Seminar
	Thiruvananthapuram				
1	Kottukal	February 2014	131	31/05/2014	175
2	Anchuthengu	January 2014	104	2/5/2014	75
3	Vithura	August 2014	204	8/7/2014	NA
	Ernakulam				
4	Edavanakkad	January 2014	110	28/1/2014	110
5	Cheranallur	February 2014	127	28/2/2014	67
6	Kuttampuzha	NA	NA	1/2/2014	NA
	Thrissur				
7	Erumappetti	December 2013	135	23/12/2013	71
8	Nattika	December 2013	120	25/01/2014	160
9	Puthur	December 2013	177	30/2/2013	128
	Kozhikode				
10	Narippatta	January 2014	129	27/1/2014	NA
11	Kadalundi	January 2014	146	12/2/2014	203
12	Unnikulam	January 2014	155	12/2/2014	228

Source: Primary data collected from the LGs.

technical sanctions and starting execution. Table 20.4 gives the date of approval given by the GP committee and the month in which execution started. Of the GPs, only seven had approved the annual plans prior to the financial year 2014–2015. In the case of others, the plans were approved in May, June and October 2014. There were further delays to get approval from DPC, technical sanction and steps to start the execution. It is reported that the actual execution of projects in five GPs started in the months of September 2014, November 2014 and January 2015.

Execution of Projects

Here the projects are entrusted to contractors or beneficiary committees for execution. Usually, more than a month is required for

Table 20.4 *Date of Approval of Annual Plan Projects of GPs for 2014–2015*

S. No.	Name of GP/ District	Date of Approval of Annual Plan by GP Committee	Period of Starting Execution of Projects
	Thiruvananthapuram		
1	Kottukal	16 June 2014	Since January
2	Anchuthengu	2 June 2014	Since June
3	Vithura	6 October 2014	Since July
	Ernakulam		
4	Edavanakkad	19 February 2014	NA
5	Cheranallur	6 March 2014	Since November
6	Kuttampuzha	10 February 2014	NA
	Thrissur		
7	Erumappetti	30 June 2014	June to September
8	Nattika	10 February 2014	April to March
9	Puthur	28 February 2014	July to September
	Kozhikode		
10	Narippatta	13 February 2014	June to September
11	Kadalundi	15 February 2014	October to January
12	Unnikulam	6 May 2014	Since May

Source: Primary data collected from the LGs.

completing the procedures of tendering a work. The data given by the GPs reveal that except in a few GPs, the rest are executing the majority of the projects through beneficiary committees and others. Table 20.5 gives the number of projects executed by the contractors. The practice followed in the majority of the GPs is to entrust the execution of projects to beneficiary committees. Even road construction, tarring, construction of buildings, etc., are given to beneficiary committees without assessing their capability to execute the projects. The civil engineers of the GPs told us that they face serious problems in the execution of projects through beneficiary committees. Most of the beneficiary committees do not have expertise, skilled staff and

Table 20.5 *Number of Projects Executed in 2014–2015 in GPs*

S. No.	Name of GP/ District	Contractor	Beneficiary Committee and Others	Total	Percentage Executed by Contractors
	Thiruvananthapuram				
1	Kottukal	2	223	225	0.89
2	Anchuthengu	9	80	89	10.11
3	Vithura	17	153	170	10.00
	Ernakulam				
4	Edavanakkad	78	47	125	62.40
5	Cheranallur	0	109	109	0.00
6	Kuttampuzha	23	243	266	8.65
	Thrissur				
7	Erumappetti	10	123	133	7.5
8	Nattika	22	138	160	13.8
9	Puthur	113	119	232	48.7
	Kozhikode				
10	Narippatta	45	108	153	29.41
11	Kadalundi	50	104	154	32.47
12	Unnikulam	10	291	301	3.32
	Total	379	1,738	2,117	17.90

Source: Primary data collected from the LGs.

equipment for undertaking road construction, repair, building construction and other civil works. In some cases, the beneficiary committee sublets the work to contractors and executes it. Second, settling the payments also involves difficulties due to the lack of production of proper receipts and other documents. Engineers also told us that they also found it difficult to have an effective supervision of work executed by beneficiary committees. It was also pointed out that in majority of the cases, the quality of the work executed was not up to the standard. The engineers told that the execution of projects through the contractors is a better option for effecting speedy execution, ensuring quality of the work and fixing accountability of the work executed, and effecting prompt payments.

A disturbing development is the implementation of a large number of projects by GPs. The representatives of LGs told us that the practice followed in almost all GPs is to divide the total annual plan amount among the members equally. The general requirement of the development projects of the GP is seldom taken into consideration. The members are mostly concerned about the developmental activities in their wards, and distribution of benefits, subsidies, etc., to the people in the ward. The clashes between ruling and opposition members also prevent them from going for major development projects spread over in more than one ward. Another tendency is to formulate and implement very small projects.

The GPs reported that the engineering projects are prepared by the engineers. The others are prepared by the implementing officers of the GP and transferred institutions. A problem raised by the engineers of the GP is that they find it difficult to prepare a large number of projects within a short period. They pointed out that the same amount of work can be executed by reducing the number of projects by one-third or one-fourth.

In some of the GPs, an assistant engineer is in charge of more than one GP and finds it extremely difficult to attend to the project-formulation and implementing activities in a satisfactory manner. The lack of a sufficient number of overseers to supervise the execution of the work also affects the quality of the work. The engineers also pointed out that they do not get any clerical support for preparing the bills and other administrative work required for project formulation, execution and payment of bills.

A major reason for the poor execution of projects in the GPs is the large and unmanageable number of projects formulated and executed. The number of total projects ranged between 81 and 301 in the year 2014–2015. The average number of projects including spillover executed in the GPs for the financial year 2014–2015 is 176. Table 20.6 gives the total number of projects executed including the spillover, and the percentage of projects completed. The data indicates that except in one GP, there has been an increase in the number of projects executed

Table 20.6 *Details of Implementation of Projects in GPs*

S. No.	Name of GP/ District	Number of Projects Implemented		Percentage of Projects Completed	
		2011– 2012	2014–2015	2011– 2012	2014–2015
	Thiruvananthapuram				
1	Kottukal	0	225	0	52.44
2	Anchuthengu	78	89	67.95	78.65
3	Vithura	0	170	0	71.18
	Ernakulam				
4	Edavanakkad	95	125	57.89	66.40
5	Cheranallur	89	109	57.30	51.38
6	Kuttampuzha	183	266	61.75	59.40
	Thrissur				
7	Erumappetti	139	133	55.40	54.89
8	Nattika	0	160	0.00	83.13
9	Puthur	149	232	63.09	82.33
	Kozhikode				
10	Narippatta	102	153	0.00	67.32
11	Kadalundi	0	154	0.00	47.40
12	Unnikulam	265	301	63.02	66.11
	Total	1,100	2,117	57.70	65.85

Source: Primary data collected from the LGs.

in all sample GPs. As the GPs are handling more projects beyond their administrative capacity, and the percentage of uncompleted projects is high. Due to this, a good number of projects become spillover projects to be completed during the subsequent financial year. During the financial year 2014–2015, out of the total 2,117 projects implemented, only 66 per cent was completed. In four GPs, the number of projects completed was less than 55 per cent. Thus, the root cause for the very poor execution of projects is the large number of projects implemented by the GPs.

ACHIEVEMENT OF FINANCIAL TARGETS

We may examine the monitoring and achievement of financial targets. The percentage of plan spending to total plan outlay gives an indication of achievement of financial targets. Here the utilisation of funds includes both plan and maintenance. Table 20.7 gives the percentage of fund utilisation of the 12 GPs for four years. During the financial year 2014–2015, the average total plan and maintenance expenditure of the sample GPs was 66 per cent. The plan spending was not better in the early years. This indicates very poor plan fund utilisation and plan performance.

Bunching of plan expenditure to the last quarter or last month of the financial year is a common practice seen in the spending pattern of GPs. In order to assess the pattern of plan spending, we have estimated the quarter-wise spending of the sample GPs for 2014–2015 (Table 20.8). During the first quarter of the financial year, out of 12 GPs, seven had not spent a single rupee. The share of plan spending during the second quarter for the sample GPs was 19 per cent. Another 24 per cent was spent by the sample GPs during the third quarter. A notable thing is that the major share of the plan was spent during the last quarter of the financial year, namely, the months of January, February and March 2015. An examination of the month-wise plan spending of the 12 GPs revealed that out of the total plan expenditure for the financial year 2014–2015, 36 per cent was spent in March 2015. This indicates hasty spending of the plan outlay during the last quarter or last month of the financial year.

Table 20.7 *Percentage of Fund Utilisation (Plan + Maintenance) in GPs*

S. No.	Name of GP/ District	2011– 2012	2012– 2013	2013– 2014	2014– 2015
	Thiruvananthapuram				
1	Kottukal	0	65	60	65
2	Anchuthengu	38.6	59.85	74.2	69.7
3	Vithura	0	74.74	81	72.3
	Ernakulam				
4	Edavanakkad	75.2	49.7	78.5	69.5
5	Cheranallur	80	55	75	70
6	Kuttampuzha	23.46	58.81	72.13	53.8
	Thrissur				
7	Erumappetti	62.6	62.01	61.6	74.7
8	Nattika	0	75.47	79.68	75.35
9	Puthur	68.42	57.86	60.99	58.29
	Kozhikode				
10	Narippatta	NA	NA	NA	NA
11	Kadalundi	39.5	54	69	54
12	Unnikulam	44.5	49.62	63.15	60.61
	Total	44.89	50.65	68.58	66.49

Source: Primary data collected from the LGs.

CONCLUSION

The analysis may be concluded with the following observations. The plan formulation guideline has given too much emphasis for the elaborate procedures at the pre-project preparation stage, and it gives little priority for actual project preparation, getting approvals and efficient execution. Major part of the effort and time of LGs is spent in completing the elaborate and irrelevant procedures at the pre-project preparation stage. Though grama sabhas are assigned a key role in the formulation of development plans, they are mainly concerned about distribution of benefits and selection of beneficiaries, etc. The root cause for the poor plan performance is the

Table 20.8 *Plan Spending: Quarter-wise in 2014–2015 of GPs*

| S. No. | Name of GP/ District | Total Percentage | | | | |
		1st Quarter (April–June)	2nd Quarter (July–September)	3rd Quarter (October–December)	4th Quarter (January–March)	Total
	Thiruvananthapuram					
1	Kottukal	0.00	27.79	31.09	41.13	100.00
2	Anchuthengu	1.71	16.91	28.39	52.99	100.00
3	Vithura	0.00	17.26	26.75	55.98	100.00
	Ernakulam					
4	Edavanakkad	1.54	25.57	29.74	43.16	100.00
5	Cheranallur	0.00	4.81	50.98	44.21	100.00
6	Kuttampuzha	16.13	15.37	12.09	56.41	100.00
	Thrissur					
7	Erunappetti	10.30	12.93	30.72	46.05	100.00
8	Nattika	0.00	23.42	18.72	57.86	100.00
9	Puthur	0.22	16.27	9.89	73.63	100.00
	Kozhikode					
10	Narippatta	0.00	18.58	33.36	48.06	100.00
11	Kadalundi	0.00	12.83	30.53	56.64	100.00
12	Unnikulam	0.00	23.66	22.56	53.79	100.00
	Total	2.03	19.36	24.28	54.34	100.00

Source: Primary data collected from the LGs.

implementation of a large and unmanageable number of projects. The execution of projects through beneficiary committees and lack of adequate number of engineers and supporting staff also contribute to poor plan performance. The projects implemented give emphasis on ward-wise interests and neglect the overall development of the LG. Due to the enormous delays in completing the pre-execution formalities of the projects; they are hasty executed during the last quarter or last month of the financial year. And bunching of plan expenditure to last quarter or the last month of the financial year is a common practice.

REFERENCES AND SELECT BIBLIOGRAPHY

GoK (Government of Kerala). (2009). *Report of the Committee for Evaluation of Decentralised Planning and Development.* Thiruvananthapuram: GoK.

————. (2011). *Report of the Fourth State Finance Commission, Kerala, Part I and Part II.* Thiruvananthapuram: GoK.

————. (2016). *Report of the Fifth State Finance Commission, Part I and Part II.* Thiruvananthapuram: GoK.

LSGD (Local Self Government Department). (2013). *12th five year plan (2012–2017). Plan guidelines, subsidies and other subjects of local self governments.* Thiruvananthapuram: LSGD.

About the Editors and Contributors

EDITORS

B. A. Prakash is Former Professor and Head, Department of Economics, University of Kerala, Kariavattom, Thiruvananthapuram. Earlier he was a Professor at the Department of Economics, University of Calicut, where he had been teaching since 1976. After retirement from the university, he was appointed as Chairman of Kerala Public Expenditure Review Committee for three years. The latest official position held by him is Chairman, Fifth State Finance Commission, Kerala. Professor Prakash has been conducting research on different topics relating to Kerala's economic development during the last four decades and has published a number of papers in leading journals, research reports and monographs. He has also edited six books on India's and Kerala's economy. SAGE had previously published three of his edited books, namely, *Kerala's Economy: Performance, Problems and Prospects* (1994); *Kerala's Economic Development: Issues and Problems* (1999); and *Kerala's Economic Development: Performance and Problems in the Post-Liberalisation Period* (2004).

Jerry Alwin is Assistant Professor of Economics, Department of Economics, Sree Narayana College, Sivagiri, Varkala, Kerala. He got his PhD in economics from the University of Kerala in 2012. He has published papers in journals, and a book titled *Recent Trends in Kerala State Finances* (2014). He was also a member of Kerala State Planning Board Working Group on Non-banking Financial Institutions (2015).

CONTRIBUTORS

M. P. Abraham is Assistant Professor, Government Women's College, Thiruvananthapuram, Kerala.

P. Aravindh is Doctoral Scholar, Department of Applied Economics, Cochin University of Science and Technology, Kochi, Kerala.

K. Gangadharan is Professor and Head, Department of Applied Economics, Kannur University, Thalassery Campus, Palayad, Kerala.

S. Harikumar is Professor and Head, Department of Applied Economics, Cochin University of Science and Technology, Kochi, Kerala.

Brigit Joseph is Associate Professor, Kerala Agricultural University, Vellayani Campus, Thiruvananthapuram, Kerala.

K. J. Joseph is Ministry of Commerce Chair, Centre for Development Studies, Thiruvananthapuram, Kerala.

Tomy Joseph is Associate Professor, Department of Economics, St. Xaviers College, Vaikkom, Kerala.

K. P. Mani is Former Professor and Head, Department of Economics, University of Calicut, John Mathai Centre, Thrissur, Kerala.

Shijo Philip is Assistant Professor, University College, Thiruvananthapuram, Kerala.

N. Vijayamohanan Pillai is Associate Professor, Centre for Development Studies. Thiruvananthapuram, Kerala.

V. Prakash is Head, Department of Economics, DB Pampa College, Parumala, Pathanamthitta, Kerala.

Rony Thomas Rajan is Assistant Professor, University College, Thiruvananthapuram, Kerala.

S. Irudaya Rajan is Professor, Centre for Development Studies, Thiruvananthapuram, Kerala.

A. Abdul Salim is Professor and Head, Department of Economics, University of Kerala, Kariavattom, Thiruvananthapuram, Kerala.

Jose Sebastian is Associate Professor, Gulati Institute of Finance and Taxation, Thiruvananthapuram, Kerala.

A. S. Shibu is Assistant Professor, University College, Thiruvananthapuram, Kerala.

S. Sunitha is Research Associate, Centre for Development Studies, Thiruvananthapuram, Kerala.

Arun Shyamnath is Research Officer, State Planning Board, Thiruvananthapuram, Kerala.

Index